The Acquisition of Literacy:

Ethnographic Perspectives

Bambi B. Schieffelin   Perry Gilmore

University of Pennsylvania   University of Alaska

EDITORS

VOLUME XXI IN THE SERIES
ADVANCES IN DISCOURSE PROCESSES
ROY O. FREEDLE, EDITOR

ABLEX PUBLISHING CORPORATION
NORWOOD, NEW JERSEY

Library of Congress Cataloging in Publication Data

Main entry under title:

Acquisition of literacy.

    (Advances in discourse processes ; v. 21)
    Bibliography: p.
    Includes index.
    1. Literacy—Addresses, essays, lectures.
2. Reading—Addresses, essays, lectures.   3. Children—
Books and reading—Addresses, essays, lectures.
I. Schieffelin, Bambi B. II. Gilmore, Perry. III. Title.
IV. Series.
LC149.A27   1986   370.19   86-1037
ISBN 0-89391-206-9
ISBN 0-89391-379-0 (pbk.)

Ablex Publishing Corporation
355 Chestnut Street
Norwood, New Jersey 07648

Contents

iii

PART III   SCHOOL COMES HOME: WHAT CAN PARENTS DO?

PART IV   LITERACY AFFECTS THE SOCIAL ORDER

For our parents
Sylvia & David Bernhard
Helen & Solomon Raefsky

Preface to the Series

Roy O. Freedle
Series Editor

This series of volumes provides a forum for the cross-fertilization of ideas from a diverse number of disciplines, all of which share a common interest in discourse— be it prose comprehension and recall, dialogue analysis, text grammar construction, computer simulation of natural language, cross-cultural comparisons of communicative competence, or other related topics. The problems posed by multisentence contexts and the methods required to investigate them, while not always unique to discourse, are still sufficiently distinct as to benefit from the organized mode of scientific interaction made possible by this series.

Scholars working in the discourse area from the perspective of sociolinguistics, psycholinguistics, ethnomethodology and the sociology of language, educational psychology (e.g., teacher–student interaction), the philosophy of language, computational linguistics, and related subareas are invited to submit manuscripts of monograph or book length to the series editor. Edited collections of original papers resulting from conferences will also be considered.

Volumes in the Series

Introduction

Bambi B. Schieffelin

University of Pennsylvania

In the last 10 years the nature and role of literacy in society has become a topic of interest and debate among academicians, politicians, practitioners, and parents. The definition and boundaries of literacy remain beyond agreement, but most people will agree that the meaning of "being literate" varies according to one's time and place in society and history. Literacy has been viewed as a way of knowing, a way of "speaking," an economic necessity, a cognitive advantage, a political excuse. From a social perspective, it is difficult to examine literacy "objectively." The process of acquiring literacy always has serious cultural consequences, for individuals, social groups, societies. The fact that many have sought to claim credit when literacy is achieved and to locate blame when it is not is evidence of the fact that no matter what else, literacy is universally considered to have social and cultural consequences.

The authors in this volume share a view of literacy as a social and cultural phenomenon, something that exists between people and something that connects individuals to a range of experiences and to different points in time. These essays demonstrate that literacy, viewed as a cultural phenomenon that interacts with certain social processes, is best studied by adopting an ethnographic perspective. By ethnographic we mean descriptions that take into account the perspective of members of a social group, including the beliefs and values that underlie and organize their activities and utterances. An ethnographic perspective allows the researcher to find out the meaning of events for those who are involved in them. This entails investigating the contexts of the uses of literacy, the meanings of literacy, and the forms of literate communication as it is organized in and plays a role in organizing particular social interactions. As will become apparent in these essays, the Ethnography of Speaking perspective (Hymes, 1972; Basso, 1974; Szwed, 1981) has been critical in providing a conceptual framework in which such notions as a literacy event—that is, "any occasion in which a piece of writing is integral to the nature of the participants' interactions and their interpretive processes" (Heath, 1982)—can be examined and understood.

The essays that follow focus on the social and cultural contexts and processes involved in the acquisition of literacy. They use an ethnographic approach to study socialization for literacy; this involves an important research focus on the relationship between attitudes, values, beliefs, and skills that are culturally transmitted to learners in relation to the development of literacy skills. Fundamental to understanding these contexts and processes are the social relationships and interactions in which an orientation to literacy is presented to novices. Particular concern is directed to the organization of the discourse in which these interactions occur and the affective nature of these interactions. By exploring literacy and literacy-related activities in social groups both within and outside of the United States, these essays document a range of meanings and consequences of literacy acquisition, presenting a broad spectrum of the implications of this communicative mode. Finally, an important aim of these studies is to raise new research questions and offer new ways to formulate investigations into the acquisition of literacy and the nature of literacy itself.

The chapters in this volume have been organized into four sections. Part I, "Taking from texts: Cultural variations on a theme," examines the organization and meaning of literacy events that involve adults reading to and using written texts with young children in both mainstream and nonmainstream American communities. In these essays information about a group's values and beliefs is used to help make sense of the structure of the discourse of these literacy events. The structure and meaning of these events are not assumed to be universal or natural. Instead, the investigators focus on the sociocultural organization of these events and the ways in which an orientation to literacy is displayed to young children. It is through the participation in these literacy events that the culturally specific ways of taking information from written texts is acquired.

In Chapter 1, "Early reading at home: Its practice and meanings in a working class community," Miller, Nemoianu, and DeJong examine events in which working class mothers and their 2-year-old children look at books in the context of play activities. They analyze the discourse structure of these events as well as the affective aspects of this first tutorial relationship. In comparing these early informal literacy events with the way literacy is instructed in school, Miller et al. discuss a number of factors that may present problems to these nonmainstream children, including teaching style and social class of the teacher, competitive relationships with peers, public performance issues. The authors make the very important point that to the degree that the academic skills of these mothers were limited, they were dependent on the schools for the education of their children in a way that highly educated parents are not. While schooling and literacy were valued, hoped for, and sought after, they could not be taken for granted by these mothers.

In Chapter 2, "The book as narrative prop in language acquisition," Heath and Branscombe investigate what children from mainstream and nonmainstream families learn about narratives from books. They distinguish four types of narratives (recounts, accounts, eventcasts, and stories) and suggest that children must not only learn how to tell these different types of narratives, they must learn to frame occasions for these tellings. Working collaboratively with a nonmainstream mother whose traditional patterns of talk in the family were more adult-centered than child-centered, the authors describe the mother's changing mode of response to her child's narratives. This chapter also documents the language socialization of the preschooler, focusing on the acquisition of different narrative skills between the 2d and 3rd birthdays. Labeling, embedded in a "school-like discourse structure," was learned early on in these interactions, and later on bookreading became a major occasion in which to recount fantasies and factual stories.

These interactional patterns represented a major shift in the ways of learning about taking from text. Heath and Branscombe emphasize the importance of adult-child interactions around books, especially in learning the rules for appropriate sequencing and for
making inferences. The mother's role in these events was crucial in providing the necessary scaffolding to facilitate the learning of mainstream literate behaviors seen as critical
for school achievement.

Chapter 3, "Reading stories to children: A model for understanding texts," is based
on a study of nursery school children in middle-class, school-oriented families.
Cochran-Smith calls attention to the ideological underpinnings, the culturally patterned ways of taking meaning from text that are bound up with assumptions about
literacy and success in school. She found that these families are not interested in early
deliberate literacy instruction. Instead, they prefer that their young children engage in
literacy activities that fit into more general patterns of social interaction. For this social
group story reading is a regular activity at home and is expected to occur in the nursery
school. These literacy activities ideally extend from the personal relationships in the
home, where adults make texts comprehensible by building on existing and developing
communicative resources that the child brings to the situation. The emphasis here is on
adults making connections between oral experiences and later literate experiences.
Cochran-Smith demonstrates how these interactions build on a culturally specific model
of conversation and turn taking, and model of narrative.

In Chapter 4, "For the Bible tells me so: Teaching children in a Fundamentalist
church," Zinsser reports on a situation that is one of the early contexts for literacy socialization for many children in the United States. She examines classroom interactions
between teachers and young children in a fundamentalist Sunday school and vacation
Bible school as a variation on mainstream patterns of teaching children how to take
from texts. From an analysis of this particular type of pedagogical discourse that maintains textual authority, she concludes that what is most valued is the learning of the
Bible text, not general literacy. Given the fact that many children are involved in this
particular type of literacy, Zinsser posed the question as to what extent children who are
socialized into these particular patterns of pedagogical discourse are advantaged or dis-
advantaged in other educational contexts.

Part II of the volume is entitled "Connecting oral and written modes: What children
can do in school." These essays examine another important set of questions concerning
how children acquire an orientation towards literacy as well as the skills required to
achieve it. They examine the contributions of the child's already existing communicative resources and knowledge about literacy to the development of literacy skills. Several different routes into literacy are explored—using different genres of oral language,
orally presented written language, and dialogic written language.

In Chapter 5, "I want to talk to you about writing: Five-year-olds speak," Blazer
reports on the relationships between oral and written language during the development
of early writing in a kindergarten classroom. Toward examining the social and psychological processes involved in the development of beginning writing, she focuses on what
children know about the social functions of writing and how they use oral language in
the context of social interactions to create early written texts. She demonstrates that the

child's oral language produced while writing provides the necessary scaffolding for that writing, as well as helping to organize early writing events. Blazer suggests that the eventual internalization of this "scaffolding" oral language as writing develops, fits the Vygotskyian (1962) notion of inner speech.

In Chapter 6, "Six authors in search of an audience," Braig presents findings from a longitudinal case study of the development of a sense of audience in the early writing of six children (ages 6–8). Using dialogue journals, the researcher as the child's responsive partner drew on the child's existing communicative resources, providing scaffolding through a personal relationship for the acquisition of literacy skills. She found that given a meaningful basis for communication, writing became relevant, which facilitates the acquisition of the conventions of written language. Braig emphasizes the importance of affective factors in making the connection between oral and written modes in the acquisition of literacy.

In Chapter 7, "Teacher/child collaboration as oral preparation for literacy," Michaels and Cazden investigate the relationship between oral style and developing literacy skills. Analyzing the structure of discourse in collaborative exchanges in school settings ("Sharing Time"), in which, ideally, children together with teacher co-construct lexically explicit narratives, they found that not all children gained equal access to this kind of help. Those who started out sharing a set of discourse conventions and interpretive strategies got more practice and informal instruction in producing expanded literate style narratives. Michaels and Cazden characterize two major styles, each found more frequently with a particular group of children: topic-associating style characterized the style of black children, and topic-centered characterized white children. Teachers try to help children clarify and organize their discourse according to their own expectations. Their study indicates that some children are helped, while some aren't, depending largely on differing ethnically specific patterns of speaking. In addition, they elicited value judgments on the children's Sharing Time narratives and found that black and white adults responded differentially to topic-associating narratives. White adults evaluated the black children's stories quite negatively; black adults appreciated the form of both black and white children's talk. They suggest that one factor for the successful development of literacy skills seems speaking topically, with explicitly lexicalized thematic connections, and they see extended discourse activities as key situations influencing children's access to literacy instruction.

In Chapter 8, "Sub-rosa literacy: Peers, play, and ownership in literacy acquisition," Gilmore contrasts the literacy and literacy-related competencies displayed by male and female school and peer-group contexts. She presents an analysis of peer culture activities including girls' performances of street rhymes, locally referred to as "steps," and boys' participation in group literacy activities when playing the game Dungeons and Dragons. These literacy events, owned and demonstrated in peer contexts which she terms "sub-rosa," provide examples of student competencies in a range of oral and written performances. Gilmore points out that the skills demonstrated in these activities had been identified by the school as the very ones in which the students were considered deficient. Gilmore ties these findings to pedagogical implications.

The two chapters that form Part III, "School comes home: What can parents do?"

consider issues of school success and failure, specifically with regard to literacy development from different perspectives. Both chapters discuss interactions in which children
need assistance in homework activities and the effects of school impinging on home and
family organization. Both are drawn from larger observational studies of literacy in families that live in the Northeastern United States.

In Chapter 9, "Parents as teachers: Observations of low-income parents and children
in a homework-like task," Chandler, Argyris, Barnes, Goodman, and Snow argue that
for 31 low-income families belonging to a range of cultural groups that they followed,
failure in literacy acquisition cannot be explained by discontinuities between home and
school. They found that parent–child interaction over a homework-like task was very
similar to dyadic interactions that occurred between teacher and child. Both below- and
above-average readers came from families where the observed interactions and inferred
education theories were similar to what they experienced at school. They cite the long-
term stability of this racially and ethnically heterogeneous neighborhood as contributing
to their findings of continuity between home and school and suggest searching for additional factors to explain the tendency of the low-income child to be nonsuccessful in the
achievement of literacy.

Chapter 10, "'Why' Sheila can read: Structure and indeterminacy in the reproduction of familial literacy," by Varenne and McDermott, questions why the American
institutional framework creates a system of evaluation such that school failure is used to
affirm individualism by differentiating persons. They argue against focusing on individual children in favor of looking to larger cultural systems to understand the conditions
of the practice of literacy in and out of school. They make the point that there are
different literacies in the family, some of which are not school-evaluated and some of
which are (homework). Their analysis frames homework as a ritual in which individuals
differentially display knowledge and places it in the context of the larger organizational
issues of everyday life.

The final section focuses on the impact literacy has on different aspects of the social
order, and draws on examples from Western Samoa, Morocco, and the United States. In
Chapter 11, "Literacy instruction in a Samoan village," Duranti and Ochs describe the
consequences of literacy instruction in a traditionally nonliterate society. They report
that in the context of explicit literacy instruction a wide range of social and cultural
skills and knowledge as well as a particular set of expectations are introduced. With
school achievement there is an emphasis on individual achievement, rather than on cooperative accomplishment. There are issues of change of identity for the person who
becomes literate, as well as changes in social responsibility. They found significant
changes in traditional modes of adult-child relationships as a result of new schooling
experiences in Western Samoa. There is a shift to child-centered interactions, a change
in the traditional definitions of task and achievement, and changes in the social meaning of praise. Based on an analysis of the discourse patterns of literacy instruction they
document the influence in this society of Western patterns of organizing instructional
sequences, and conclude that literacy instruction is teaching a far greater range of information than decoding. This is especially significant given the influence of the Christian
church in introducing orthography, preparing literacy materials, setting up literacy

training, and packaging literacy within a specific framework with clearly defined goals in Western Samoa as well as elsewhere in the world.

In Chapter 12, "Studying literacy in Morocco," Wagner, Messick, and Spratt report on a study carried out in a complex multi-lingual, multi-literate, multi-class society, Morocco. The major domains of investigation are the uses and mediators of literacy (societal structures and individual circumstances in which literacy plays a significant role), institutions of transmission (school and home settings), and the material culture of literacy (an historical inventory of the instruments and artifacts of this literate society). To tap some of the complexities of literacy in Morocco they work within a framework of "culture" of literacy (cf. Smith, Chapter 13) to explore connections between the ideology and practice of literacy. They explore the issue of restricted literacy, and the stigmatization of not being literate, and raise the question of whether literacy is understood as a social and communicative resource that is shared, or is personally held, privately dispensed.

In Chapter 13, "The anthropology of literacy acquisition," Smith's essay provides a number of perspectives on social problems of literacy and illiteracy. He argues that literacy must be understood in terms of a set of valences, which he refers to as a group's "culture of literacy." Smith focuses on the consequences (costs) of being viewed as illiterate or literate, and argues that an ethnographic perspective is critical in examining literacy and illiteracy as a relational problem for individuals in contemporary American society.

REFERENCES

Basso, Keith. (1974). The ethnography of writing. In R. Bauman & J. Sherzer (Eds.), *Explorations in the ethnography of speaking.* New York: Cambridge University Press.

Heath, Shirley. (1982). Protean shapes in literacy events: Ever shifting oral and literate traditions. In Deborah Tannen (Ed.), *Spoken and written language: Exploring orality and literacy.* Norwood, NJ: Ablex.

Hymes, Dell. (1972). Models of the interactions of language and social life. In John J. Gumperz & Dell Hymes (Eds.), *Directions in sociolinguistics: The ethnography of communication.* New York: Holt, Rinehart and Winston.

Szwed, John. (1981). The ethnography of literacy. In M. F. Whiteman (Ed.), *Writing: The nature, development and teaching of written communication* (Vol. 1). Hillsdale, NJ: Erlbaum.

PART I

Taking from Texts:
Cultural Variations on a Theme

1

Early Reading at Home: Its Practice and Meanings in a Working-Class Community

Peggy Miller
University of Chicago

Anca Nemoianu
Catholic University

Judith DeJong
Center for Human Development
Washington, D.C.

How do families prepare their children for school? Surprisingly, we know little about this question, particularly as it applies to low-income and minority groups. Yet it is these children more than others who risk not learning to read. In this chapter we are concerned with three young children from an urban, working-class community. We examine their preschool experience in light of observations of first-grade classrooms in the same community. The objective is to describe and generate questions about early socialization for schooling, focusing on reading at home during the third year of life. We attempt to contextualize early reading by incorporating into our description the ordinary circumstances in which the activity occurs, the expressed experiences and understandings of adult caregivers, and the personal and qualitative aspects of the interactions.

THE STUDY

The study is part of a larger investigation of early language development in South Baltimore, a community of mixed German, Polish, Irish, Italian, and Appalachian descent (Miller, 1982). Many families have lived there for generations, inhabiting modest rowhouses that were built for immigrant laborers in the mid-19th century. Amy, Wendy, and Beth were first-born children of mothers who were 18 to 20 years old and unmarried at the time of the child's birth. Two of the children lived in extended family households, and all of the mothers received practical assistance, such as babysitting and sharing of household expenses, from the maternal grandparents.

Beth's mother dropped out of high school in the eighth grade and could not read. Amy's mother also left school in the eighth grade. Wendy's mother was a high school graduate. Two of the mothers received public assistance, and Amy's mother worked as a machine operator in a factory. Other family members were employed as factory workers, custodians, truck drivers, and secretaries.

The study was longitudinal in design and ethnographic in approach, combining intensive observations of the children in the contexts of everyday life with an inquiry into the beliefs and values of their families. Following a preliminary get-acquainted phase, a series of 12 video recordings was made during the third year of life (age at outset varied from 18 to 25 months). At each taping session the child was observed for one continuous hour in the rowhouse livingroom as she interacted with her mother and other family members. Audio-recorded interviews with the mothers provided another source of data.

The videotapes were transcribed in detail, with each transcript including a record of what the child said, a record of what other speakers said, a running description of the child's nonverbal behaviors, and a description of contextual features and of other speakers' behaviors. (See Miller, 1982, for transcription procedures.)

For the present analysis we made additional observations in two first-grade classrooms in South Baltimore. Handwritten observations of reading and related activities were made every two to three weeks during the spring semester. During summer vacation we tutored three of the students who had not learned to read, according to the teacher's assessment and our own observations. All three were from low-income families. Our class met at the school once a week for three hours. One of us acted as teacher, another took notes on the interaction and on the children's activities with printed materials.

THE FIRST TUTORIAL RELATIONSHIP

A previous analysis revealed that the mothers of Amy, Wendy, and Beth believed in the importance of teaching young children to talk and that they routinely gave direct instruction in various aspects of language and speaking (Miller, 1982). That is, they explicitly told the child what to say or how to say it or quizzed her on these matters, using such teaching devices as elicited imitation, prompts, directions to ask or tell, and tutorial questions. These interactions provided opportunities for the child to acquire various kinds of social and linguistic knowledge—to answer and ask what-questions; to assert and comply verbally and nonverbally; to participate appropriately in conversation; to take care of "babies" in mothering play with dolls; and to rhyme, sing, and play verbal games. In addition, a developmental analysis of one category of direct instruction (naming people and things) for one of the mother-child pairs revealed that the mother's instructions were well adapted to the child's level of understanding about naming.

Not only did family members issue direct instructions at least twice per (one-hour) sample,[1] but the children participated enthusiastically in these interactions. They responded at a very high rate to direct instructions of all kinds. They were highly atten-

---

[1] The frequency of direct instruction varied from child to child and sample to sample. Across the eight samples per child examined for this analysis, the frequency of interactions involving direct instruction ranged from 3 to 31 for Amy, 3 to 14 for Wendy, and 2 to 20 for Beth.

tive for lengthy periods as mothers named pictures in books or ran through lists of relatives and friends. In the later samples the children took a more active part in initiating teaching interactions, requested the names of people and things, and even adopted the role of teacher in pretend play with dolls. The mothers counted on their children's cooperation, using direct instruction as a way of entertaining the child or redirecting her activity.

Now, what is important about direct instruction for the issue of schooling is that learning in the context of an informal teacher/pupil relationship was a significant part of the preschool experience of these children. By the age of three, Amy, Wendy, and Beth had had extensive, positive experience of learning in relation to mother or grandmother or cousin as tutor. Being a successful learner was part of the child's identity just as being a successful teacher was part of her mother's identity. Obviously, there are major differences between learning at home in one-to-one interaction with a close relative and learning at school with many children and an unfamiliar adult. Nevertheless, in the critical matter of teaching and learning, the values of home and school intersected. Amy, Wendy, and Beth's preschool socialization equipped them to understand and appreciate a teacher/pupil relationship.

Of course, one can imagine a culture in which teaching occurs as an indigenous language socialization strategy for presenting content that bears no relation to schooling. And, indeed, the Kaluli of Papua New Guinea (Schieffelin, 1979) and the Zuni of New Mexico (Bunzel, 1932) are two such cases. For Amy, Wendy, and Beth, however, the largest category of direct instruction involved naming people and things, including pictures in books. That is, direct instruction framed the child's first experience of reading.

For the present study we extended the earlier analysis of direct instruction, asking whether the children engaged in early forms of the kinds of academic activities we had observed in first-grade classrooms in the community. For this analysis we examined the transcripts of 12 hours of video-recorded observations per child. We found that in addition to reading, the children engaged in at least one episode of each of the following activities: writing, counting, identifying colors, reciting rhymes, telling narratives, and identifying other kinds of pictorial representations (e.g., pictures on walls). Spelling, reciting the alphabet, telling time, and providing identifying information about the self (e.g., name, age, address) were engaged in by one or two of the children but not all three. In other words, Amy, Wendy, and Beth not only experienced a teacher/pupil relationship at home but were encouraged to perform various school-related activities.

THE STRUCTURE OF READING AT TWO

Because of the central place of reading in the early grades, we singled out for closer examination the children's preschool activities with books. Following Anderson, Teale and Estrada (1980), we defined *reading* as any event in which the child performed reading-like behaviors in relation to a book, magazine, or other printed material, either with or without a partner, in silence or with accompanying talk. Caregivers and children themselves used the word *reading* in reference to such activities. Reading events could be very brief, as the child quickly leafed through a book or several minutes long as she gazed at page after page in one after another book. Events consisted of episodes, corresponding to each of the different books read during a single, continuous event. When the child read only one book, the event and the episode were coterminous. Reading occurred both with and without a partner, usually the mother, and, in the majority of cases, the child initiated the activity. The following analysis is restricted to reading events with a partner. These occurred relatively infrequently: we found a total of 13 over the course of the 36 hours of video-recorded observations.

It is important to emphasize here that the original purpose of the study (understood as such by the mothers) was to document the naturally occurring contexts for language learning—not specifically to document early reading. Two of the mothers reported that they read regularly to the child (one at bedtime) but unfortunately, we do not have a systematic sampling of these events. Thus, we cannot draw strong inferences about the frequency with which reading occurred in these homes. We are limited to describing those events that happened to occur during the taping sessions. However, since our focus was *not* on reading and since care was taken during the preliminary phase of the study to establish rapport with the mother and to assure her that we did not wish to change her behavior (Miller, 1982), we assume that the reading events that did occur are reasonably representative.

Reading with a partner involved several preliminary steps. First, child and caregiver had to agree on a common activity. This was accomplished in a number of ways. Child or caregiver initiated the event by simply taking the book to the partner. Or the child began to read, and then invited the caregiver to participate, for example, "You take em (magazine)," or the caregiver spontaneously joined in. In other cases the caregiver initiated the event with an explicit proposal, for example, "Read it to me," or "Let's look at your books."

The need to agree upon a joint activity is, of course, a necessary part of any social interaction. There were also preliminary steps that were specific to reading. These included selecting a book and holding it open within easy view of both participants. The conventions of holding the book are best exhibited in the following event in which Beth holds the book upside down and mother attempts to correct her:[2]

(Beth 1, 25 mo.)

	Beth	Mother
B holds book on lap, upside down		Read it to me.
B pages	hey rabbit!/	
	- - -/	
		It's upside down.
		Turn it around.
		Turn it around.
		It's upside down.

---

[2] The format for examples is as follows: nonverbal behaviors in the left column, child's speech in the middle column, mother's speech in the right column. Unintelligible utterances are indicated as - - -/.

		Turn the book around.
M turns book right side up on B's lap		Here. Here's around.
		There. Now open it.
		Now it's right side up.
B opens book		
		There. See?
M points to picture		What's that?
B closes book and turns it upside down	mm want like that/	
		Well, then keep it backwards.
B opens book	there/	
M points to picture		Now you can't see what it is.
M points to picture		What is it?

Interestingly, the mother does not insist that Beth hold the book right side up and the event proceeds nonetheless. (We discuss below individual differences in styles of reading.) In order to see the pictures readers had to be in close proximity to one another. Moreover, the lap figured importantly in these events. Mother and child sat next to one another, book open on child's lap. Child stood next to mother, book open on mother's lap. Or, the most intimate, mother held child on her lap, arms encircling child, holding book open on child's lap.

Once partners were situated and book opened, reading itself began. This consisted of paging and pointing to pictures, accompanied by several types of verbal activity, the most frequent of which was naming. Naming resembled the joint bookreading cycle identified by Ninio and Bruner (1978) for one middle-class mother-child pair. The first part of the cycle was the *attentional vocative,* which included such forms as *let's see, look, look X,* and *see X.* The mothers in our study used these same forms, which were accompanied by further elaborations. For example, Wendy's mother said "Look. He's got wings! He's flying!" and "Look. He's lookin at the flowers!" This contrasts with the children's use of the attentional vocative which consisted of the "notice verb" alone or together with a name. For example,

(Amy VIII, 24 mo.)

	Amy	Mother
A flips magazine open	look/	
A stands in front of M, holding magazine, looking at M	Marlene, Russell!/	
A looks at magazine and back at M	look Russell/	
A still looks at M, M interrupts	look a _____/	Yeah.
A pages through magazine		
	look Russell/	
	see Russell?/	
A points to picture	see Russell, Mar?/	
	see Russell there?/	
		Russell.

The notice verbs were accompanied by specific prosodic features which differed for mothers and children. The mothers uttered the notice verb in a neutral manner, but marked their comments with an excited, high-pitched voice and exaggerated intonation contour. By contrast, the children used these prosodic features redundantly with the notice verbs.

Once the attention of the partner was secured, the reading event developed further. The second and third parts of the bookreading cycle identified by Ninio and Bruner (1978) are the *query* followed by a *label*. In our data queries took two forms: *What is this/that* and *Say X*. In the *Say X* request the label (*X*) was uttered with a listing intonation and the child's response echoed the mother lexically and prosodically; the sequence was thus marked as a recurrent one. This is exemplified in the following excerpt in which Wendy's mother said "Say 'bird' " and Wendy replied "bird," followed by a long sequence of identically marked elicited imitations:

(Wendy III, 25 mo.)

	Wendy	Mother
M points to picture		What's this? Bird?
W looking at page	bird/	
M looks at W, speaks louder on 'bird'		Say 'bird.'
	bird/	
M points to picture		
		Say 'butterfly.'
W looking at page	butterfly/	
		Say 'bunny.'
W looking at page	bunny/	
		Say 'deer.'
	∂ deer/	
M turns page		
		Say 'bear.'
W looking at page	bear/	

The mothers of Amy, Wendy, and Beth did not offer explicit *positive feedback* as regularly as seems to be the case in the Ninio and Bruner study. One possible explanation for this difference is the more advanced age of the children from South Baltimore. A smooth exchange is, of course, positive feedback in itself.

In addition to identifying the pictures, readers also described the named characters, scenes, and activities. For example,

(Wendy III, 25 mo.)

	Wendy	Mother
M points to picture		Look. He's got wings. He's
M glances at W		flying.
	hm?/	
		The bunny rabbit's flying.
W looking at page	yah/	

		Look. He's lookin at the flowers.
•[3]		
•		
•		
W looking at page		Here's a squirrel. Say 'squirrel.'
	squirrel/	
	squirrel/	
		Oh look. He's talkin to the frogs.
	huh?/	
		Say 'frog.'
W looking at page	frog/	
		Look at all them frogs hoppin.
	huh?/	
		See em?
W nods	yah/	
•		
•		
•		
W looking at page	∂ bunny/	There's the bunny.
		And there he is asleep.
	huh?/	
		Asleep.
	asleep/	
W still looking at page		Mmhm. He's sleepin.

The third and least frequent type of verbal activity that occurred in relation to books was storytelling. It is possible that telling narratives in association with printed materials was a later development, as we do find narratives in other contexts. In fact, our data contain many narratives told by adults and some fascinating narratives told by the children, but these tended to be factual accounts, drawn from personal experience and accompanied by nonverbal dramatization. In the following narrative, for example, Beth relates and enacts a fight with her younger cousin, Kathryn:

(Beth IX, 30 mo.)

	Beth	Other Speakers
B tugs on her hair in back, turning the back of her head toward audience	pull my hair like that/pull my hair like that too/	
		Mother: Kathryn pulled your hair?
B demonstrates again	yeah/like that too/there/	Mother: Uh huh.

---

[3] The three vertical dots indicate that material has been omitted here. This is a lengthy episode, and we excerpted segments that include descriptions of the characters, scenes, and activities.

		Investigator: What did you do to Kathryn then?
B with back to audience, climbing to look out window	I do nothin ∂ her	Mother: You did too. You bit her.

Thus, for Amy, Wendy, and Beth storytelling at two tended to involve the verbal and nonverbal re-creation of an experienced or witnessed event, without accompanying text. In this way, they differed from Scollon and Scollon's (1981) "literate two-year-old" whose personal stories were first written down and then read.

Framing reading, with its three types of verbal activity, was a distinctive pattern of gaze. Child and caregiver gazed at one another at the beginning and end of the episode. During the episode both gazed at the page. Momentary departures from a smoothly flowing interaction were marked by glances at the partner. For example, the caregiver glanced at the child when there was a delay in the child's response or when the child failed to acknowledge an attentional vocative.

In addition, glances at one another tended to occur when child or caregiver made explicit connections between the content of the book and real-life events or characteristics of the child. For example:

(Beth I. 25 mo.)

	Beth	Mother
B and M have been reading		
B points to ear of depicted rabbit	it ear/	
M uses baby talk		That it ear?
M speaks loudly		Ears.
B touches own ear, looks at M	∂ like that ear/	
M returns gaze		Yeah, you got yours.

In another example, Wendy's mother, referring to a picture of puppies, said, "There they are. Look. Look at em dancin." Wendy said, "hm?" Mother gazed and smiled at her, "See em dancin? Wendy gazed back at mother, shook her body in a "dancing" motion and sang, "dá da dá da!"

We suspect from our observations of reading in first-grade classrooms in South Baltimore that a later development involves the elaboration of these real-life connections into narratives of experienced or witnessed events. In other words, the printed story eventually becomes an occasion for relating a personal story. (This contrasts with the Maintown practice, described by Heath, 1982, in which the child's personal experience becomes an occasion for referring back to a printed story.) If this finding is borne out in subsequent observation, it provides a unique opportunity for classroom teachers to make reading meaningful to children like Amy, Wendy, and Beth by building on the child's spontaneous tendency to relate the printed to the personal.

PERSONAL ASPECTS OF READING

The foregoing description centers on the basic structure of early reading. At the risk of belaboring the obvious, we emphasize that this structure was realized in personal relationships. The meaning of reading at two derives less from books than it does from the character of those relationships. Reading as interaction has certain peculiarities but it also abides by the more general rules that govern those relationships.

Or. to put it another way, individual differences in styles of reading reflect, in part, differences in attitude and in general style of interacting. In the episode quoted on pp. 6–7, for example, the mother does not persist with her corrections when Beth is determined to hold the book upside down. Later in the same event Beth accidentally tears a page from the book, and mother delivers a mock scolding. Mother notices but tolerates these departures from the conventional reading format. She was not concerned with the physical integrity of books. She did not encourage Beth to handle or store books carefully or to take them out and read them at regularly-scheduled times. But this attitude extended beyond reading. Beth was permitted to bounce on the bed, climb on the coffee table, play with mother's beaded necklace, "help" with the cooking— regardless of the risk of damage to the objects involved. That risk, in this mother's view, was a necessary part of learning. Interactions between Beth and her mother, whether they involved books or not, were warm, casual, loosely structured.

By the same token, many of Amy's interactions with mother—reading books, performing jumping jacks, reciting rhymes—involved displays of competence. Mother would encourage the display, Amy would eagerly comply, and mother would convey her pride nonverbally, with a smile or rolling of the eyes. The display dimension was also apparent in Amy's interactions with the older children in her extended family (a 5-year-old cousin and an 8-year-old aunt). Their relations were characterized by a combination of rivalry and emulation. Amy showed off her ability to do flips, forward rolls, and clapping games and insisted that she was big enough to be included when they played school or ventured out to the corner store.

For Wendy and her mother reading together was characterized by a special closeness. It offered the pleasures of a family ritual, of quiet, mutual concentration, and shared imaginings. Reading was highly structured, slow-paced, with an undercurrent of excitement (a squirrel!; hi skunk!), and explicit references to feelings, the readers' own and the depicted characters'. Wendy and her mother were both highly expressive, volatile personalities, whose interactions, with and without books, tended to be emotionally intense.

Thus, the initial experience of reading for these children occurred informally in the company of mother and other intimates, and while the structure of the activity was more or less the same, the tone was set by each individual mother-child pair. One of the challenges that the classroom presents is the transition to reading with strangers. Although all children face this transition, it may be a good deal harder for those from non-middle-class backgrounds. The teacher is likely to be from a higher class background, to act and talk and dress differently.

In addition, at school reading takes place in front of peers, who are not necessarily seen as allies. When we tutored three first-graders from South Baltimore, we were struck by the competitiveness of our tiny class of unsuccessful readers. Each child spent a considerable amount of time monitoring the others' performance, covering up mistakes, and showing off in various ways, to the detriment of his or her ability to concentrate on the task at hand. Their efforts to "save face" and demonstrate what they *did* know revealed that they understood all too well the basic rule of classroom interaction that dictates a public display of knowledge.

Moreover, this rule may represent continuity with the child's preschool experience of rivalry with other children. For example, Miller (1982) described an episode in which 5-year-old Cousin Kris assumed the role of teacher, quizzing 2-year-old Amy about the names of her stuffed animals. Kris asked what-questions, and when Amy was unable to answer, she prompted her until the correct name was given. However, when Amy gave an incorrect answer, Kris said, "you don't known nothin," a type of response rarely heard from mothers as tutors. Amy, for her part, was not as attentive or cooperative with Kris as she was with mother. This episode, then, illustrates both the tendency of the older child to spontaneously teach the younger and the rivalry that characterized their relations.

To return to our class of three, our students' efforts to outshine their peers had the ironic effect of interfering with their ability to process the reading materials. This is an example of Cazden's (1982) point that "characteristics of setting may affect not only what children say and do, but even what comes into their minds" (p. 210). When the children were seen privately, concentration improved markedly. That is, the child performed far better in the context of a one-to-one relationship with a friendly adult, a teaching situation that more closely resembled the earlier experience with mother.

MEANINGS OF SCHOOLING AND READING

So far we have considered the informal teacher-pupil relationship at home, the structure of early reading-like activities, and the personal aspects of reading together. Interviews with the mothers contain further glimpses of the complicated meanings of schooling and reading for these families.

Consider, first, Beth's mother who left school in the eighth grade without having learned to read and who currently lived on public assistance. She described a school experience of repeated insults and humiliations which led to violent confrontations with teachers and fellow students. She was in a classroom for slow learners when the final confrontation occurred, and the principal told her to leave. Nora related these experiences with much feeling and concluded, "That's why I hope she (Beth) don't have trouble in school." She believed that her daughter was smart, bought second-hand books for her, and worried over who would teach her the "high-class words."

Amy's mother, employed as a machine operator, had completed eight years of schooling. She was a fluent reader who enjoyed the daily newspaper. She expressed pride in her younger brother's excellent scholastic record and predicted that he would be the first family member to graduate from high school, as, indeed, he was. Amy was particularly close to this uncle, who allowed her to play school with the older children.

Wendy's mother was a high school graduate who received public assistance for a time, sought further training, and eventually found work as a secretary. She occasionally read magazines and romantic novels. She hoped that Wendy would "go all the way through school. And if there's enough money and she wants to go to another type of school, even a college, or something, if she's smart enough to go there I'd like to see her do that. I'd just like to see her have a better education than what I had so she'll be able to get a better job. So she'll be able to support herself."

One hears in the mothers' words the desire for the child to get a better education; the hope that the child will be intelligent or "good" enough to succeed scholastically and that the mother will be capable enough to help; and, for some more than others, forebodings stemming from the mother's own troubles in school. To the degree that their own academic skills were limited, these parents were dependent on the schools for the education of their children in a way that highly educated parents are not. Schooling and literacy were valued, hoped for, and sought after, but not taken for granted by these mothers.

THE IMPORTANCE AND UNIMPORTANCE OF EARLY READING

Our observations suggest that reading was located primarily in school, secondarily at home. Amy, Wendy, and Beth did not live in households where reading was omnipresent. Their families did not cover their walls with books or read or write for a living. At the age of two the children owned and read books, but reading was not so frequent or pervasive as it is for children from more privileged backgrounds (Ninio & Bruner, 1978; Scollon & Scollon, 1981).

Yet the basic structure of the reading cycle was very similar to what has been described for these other groups (Ninio & Bruner, 1978; Snow & Goldfield, 1982). Perhaps this is not surprising, for at this age the activity of reading is dictated to a large degree by the nature of the materials themselves. The differences that we found—the *Say X* version of the query, the infrequent use of explicit positive feedback—were minor variations, functional equivalents of the forms used by middle-class families. Unfortunately, it is differences of this order that tend to get foregrounded in class and ethnic comparisons.

For example, Ninio (1980) compared two Israeli groups, which differed by class and ethnicity, as to the ways in which mothers and young children read books provided by the investigator. She found that the groups did not differ in structural aspects of reading such as turn-taking or length of interactional cycles; in the quantity, positiveness, or informativeness of feedback; or in the readiness of infants to initiate or participate in reading, or to emit vocalizations or well-formed labels. However, it is the differences—the preference for where-questions rather than what-questions on the part of lower-status mothers, the tendency for lower-status mothers to use fewer words, utterances, and attribute and action labels—that are emphasized and taken to indicate a teaching style that impedes the child's linguistic and educational growth.

We question not only the importance of such differences but the importance of early reading itself. On the one hand, it quite clearly *is* important in providing a bridge into school. The emotional quality of the child's first experience of books, whether it is happy or unhappy, surely bears on her attitudes toward school. Through early reading she expands her vocabulary, and learns the basic conventions of reading. The more frequently reading occurs at home the more familiar the child is with the core of the elementary school curriculum. For all these reasons it can be argued that the child who is exposed to books on a daily basis during the preschool years has an edge upon entering school.

On the other hand, early reading clearly is of limited importance in the whole scheme of things. Whether the child eventually succeeds in school—whether she learns to read and write, experiences curiosity and joy in learning, scores well on standardized tests, and graduates from high-school—depends on any number of factors besides the preschool reading experience. These include the quality of the educational resources at school (e.g., the teacher's attitude toward the child, the school budget, the teacher/pupil ratio); the quality of the educational support provided by the child's family during the school years (e.g., the parents' expectations, hopes, and fears about school achievement; the parents' ability and willingness to help with academic tasks); the extent to which teacher and parent understand, respect, and cooperate with each other; and the shared beliefs and values about education held by the child's peer group and the community at large. Each of these factors may be expected to correlate with social class independent of preschool exposure to reading. Together they comprise the cultural context in which some children learn to read and others do not.

REFERENCES

Anderson, Alonso B., Teale, William H., & Estrada, Elette. (1980). Low-income children's preschool literacy experiences: Some naturalistic observations. *Quarterly Newsletter of the Laboratory of Comparative Human Cognition, 2,* 59–65.

Bunzel, R. (1932). *Zuni ritual poetry* (47th Annual Report). Washington, DC: Bureau of American Ethnology.

Cazden, Courtney (1982). Four comments. In P. Gilmore & A. A. Glatthorn (Ed.), *Children in and out of school: Ethnography and education.* Washington, DC: Center for Applied Linguistics.

Heath, Shirley B. (1982). What no bedtime story means: Narrative skills at home and school. *Language in Society, 11,* 49–76.

Miller, Peggy J. (1982). *Amy, Wendy, and Beth: Learning language in South Baltimore.* Austin: University of Texas Press.

Ninio, Anat. (1980). Picture book reading in mother-infant dyads belonging to two subgroups in Israel. *Child Development, 51,* 587–590.

Ninio, Anat, & Bruner, Jerome. (1978). The achievements and antecedents of labelling. *Journal of Child Language, 5,* 1–15.

Schieffelin, Bambi B. (1979). Getting it together: An ethnographic approach to the study of the development of communicative competence. In E. Ochs & B. B. Schieffelin (Ed.), *Developmental pragmatics.* New York: Academic Press.

Scollon, Ron, & Scollon, Suzanne B.K. (1981). *Narrative, literacy, and face in interethnic communication.* Norwood, NJ: Ablex.

Snow, Catherine, & Goldfield, Beverly B. (1982). Turn the page please: Situation-specific language learning. In D. Tannen (Ed.), *Analyzing discourse: Talk and text.* Washington, DC: Georgetown University Press.

2

The Book as Narrative Prop in Language Acquisition

Shirley Brice Heath

Stanford University

Amanda Branscombe

Ridgeview Institute

(with Charlene Thomas)

Since the early 1970s, investigators from a variety of disciplines have undertaken research on children's stories. The majority of these researchers have focused either on the linguistic construction of children's tales (e.g., Umiker-Sebeok, 1979; Scollon & Scollon, 1981) or the cognitive aspects of producing and understanding narratives (e.g., Rumelhart, 1975; Mandler & Johnson, 1977; Stein, 1982; and Stein & Trabasso 1982). Anthropologists, however, have focused on the contexts as well as the structural and performance norms of stories across cultures. By re-evaluating the attention they have previously given cross-cultural forms of play and by attending increasingly to forms of discourse used during leisure time in different societies, anthropologists have turned their attention to the variety of narratives, of which stories may be only one form, which exists across societies (e.g., Schwartzman, 1979; Sutton-Smith & Heath, 1981; Ochs & Schieffelin, 1984; Bruner, 1984).

For most anthropologists, the question of "What is a story?" (Stein, 1982) can be answered only according to judgments of members of the social group performing, telling, and listening to narratives in context (Colby, 1966). For some groups, a "story" implies only a fictional narrative; the accounting of real events or the recounting of events known to all listeners is not considered a story (Heath, 1983, chap. 5). For other groups a story is not defined by its basic plot structure, but by the audience and purpose of the telling; a basic narrative becomes different story in some settings, but instruction in others (Rosaldo, 1983). For still other groups, a story is any connected discourse which presents state-event-state changes (e.g., Prince, 1982), even though no goal-directed behavior is contained in the story (for a full discussion of definitions of story, see Stein & Kilgore, forthcoming).

To enable us to discuss children's narratives cross-culturally, we use the term *narrative* here to include expression of experiences which have been stored in memory by the teller, are selected for attention in the telling, and are organized in knowledge structures which can be anticipated by the listener. Recent work on comprehension of narratives has indicated that listeners must, in order to store and recall narratives, be able to anticipate some order and some constituents of incoming extended discourse. Listeners must share a general knowledge of the world, specific sociocultural knowledge, and expectations of text structures. The extent to which listeners and readers will comprehend oral and written texts depends on the extent to which they share schemata and semantic networks, as well as a generalized acceptance of the genre and its appropriateness to a given context. Along the narrative continuum, a range of genres is possible, and each society or social group may accept only some combination of possibilities along this range.

For our purposes of comparing the narratives of children in mainstream and nonmainstream families, we distinguish among four types of narrative: recounts, accounts, eventcasts, and stories. *Recounts* are retellings—either voluntarily or in response to questions providing a scaffold for experiences or information known to both teller and listener; examples include children's retellings of events in which they and their listener have participated, well-known stories or stories familiar to their listeners, or school lessons in response to the teacher's request for recitation. Adults' recounts include familiar childhood tales or recounts of infamous events in their own or others' lives. Recounts depend upon a power differential; one party asks another to retell or perform for the sake of performance or to transmit to a third party information known to both the teller and the questioner.

Accounts, on the other hand, are narratives generated by either the teller or another party to provide new information or new interpretations of information which may already be known to both teller and listener. Examples include children telling parents about an afternoon spent at a friend's house or an incident at nursery school. Adults share news of a day at work, retell an item read in the newspaper, or describe a scene unknown to the listener. To give an account, the teller must insert his communication into either an existing silence or a stream of discourse; unlike recounts, accounts are not usually invited or scaffolded by listeners. Once the frame has been established and the teller is into the stream of discourse, control of the account usually rests primarily with the teller.

Eventcasts provide a running narrative on events currently in the attention of teller and listeners; this narrative may be simultaneous with the events or precede them. A child narrating his block-by-block construction of a castle or telling a friend what he plans to do when he gets to the carnival creates eventcasts. A sportscaster's account of a game during play, a preplay of a travel plan, and a mother's explanation to a preverbal infant of what she is doing as she prepares a baby's bottle represent eventcasts. Finally, according to our definition, *stories* are fictional narratives which include an animate being who moves through a series of events with goal-directed behavior. Most prose (and some poetic) literary forms are stories, as are exaggerated accounts of the behaviors of contemporaries if their movement through goal behavior to an outcome is the basis of the telling. A child's retelling of a story from a book or an adult's fanciful tale of a colleague's successful completion of a contract negotiation are familiar examples.

Psycholinguistic research on the production and comprehension of narratives by mainstream school-oriented populations has, in recent years, focused almost entirely on stories (but see Goelman, 1982). Scholars in psychology and linguistics have found it difficult to identify the knowledge structures of expository or descriptive narratives (Brewer, 1984), and they have given much attention to testing the concept of *story* and refining this concept through experiments designed to determine judgments of "good" stories (e.g., Stein & Kilgore, forthcoming; Stein & Policastro, forthcoming). This research has shown that members of mainstream school-oriented institutions expect stories to contain goal-based actions on the part of an agent capable of reactions. For mainstreamers, the criterion of whether or not the events of the story actually occurred in just the way they are told is not critical to *definitions* of stories (though it may be pertinent to judgments of the "goodness" of a story).

Calfee (1981) and others have argued that the concept of story and knowledge of the rules of story grammar are learned through exposure to book-reading in the mainstream child's preschool years and reinforced by the repeated practices teachers use in school to frame reading activities. Studies of mainstream families interacting with their preschool children have shown that from an early age, children in these households hear stories from books, are asked questions about stories which enable them to build an internal story schema, and are prompted to tell and required to listen to imaginary or fantasy stories based on this schema (Ninio & Bruner, 1978; Heath, 1982; Cochran-Smith, 1984).

Most of these studies describe mother and child reading or telling stories during leisure time, when the adult's attention is focused on the infant or child. These modes of interaction include exchange of routines in which the child imitates the mother reading the story; central-person routines, in which either the child or the mother is the teller or reader, and the other is the listener or spectator; and questioning routines in which the mother questions the child about a book, an event they both shared, or about feelings or desires she infers from the child's actions or talk. On such occasions, actions surrounding these routines are either stopped or given backstage focus. The mother stages or frames these routines, inviting the child to participate; for example, "Can you tell daddy about the story you heard at the library today?." Some children go on to practice these routines in solitary play (Ferguson & Macken, 1980), transmuting their prior interactional play with parents. In the second or third year, youngsters begin to frame occasions for introducing story-like routines into play with their peers and with adults on those occasions when adults do not initiate these routines. They must build a context, a way into the stream of activities of others. Props are helpful, since if a child brings a book or an object connected with a story to an adult, the adult will often initiate the story-time. On other occasions the child may have to establish the frame verbally—"Book, mama," "Read book."

Scholars have given far less attention to nonstory forms of narrative than they have to stories in mainstream families. Though many studies include mention of the running narratives mothers model for children while dressing the child or verbalizing childcare or travel plans (e.g., "and then we'll have our bath, and then our bottle and . . . ."), the structure and occasion of these throughout the preschool years have received relatively little analysis. Children practice these running narratives during their solitary play, often talking to themselves about putting "this block on top of that block . . . ." Adults in the vicinity of children verbalizing their play will often ask, "And then what will you do?", leading the child to frame actions of the future as well as the present. In captive audience situations (e.g., in the waiting rooms of the doctor's office or on long car trips), parents surround their children with eventcasts which focus on current or pending actions and the immediate environment.

At any time after events have been jointly shared by a mainstream parent and child, the parent may ask the child to give a narrative recounting of shared actions to a third party, who questions portions of the recount which have not been understood or do not make a coherent narrative. Once mainstream children are old enough to go to playschool or engage in other experiences to which their parents are not parties, the mother or father may ask for an account of the child's actions. These accounts often cannot be checked against the facts, so the coherence of the child's narrative accounting is one way adults decide whether to accept or question the child's account. Mainstream families and preschool institutions place considerable emphasis on children's accounts of experiences which are testable only insofar as the narrative through which they are presented makes sense to listeners. The accounts told to children, the questions asked by adults, and the retellings elicited from children help them learn the schema for accounts.

However, the children's narrative recounts of shared experiences, their accounts of experiences not shared with the listener, and the questions they are asked regarding cohesion, the logical occurrence of events, and expected outcomes do more than help them learn a set of schemata for different types of eventcasts, recounts, and accounts; they also teach children to frame occasions for offering these types of narrative. The preschooler (unlike an adult) can carry on a running monologue during his actions, and adults will not consider his verbalizations inappropriate (cf. Goffman, 1981 on "self-talk"). The child may later be encouraged to do such eventcasting while watching an animal at a zoo or a guest wrapping a birthday present ("What's the giraffe doing? Where's he going?"; What's Aunt Marge doing?") To make his own way into a conversation and to establish a frame through which he can share a recount, a child may ask of a third party in the presence of a person who shared the event: "You know what?" "You want me to tell you what mama and I did today?" To provide an account, children often ask, "You wanna hear about . . . ?" or announce what they hope will be a piece of information which will stop the ongoing conversation: "Jimmy's got a new bird," said as an opening to an accounting of an afternoon's play at a friend's house (cf. Dore, 1979). Either leisure time or a shift of focus from other actions or topics of conversation form a backdrop for this kind of talk from young children. Since in mainstream homes, social convention dictates that only one person talk at a time, children are usually granted the floor for at least a brief framing and ensuing narrative. At the very least, adults usually give some signal they are listening, even though they may continue with their activities; a common signal of listening is a question which is a probe or a request for clarification (Corsaro, 1977).

CHARLENE AND DE

We examine here a very different context, one in which stories as defined by mainstreamers were introduced through children's books to a family which carried a different definition of story from that held by mainstreamers. The extended family household of eleven members observed conventions which sanctioned talk by more than one person at a time and the dominance of adult conversations over young children's talk. Stories told by adults fit the basic structural norms of those described by psycholinguists for mainstream children and adults; however, oral stories were based on real actions, the details of which were elaborated in the telling. Stories from television or written sources did not form the basis for adults' stories but might be used as elaboration of real events (cf. the Trackton community described in Heath, 1983). Reading in this household consisted of reading to meet daily practical needs (e.g., scanning the newspaper and sports magazines, and reading personal and business letters and forms from various local and state bureaucracies). Neither reading to preschoolers nor by adults as a solitary activity occurred in the daily routines.

In response to the intervention of being read to ten minutes per day from children's books, the preschooler in this household evolved basic schemata both for telling goal-based stories and for providing eventcasts and accounts which included physical descriptions and time-ordered accounts of events. With minimal prompting or focusing of his attention on the components of stories from books, the preschooler in this family became a narrative-maker and set up frames in which he could tell narratives of various types to his mother. Though she initially rejected these stories as "lies," she came to accept his accounts and to provide frames for him to tell his narratives. This chapter will summarize the language socialization of this preschooler from 18 to 24 months (reported in Heath & Thomas, 1984) and will describe the acquisition of varieties of narrative skills that took place in the year between his second and third birthdays. We identify the evolution of narrative structures and the frames which he provided and his mother gradually evolved to help organize and shape his expression of remembered experiences.

THE ACHIEVEMENT OF PRESCHOOL LITERACY FOR MOTHER AND CHILD

Elsewhere we have detailed the development of preschool literacy for Charlene Thomas and De, her preschool son (Heath & Thomas, 1984). We provide here only a summary of the changes which took place in their uses of oral and written language in the six months between April and September 1982, the period just prior to the year in which data reported in this chapter were collected.

In September 1981, Charlene Thomas entered the ninth grade Basic English class of Amanda Branscombe, a teacher who worked with Shirley Brice Heath during the academic year 1981–82 in a teacher-researcher relationship.[1] Branscombe's class was in a high school in a town of 30,000 in the deep South of the United States. The school provided two academic tracks for grades nine through twelve: "general", for students who planned to attend college or technical school, and "basic", for those who had previously been in the special education lane or who scored below the fifth-grade level in reading and language arts skills. Heath wrote to the ninth graders, introducing them to methods of collecting language data and asking them to take fieldnotes and to audiotape some of the occasions for the use of oral and written language in their homes and communities, and in the workplaces of their parents. In November, when this ethnographic work of the students had barely begun, Charlene dropped out of school. She was the mother of a son, De, born the previous September, and she was expecting another child who would be born in mid-April, 1982. Heath continued to write to Charlene and asked her to record her reading with De for ten minutes a day, leaving the tape-recorder on for twenty minutes after the reading. Branscombe took children's books and a tape-recorder to Charlene; during these visits, Charlene went over the tape-recordings, filling in details of background actions which had taken place during the tapings. In addition, Charlene took fieldnotes on her son's language development and wrote brief histories of his growth and play patterns. Branscombe gave Charlene minimal instructions on the procedures she thought Charlene should follow as she read to De.

Prior to June of 1982, the tapes, Charlene's fieldnotes and oral commentary on the tapes, and her case histories indicated that the adults in her household surrounded De with talk, but they usually did not direct talk to him. When they did address him directly, they gave brief commands, usually repeated three times. They used no baby talk or other simplified language addressed to the preschooler (cf. the Trackton community in Heath, 1983). In April, Charlene began to read to De; until June, she used the book as a prompt for a string of requests that he name items in the environment around him, call members of the family by name, and give others commands. She transferred the previous command mode for addressing De to the bookreading interaction and issued commands such as "Say dog," "Say A, say B." Between April and June, Charlene made few efforts to focus De's attention on the book, its pictures, or its story. However, between June and September, Charlene increasingly focused on the text and read to De, who often repeated names of items pictured in the book, and, on several occasions, after hearing a story only twice, showed his anticipation of a story's text by repeating phrases before his mother read them. By September 1982, the month of his second birthday,

---

[1] The "subjects" of this research have been identified with the full written consent of Charlene Thomas and her father. Charlene has played a role similar to that of graduate students who compile data, provide summary reports, discuss and interpret their professors' write-up of the material they've contributed, and provide suggestions for revision and additions to drafts of the article. Heath made an agreement with the students of Branscombe's ninth-grade class that they were to be acknowledged as research associates to the fullest extent possible (see Heath & Branscombe, 1985).

De was completely toilet-trained; could give his baby brother, Tutti—born in April 1982—his bottle; went to bed upon direction; got his own water from the kitchen sink; and enjoyed playing with the electronic games of older children in the neighborhood. Charlene reported of his reading:

> He calls hisself readin'—tryin' to read, but the only thing he's done is readin' the picture book. After a while, he can soon learn how. And now he gets where he had learned to count a little bit, but he can't put 'em in order. He will just say the numbers just out of order. But then you sit down and teach him how to say his ABCs, he'll mock you n' stuff like that.

By De's second birthday on September 21, 1982, the tapes of the readings and the talk that sometimes followed between mother and child had begun to include modified talk, with a high proportion of teaching questions directed to the child—a language interaction feature commonly reported from studies of mainstream mothers and children.

On a tape made two days before De's second birthday, Charlene had the first recorded conversation with a preschooler (De's 30-month-old cousin) in which she responded in a conversation initiated by the child, restated the child's utterances into well-formed sentences, and participated with the child as a conversational equal, building cooperative propositions about events which were not pictured in books. The introduction of books and regular occasions for mother and child to interact together when nurturing routines were not the focus of the interaction co-occurred with Charlene's simplified language input to her preschooler and other initial steps toward mainstream habits of talking with De and his preschool peers. She sought leisure time to read with him and ask him questions about the books.

As Tutti grew older, he became a third party to the book readings, sitting on one side of Charlene, while she read to De from a book she held between the two children. By late August of 1982, De sat beside Tutti on the floor, "read" to him by pointing to items in the books, and watched his eyes to see if he followed De's deictic gestures. Charlene had begun to attend to De and his older cousin consistently as conversational initiators, to adapt conversational topics to the children's expressions of interests, to expand the children's propositions into well-formed sentences, and to build cooperative propositions with them (cf. cases included in Ochs & Schieffelin, 1984).

During the months between the time Charlene dropped out of school and De's second birthday, reinforcement for these changed ways of talking and for the maintenance of the taping and taking of field notes had been minimal: Heath had written six letters but had never met Charlene. Branscombe had visited approximately ten times, taking books, a tape-recorder and audiotapes, and spending time listening to the tapes with Charlene. Neither Heath nor Branscombe had given specific directions to Charlene about how to read with De or how to talk with the children; she had learned through trial and error and perserverence when and where to read with De, how to hold him and the book, and how to focus his attention on the reading. She had learned to call his name to direct his attention to items in the book, and she had begun to wait and let De make his contribution to the reading. She had moved away from simply trying to get

De to label items in the books to making topic comments about the books and their pictures. She had mastered the basic features of dialogues with De about a book's contents and the difference between different types of books. Charlene had also begun to provide him with crayons, pencils, and papers, and to encourage him to draw his name and to "write stories." She had begun to speak of De as "going to school," and De had begun to push for his early entry to "school" (Head Start). Charlene offered him frames for telling about his books ("What's that book?"), allowed him to negotiate frames for book reading to Tutti and with her ("Read book, Ma?"), and provided him with a model of a book reader as she read to him and questioned him about the books. De sometimes repeated her entire utterance, sometimes selected segments for repetition, and sometimes volunteered topic comments.

There were, however, no occasions on which Charlene modeled eventcasts for De or asked him questions which would have led him to talk aloud about his activities during play, verbalizing what he was doing. De had few opportunities for activities outside the home without his mother, so she did not have cause to ask him to give account of events or actions in which he had participated but in which she had not shared. There were numerous occasions on which she asked him to recount information known to both mother and child ("What color is your grandmother's car?" "Where does your daddy work?"), but only two of these (in eighteen hours of taping) included as many as three turns exchanged between mother and child on a single topic. In September 1982, when we summarized the achievement of literacy for Charlene and De, we could not predict whether Charlene would retain the language socialization patterns acquired in the first few months of the research project or whether she would extend her ways of talking with De and Tutti. We had as yet no evidence that she had engaged De in the common mainstream ways of extending the functions and uses of literacy—providing extended discourse about real-world events related to book-based knowledge, offering running explanatory narratives during activities, forecasting future events, or accounting for events and feelings not shared by the listeners.

THE ACHIEVEMENT OF NARRATIVES

From September 1982 through August 1983, in De's third year, Charlene continued to read with De and Tutti as often as possible, recording the readings and leaving the tape recorder on for twenty minutes afterwards. However, Branscombe was no longer living near Charlene, and most communication was by letter and the mailings of audiotapes. Often Branscombe could not listen to the tapes with Charlene until several months had passed since the original taping. Thus the data and analysis presented here come only from the twenty-four audiotapes (twenty-six hours recorded between September 1982 and August 1983) and six general interviews with Charlene held between May and June 1983 and in August and September 1983. We note here to the extent possible the stages of De's production of accounts and stories, his mother's initial denial of these when they were not linked directly to book-reading routines, and her eventual acceptance and framing of occasions for his narratives.

In the tapes recorded in September and October 1982, Charlene continues to read to De, responding to his interjections with "yeah" or "look." De appears to focus intently on the order of events in the stories, remembering and anticipating what comes next. As Charlene reads the text aloud, De often anticipates segments before she says them, and he can be heard on the tape "preplaying" the actual words of the text. His favorite preplays are the sounds animals make of the names of animals.

In October, at age 25 months, De appears to begin to focus on the themes of books and to link these themes to real-world knowledge in which he has not participated directly, but about which he has heard talk. For example, as Charlene reads a book filled with pictures and labels about different kinds of workers and work, De extrapolates the book's theme and adds his own contribution to the text by breaking into Charlene's reading with an utterance about his father's work:

Sedrick, Sedrick work (10/82:218)

Charlene had not pulled him out of the text with comments about real-world events, but here De links information from the written text to knowledge gained, not from direct experience, but from hearing others talk about Sedrick going to work. In the following two weeks, he consistently interrupts Charlene's reading to make new texts modeled either on statements made in the book, or on statements he has heard which he links to the theme of the book.

In early November, as Charlene was reading a book about animals, De stops his mother, points to a wolf, and his mother responds by saying "wolk" [sic]. De repeats this term with questioning intonation, pauses 1.2 seconds, and then says "dog says woof, woof." He appears to try to make sense of the term "wolk" his mother has given him by interpreting the pictured wolf as a dog. He then restates her utterances into a well-formed sentence which enables him to make sense of the unknown term "wolf." Charlene does not respond to his statement, but resumes her reading of the names of the animals in the book. For the next few weeks, he appears on the tapes to tell himself a story based on the pictures, focusing most often on a book about a puppy. He "reads" as he creates a story about a puppy: "Pup, puppy, pup, woof, woof, puppy says woof, woof." He goes over the same text repeatedly, in a patterned practice routine offering little variation except in the order of his words. At several points, he asks his mother to help him find another of his books about puppies, or he tries to engage her in extended talk about puppies, but she replies that she doesn't have the book, and then shifts his attention to naming items in the room.

In mid-October, in the midst of a book-reading session which has focused exclusively on De's answering questions such as "What's that? Who's that?," Charlene shifts to try to create the first recorded eventcast with De.

Charlene: Who you gonna go trick or treating with?
            Who gonna take you trick or treating?

When De does not respond to this request to talk about the future, Charlene shifts to another type of narrative, asking for a recount of a recent expedition in which De was taken for ice cream and given a dollar by a family friend whose name is Mel. (Charlene

was not along on the trip, but she had been told about the outing by Mel.) Charlene
does not give an orientation to her request for a recount of the outing (10/82:28-103).[2]

Charlene	De
Where your money?	money
How much money you got?	
What dat is? What dat is?	unintelligible
	utterance beginning with /d/
How much money?	repeat of above
How much money is dat?	repeat of above
Say a dollar.	above utterance elongated
Who gave you dat?	Mel
Mel gave you dat dollar?	repeat of sound for dollar
She did?	did
You had some ice cream?	cream
'n drink	yeah
You did?	did
You had a good time?	yeah
Huh?	dollar
You got a dollar? Where Babe dollar? Where his dollar at? Mel didn't give babe no dollar?	no
Huh?	no
She didn't give babe no dollar?	no
Where Babe dollar at?	gone
Mel got it?	it gone
It gone? He spent it?	yeah
Babe spent dat dollar?	yeah
He did?	yeah
Uh hum	

Charlene then switches to asking De where various members of the family are; among
those named is King, De's dog which had been killed by a car. The exchange shifts then
to an eventcast of Christmas; she asks De what he wants for Christmas and what he
thinks Santa Claus will bring the baby. De does not respond, and she shifts to a request
that De tell how old he is and count, repeating each number after Charlene. The exchange continues for nine minutes before Charlene asks De to get her a book to read to
him. In this lengthy exchange, Charlene tries for the first time in a recording of a single
book-reading session to elicit an eventcast and a recount from De; when he does not
respond to her invitation to talk about a future event, she switches to a past event familiar to both of them. However, she turns this recount away from actual events to questions which try to structure a fantasized event—Mel's giving the baby money and the

---

[2] Charlene is a speaker of Black English, who shifts toward some standard English features in some registers. No attempt is made to represent the exact sounds of her speech. The modified spellings are used here to
represent the natural flow of her speech and in full awareness that all natural English speech differs from what
the standard orthography seems to indicate.

alternative solutions which might solve the problem of where the baby's money is now. De, however, tries to stay in a reality mode—to stick to the known text—telling Charlene that Mel did not give the baby a dollar, first through three repetitions of "no" and then through the summative statement "it gone." Only when she insists on continuing the fantasy does he seem to join in by offering her "yeah," the same rein-forcement she gives him when he creates texts different from that of the book while she is reading to him. In the final portion of this episode, mother and son switch the cus-tomary roles they play when she is reading to him; on those occasions he deviates from the known text—the book—and Charlene offers denial sometimes, silence occasionally, and at other times, a series of "yeah's" when De persists in creating his own text. Here Charlene creates her own text, which De initially denies and then weakly acknowledges with a series of "yeah's."

Tapes between October and January show a continuation of Charlene's requests for item or event labels and brief elaborations on these (e.g., "What dat?" "Duck in water, ain't it?") Between October 1982 and January 1983, Charlene did not make any tapes, but she said she had occasionally read to De. On the tapes made in January, De listens for longer stretches than he had previously done. Between April and October 1982, two minutes was the maximum time he listened without interrupting Charlene. In January, he listens as long as six minutes without breaking into the text with either questions or his own text additions. In late January, he asks the first "Why?" of the text recorded (Charlene is never recorded asking De a why- or how-question about the text of a book); previously, De (and Charlene) asked only what-questions or offered elaborating com-ments on the sounds animals made, the actions of characters, and the location of items in the pictures. In late January, Charlene reads a book on ducks, and she stops the reading to comment: "Duck crying." De asks "Why?" twice (1/83:234). Charlene re-sponds "Yeah, duck cryin'" and asks "What dis?" pointing to an item and then naming it "Bird." She continues naming items in the book and asking De to give labels. Near the end of January, Charlene, after reading several books to De, asks him to read to her. He does so, telling her to "Look, look, look" and repeating names of items in the book for her (1-27/83: 559). Charlene refers to this activity as "readin' the pictures."

In April, when Tutti was one year old, Branscombe and Heath sent books to Tutti as well as to De and asked Charlene to include Tutti in the talk surrounding her reading of books. On a tape recorded in early April, she gives De directions on how to read to Tutti: "Get down and read Tutti a story. Let him see one [book] and you read him one" (4/83:180). While De reads to Tutti, Charlene plays a color-and-counting game with Reka, De's three-year-old cousin. De eventually joins the game and a triadic conversa-tion about the colors of the eggs pictured in the book takes place. Charlene asks Reka to "tell a story"—the first such request recorded. Reka begins: "That puppy . . . (pause 3 sec.) puppy run." Charlene asks: "What kinda puppy?" De asks something which is unintelligible, and Reka answers "Puppy." Charlene then begins to count the number of puppies in the pictures and asks: "What puppy doing?" Reka answers "Gone to bed." Charlene and Reka continue talking about the puppy for several minutes longer, but Charlene does not try to reinstate a story form.

On April 7, Charlene provides the first invitation to read with De which is longer than a single utterance: "Come on and let Mama read about the little elephant. Come on up here. Come sit right here. Say Little Elephant." (4-5/83:93). Charlene's intonation here is invitational, as a teacher's might be, and she announces the topic to De before opening the storybook. Throughout the story, she asks De questions, but he interrupts, saying "Mama, dere cat [or other animals pictured in the book], mama." Throughout the story, De connects the text to his own experiences. In a portion of the text which shows animals playing cards, De comments: "Playing cards right dere. I played cards up at Jack's house" (4-7/83:144). In a story about a rabbit, he interrupts Charlene's reading to give the first recorded voluntary account of an event in which Charlene has not shared (4-7/83:198):

Look Ma, look Ma, look Ma, at that rabbit. I get another one. I get another one, a rabbit. Get rabbit up Mel's house, Get rabbit up Mel's house. Get rabbit up Mel's house.

During the next month, De consistently stops the reading to give an account of his own experience with events or items from the stories: a birthday cake, a cat in a tree, cars, and so on. In mid-April, when Charlene and De are reading a book about an elephant's birthday party to which a cat is invited, De notices a box of cornflakes pictured in one of the illustrations. De has recently been to his cousin's house, where he had cornflakes for the first time. He reads to his mother, and then breaks in with his account:

One el go
    el go
    el go walk
Two el right there
De and the el eat cornflakes. De eat cornflakes at Re's house. De eat cake at
Re's house. Look Ma, happy birthday to you (He then sings "Happy Birthday")
(4-18/83:423)

Tutti's birthday is to be in a few days, and De has been practicing the happy birthday song. In his mingling of the book's story and a real-life account, De fictionalizes himself (he and the elephant eat cornflakes), and he adds background information to which Charlene has no access (his eating of cornflakes at Re's house). De then returns to the book, however, repeating "birthday cat" several times and telling his mother to look at the cat eating birthday cake. Charlene asks, "Whose birthday is it?" De responds "cat," but Charlene says, "Tutti's birthday." De has, however, continued to focus on the book, ignores Charlene, and goes on to talk about the cat eating cornflakes and the elephant's birthday party.

Later in April, De and Charlene play a game of "Where's ————?", filling in names of various members of the family. Charlene suddenly breaks the pattern of routine questions by asking a question about the future: "You wanna go to school?" (4-18/83:332). De answers with the following eventcast, interrupted only by his mother's occasional "Yeah."

Me go to school. Go school bus. School bus come down house. School bus come down house. Ma [Mama] go school, Ma go school?

Charlene tells him that she will have to sign him up for school; he repeats "sign me up," and the eventcast and surrounding conversation end. The topic of school does not appear on the tapes again until mid-May, when Charlene and several adults are carrying on a conversation, and De is playing alone, while narrating an eventcast about himself as he plays:

I read. I play football. I got my foot. I got my schoolwork. I play football. I played basketball. I played baseball. I go school. I get my book. (5-18/83:30)

Charlene interrupts her conversation with other adults to say, "You don't go to school. When you go to school?" De answers "Today." Charlene says "No" and De tries "Tomorrow?" Charlene says "You have to wait for you to go to school."

In May of 1983, Branscombe began a series of regular visits with Charlene, going over tapes from the previous months and taking De in her car for short trips to visit a local farm and to see the animals at a small wild animal compound. When he returns from the trip, Charlene asks, "Where you and Miss Branscombe went?" This frame allows De to tell his mother about his visit to see the monkeys, how many monkeys he saw, and what they were doing. She interrupts with questions: "You see monkeys eat?" "Ya'll see birds?" urging him to fill in his story with more details. When Branscombe is not present and De gives an account of his trip to the monkeys, he includes elements Charlene does not think happened. She cuts him off, saying "You didn't see no fish" (implying she knows he saw monkeys and not fish on his outing with Branscombe). During May, De also creates fictionalized accounts of himself riding a motorcycle he says his daddy has given him, and he also tells about catching fish. When Charlene and Branscombe went over the tape, Charlene expressed her dismay at his "lies"; Branscombe assured Charlene that De was not being "bad," and that the going-to-zoo eventcast noted above was, for example, the kind of story he might be asked to tell at school. She described De as making up "stories" for himself, and said this activity may be good practice for talk about reading or for sharing time at school, so Charlene should not worry about his telling these narratives at home.

During subsequent trips in the car with Branscombe, De provides a running narrative on their whereabouts, names items and elaborates on their features, and often puts himself into an action he describes as taking place; for instance, while pointing to a ballfield, he says, "I play ball with my daddy there." Branscombe's check with Charlene indicated these events did not, in fact, take place.

From June until September, De fictionalized other members of the family in stories which drew from his car trips with Branscombe and his book reading, and, no doubt, from events he had seen on television. His favorite story motif was fishing, and during play he created stories about fishing trips with his daddy, his mother cooking the fish they caught, and the birds they saw on their fishing trips. Charlene did not ask him to tell these stories, and she did not try to "correct" his excursions into fantasy. When asking for accounts after his car trips with Branscombe, Charlene focused primarily on questions, such as, "What did you [or the animals] do?" In late June, De saw the zookeeper feed an eagle a large rat. He returned home to tell his mother: "I see a bird." She asks "What did the bird do?" He answers: "The bird cried." Charlene asks the only recorded why-question about De's talk: "Why did the bird cry?" De answers: "Because he had to eat a rat for his supper," inferring the cause of the bird's reaction.

By late June, on occasions when De used crayons to draw, he referred to his activities as "writing." When asked by Branscombe or Charlene, he refused to label separate items in his drawings. In response to adults' pointing to portions of his writing and asking "What's that?", he was silent. Usually only after he had finished his writing would he announce "a story," and he would then tell about what had occurred in the writing by giving a script: "A bear. A bear comes and eats the fish" (6/83:210). His drawings exemplify the representation of motion described by E. Ferreiro and Teberosky (1979) for preschoolers who embellish their drawing with long upward strokes to denote forward movement of vehicles, and repeated strokes for the sounds of trucks or motorcycles. (This self-generation of a stylized device parallels the internalization of literary style by preschoolers described by Green, 1982. In both cases adults gave children no explicit instruction on how to represent motion in art or to distinguish among authors' styles; yet children learned these abstract characteristics about books.)

CHILD AS NARRATIVE-MAKER: THE NECESSARY CONDITIONS

During the year between September 1982 and September 1983, Charlene and De grew together in several ways around stories, eventcasts, recounts, and accounts. Independent of repeated, redundant, or multiple scaffolds of various types by Charlene, De learned to produce narratives ranging from eventcasts to stories of fantasy. Charlene's questions about the books they read together focused primarily throughout the third year on "What's that?" and "What's that doing?" questions. Only twice on the tapes made during the twelve months (a total of twenty-six hours) did she ask questions which would have led De to focus on the motives or causes of events. On four occasions, she asked De to relate the book's events to real-life events (such as Tutti's birthday). On no occasion did she offer an evaluation of characters or events in the books' stories (e.g., "He a bad duck, isn't he?").

Snow and Goldfield (1982), in describing the book reading of Nathaniel, a mainstream child (from 2;5 to 4;21), and his mother, suggest seven functions which describe the "information categories" (illustrated below in the questions given) and "information content" (illustrated below in the answers to questions) that mother and child use in reading a picture book (p. 133). These include:

item labels (e.g. "What's that?" "That's a Dingo.")
item elaborations ("What kind of car?" "How many?" "Red." "Two")
event labels ("What's happening?" "He's climbing a tree.")
event elaborations ("Duck's in the water." "Duck can swim in the water.")

motive/cause ("Why?" "His mother's gone.")
evaluation/reaction ("What do you think?" "He's sad.")
relation to the real world ("What's that like?" "My bike.")

Snow and Goldfield point out that as Nathaniel grew older, his mother increased her requests for motive/cause, evaluation/reaction, and real world comments. Increasingly Nathaniel took responsibility for providing information content through his answers to questions asking for item labels and elaborations and event labels and elaborations; his mother carried major responsibility for motive/cause, evaluation/reaction, and real world categories and information—questions and answers.

In contrast, Charlene's conversations about books and subsequent talk around the narratives De created do not show movement away from her earlier focus on labels and elaborations. De, however, begins to create fictional stories of a state-event-state order, to fictionalize himself and others in events for which he provides comments on motive/cause, evaluation/reaction, and real-world links, and to add comments on the motivations and evaluations of actors included in his accounts of real events. In his drawings, he does not focus on discrete pieces or items, but talks of the picture as a whole story and of portions of the drawing as representing actions. By the time he was three years old, with the minimal modeling he received, De had acquired the following behaviors related to reading and talking about reading:

1. Producing spontaneous frames for opening conversations about books or real-world events ("This a book about trains." "Did you see it's raining out there?").
2. Voluntarily counting objects in books and naming their colors.
3. Voluntarily "reading" books to himself and Tutti.
4. Sustaining the topic of narratives he created, even when adults tried to divert him from the telling by asking questions.
5. Inferring causal links and internal states of both book characters and real-world animates about whom he created narratives.
6. Fictionalizing himself as a reader and writer in a future scene; explaining his current actions as "reading" and "writing."
7. Issuing imperatives to other preschoolers about "taking care of books."
8. Engaging in forecasting events to come, based on limited experiences with those events; laying out steps to be followed in a car trip, preparation of cards for a game, and so on.

In September 1983, at the age of three, De began attending the local Head Start program. Within a few weeks, the teachers told Charlene he was "too fast" and wanted to "talk too much." A shift of teachers several months into the year brought De more acceptance, and by January 1984, he was seen as the star performer of the class. He was able to count to ten, label colors, recognize his name in print, and answer questions such as "What does your Aunt Mimi's name start with?" He voluntarily gave Charlene accounts of his day at school, and he read to Tutti as well as with both his mother and father.

CONCLUSIONS

This is the second report of a longitudinal study of a child in a family in which book reading and simplified language routines with preschoolers developed in connection with the introduction of brief periods of mother-child interaction over books. With minimal modeling and scaffolding from adults, the child "lessoned" and practiced in self-talk and in solitary activities of reading and writing many key behaviors which educators judge important for school success. Just as in the period between 18 and 24 months, book reading was the primary occasion in which De learned labeling (Heath & Thomas, 1984), so in his third year, book reading was the primary occasion in which he had a frame to interact with others to give recounts, to interject his knowledge in accounts about the real world, to combine factual and fictional elements to create stories, and to ask and answer questions about written texts. Near the end of the year, as De had more experiences outside the home, requests for accounts of these events began to occur with more frequency during periods when mother and child sat down to read books. According to his mother, the book-reading episodes were her only leisure times ("rests") to "be with De" and to "teach him." In periods in which the tape-recorder was left on after the book reading, family members—including Charlene—often seemed to forget about the audio-recording; these conversational interactions outside the book-reading occasions do not contain frames for De's narratives or efforts to include De and Tutti as conversational partners.

What cannot now be known is whether Charlene will maintain the book-reading, retain her present style of questioning, or extend her requests from item and event labels and elaborations to queries about motives, causes, reactions, evaluations, and real events in the next year. If Charlene does not extend her questioning, we do not know whether De will, in the absence of help from his mother, develop more complex narratives which will move him closer to the kinds of narratives needed for successful school performance. We also cannot know whether or not Charlene will encourage or model fantasy in her talk about books or in fictionalized narratives about De; she has not yet done so on more than three occasions (cf. Kavanaugh, Whittington, & Cerbone, 1983 on the use and importance of fantasy in speech with mainstream preschoolers). Studies of mainstream children indicate that adult-child interactions around books and through told and retold stories help prepare preschoolers for behaviors valued in school reading: finding the main or most important idea in a narrative; reordering narrative events in "correct" temporal sequence; making inferences from text information and subsequent judgments about the texts; and summarizing the events of a narrative (cf. Stein & Trabasso, 1982, p. 213).

We have shown, from the data presented here, that from the relatively minimal scaffolding he received in episodes centered around books, De learned numerous language forms and specific behaviors associated with mainstream literate behaviors. He used items, events, causes, reactions, and comparisons of events to organize factual and fantasized narratives about past, current, and future events. During the period from 24 to 36 months, he and his mother continued a sociocultural event which began as an intervention in their daily routines. With this book reading intervention, De developed a perception of himself as reader and writer; and his mother developed a consciousness of her child's roles as a coparticipant in talk, a fictionalized character in his created tales, a fiction-maker, an elaborator of meaning, and a possible source of new information.

This study underscores the importance of considering the sociocultural contexts which support the development of certain types of narratives. The systematic structures which story-grammar theorists have found in their studies of mainstream children have been strongly influenced both by the literate organization of past experience used in families which have language habits similar to those used in formal schooling, and by assumptions that language development proceeds through an invariant series of stages. Researchers have thus been strongly inclined to infer that these patterns are—or should be—common to all children learning all languages in all types of sociocultural settings.

However, the way a child learns of different genres, organizational schemata for different types of narratives, and questioning routines to extract meaning from narratives depends very much on the language to which he is exposed and the frames and occasions open to him in his early language socialization. The basic order of acquisition and the set of narrative features used and heard in mainstream homes and expected in school are not universal. Neither a single model of a story grammar nor a single set of schemata for organizing certain genres of narrative is likely to be ecologically valid across cultures. Children do not have psychological proclivities toward some narrative schemata and not others. In the words of Rosen:

> However universal our human bent for narratizing experience, we encounter our own society's modes for doing this. There is no one way of telling stories; we learn the story grammars of our society, our culture. Since there are irreconcilable divisions in our society of sex, class, ethnicity, we should expect very diverse, but not mutually exclusive, ways of telling stories. The composer of a story is not a completely free agent (1982, pp. 11–12).

Children learn to "play the game of free choice according to the rules" of their own cultural community.

We need, however, to know more about the environmental factors which condition these rules. We provide here further evidence to support the suggestions of Goody (1977), Bruner (1984), Olson (1984), and others, that the focused activity of book reading—even in relatively limited amounts and without the development of complex interactional scaffolding—provides a "playful setting" in which children learn to use language in "daring" and "advanced" (Bruner, 1984, p. 196) ways. The book as prop allows numerous frames through which children learn to create narratives of various genres on both information in books and knowledge beyond books. The book, unlike comics, television, or routine conversation, forces adult and child to focus on saying what things are and what they mean—critical skills for meeting the demands of school.

As researchers collect more detailed accounts of the different patterns by which children learn to produce and comprehend narratives, we will learn more about varieties of genres and features as they co-occur with certain structural and functional aspects of sociocultural environments. We speculate that after numerous cross-cultural comparisons, researchers will be able to posit a human bioprogram which carries the potential for enabling an individual to play, monitor, and evaluate incoming information presented in narrative form. Researchers should then also be able to demonstrate that particular orderings and stages of these processes are dependent on contexts of learning which have specifiable features (cf. Sternberg, 1984). The particular sociocultural environments of children will vary depending on whether or not the adults around them respond, consciously and unconsciously, to children as information-givers and perceive adults as the agents responsible for teaching, modeling, and reinforcing a particular set of skills and a body of knowledge for the child. Thus our models of the order in which children acquire narratives will have to include key features of the social structures and belief systems which surround the child and determine the sequence and types of information offered to the child. In short, our models will have to account for the types of narrative structures that result from different contexts for narrative building which co-occur with certain sociocultural environments.

REFERENCES

Brewer, W. (1984). *The structural affect theory of stories.* Paper given at CORR–5, Annual Meeting of the International Reading Association, Atlanta. Manuscript.

Bruner, J. (1984). Language, mind and reading. In H. Goelman, A. Oberg, & F. Smith (Eds.), *Awakening to literacy.* Exeter, NH: Heinemann Educational Books.

Calfee, R. (1981). Some theoretical and practical ramifications of story grammars. *Journal of Pragmatics, 6,* 441–450.

Cochran-Smith, M. (1984). *The making of a reader.* Norwood, NJ: Ablex.

Colby, B. (1966). Cultural patterns in narrative. *Science, 151,* 793–98.

Corsaro, W. A. (1977). The clarification request as a feature of adult interactive styles with young children. *Language in Society, 6,* 183–207.

Dore, J. (1979). Conversational acts and the acquisition of language. In E. Ochs & B. B. Schieffelin (Eds.), *Developmental pragmatics.* New York: Academic Press.

Ferguson, C. A., & Macken, M. (1983). The role of play in phonological development. In K. E. Nelson (Ed.), *Children's language* (vol. 4). Hillsdale, NJ: Erlbaum.

Ferreiro, E., & Teberosky, A. (1979). *Literacy before schooling.* Exeter, NH: Heinemann Educational Books.

Goelman, H. (1982). Selective attention in language comprehension: Children's processing of expository and narrative discourse. *Discourse Processes, 5,* 53–72.

Goffman, E. (1981). *Forms of talk.* Philadelphia: University of Pennsylvania Press.

Goody, J. (1977). *The domestication of the savage mind.* Cambridge: Cambridge University Press.

Green, G. (1982). Competence for implicit text analysis: Literary style discrimination in five-year-olds. In D. Tannen (Ed.), *Georgetown University round table on languages and linguistics.* Washington, DC: Georgetown University Press.

Heath, S. B. (1982). What no bedtime story means: Narrative skills at home and school. *Language in Society, 11*(2), 49–76.

Heath, S. B. (1983). *Ways with words: Language, life, and work in communities and classrooms.* Cambridge: Cambridge University Press.

Heath, S. B., & Branscombe, A. (1985). Intelligent writing in an audience community: Teacher, students, and researcher. In S. W. Freedman (Ed.), *The acquisition of written language: Revision and response.* Norwood, NJ: Ablex.

Heath, S. B., & Thomas, C. (1984). The achievement of preschool literacy for mother and child. In H.

Goelman, A. Oberg, & F. Smith (Eds.), *Awakening to literacy*. Exeter, NH: Heinemann Educational Books.

Kavanaugh, R. D., Whittington, S., & Cerbone, M. J. (1983). Mothers' use of fantasy in speech to young children. *Journal of Child Language, 10*, 45–55.

Mandler, J. M., & Johnson, N. S. (1977). Remembrance of things parsed: Story structure and recall. *Cognitive Psychology, 9*, 111–51.

Ninio, A., & Bruner, J. (1978). The achievement and antecedents of labelling. *Journal of Child Language, 5*, 1–15.

Ochs, E. (1982). Talking to children in Western Samoa. *Language in Society, 11*(2), 77–105.

Ochs, E., & Schieffelin, B. B. (1984). *Acquiring conversational competence*. London: Routledge & Kegan Paul.

Ochs, E., & Schieffelin, B. B. (1985). Three developmental stories and their implications. In R. A. Schweder & R. A. LeVine (Eds.), *Culture theory: Essays on mind, self, and emotion*. New York: Cambridge University Press.

Olson, D. (1984). "See! Jumping!" Some oral language antecedents of literacy. In H. Goelman, A. Oberg, & F. Smith (Eds.), *Awakening to literacy*. Exeter, NH: Heinemann Educational Books.

Prince, G. (1981). *Narratology: The form and functioning of narrative*. Berlin: Mouton Publishers.

Rosaldo, R. (1983). *Ilongot headhunting*. Cambridge: Cambridge University Press.

Rosen, H. (1982). *The nurture of narrative*. Paper given at Annual Meeting of the International Reading Association, Chicago. Manuscript.

Rumelhart, D. E. (1975). Notes on a schema for stories. In D. G. Bobrow & A. Collins (Eds.), *Representation and understanding*. New York: Academic Press.

Schwartzman, H. (1979). *Transformations: The anthropology of children's play*. New York: Plenum.

Scollon, R., & Scollon, S. (1981). *Narrative, literacy, and face in interethnic communication*. Norwood, NJ: Ablex.

Snow, C., & Goldfield, B. A. (1982). Building stories: The emergence of information structures from conversation. In D. Tannen (Ed.), *Georgetown University round table on languages and linguistics*. Washington, DC: Georgetown University Press.

Stein, N. (1982). What's in a story: Interpreting the interpretations of story grammars. *Discourse Processes, 5*, 319–335.

Stein, N., & Kilgore, K. M. *The concept of a story*. Manuscript submitted for publication.

Stein, N., & Policastro, M. (forthcoming). The concept of a story: A comparison between children's and teachers' viewpoints. In H. Mandl, N. Stein, & T. Trabasso (Eds.), *Learning and comprehension of text*. Hillsdale, NJ: Erlbaum.

Stein, N., & Trabasso, T. (1982). Children's understanding of stories: A basis for moral judgment and resolution. In C. J. Brainerd & M. Presley (Eds.), *Verbal processes in children*. New York: Springer-Verlag.

Sternberg, R. (1984). *Beyond IQ. Toward a triarchic theory of intelligence*. Cambridge: Cambridge University Press.

Sutton-Smith, B., & Heath, S. B. (1981) Paradigms of pretense. *The Quarterly Newsletter of the Laboratory of Comparative Human Cognition, 3*(3), 42–5.

Umiker-Sebeok, J. (1979). Preschool children's intraconversational narratives. *Journal of Child Language, 6*(1), 91–109.

3

Reading to Children:
A Model for Understanding Texts

Marilyn Cochran-Smith
University of Pennsylvania

Becoming a reader requires shifting from the language strategies used to interpret face-to-face oral interactions to the language strategies used to interpret decontextualized essayist literacy. We know little, however, about the ways adults (in literate communities) help children make this shift. This chapter describes some of the experiences of one group of preschoolers involved in the process of making this transition. The chapter is drawn from a larger study concerning the ways adults help preschool children acquire and develop the literary and social knowledge needed to appropriately approach, interpret, and use texts and other printed materials (Cochran-Smith, 1984).

The larger study was based on participant-observation, interviewing and audio-recording of storyreadings over a period of 18 months at a private nursery school in a Philadelphia community. Members of this nursery school community identified themselves as middle-class, school-oriented families. Individual interviews with each family revealed an out-of-school environment in which literacy was assumed. Reading and writing were preferred activities for both adults and children, and preschoolers were regularly exposed to bookreading for a variety of purposes. Underlying bookreading practices was a system of adult values and beliefs that centered heavily on the importance of reading for lifetime academic and intellectual success, personal growth and development, and individual entertainment.

Although nursery school families assumed that education was the key to their children's futures, they were decidedly not in favor of preschool programs that stressed reading and writing instruction. They reported that they make little or no conscious effort to teach reading and writing at home or at nursery school, and they made no overt acknowledgment that their children were being taught a particular orientation to literacy. Nevertheless, bookreading and other print-based activities were pervasive in nursery school life. The children were daily exposed to a variety of uses of literacy and very early demonstrated considerable competence in using reading and writing for these purposes.

The adults in this community saw no incongruity between a nursery school program laden with literacy activities and a nursery school philosophy that deemphasized literacy instruction. They saw no incongruity precisely because the context of literacy activities at the nursery school was *not* instruction. That is, literacy events did not occur within

35

contexts artificially constructed for educational purposes. Rather they were embedded within routine adult-child social transactions; adults chose to use print in these transactions not in order to teach literacy skills, but because print was effective in many aspects of their everyday lives.

Adult-child storyreading emerged as the key literacy event in the nursery school; hence the primary data base for the larger study was a corpus of 100 annotated storyreading transcriptions. Storyreadings and all other literacy events that occurred in the nursery school were analyzed according to their structures of interactional and interpretive norms in relation to the contexts in which they occurred. This chapter discusses several aspects of the adult-child oral storyreading process itself.[1]

INTRODUCTION

In his preface to *S/Z*, Barthes' (1974) work on ways in which readers read, Howard (1974) argues that "we require an education in literature . . . in order to discover that what we assumed . . . was nature is in fact culture, that what was given is no more than a way of talking" (p. ix). What Howard seems to be suggesting is that we tend to consider our ways of reading as "given" or "natural" rather than learned. Barthes' analysis urges us to instead examine the "givens" in literature as learned, and perhaps culturally specific "ways of taking."

Ways of making sense of the relatively uncomplicated narratives in children's picture books are easy to take for granted, to consider given. What *is* actually given, however, is the assumption that the readers/listeners of these picture books will have had particular kinds of experiences in the world and will use (or be helped to use) particular strategies for understanding texts. That is, it is assumed that readers will take the knowledge that they have gained from primary or secondary experiences outside of texts and use this knowledge in particular ways in order to make sense inside texts. Children, however, are not born knowing how to connect their knowledge and experience in "literate" ways to printed and pictorial texts. Rather, they must learn strategies for understanding texts just as they must learn the ways of eating and talking that are appropriate to their cultures or social groups. In the community I studied, much of the learning of ways to make connections between experience and texts (or "literacy socialization") seemed to be taking place within adult-child oral storyreadings. In other words, during the process of reading to children, adults were helping children learn to understand texts, and storyreadings were serving as an important part of the process of children's becoming literate.

The discussion that follows examines this process of group oral storyreading in one literate community. In order to provide some insight into the process, the discussion begins with a description of two of the major features of group storyreading. First,

---

[1] A shorter version of this chapter, " 'What Is Given Is No More Than a Way of Taking': Children Learning to Make Sense of Texts," was prepared for the World Congress of Sociology X, Mexico City, Mexico, August 16–21, 1982.

storyreadings were socially interactive, conversational events that included active participation by both adult readers and child listeners. In this first section, I make the
argument that these storyreadings were scaffolded by both the children's prior achievement of the norms of conversation *and* by the design and language style of picture books
themselves. Second, storyreadings were joint ventures in which the meanings of storybooks were cooperatively negotiated. In this section, I argue that the storyreader served
as mediator between children and texts by providing frameworks within which the texts
could be read. In this way the storyreader gave the decontextualized language of essayist
literacy *a context* and effectively transformed storyreading events so that they allowed for
joint construction or negotiation of meaning. Following discussion of these two major
characteristics of group storyreading, I analyze storyreading as a model for understanding texts. In this third section, I examine storyreading conversations more closely and
describe some of the sense-making strategies that the storyreader was modeling for the
children.

A CONVERSATIONAL EVENT

The nature and course of children's early language acquisition and development in the
primarily middle-class families of white, western literate societies have been studied
extensively.[2] The research has documented well the fact that children who are part of
these social groups learn to make sense of oral language via social interactions with
adults. Very early on these interactions take the form of dialogues wherein children are
treated as conversational partners who are capable of intention and meaning. Within
these dialogues and through a process of oral turn-taking, adults shape and guide both
the meanings of children's speech and children's interpretations of others' speech. The
turn-taking model is learned early in these social groups and, as Ninio and Bruner
(1978) point out, it often allows for or "scaffolds" the acquisition of other language
concepts and skills, such as lexical labels (Ninio & Bruner, 1978) or particular lexical
and syntactic forms (Snow & Goldfield, 1980, 1982).

My research on storyreading coupled with several other studies that look at children's early experiences with texts (see, for example, Taylor, 1983; Magee & Sutton-
Smith, 1983; Miller, Nemoianu, & DeJong, this volume) begins to make the case that
the turn-taking, conversational model that scaffolds much of early language learning in
particular social groups also scaffolds children's early learning of ways to understand,
deal with, and talk about storybook texts. In the community I observed, the adult
storyreader shaped and guided children's understandings of story texts by conversing
with them *during* storyreadings that were governed by turn-taking norms and often patterned by adult-directed couplets of question-answer or incomplete phrase-completion.
In this way storyreadings were not oral renditions of printed texts, as the conventional
use of the term implies, but were, instead, conversations themselves. These conversa-

---

[2] For an insightful discussion of oral language in these social groups and a review of much of this research,
see Ochs and Schieffelin (1982).

tions *did* contain readings of printed texts, but the readings were continuously broken apart by, and intertwined with, talk. The conversational patterning of storyreading served as a scaffolding as adults helped children understand printed and pictorial texts.

Key illustrations of the conversational scaffolding of storyreadings occurred when the adult storyreader shared wordless picture books with the nursery school children. In wordless books narratives are implicit within the pictures of a book, but are not explicitly stated as written texts. During "readings" of books of this kind, reader and listeners took conversational turns as they jointly constructed oral texts across utterances. In this way each storyreading became, essentially, a conversation—a network of verbal give-and-take, and *not* an adult's performance of text for a passive audience.

Example 1 is excerpted from a storyreading of a wordless picture book. In this example we can clearly see the active participation of both adult reader and child listeners as they constructed the text implicit within the book's illustrations. We can also see how this story construction was scaffolded by the children's prior achievement of the norms of conversational turn-taking.[3]

Example 1

Reader		Listeners	
Verbal	**Nonverbal**	**Verbal**	**Nonverbal**
Amy:			
All right . . .			
	holds up book	(many children talking)	
[PIC: bird flying downward toward evergreen tree]	opens to first page		
Once upon a time . . .		Mark: Once upon a time . . . (exact intonation as reader)	
there was a . . .	pats picture of bird	Curt: Birdie!	points to picture
		Mark: Birdie	
		Suzie: Birdie	
		Curt: Flying! (excited)	
This is called the . . .	turns back to cover, points to words of title	Susie: I want a scary, scary story.	on knees
good . . .			
/beh/. . .			

---

[3] The transcription system used in examples is adapted from Ochs' (1979) "basic transcript." The behaviors of the storyreader appear on the left and behaviors of the storylisteners appear on the right side of the page. In each case, verbal behaviors are in the first column and nonverbal behaviors in the second column. Information about the situational and discourse contexts is enclosed in parentheses. Except for overlapping behaviors (indicated by horizontal placement), the transcript is temporally arranged and should be read in a continuous left-to-right, top-to-bottom manner. Utterances follow the usual conventions of capitalization and punctuation. Book information appears in the first column of the left side of the page. Description of illustrations (LP, RP or PIC) appears in the transcript immediately after the storyreader has turned the page (TP). Picture information is enclosed in brackets. The words of picture book texts are enclosed in quotation marks; within quotation marks reader modifications are enclosed in parentheses, and original text materials are marked "t."

Example 1 *Continued*

Reader		Listeners	
Verbal	Nonverbal	Verbal	Nonverbal
	TP		
[PIC: bird sitting on tree; house with fishbowl in window off to side of picture]			
And he flew . . .	makes downward motion with hand tracing path of bird	Curt: To a tree Andrew: De tree, and then he flew to a house Mark: A house!	
Near a house . . .		Susie: With a fish!	

A striking feature of this storyreading is its socially interactive, conversational nature. That is, the storyreading was an event in which both adult reader and child listeners continuously played very active verbal roles. It is readily apparent from this example that to analyze storyreading events of this kind, there is no way to separate out what the children were saying or understanding of the text from the conversation itself. Rather the children's experience of the text occurred *within* the social interaction of their conversation with the reader. Much of the children's experience had to do with what the reader was saying and doing as she guided the verbal interaction around the pictures so that it became a dialogue in form and shape. For example, the storyreader repeatedly uttered incomplete phrases and then paused for several seconds. The contour of these phrases was consistently a rising intonation with a long drawn-out emphasis on the last word. This rising intonation coupled with the long pause functioned both to allow the children their turns in the story-reading conversation *and* to provide them with many of the connectives and temporal markers needed to understand the story.

Like both Ninio and Bruner's (1978) analysis of adult-child picture book labeling and Cazden's (1980) analysis of child-adult peek-a-boo games, the conversational nature of storyreading can be seen as a kind of scaffolding in which the specific questions, comments, and incomplete phrases of the adult reader provided slots for child listeners to sort out and integrate various aspects of stories.

The children's prior achievement of the norms of turn-taking was not the only factor that encouraged and supported the children's understanding of, and experience with, storybooks. The style and design of the picture books themselves also supported the storyreadings. Picture book language, style, and design implied both joint adult-child readership and a dialogic relationship between adults as storyreaders and children as listeners. For example, it was a stylistic feature of many of the picture book texts shared during group storyreading to directly address the reading/listening audience with open-ended questions (e.g., "Do you know what you like?" or "What makes you mad?"). Through direct address these texts seemed to imply that some adult reader would address "you" phrases to child listeners and would then hold the floor open for the child listeners to respond. In this way, the language of the texts themselves often invited audience response through verbal participation.

Example 2 illustrates how the conversational style of picture book texts fed directly into a dialogic, socially interactive pattern of storyreading. The book shared in Example 2 was a comical play on both books of politeness and parental reminders to children to repeat politeness formulae. The conversational text of the book, which was directly addressed to the audience, invited listeners to participate by repeating the correct formulae and, at the same time, laughing at the absurd situations posed by pictures and text. This excerpt points out both the stylistic feature of direct address and the way it helped the storyreader invite listeners to become actively verbally involved in the storyreading.

Example 2 points out the relationship between the verbal style of the text and the conversational style of the reading of the text. The stylistic feature of direct address used in the text invited the audience to become involved with the book and to very actively participate in co-creating its meaning. It also assumed and built on a conversational relationship between adult storyreaders and child listeners. In this way the design and style of the printed text itself helped to scaffold the children's experience with, and understanding of, the text.

Example 2

Reader		Listeners	
Verbal	Nonverbal	Verbal	Nonverbal
Amy: [PIC: man with elephant under arm; children walking away, carrying elephant]			
"You are downtown and there's this gentleman giving baby elephants to people. You want to take one home because you've always wanted a baby elephant, but first the gentleman introduces you to each other. What do you say dear?"			
		Ben: Thank you	
What do you say dear?			
		Kris: Thank you	
		Curt: Thank you	
What do *you* say?	nods toward Andrew		
		Andrew: Thank you	
If he's introducing you . . . He's getting you so that you know. What do you say . . .			
		Ben: Thank you	
		Andrew: Thank you	

Example 2 *Continued*

Reader		Listeners	
Verbal	Nonverbal	Verbal	Nonverbal
When you first meet some- body, you say . . .	mimes shaking hands with someone	Ben: Hello Kris: Hello Curt: Hello Andrew: Hello	(in rapid succession)
Introducing a person, you say . . . [PIC: boy and elephant bow to one another] "How do you do?"	TP		
		Ben: How do you do, mister!	

Examples like this one help us to make the case that there is a direct tie, in particular groups, between the texts to which young children are exposed and the language and cultural assumptions that underlie these texts. That is, for the community studied here, children's texts were written and produced by people whose language backgrounds were, by and large, the same as the language backgrounds of those for whom the books were intended. This interrelated network of producers and consumers of early texts for children built on and assumed certain language patterns and experiences.

Some of the assumptions underlying the design and style of picture books and the assumptions of those who both produced and used these books can be stated as follows:

1. Bookreading (booksharing, booklooking, picture labeling, etc.) is an appropriate and desirable activity for young children who cannot yet read or write in the conventional sense.

2. Books designed exclusively for young children are appropriate and desirable materials for use during these bookreadings.

3. Bookreadings are interactive activities wherein adults (or other experienced readers of the community) read and share texts with young children who listen, respond, and actively verbally participate.

4. Adults and children have a conversational relationship already established which supports their bookreadings and scaffolds their interactive construction of meaning in texts.

This is not to suggest that the language of early picture books for children is simply an imitation of adult-child "talk" written down. To the contrary, book language is by its very nature quiet different from face-to-face oral conversation. And the task of becoming literate and learning to make sense of printed and pictorial texts requires more than simply breaking the sound-symbol code. This *is* to suggest, however, that the texts and design of picture books for young children assume, and are directly tied to, the adult-child oral language patterns of the social groups that produce and use them

In addition to their experiences with many storybooks, young children who have participated in conversational storyreadings of the kind described here have been exposed to the idea that textual meanings are negotiable. That is, they have participated in storyreadings that operate on the principle that textual meanings are constructed by connecting one's knowledge and experience of the world to the printed or pictorial text. This idea is discussed below.

A NEGOTIATED EVENT

Storyreadings in the literate community I observed were joint ventures not only in the sense, discussed above, that they were actively participated in by both reader and listeners, but also in the sense that storybook meanings themselves were cooperatively negotiated. Examples 1 and 2 indicate that the storyreader's role was an active and flexible one. This role is in contrast to other oral readings we can envision (for example, a professor delivering a paper at a conference, a minister reading a Biblical passage to his or her congregation, a Congressman presenting a statement to the legislature) wherein there is usually little or no commentary or glossing of the text while it is being read. Rather during oral readings like these, even when the reader is himself or herself the author of the text, the reader functions primarily as spokeperson for the text by translating from the written to the oral channel. Reader-as-spokesperson-for-text was not an adequate description of the reader's role in nursery school storyreadings in the community studied. To the contrary the reader almost never functioned simply as spokesperson for a text. In fact as many as 80% of her utterances during a single storyreading were commentary and annotation *on* the printed or pictorial text rather than direct reading *from* the text.

The texts of stories were not simply read to the children; nor did the children respond as passive listeners or as participants only through ritualized responses. Rather the storyreader was very much aware of the responses of each particular group of listeners, and individuals' responses influenced the storyreader's guidance of interaction around the text. Again we see a contrast with other oral reading situations (for example, responsive readings or church prayers where congregations read ritual phrases at specific times). These situations are socially interactive (that is, both readers and listeners actively participate) but are not cooperatively negotiated (that is, the nature of readers' and listeners' utterances are not mutually dependent). In responsive readings and the like, standard phrases are uttered by both readers and listeners; neither is free to deviate from the text. In nursery school storyreadings, however, just the opposite was true. Both reader and listeners deviated from the text, and the responses of each depended to a great extent on the prior responses of the other. Especially for the storyreader, who dominated the interaction, the meaning that the listeners seemed to be making of the text directly shaped her own role in the storyreading. Hence two readings of the same book by the same storyreader did not call forth the same interactive patterns. Rather the cooperative negotiation of the story by the reader and the listeners depended on what listeners noticed in texts and pictures, what they understood or were confused by, and how they were interpreting the story—in short, the meaning that the listening group seemed to be finding in the picture book.

In their comparison of bard and formula oral narratives with Athabaskan oral narrative, Scollon and Scollon (1980) have suggested a distinction between "focused" and "non-focused" interactions that is useful here. Focused situations, such as formularized oral narratives, "force the adoption of some non-negotiated way of making sense" (p. 27) and allow for little repair or recycling. Non-focused situations, such as Athabaskan oral narratives, on the other hand, are interactive and "mutually negotiated . . . (they) emphasize respect for the sense the other is making of the situation . . . " (p. 27). Scollon and Scollon argue that essayist literacy necessitates focused situations because writers of essayist literacy know little or nothing about their distant audiences and hence must "assume responsibility for unilateral sense-making" (p. 28).

The arguments posed by Scollon and Scollon help to point out an interesting and significant aspect of preschool storyreading: it involved *both* the reading of essayist literacy (Scollon and Scollon's focused interaction) *and* cooperative negotiation of story by reader and listeners (Scollon and Scollon's non-focused interaction). While this may present a contradiction in Scollon and Scollon's terms, it provides some insight into the nature of nursery school storyreading and its role in the literary socialization process of this particular literate community.

Because it centered on the reading of essayist literacy but also accommodated the sense-making of individual listeners, nursery school oral storyreading had some of the characteristics of both negotiated and non-negotiated interactions. The books read to the nursery school children were characterized by a non-negotiated kind of communication: to understand the texts readers/listeners had to make sense of language that was decontextualized, or independent for its meaning on a particular writing or reading context. And yet the conversational storyreading context within which these books were read was characterized by a negotiated kind of communication as well: the story reader, who was translating the text from written to oral mode, very much respected and responded to her listeners' sense-making efforts. Specifically, there *were* opportunities for repair and recycling of textual meanings within storyreadings, and there *was* a two-way effort at making sense of the texts. In this way storyreading functioned to provide the nursery children with oral and group opportunities for practice at "making sense of texts," or book reading, an activity that was essentially silent and solitary for the adult members of this community, and would eventually be silent and solitary for the children as well.

The story reader played a key role in these readings.

The Storyreader as Mediator between Children and Texts
Several literary theorists (see, for example, Booth, 1961; Iser, 1974, 1980) have described the phenomenon of spatial and temporal separation of writers and readers of essayist literacy by developing the literary notion of "implied" or fictionalized reader. This concept can be summarized something like this: writers of essayist literacy are separated from their audiences by greater or lesser distances in both time and space. Because writers of essayist literacy never know their readers, they cannot rely upon the personal experiences or knowledge stores of particular individuals to provide a background against which texts can be read and interpreted. Instead interpretive information must be contained in the text. Of course for writers to include in written texts everything that readers need to read their texts or to explain to them all that there is to

be explained is impossible. Instead readers actively and continuously participate in the creation of meanings in texts by bringing their own life and literary experiences to bear upon texts. Writers, however, have no way of knowing specifically what their anonymous and distant readers bring to texts. Furthermore during actual readings of texts, there is no face-to-face interaction between authors and readers and hence there is no opportunity for writers to repair misunderstood passages or offer further explanations where needed. As a result either consciously or subconsciously, writers create or imply readers within texts themselves.

Booth (1961) argues that an *"author creates . . . his reader; he makes his reader,* as he makes his second self, and the most successful reading is one in which the created selves author and reader, can find complete agreement"* (emphasis added, pp. 137–138). Booth's description proposes that the real reader of a work must, to a certain extent, take on or match up with the characteristics of the reader implied in the work in order to read that work "successfully."

I have already suggested that preschool storyreading in the community I studied was conversationally interactive and jointly negotiated. What I wish to argue now is that as the storyreader guided the children in interactive sequences, part of what she was doing was mediating between child listeners and texts. That is, in order to make for Booth's "successful" reading, the storyreader was continuously monitoring the "match" between the reader implied in the text and the real readers who sat before her listening to the text. To help the children make sense of the text, the storyreader guided them to take on the characteristics of the readers implied in individual works. To shape real readers into implied readers or whenever a mismatch between the two occurred or seemed about to occur, the storyreader overrode the textual narrator and became the narrator herself, annotating the text and trying to establish some sort of agreement between real and implied readers. Hence the storyreader was constantly mediating by alternating between two roles—spokesperson for the text and secondary narrator or commentator on the text.

To mediate the storyreader had to continuously assess and interpret both the text (e.g., its lexical and syntactic structures, its storyline, temporal and spatial sequences, amount and kind of information carried by the pictures and by the words and the interrelationships of these two kinds of information) *and* the sense that the listeners were making of all of these. Listeners' sense-making was monitored by the reader's paying close attention to the responses of the listeners.

This process of storyreading mediation is clarified somewhat by the following excerpt from a single storyreading. In the storyreading in Example 3 the reader continuously monitored the coincidence between implied and real readers and mediated between the two. The book being read was a simple story of two boys who built a snowman, argued about its ownership, destroyed it during a snowball fight, reconsidered their feelings, and then returned to build together a series of little snowmen. To the right of the actual verbal interaction around the storyreading, I have superimposed a description of the reader's mediation between real and implied readers by suggesting some of the messages about making sense of texts that are implicit in the reader's comments. This is not to suggest that the reader was consciously or deliberately motivated

by an inner-commentary of the sort I have constructed. To the contrary, for this particular storyreader in this particular community, storyreading mediation was more or less
automatic; it was taken for granted and considered routine by adult members of the
community. In this example we can clearly see how the storyreader mediated between
implied and real readers and, in doing so, helped the children make sense of the text.

Example 3 makes clear that storyreading mediation involved a process of mediated
sense-making. The very young literary apprentices who participated in the storyreading
were not faced with the task of making sense of an author's unilateral text. Instead they
received a great deal of explicit instruction—confirmation of their correct, and negation
of their incorrect, attempts at sense-making. If they misunderstood or became confused, they were allowed to try again; specific textual passages or pictorial features that
caused confusion were pointed out and the proper ways to make sense explained. In the
storyreading in Example 3, the key event in understanding temporal sequence occurred
between two pictures and hence had to be inferred, but the children had difficulty with
this sequence. To guide the children closer to the image of the reader implied in the
text, the storyreader initiated an interaction sequence in which she recycled several
pages of text and illustration, emphasizing temporal language and pointing out the
ways in which the pictured actions were temporally related to one another. Through a
mediated story-reading experience, the children were receiving instruction in how to
take information from their pool of world knowledge and experience in order to make
sense of a text. Primarily through this sort of mediation, oral storyreading became a sort
of intermediate step between making sense of face-to-face, oral interaction and making
sense of decontextualized literary texts.

The Role of Metanarrative in Storyreading

One way of looking at these sense-making interactions is to consider them in relation to
what Prince (1980, 1982) has called "metanarrative" signals to readers concerning ways
in which particular parts of texts are to be read and interpreted. Prince has suggested
that narrative texts include both narrative statements that advance the narrative itself
and metanarrative signs or narrative self-references that concentrate on the codes according to which readers read and make sense of narratives. For example, as Prince has demonstrated, "Mary was crying" is a narrative statement; it advances the plot or action of a
narrative. In the sentence, "Mary was crying; this was a mystery," however, the second
clause is not a narrative statement but a metanarrative signal to the reader about how to
read and interpret the first clause concerning Mary's actions and/or state of mind
(Prince, 1980).

Children's narratives, of course, contain metanarrative signals to their readers just as
adults' narratives do. The point I wish to make here, however, is that in adult-child
verbal interactions around printed or pictorial narratives, the adult story reader provided a wealth of metanarrative information *in addition to* that which was provided
within the text itself. Hence the storyreader essentially transformed the usually
internalized and automatic reading process common to the adult readers of this literate
community into an outwardly explicit and very gradual sense-building process for the
group of young literary apprentices who sat before her listening to stories. This brings

Example 3

Reader		Listeners		Metanarrative Commentary
Verbal	Nonverbal	Verbal	Nonverbal	
"'Hooray for *my* snowman,' cheered Calvin."	points to herself			text: reading
Whose is it?	looks up at children TP	Ben: Both of 'em		There is going to be a conflict here. It revolves around ownership of the snowman. Pay attention to what the characters say about who owns the snowman
"'But he's my snowman,' said Berkley. 'I thought of him first.' 'But I did most of the work,' said Calvin. 'So he's mine.' 'Ah, nuts to you!' said Berkley."	points to herself			text: reading
	waves hand in a dismissing gesture TP			
[Pic: Boys begin to throw snow at each other]				

Notice facial expressions in the drawing; they give you a clue about the moods of the boys. Relate these moods to what the boys just said. Remember the temporal sequence we just read; the boys started out as friends, but now the situation has changed.

Be ready! Pay attention; something bad is beginning to happen! This snowball fight is not for fun.

This picture portrays a series of actions; relate those actions to one another. The boys are fighting. The snowballs in the air have been thrown by the boys. The boy getting hit on the head was aimed at by the other boys.

"Ah, nuts to *you*," said Calvin." (angry voice)

Boy, look at 'em! Getting madder by the minute, those two. I thought they were friends.   *points to picture of snowball fight*

Oh oh! Got a snowball right in the head   *points to boy being hit in the head*

TP

[PIC: no text, picture shows snowball fight continuing]

Before you know it, look! Snowball, snowball, and splat! Right on the head   *points to boy throwing ball* *points to boy hit in head*

47

us back to the idea, following Barthes (1974), of literary sense-making as a "way of taking" rather than as a given.

This is not to argue that the reader consciously engaged in metanarrative activity. To the contrary the storyreader's metanarrative commentary occurred because the reader wanted to share a good (i.e., funny, entertaining, interesting, informative, pertinent, scary, timely) story with the children. To the members of this community, the context of storyreading was never "teaching the children how to read or understand a story," and the goal of storyreading was never "instruction in how to enjoy a story." Rather for this community, the context of storyreading was understanding itself, and the goal was enjoyment itself. What I am essentially suggesting here is that the preschool children in the community I studied were instructed, both directly and indirectly, in a model for taking various kinds of knowledge of the world and using these as frameworks or codes for reading particular parts of texts. This idea is described in the following section.

A MODEL FOR UNDERSTANDING TEXTS

As the examples above have already alluded, the storyreader offered metanarrative information and hence instructed the children in how to make sense of texts by signaling them to use or using for them several kinds of knowledge in order to read and interpret texts.[4] Four major kinds of knowledge as frameworks for reading emerged from the data (a corpus of 100 story readings collected over an 18-month period):

1.   General knowledge of the world
2.   Knowledge of literary conventions
3.   Knowledge of narrative structure
4.   Knowledge of how to respond as members of a reading audience.

Despite the fact that instruction was neither the goal nor the context of storyreading, implicit in the reader's interactions with the children was a model of ways of taking information from these four kinds of knowledge in order to make sense of texts.

Within their storyreading conversations, the storyreader encouraged the children to use information from their stores of knowledge and experience as frameworks for understanding texts. One kind of knowledge that functioned as a framework for reading, "general knowledge of the world," is briefly described below in an effort to illustrate the idea of storyreading as a model for understanding texts.

In many reader-listener interaction sequences, the reader guided the children to use their world knowledge to recognize the objects, persons, places, and actions that were verbally or pictorially presented. In these sequences the reader either called the children's attention to items, invited them to identify items, or, when they seemed unable to do so themselves, identified items for them. These sequences were often introduced

---

[4] Adult-child storyreading interactions that centered on strategies for making sense of texts occurred primarily in what I have called Type II, "Life-to-Text Interactions." These, along with Type I "Readiness Interactions" and Type III "Text-to-Life Interactions" are discussed in detail in Cochran-Smith, 1984, and will not be discussed here.

by reader language such as "What's that?", "*Is* that a . . . ?", "Look at that . . . ", and "That's a . . . ".

Using Knowledge of the World—Labeling

One way of taking information from general knowledge of the world was to identify and correctly label the items, actions, and characters in books. In story-reading interactions of this kind, the storyreader guided the children to use their knowledge of the attributes of various items in order to figure out and correctly label storybook items. She also frequently helped the children with definitions of words that the children did not seem to know or that she assumed they would not know by substituting synonyms for troublesome words or simply providing explicit lexical information (e.g., "He painted a *big picture;* a mural is a bi-ig picture").

Taking information from one's knowledge of the world was important not only for labeling items but also for pointing out the particular attributes of items that allowed one to make appropriate inferences about characters, time and place settings, and actions. In the story-reading segment below, for instance, the book being shared was a loose retelling of "king Midas" featuring a young genie. In Example 4 we can see how the reader guided the children to infer that the genie's mother, who had just appeared on the scene, was a magical creature just like her son.

Example 4

Reader		Listeners	
Verbal	Nonverbal	Verbal	Nonverbal
Amy:			
Then "they were both sound asleep when Oliver's mother flitted (right) into the room. She had been looking for Oliver all that night. 'My, what a mess,' she murmured softly. 'What am I gonna (t: going to) do with that boy?' "			
See his mother is a magical person too.	point to mother		(children look over, blankly)
She's a magical person			
Does she look like a *real* little lady?			
		Nat: Mmm hmm (quietly)	
She's kind of tiny. And what does she have on her shoulders like Oliver? What does she have up on her shoulders?	points to wings		
		Mark: I don't know	
		Nat: Wings! (exclaiming)	
		Nat: Wings!	

Example 4 *Continued*

Reader		Listeners	
Verbal	Nonverbal	Verbal	Nonverbal
Can you see those wings?			
That's right, Nat knows. Just like little Oliver has wings, and I think she doesn't have any color on her clothes, does she?			
		Anna: She has white on her color	
Yes, she's all white			
	TP		

In this example the text specifically revealed the identity of the female character who was pictured (i.e., she was Oliver's mother), and the reader remarked that she was a magical lady. When the children seemed rather blank about all this, however, the story reader made explicit the process according to which she herself had inferred this information about the character. She urged the children to notice certain pictured details—the mother didn't look like a real mother, she was very small, she had wings on her shoulders like her son did, and she was dressed all in white—in order to infer the mother's most important attribute. To reach the conclusion that the mother was a genie like her son, textual information had to be considered in relation to both the children's knowledge of the world (e.g., comparison of the size of Oliver's mother with the size of other adult women) and information already presented in the text (e.g., Oliver had wings in this story and *he* was a genie). In this interaction sequence, initiated in response to the children's confusion about the identity of the mother character, the story-reader modeled one strategy for making inferences in picture books.

In many interaction sequences the children were called on to recognize or identify items and objects. Many of these sequences resemble the mother-child picture book dialogues described by Ninio and Bruner (1978), who suggested that very young children achieve labeling through the adult-dominated conversation that surrounds the activity of looking at the pictured items in books. The initial questioning pattern used by the mother in both Ninio and Bruner's study and by the storyreader in this study is particularly similar (i.e., "What's that?", "That is a . . . ", "is this a . . . ?"). The differences between the two, however, are very important. Ninio and Bruner's description indicates that via an adult-child dialogue, a 10–18 month old child was learning both the concept of lexical labeling and specific labels for various pictured items. The three to five year old children in the community I studied, on the other hand, had long since achieved the concept of lexical labeling; furthermore, although they were introduced to some new labels, they were already familiar with the names for most of the items that they were called upon to identify. Hence, nursery school storyreading interactions built upon *both* the children's prior achievement of lexical labels *and* the adult-child dialogue of early story readings.

Ninio and Bruner's child was exposed to labels in isolation; that is, the child in their study was called upon to identify or confirm the identity of discreet, specifically-pictured objects in picture books. The nursery school children, however, were guided to identify and/or recognize the attributes of objects, characters, places, and actions in relation to the overall context of the individual story being shared. The reader called the children's attention to relationships among the individual parts of pictures and to the relationships implied between the pages. Hence the nursery school children were called upon to continually balance their world knowledge with textual information in order to make sense of texts.

That the children were expected to see relationships between items and in relation to overall texts is indicated by the language patterns used in these interaction sequences. Frequently the children were asked to make comparisons (e.g., well, it's kind of oval *like a tangerine . . .r*"; "Does it look more *like a tangerine?*"; "Does she look *like a real live lady?*"; "And what does she have on her shoulders *like Oliver?*"; " . . . just *like little Oliver* has wings."). These analogic relationships imply a more complex use of world and textual knowledge than does simple identification of discreet items. Furthermore the nursery school children had to do a great deal of inferring in order to achieve the identification of items. They had, for example, to conclude that a pictured item was an orange and not a carrot because of their world knowledge that oranges are round and orange-colored and their textual knowledge that the nose of the snowman in the picture was round and not long and skinny.

In interactions of this sort in which children were, in a sense, taught to take information from their knowledge of the world to make sense of printed texts, two very important rules of reading were made explicit. First *when one reads a book, one must integrate all the information one has*. Items cannot simply be identified in isolation; rather, the relationships that objects, characters, places, and actions have to one another must be figured out and accounted for. That is, everything in the text ought to make sense on a holistic level and also ought to be consistent with one's knowledge of the world. Secondly the *reading process requires that the reader make many inferences*. Neither the text nor the pictures explicitly provide all the information needed; instead the reader/listener uses the information that is provided in conjunction with the information he or she already has of the world. Hence the reader/listener takes an active role in the process of making sense of texts.

Using Knowledge of the World—Connotations

Barthes' *S/Z* (1974) is helpful when considering ways in which readers use their knowledge of the world to make sense of text. Barthes describes five narrative codes or groups of norms in terms of which narrative is made legible (i.e., made readable). His fifth code, the cultural, is used to describe the many codes of knowledge or wisdom to which texts implicitly refer. Barthes suggests that fluent readers continuously and more or less subconsciously call up needed information from a broad array of past experiences in order to understand texts. Thus they read and interpret texts in terms of their concepts of, for example, "Italian-ness" of "The Code of Psychology" when these are implicitly referred to in various parts of texts. The kind of knowledge Barthes describes is more complicated than knowledge of the labels for, or the physical attributes of, objects and places. What Barthes is describing is a way of taking information from a broader kind of knowledge that acts as a framework within which parts of texts can become accessible or readable. Example 5 illustrates how this way of taking information from world knowledge was integral to story reading. In this example you will see how the storyreader

Example 5

Reader		Listeners	
Verbal	Nonverbal	Verbal	Nonverbal
Amy:			
Wait a minute! (excited) What's happened to her here?	points to Shirley on plank		
		Andrew: Walk the plank!	
Walk the plank like in Peter Pan? Like when they tried to get Wendy to walk the plank?			

helped the children frame their reading of one part of a pirate adventure in terms of connotations for the phrase "walk the plank."

We can see in this example that in order to understand what was happening to the little girl in the picture, it was not enough for the children to label "plank" and the action "walking." Rather, "walking the plank" needed to be related to all of the things that the phrase commonly connotes—pirate ships and treasure and rescues—or, all of what Barthes might call "The Code of Pirate-ness." The world experience that the nursery school children had had with "pirateness" was their own dramatization of "Peter Pan." Thus when a child labeled the story character's action as "walking the plank," the storyreader built on this label by relating it to Wendy's walking the plank in the Peter Pan story. Mention of this literary reference called upon the children to take information from their previous knowledge of pirateness and use it as a framework for understanding pirates and pirate ships, walking the plank, falling overboard, and using a map to dig for buried treasure (all of which were to be parts of the story).

To make sense of the humor in a book featuring comical drawings of animals dressed in clothing, listeners needed to take information from their knowledge of the habitats and characteristics of various kinds of animals. For most of the pages of the text, however, the children did not seem to "get it." Consequently the storyreader attempted to fill in for them and prod them toward the information needed. As she supplied this information, it served as a framework within which the children could interpret the text and pictures and hence make sense of the text as a "joke," as something that was amusing.

Like knowledge of labels, connotative knowledge of the world had to be related to the events of texts as wholes. There was consistent encouragement by the storyreader for the listeners to take information from their prior experiences of the world in order to make sense of texts holistically. As the storyreader encouraged the children to label items and to relate events in stories connotatively, she exposed them to some new knowledge. More importantly, however, the children were being consistently instructed in how to take information from their knowledge of the world (both old and new) in order to make sense of whole texts. In other words, they were being exposed to a model for understanding texts.

CONCLUSION

Making sense of decontextualized print is an activity that is essentially solitary. Indeed literacy progress and reading success are especially marked in American schools by children's abilities to read and understand independently. For the group of preschoolers I studied, the negotiated, socially interactive, and oral aspects of early storyreadings seemed to introduce and allow opportunities for practice in the solitary, unilateral, and silent process of decontextualized book reading. Hence storyreading was intermediate between making sense of contextualized language and making sense of decontextualized language. As such, it served in this community as a part of the children's transition from oral to written language strategies.

This chapter is based on one particular case and is not intended as a prototype that can be generalized to other communities. Nevertheless, the nursery school community described is one that is linked to formal education in America. The preschool literacy experiences of the children in this community are often the experiences that public school teachers take for granted. Further research will indicate the extent to which preschool storyreading practices of this kind are common in other communities.

REFERENCES

Barthes, Roland. (1974). *S/Z* (R. Miller, Trans.). New York: Hill and Wang. (original work published 1970)

Booth, Wayne C. (1961). *The rhetoric of fiction*. Chicago: University of Chicago Press.

Cazden, Courtney. (1980). Peekaboo as an instructional model: Discourse development at home and at school. Papers and Reports in Child Language Development 17.

Cochran-Smith, Marilyn. (1984). *The making of a reader*. Norwood, NJ: Ablex.

Howard, Richard. (1974). *Introduction to S/Z (Roland Barthes)*. New York: Hill and Wang. (original work published 1970).

Iser, Wolfgang. (1974). *The implied reader: Patterns of communication in prose fiction from Bunyan to Beckett*. Baltimore: Johns Hopkins University Press.

Iser, Wolfgang. (1980). *The act of reading: A theory of aesthetic response*. Baltimore: Johns Hopkins University Press.

Magee, Mary Ann, & Sutton-Smith, Brian. (1983, May). The art of storytelling: How do children learn it? *Young Children*, 4–12.

Ninio, Anat, & Bruner, Jerome. (1978). The achievement and antecedents of labeling. *Journal of Child Language*, 5, 1–15.

Ochs, Elinor. (1979). Transcription as theory. In E. Ochs & B. Schieffelin (Eds.), *Developmental pragmatics*. New York: Academic Press.

Ochs, Elinor, & Schieffelin, Bambi B. (1982, December). *Language acquisition and socialization: Three developmental stories and their implications*. Working Papers in Sociolinguistics. Austin, TX: Southwest Educational Development Lab.

Prince, Gerald. (1980). *Metanarrative*. Paper presented at Language in Education Colloquium Series, Graduate School of Education, University of Pennsylvania, 1979–1980.

Prince, Gerald. (1982). *Narratology*. Hague: Mouton.

Scollon, Ron, & Scollon, Suzanne. (1980). Literacy as focused interaction. *The Quarterly Newsletter of the Laboratory of Comparative Human Cognition, 2*(2), 26–29.

Snow, Catherine, & Goldfield, Beverley A. (1980). Turn the page please. Situation-specific language learning. Manuscript. Harvard University.

Snow, Catherine, & Goldfield, Beverley A. (1982). Building stories. In Deborah Tannen (Ed.). *Analyzing discourse: Text and talk.* Washington, DC: Georgetown University Press.

Taylor, Denny. (1983). *Family literacy.* Exeter, NH: Heinemann Education Books.

4

For the Bible Tells Me So: Teaching Children in a Fundamentalist Church

Caroline Zinsser

University of Pennsylvania

In the study of how children become literate, researchers have observed both home and school settings as social contexts for literacy acquisition. (Cochran-Smith, 1984; Heath, 1983; McDermott & Gospodinoff, 1977; Michaels, 1981; Miller, 1982; Philips, 1972, 1983; Scollon & Scollon, 1981). In this study, another setting—the Sunday school and vacation Bible school—was investigated from an ethnographic point of view, looking at how information is organized and presented to children in a church setting and how this can be related to their becoming literate.

Considering the large population committed to religious education for children, the prevalence of Sunday schools for children of all ages, the fact that many children experience their first classrooms at Sunday school, and that these schools are based on sacred textual material, this subject has received surprisingly little study as a source of literacy socialization.

Heath (1983) has noted that Bible reading was one of the few examples of solitary reading in the black community that she studied and that Sunday school books and single-page handouts from Sunday school provided homes with the small number of pieces of writing produced especially for children.

In the white mill workers' community Heath studied, parents and children attended Sunday schools in Protestant churches, many of which were termed "fundamentalist." She found that Christianity influenced ideas of good parenthood and there were "striking similarities of the teaching methods used in church and home."

The two churches chosen for this study were self-identified as "fundamentalist" and were characterized by an emphasis on Bible reading. The Bible was believed to be the actual work of God and was taken literally, word for word, rather than being considered, as in other more liberal branches of Christianity, the inspired word of God, not necessarily to be taken literally.

Fundamentalists are in the conservative wing of evangelical churches whose distinguishing characteristics are that members describe themselves as "born again" (having experienced a turning point when they committed themselves to Jesus Christ), that they have encouraged other people to believe in Jesus Christ, and that they believe in a literal interpretation of the Bible.

Using this three-part definition, the latest Gallup religious poll shows that one out of six American adults can be classified as evangelical. Nationally, certain groups are overrepresented in the evangelical ranks—women, nonwhites, persons with less than a college education, Southerners, older people, Protestants, rural residents, and the less well-to-do. The survey also reveals that over one-third of the adult population believes in a literal interpretation of the Bible, that nearly one out of five reads the Bible daily, and that over four out of five want their children to receive religious instruction (Princeton, 1982).

My observations in fundamentalist Sunday school and vacation Bible school were of pre-primary classes of four- and five-year-old children who had not yet entered first grade and who had not been "officially" taught to read and write. Their teachers were nonprofessionals, largely mothers of children in Sunday school. Yet these children were learning a great deal about literacy.

They were becoming familiar with what Heath (1982) calls literacy events, the occasions in which "a piece of writing is integral to the nature of participants' interactions and their interpretive processes." But Bible literacy is a particular kind of literacy within this context.

Children were taught in a literate environment, surrounded by printed materials and literate adults. They became familiar with Bibles as books, both as objects to be handled in prescribed ways, and as a source of important textual material.

Children learned the rules for church classroom behavior. They learned how to handle materials and how to perform routines. They were taught text through distinctive methods of listening, repeating, memorizing, and singing. They became familiar with rules of a particular kind of pedagogical discourse which included turn-taking, forms of questions and answers, and contextualization cues.

The function of the text, as taught in these settings, was to provide divine inspiration as a guide to daily behavior and as a means to personal salvation. Pre-primary children were considered old enough for the experience of being "born again," a most valued consequence of learning text.

In fundamentalist Sunday schools children are taught specific skills for Bible literacy, they are taught by a systematic form of classroom discourse, and the sacred text differs markedly from secular text in its significance for the reader, its establishment of authority, and in the sequencing of presentation.

These findings raise questions about literacy acquisition within the dominant culture. The children in this study belong to a group which is neither minority nor stigmatized. Yet their early Bible school training differs from that in public school classrooms. What this suggests is that even within the dominant culture we might be more accurate in describing the acquisition of literacies as being dependent on specific, local contexts, rather than assuming a single literacy process for young children.

SETTINGS FOR THE STUDY

The churches I chose for my observations were in a Northeastern state. The first, which I will call the Bible Chapel, was located in a town of 50,000; the second, which I will call River Baptist, was located in a rural area. The congregations of both were almost totally white and of working and business classes.

My own professional background includes elementary public school teaching, and although I am a Protestant, I am not a member of an evangelical church. At the Bible Chapel I spent two weeks as a participant-observer helping with a group of 75 pre-primary children during daily vacation Bible school and observing a Sunday school class of 50 children for five weeks. At the River Baptist church I observed a Sunday school class of six children for one month. At both locations I was able to make running field notes and at River Baptist I tape-recorded classroom sessions.

Both the Bible Chapel and River Baptist took pride in their conservative position in regard to Bible interpretation. The Bible Chapel had, two generations earlier, been a part of the Plymouth Brethren, Dispensationalists who "insisted undeviatingly on the absolute verbal inerrancy of the Bible as the 'inscripturated' Word of the unchanging eternal God, every word and phrase was deemed capable of revealing in divine truth " (Ahlstrom, 1972, p. 810).

Despite their independence, both churches used Sunday school curriculum materials published by a variety of nonsectarian religious publishers in the Midwest.

THE BIBLE AS BOOK

The Bible was central to these programs. All children were expected to bring Bibles to Sunday School. At River Baptist each classroom session began with a Bible Count; children received stars for having remembered to bring their Bibles. Sometimes these were small pocket versions of the New Testament, which were easier for a small child to hold, but usually they were standard-sized Bibles. Nearly all were the King James version, the version used in instructional materials as well as for readings from the Bible itself.

Many of the Bibles were "presentation" copies with a printed page where the donor's and recipient's names could be inscribed with a date. Although I saw one inscribed by a neighbor (for a boy who was not a church member), the others were presented by parents or grandparents. One inscription, written by a child's parent, read: "May this be the door to lead you to Christ and Christ lead you to heaven. See you there!" One Bible was inscribed to the child's mother indicating that she had received the book during her own childhood.

Because daily Bible reading was so emphasized by the church, each member of the family was likely to have his own Bible, as indicated by the following exchange which took place in the parking lot on the way to the car:

> Mother: (to daughter) Does David have his Bible?
> Daughter: (who is carrying her Bible) He'd better!
> Mother: Rachel, go back and look. It was right on top of Mommy's Bible.

Some of these Bibles were new but most had the well-worn look of a book that had been used—although not necessarily for reading. Although Bible publishers produce books with a precious appearance (imitation leather covers in black or white with gold lettering, place markers, zippers to enclose the pages, plastic protective covers) indicating the sacredness of the text, children handled their Bibles with easy casualness as toward a familiar talisman.

During daily vacation Bible school:

A boy chases a girl before class begins. Both hold Bibles. The boy hits the girl with his Bible.

During assembly time a girl sucks on the end of a Bible zipper which has torn loose.

Required to join hands in a circle, a girl holds her small Bible in her teeth.

During aggressive play two boys shove a Bible back and forth across a table.

A boy sits on his Bible so he can use both hands to perform motions to a song.

THE BIBLE AS TEXT

Aside from curriculum workbooks or worksheets, the Bible was the only book used. A single incidence of a girl bringing a non-Bible storybook to the vacation Bible school assembly area caused an adult to tell her to close it.

At River Baptist, Bibles were referred to metaphorically as "swords":

Teacher: Anna? Do you have your Bible with you? (Anna holds up her Bible.)
Teacher: There it is. What can we call our Bibles? Who knows what another name for our Bible is? Charlie? What do you have with you?
Charlie: Sword.
Teacher: Your sword. That's right. What do you do with your sword? James?
James: Stab the devil.

Although none of the children in the River Baptist class was able to read the Bible, the teacher opened each child's book to the appropriate passage during the Bible storytelling.

A central part of each morning's program was hearing a Bible story. Teachers took their responsibilities for telling the stories very seriously. Although they used the curriculum material as a guide to the order in which stories were to be told, teachers told the stories in their own words and used the Bible text itself as their main preparation:

Child: What happened to the ark?
Teacher: I don't know. I'll have to read (consult Biblical text) a little more.

A teacher in the vacation Bible school begged off after two days because she felt "overwhelmed" by the responsibility of storytelling. In the first day's meeting of teachers, while the children were at recess, the teachers prayed earnestly together that they might "reach the souls of the children."

On the vacation Bible school schedule 20 minutes were allotted for telling the Bible story. During this period the children were generally quiet, and the tone was one of solemnity, sometimes reinforced by the children themselves:

Child: Shh, pay attention! This is the Bible story.

Children were taught that the Bible was the direct word of God:

Teacher: What is the Bible?
Child: God's word.
Teacher: God's word. Who wrote the Bible?
Child: Men
Teacher: Men. But who told them what to write? Anne, who told those men what
            they should put into the Bible?
Anne: God.
Teacher: God. He told them just the right words to write.

APPLICATION OF TEXT TO LIFE

As a follow-up to the Bible story, teachers read what the curriculum guide called "application stories." These were stories in which the lesson from the Bible story was applied to a situation in everyday life. For example, following the Bible story of Jacob's ladder, the curriculum guide included an "application story" about a little boy's first day at school when he was apprehensive about making friends. By remembering that his best friend was Jesus and that, "He said He would be with me" (a reference to "The Lord said . . . I will be with you," Genesis 31:3), the boy was comforted and was able to make friends.

During vacation Bible school a mother volunteered to take over the "application story" part of the daily program. After one day of following the curriculum guide's suggested story but telling it in her own words, she substituted during the rest of the sessions stories of her own experiences stressing the importance of her conversion. These conversion stories or "testimony" were a common part of Sunday school programs by which converts "witnessed" to their salvation.

In both churches four and five-year olds were urged toward a conversion experience—being "born again." During my observations no child reported a conversion experience during a Sunday school session although two reported such conversions having taken place at home during the previous week:

Teacher: Something important happened to Mary this week. Do you want to tell
            us about it, Mary?
Mary: I got saved.
Teacher: Tell us how you got saved.
Mary: I prayed.
Teacher: How did you pray, Mary? What prayer did you make?
Mary: I asked Jesus into my heart.

The vacation Bible school sessions ended with conversions of children of all ages. In the pre-primary group, the woman in charge of the "application story" who had turned instead to personal testimony, told a story using a "Wordless Book" as a prop. The book was made up of blank pages in colors whose symbolism she explained: gold for "the kingdom of heaven," black for sin "which everyone is guilty of," red for "Jesus' blood who took our punishment," white for "white as snow" when sin is removed, and green for "GROW, Go to church, Read the Bible, Obey, and Witness for the Lord."

After explaining the Wordless Book, she asked, "If anyone wants to be washed white as snow . . . Any little boy or girl here who would love to ask Jesus into your heart, raise your hand." About fifteen children raised their hands, and at the end of the session they were met individually by teachers who questioned them and decided which of the children were "truly born again." The teachers viewed the conversion experience as a child's own decision "to let Jesus into their heart." They were definite in saying they could tell if a child's claim to being "saved" was valid:

> Teacher: (speaking about past experience with childrens' conversion) One girl. I
>   telephoned her mother. She didn't go to church. She was doubtful. But
>   I didn't doubt.

Learning Bible text was viewed as the means of mastering personal problems and of achieving salvation. Both textual accounts and oral accounts of such experiences included quotations from Biblical text and ritualistic or stylized expressions of life experiences.

LISTENING

For these nonreaders listening was the principal way of learning Bible text. The importance of listening was constantly stressed. In the vacation Bible school one of the craft activities was making a set of "earphones" from styrofoam disks and pipe cleaners with each disk bearing a sticker labeled, "God Speaks" and "We Listen."

At River Baptist the teacher began a lesson:

> Teacher: Does everybody have their listening ears on today?
>   (Children place their hands on their ears and turn them as though turning
>   knobs.)
> Teacher: You're going to pay attention? Screw them on, huh? All right, very good.

At River Baptist where the teacher was a compelling storyteller and there were only six children in the class, children's eyes focused on the teacher's face and there was little interaction between children. At the vacation Bible school and at the Bible Chapel Sunday school class, children sat further from the storyteller and were not so intensely involved. Despite the large size of the group, however, when the teacher would ask if anyone would like to come forward and repeat the story himself, five or six would raise hands. When called upon they were able to repeat the story in a simplified fashion, using flannelboard figures as props.

MEMORIZING

Memorization of Bible verses played an important part in Bible school curriculum. In Sunday school a new verse was presented each week and during vacation Bible school children were given a new verse every other day. When verses were memorized the Biblical citation was always included, for example, "At the name of Jesus, every knee should bow—Phillipians 2:10."

When a new verse was presented, the teacher first said the verse, then had the children repeat it several times in unison along with her. Children watched the teacher's lips or any other adult's who was nearby as an aid to repetition. The teacher would then ask if any children would like to repeat the verse solo. Several were able to do so.

Each day's craft item or workbook sheet, which was sent home with children, bore a printed verse for the day so that parents could help children to memorize. Some parents were very conscientious about this:

> Mother: (meeting child) Did you get a hard one today?

> Another Mother: (meeting child) Did you say your verse?

During the classroom period each child received a star on a chart for correctly reciting the previously assigned verse. A few children were able to do this without prompting but most needed help. Teacher persisted until each child had at least once repeated the verse following the teacher's instruction, line for line, so that everyone received a star every day.

Children were taught that the reason for memorizing Bible verses was to recite them in times of trouble or doubt. The curriculum guide included an "application story" in which Janie was frightened by thunder. With her mother's help she prayed: "Dear God, please help me not to be afraid of the thunder. Help me to really learn my Bible verse more than just the words." When the thunder came again, "Janie flinched but she said, "The Lord is my Helper, and I will not fear the thunder!"

At the River Baptist classroom the teacher made a similar point in her own words:

> Teacher: Every time you have a problem, the Lord can help remind you of memory verses—of verses in the Bible. And that is how you can make the devil run away from you.

SINGING

Another form of memory work was learning songs. During the two weeks of vacation Bible school the children learned nine new songs which they sang in addition to about 15 songs which most of the children already knew. They sang with gusto, as did their elders. Most songs were sung standing up with children automatically rising for "Jesus Loves Me," which was a favorite and whose words reinforced Bible lessons:

Jesus loves me, this I know

For the Bible tells me so.

Little ones to him belong.

They are weak but he is strong.

Jesus loves me when I'm good

When I do the things I should.

Jesus loves me when I'm bad

Though it makes him very sad.

Another favorite stressed a personal commitment to the Bible:

The B-I-B-L-E

Yes, that's the book for me!

I stand alone on the word of God

The B-I-B-L-E

(shout and hold Bible aloft) The Bible!

Children were taught new songs by "catching on" to the singing, watching lips and hand motions, rather than through explanation or speaking the lines. Sunday school rooms in both churches had pianos and songs were accompanied by competent pianists.

Songs were used as reminders of Bible lessons:

Teacher: (after telling story of Jesus calming the waves)And can Jesus protect us the same way today? Yes, because he owns everything. He made the wind and the sea. Remember our song about (quotes)
My God is so big and so strong and so mighty
There's nothing my God cannot do.
The mountains are his, the rivers are his
The stars are his handiwork too.

and of Bible verses:

Teacher: Does anyone remember the verse from that week? It was easy. Remember our song? (begins to sing with children joining in)
I will make you fishers of men (casting and reeling motions)
Fishers of men, fishers of men.
I will make you fishers of men (motions)
If you follow me.

When any child had celebrated his birthday, he was honored by standing in front of the group while they sang:

Happy birthday to you

Only one will not do.

Born again means salvation

We hope you have two.

Singing songs was a means by which the memorized texts of the songs were used as a memory aid for remembering Biblical text.

ANSWERING TEACHER QUESTIONS

Because the Bible was taught as "the word of God," children were not encouraged to think speculatively about the stories, to supply additional details out of their own imaginings, or to suggest alternative endings. Children understood this and did not make such comments during the Bible storytelling. A rare exception was when a teacher, telling the story of Jacob, asked, "Would you sleep on a stone?" The children answered with alternatives. ("He could use a sleeping bag." and "He could use his underwear and put a cover on it.") This kind of display of ingenuity drawn from experiences that did not relate to the text was not rewarded.

Wrong answers were either ignored:

Teacher:	What did Jacob do with the rock?
Child:	He put oil on it.
Teacher:	(ignoring incorrect answer) What did he do with the rock?
Children:	(no response)
Teacher:	(supplies correct answer) He marked the spot where Jesus talked to him.

or answers were corrected:

Teacher:	What would you like to sing?
Child:	"Jingle Bells"
Teacher:	That's not a Bible school song, Sweetheart. Let's sing "Oh, How I Love Jesus."

but neither wrong nor inappropriate answers were discussed.

Children were familiar with formulaic answers required in response to the curriculum guide material:

Teacher:	What could help if you were afraid?
Children:	(chorus) Pray to Jesus!

Teacher:	What have we been learning about?
Children:	(chorus) God!
Teacher:	God and his son, Jesus.*

---

* God, the Lord, and Jesus were sometimes used interchangeably, sometimes not.

> Teacher: Who can help us (to listen)?
> Children: (chorus) God!
> Teacher: Yes, the Lord. How can we ask God to help?
> Children: (chorus) Pray!

Children listened for cues which would indicate which answer was suitable. These cues were not always clear:

> Teacher: (reading "application story" about a child in a thunderstorm) What was the loud noise?
> Children: (in chorus) God!
> Teacher: No. It was thunder.

> Teacher: (reading) Do people ever interrupt God?
> Children: (chorus) No!
> Teacher: (reading) If Frankie keeps rumbling or trying to talk to his friends while the teacher is telling the Bible story, do you think he is interrupting God? Very possibly.

A child wandering from the formulaic was set straight:

> Teacher: Did God answer Janie's prayer?
> Child: Yes. She wasn't afraid . . . (adds thoughtfully) Maybe she did it herself.
> Teacher: No. God helped her.

Currciculum material was sometimes written in the form of questions which miscued the children by their appearance of being open-ended when actually, only one answer was acceptable. A teacher read the following account from the curriculum guide without pausing to acknowledge any of the children's attempts to answer the questions being put:

> Teacher: (reading) Does your dog come when you call his name?
> Child: Sometimes he does and sometimes he doesn't.
> Teacher: (ignoring answer and continuing to read) When he hears you say his name, he comes running. Does he get off the couch when your mother says, "Down"?
> Another child: My mother has a clean couch.
> Teacher: (ignoring response and continuing to read) Sometimes. When he doesn't is it because he doesn't want to obey? Are boys and girls ever like that? Sometimes. What does God want children to do?
> Another child: He wants us to be good.
> Teacher: (as though she had heard the desired answer, reads) Yes, to listen and obey.

In the River Baptist Sunday school class where the group was made up of only five or six children, they were familiar with their teacher's pedagogical style and proficient in "reading" her cues as to the expected response. Sometimes she taught by repetition:

Teacher:	And Jesus said, thy faith hath made thee whole. Say it.	
Children	and	
Teacher:	Thy faith hath made thee whole.	
Teacher:	That has a lot of "ths" in it, doesn't it? Let's try it one more time.	
Children	and	
Teacher:	Thy faith hath made thee whole.	

She also used syntactic cues:

Teacher: What can God do? He can do—
Child: Anything.

and syllabic cues:

Teacher: We have to be—
Child: Lieve.
Teacher: She got well because she be—
Child: Lieved.

Sometimes her tone of voice indicated the correct answer:

Teacher: (speaking of a dead raccoon) Could I pick up his little paw (kneels down, acts out) and say, Get up raccoon and be alive and go running off into the woods? Could I do that? (voice rises to indicate incredulity)
Children: (nod heads no)

When children were unable to read the teacher's cues, they remained silent until more cues were offered:

Teacher: She was trembling because she was—
Children: (no response)

Teacher: (imitating woman in Bible story with great expression) Lord Jesus, I touched you! Could you be made well just by touching Jesus?
Children: (no response, perhaps because the words "just" makes them cautious)
Teacher: (answering own question) No.

Sometimes the teacher miscued:

Teacher: How would you feel? Happy?
Child: (correctly reading cue to say opposite) Sad.
Teacher: You'd feel scared.

In this classroom children habitually answered questions with single words—words not from their own experience but "correct" answers that were elicited by teacher cuing. Although this might be labeled learning by rote, children were actively constructing strategies for selecting the correct responses. The teacher's repertoire for cuing was a varied one, and she did not always cue accurately. Children not only had to decide what to answer but whether the cues were sufficient to risk answering at all. Rather than acting as passive receptacles, as the term "rote" might imply, the children were actively learning and practicing rules for pedagogical discourse.

How well they had learned these rules was illustrated by an incident when I, left temporarily alone in a small classroom with ten children, asked, "Do you think we have a photograph of Jesus?" I was trying to elicit an answer which had to do with Jesus living before cameras. My question was met with what appeared to be complete blankness. The children assumed my question was a ritualistic opening to a didactic story and were waiting for cues as to what form their response should take. They were waiting for me to cue the correct answer—I was waiting for them to think about my question. We were at an impasse of unfamiliarity.

BECOMING LITERATE

The four- and five-year old children I observed had not yet entered the first grade, the public school age level at which children are "officially" taught to read and write. Neither reading, in the sense of decoding, nor writing, in the sense of composing, was "officially" practiced at Sunday school or at vacation Bible school.

The Biblical text in the King James version was recognized to be difficult for beginning readers. But because the text was considered to be the actual word of God, there were no large-type, simplified versions from which to learn to decode. Similarly, since the text was sacred, children were not expected to compose Biblical text.

Given these restrictions, however, these nonreading and nonwriting children nevertheless assumed the roles of literate people. They were surrounded by printed messages on walls and on hand-out materials. They could memorize and repeat textual material. They were practiced in listening to text read aloud. They carried their Bibles with them and sometimes opened them into reading position.

They also observed adults for whom the mastery of Bible literacy was a central part of life. Reading the Bible empowered one—provided one with a "sword"—and led to the goal of salvation. This was the "living word" that could provide the organizing experience of life: being "born again." Nonreading children were given tracts to hand to unconverted adults in the hope that the text—not its bearer—would be the means of conversion.

CONCLUSION

The findings from these observations of church settings indicate a rich source of data in the study of literacy. Although the acquisition of literacy in a sacred text has been studied in situations where the text was in a different language from that spoken in the family (Scribner & Cole, 1981; Scollon & Scollon, 1981; Duranti & Ochs, Chapter 11, this volume), American evangelical church literacy, the learning of a literal interpretation of a sacred text in one's own language, though widespread, has not been extensively studied.

Scribner (1982), in connecting theoretic cognitive processes to literacy, asks: "How do we pin down the specific activities within a given cultural milieu that contribute to a ' break ' between empirical approaches to everyday problems and theoretical approaches to problems whose subject matter does not 'count'?" In the fundamentalist church classrooms, however, the subject matter of literacy, the Biblical text, *does* "count." The progression is not from empirical solutions for everyday problems to analytic solutions for theoretical problems. The function of the text is neither to provide analytic solutions nor to consider theoretical problems. Instead it is religious.

"Application stories" were fictional accounts, geared to children's supposed interests, in which Bible verses were "applied" to practical situations, text "applied" to life, theoretical "applied" to empirical. According to the curriculum guide in which these stories appeared, the stories "will apply the Bible truth . . . to life situations."

In the story in which the little girl Janie was frightened by the loud noise of thunder, she was reminded by her mother of the Bible verse, "The Lord is my helper and I will not fear." The invocation of the words of the text enable Janie to conquer her fear.

The children in daily vacation Bible school raised points during the reading of this story that could have been explored. A child took the "loud noise" which was thunder as a reference to God, thus raising a possible question of God as creator of destructive forces. Later another child wondered if Janie was responsible for overcoming her fear ("maybe she did it herself"), thus raising a possible question of self-determination. Both these opportunities for discussion were passed by.

It could be argued that teachers ignored such questions and comments because they lacked time or they wanted to avoid digression or they considered such discussions inappropriate to the children's age and understanding. But over the course of a two-week curriculum in vacation Bible school, the repeated exclusion of such speculative questions as topic for discussion served to delineate limits for approaching Biblical text.

Janie in the story does not interpret a theoretical framework. Instead she "listens" to a directive from God by remembering words from the sacred text. The text is prescriptive for experiences delimited by teachers—loving, trusting, obeying, converting, and proselytizing.

Biblical literacy is taught with dramatic urgency toward conversion, with expressiveness of personal commitment, and within the shared community belief in God's word. It is not a "cool" experience. It shares with medieval art what Kubler (1962) has described: "This preference for reducing all experience to the template set by a few master themes resembles a funnel. It channels experience into a more powerful flow; the themes and patterns are few in number but their intensity of meaning is thereby increased" (p. 29).

Besides learning literacy the children were learning how to behave in a classroom. They learned how to use classroom furniture, tables, desks, chairs; how to use classroom materials, glue, scissors, crayons; how to perform classroom routines, line up for dismissal, accept food equally shared out at snacktime, push chairs in place on leaving. They also learned about competition and reward, competing with raised hands and winning paper stars. They learned the time schedule and its markers, such as taking attendance and saying the pledge of allegiance.

More importantly they learned patterns of pedagogical discourse. (Bellack & Davitz, 1963; Sinclair & Coulthard, 1975; Mehan, 1979; Hymes, 1982) Children learned the rules by which their teachers elicited information (Cazden, John, & Hymes, 1972). In the case of Bible literacy, the pedagogy was, to use Bernstein's terminology, strongly framed (Bernstein, 1971).

Bernstein's frame refers to "the strength of the boundary between what may and may not be transmitted." Frame refers to the range of options available to teacher and taught in the control of what is transmitted and received in the context of the pedagogical relationship. Strong framing entails reduced options; weak framing entails a range of options. The context of Bible literacy in a fundamental church setting necessitates strong framing. The Bible is set apart from other texts. Teachers can neither select nor reorder their material. Students are limited in their responses.

This strongly framed pedagogy reinforces the creation and maintenance of textual authority. Children learn that text is not the speech of its speaker but has an authority of its own. This is an important part of becoming literate (Olson, 1980). But the authority of Biblical text is not an impersonal one—it is the word of God to whom one is both responsible and connected in everyday life.

Olson (1978) speculates that in the transition from oral to written forms of language, "a more detailed study of the language of the school would show a predominance of interpersonally biased oral language in the early grades with an increasing reliance on written text and text-like language in the later grades" (p. 121). This is not the experience of the Bible school student who is immediately plunged into the task of learning text and is curtailed in both classroom display and interpersonal language during pedagogical discourse.

Some of these children will attend fundamentalist church schools. Others will attend public schools. Whether the skills Bible school students have learned—listening, memorizing, singing—in the acquisition of Bible literacy will be used in the learning of other texts and whether the rules of pedagogical discourse which they have mastered will prove to be a help in other classrooms will depend upon what kinds of schools they attend.

If the framing is strong, one in which "socialization into knowledge is socialization into order, the existing order, into the experience that the world's educational knowledge is impermeable" (Bernstein, 1971, p. 214), the child will experience a replication in kind of the pedagogical discourse he has learned in church.

If the framing is weak, as Bernstein characterizes United States education in general, where the authority relationship is tipped toward the rights of students and where the boundaries between what may or may not be taught become blurred, children will find themselves in classrooms whose rules are at variance with what they learned in their church setting. One would expect them to have difficulty, for example, in learning what Mehan calls "students' initiational rights"—ways that students contribute to discourse—getting the floor, holding the floor, and introducing news (Mehan, 1979).

Heath (1983) found that Roadville children, many of whom were fundamentalists, were criticized by public school teachers for lack of imagination, minimal answers, no extension of ideas, rarely asking questions, lack of initiative, and laconic behavior. She linked these behaviors to family background and suggested that church experiences reinforced home teaching of children.

Such teaching was not only discontinuous with that in public schools but differed in its institutional and structural patterns. When Roadville children entered public school, they came with skills of labeling, learning by prescription, abiding by the text, and acceptance of textual authority. Adults teaching children at home and at church had, within a dialogic framework, established levels of interpretation and control and set limits on children's opportunities which opposed those found in public school classrooms (Heath, 1983).

We do not know how the children in this study who enter public school classrooms will perform or how they will compare to those who enter fundamentalist church schools. These are areas for further research. One could speculate on the basis of this ethnographic study that children whose family discourse, early Sunday school pedagogical discourse, and later, school classroom discourse were consonant would acquire literacy through a process quite different from that indicated by mainstream school curriculum.

Those children who move from fundamentalist church school settings to school classrooms organized around a weakly framed or open pedagogy, one in which children are rewarded for divergent, speculative, critical processing of textual material could be expected to face the task of substituting a new set of classroom rules for the ones already learned at church.

Looking at literacy socialization in an institution whose rules are so strongly emphasized enables us to see more clearly the processes through which children learn. In a culture as complex as our own children must negotiate and interpret a wide variety of contexts and decide on appropriate behaviors for each.

Whether children are able to manage discontinuities between rules learned at home and in local communities and those taught in public schools depends also on factors beyond the classroom walls. Children such as those Philips (1972, 1983) studied from the Warm Springs Indian community faced not only deep cultural discontinuities at school but also attitudes from the larger culture which marked them as oppressed minorities and a stigmatized group.

Such children could be expected to have more problems than mainstream children, who are nonstigmatized, nonminority, and whose backgrounds are not discontinuous with school culture (Ogbu, 1974). However, as the data in this study indicates, discontinuities between home and school may also exist within the dominant culture.

Even within this study, the two churches could be characterized differently. The Bible Chapel with a larger, more transient congregation in a medium-sized town, was less rigid in its rules than River Baptist with its rural congregation and classroom of only six children. Since both churches identified themselves with conservative social values, they taught in ways that differ from more liberally-oriented Protestant Sunday schools.

In studying the acquisition of literacy, we face a multiplicity of factors which influence children in the process of learning to read and write. Even within the dominant culture children bring differing expectations of behavior according to social contexts. And even within an institutional context such as Sunday school, there is wide variation between branches of Protestantism and even individual churches.

Such multiplicity suggests that the study of literacy is as complicated as the study of culture itself and that although this precludes the application of simplistic solutions to problems in schools, it also points to the richness of our differences. No school system can afford the bland assumption of uniformity of its students. Instead, classroom life can be enriched by the recognition of a more textured, complex, and dynamic process of learning.

REFERENCES

Ahlstrom, Sydney. (1972). *A religious history of the American people.* New Haven: Yale University.

Bellack, Arno, & Davitz, Joel. (1963). *The language of the classroom.* New York: Teachers College Press.

Bernstein, Basil. (1971). *Class codes and control, Vol. 1, Theoretical studies towards a sociology of language.* London: Routledge and Kegan.

Cazden, Courtney, John, Vera, & Hymes, Dell. (Eds.). (1972). *Function of language in the classroom.* New York: Teachers College Press.

Cochran-Smith, Marilyn. (1984). *The making of a reader.* Norwood, NJ: Ablex.

Heath, Shirley Brice. (1982). Protean shapes in literacy events, ever-shifting oral and literate traditions. In Deborah Tannen (Ed.), *Spoken and written language.* Norwood, NJ: Ablex.

Heath, Shirley Brice. (1983). *Ways with words,* New York: Cambridge University Press.

Hymes, Dell H. (1982). Ethnolinguistic study of classroom discourse. Final Report to the National Institute of Education, ms.

Kubler, George. (1962). *The shape of time.* New Haven: Yale University Press.

McDermott, R. P., & Gospodinoff, Kenneth. (1977). Social contexts for ethnic borders and school failure. In A. Wolfgang (Ed.), *Nonverbal Behavior.* New York: Academic Press.

Mehan, Hugh. (1979). *Learning lessons: Social organization in the classroom.* Cambridge: Harvard University Press.

Michaels, Sarah. (1981). 'Sharing Time': Children's narrative styles and differential access to literacy. *Language and Society, 10*(3), 423–442.

Miller, Peggy J. (1982). *Amy, Wendy, and Beth: Learning language in South Baltimore.* Austin: University of Texas Press.

Ogbu, John. (1974). *The next generation.* New York: Academic Press.

Olson, David R., & Nickerson, Nancy. (1978). Language development through the school years: Learning to confine interpretation to the information in the text. In Keith Nelson (Ed.), *Children's language.* New York: Gardner Press.

Olson, David R. (1980). Some social aspects of meaning in oral and written language. In D. Olson (Ed.), *The social foundations of language and thought.* New York: W. W. Norton.

Philips, Susan. (1972). Participant structures and communicative competence: Warm Springs children in Community and classroom. In Courtney Cazden, Vera John, & Dell Hymes (Eds.), *Function of language in the classroom.* New York: Teachers College Press.

Philips, Susan. (1983). *The invisible culture: Communication in classroom and community on the Warm Springs Indian Reservation.* New York: Longmans.

Princeton Religion Research Center. (1982). *Religion in America 1981*. Princeton, NJ.

Scollon, Ron, & Scollon, Suzanne B. K. (1981). *Narrative, literacy, and face in interethnic communication*. Norwood, NJ: Ablex.

Scribner, Sylvia. (1982). Modes of thinking and ways of speaking: Culture and logic reconsidered. In R. Freedle (Ed.), *Discourse production and comprehension*. Hillsdale, NJ: Erlbaum.

Scribner, Sylvia, & Cole, Michael. (1981). *The psychology of literacy*. Cambridge: Harvard University Press.

Sinclair, J. McH., & Coulthard, R. M. (1975). *Toward an analysis of discourse. The English used by teachers and pupils*. London: Oxford University Press.

PART II

Connecting Oral and Written Modes: What Children Can Do In School

5

"I Want to Talk to You About Writing": 5-Year-Old Children Speak

Bonita Blazer

University of Pennsylvania

This chapter has been inspired by a group of 5-year-old children who took part in an observational study conducted in a kindergarten classroom. The title "I want to talk to you about writing" came from an interview with Jonethan, age 5.1 (see Figure 1), con-

Figure 1. Jonethan: November 12, 1982: "Dear / Mrs. Blazer / I like you / I want to talk to / you about writing /Love / Jonethan"

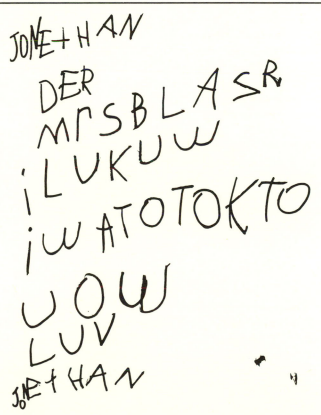

ducted during the early part of the school year. The writing sample in Figure 1 was
Jonethan's response to the interview request "write me a letter"—a probe aimed at
finding out about a child's early conception of "a letter." Jonethan, one of the more
"advanced" beginning writers at the start of the school year, demonstrated several
things in this early written sample: (a) his concept of "a letter" in regard to its form and
its function; (b) the level of his writing performance and his understanding of
directionality, spacial relationships, and sound-symbol representation; (c) his ability to
invent spellings; (d) his ability to use unconventional print to produce a sentence and to
use writing as a form of communication; and (e) his willingness to share his not-yet-
formally-acquired knowledge about writing.

Charles Read (1975) applies his work on the rule-like and systematic nature of children's early invented spellings to support the importance of uncovering and using the
initial knowledge that children bring about language to the beginning writing experience: "We are not writing messsages on a blank slate, and we cannot—and do not want
to—wipe the slate clean, even though it is incomplete and partially inaccurate. Rather,
we must strive to build upon the knowledge that the child brings to school . . . The
best we can do now is to respect the children's linguistic knowledge, try to learn from
these occasions when it shows through in children's performance, and try to build upon
it" (Read, 1980, p. 148).

Within such a perspective of respect for the child's knowledge and growing conceptions of "writing," the sometimes mystical "how" in the process of learning to write
may be described more clearly. Perhaps the child's initial knowledge about written language, as expressed through the oral language *accompanying* beginning writing and/or *in
response to* direct probes about beginning writing, will provide a link to its course of
development. Examining children's knowledge about writing via the oral language
used at different levels of conscious production (Slobin, 1979) also may generate important inferences on metalinguistic issues regarding written language acquisition.

The concern of this chapter is to explore the relationship between oral and written
language during the beginning writing experience. This is accomplished through a description and analysis of what children say *about* writing, as well as what children say
while they are learning to write in kindergarten. This aspect of beginning writing is part
of a larger ethnographic study focusing on the processes involved in learning to write
during initial informal and formal writing activities, and the social context within
which such experiences occur (see Blazer, 1984).

THEORETICAL PERSPECTIVES

Jon's response to the interview probe "write me a letter" can be analyzed when we investigate what he knows via direct investigation (Read, 1980; Ferreiro, 1978). This approach to the study of the development of beginning writing grew principally out of
two fields of study. The first is the field of psycholinguistics, concerned principally with
the study of thought or cognition and its relationship to language. This discipline focuses on the interactive psychological factors *within* the child that influence language
learning. The second field is that of sociolinguistics, which focuses on social and

situational variables and their effect on the acquisition of language and its use. It is within this discipline that the more externally interactive factors of language learning, those specifically *between* people and cultures, are considered. In an attempt to formulate a discipline that captures both the psychological and social aspects of language production and comprehension, researchers exploring initial written language acquisition have created the term "socio-psycholinguistics" (Hill, 1978; Harste, Burke, & Woodward, 1981). Incorporating the two perspectives into a research inquiry allows for a more integrated understanding of the learner as a psychologically active constructor of his learning, as a member of a social group; it underlines the importance of viewing psychological factors within the contexts (linguistic, situational, social, and cultural) in which they occur. In essence, the insight contributed by these two perspectives is that the social context of language learning must be moved to the forefront as a critical variable in any language learning process.

Although there are specifiable relationships in terms of the assumptions that each of these domains contribute to our understanding of language learning, just how the social and psychological features interact in the child's learning processes has not yet been determined. What at first appears to be an advantage (i.e., looking at written language growth through an interactive perspective) later becomes a necessity because such a perspective accounts for different aspects of child language development. My view is that the beginning writing process is a dynamic experience, created by the interaction and integration of cognitive thought processes and social contextual processes. I suggest that it is this dynamic combination of processes, including the interactions, assumptions, and cultural beliefs and values between specific people, that holds the information about learning to write. Such a joining of social and psychological perspectives for an exploration of beginning writing gains additional theoretical support by combining the distinct cognitive perspectives of child developmentalist Jean Piaget with the strong social theories of Lev Vygotsky. Piaget focused strongly on the child as an active seeker and constructor of his or her knowledge and learning (1969), while Vygotsky saw the social context as the mediator of learning between object and child (Vygotsky, 1962, 1978). By interpreting Piaget and Vygotsky as theorists who present complementary rather than opposing positions, I have begun to set up a theoretical framework for my own inquiry into the development of writing in kindergarten.

In this study, the beginning process of written language learning (i.e., "the problem") was investigated and defined by integrating psycholinguistic and sociolinguistic perspectives on language learning (i.e., "the theory") with an inductive method of inquiry in a natural setting (i.e., "the method"). The process of defining the problem became the mode of inquiry, thereby creating a study where the method is critical to the development of the theory. More specifically, because I believe that the two language modes, speaking and writing, support and facilitate each other's development during beginning writing experiences, the means of investigation required looking at the interaction of both modes through time and alongside written products that were created during social interactions at the writing table. An ethnographic methodology enabled the investigation of both social and symbolic processes involved in the construction of these beginning texts in the most authentic way—by looking at what children actually say and do, by themselves, when given an optimal and maximal environment for learning to write.

BACKGROUND

A perspective on language learning has been presented so that a backdrop may be provided for the concern of this chapter: how children learn to write as revealed by relationships between oral and written language during beginning writing experiences. Most of the past research on literacy acquisition has focused on how children learn to read rather than on how they learn to write. Inherent in this research has been a somewhat tacit assumption that writing will, in some way, naturally follow a sound beginning reading curriculum. Many years of reading acquisition research, and much debate regarding beginning reading processes, have resulted in a two-pronged explanation of optimum "methods" by which children will learn to read: whole word versus subskill approaches. Those psycholinguists who have settled on a "top-down" model claim that whole word and holistic strategies of decoding—such as close approximations, guessing, and the use of contextual clues—may be useful in explaining reading acquisition (Goodman, 1967, 1973, 1979; Smith, 1977, 1978). They treat beginning reading more like natural learning, which is aimed at making meaning and based on the learner's world views, experiences, insights, and "active constructions" about language (Spiro, 1980). In general, they see reading acquisition as more complex than a formalized process which may be accomplished by fractionated and atomistic subskill teaching. Other psycholinguistic researchers who follow a more formal model of reading acquisition treat literacy acquisition more like a linguistic information processing sequence (LaBerge & Samuels, 1976). Such "bottom-up" theorists believe that the phoneme must be learned or "accessed," and specific cognitive problems must be confronted by the beginning reader in order to decode print (Gleitman & Rozin, 1973a; Rozin & Gleitman, 1977). Such theorists lend support to specific phonics and subskill training.

At present, a third "interactive" viewpoint seems most useful pedagogically because it links the two polar acquisition positions just discussed, and offers the balance of a "combination" theory/method. By "integrating" the logical applications inherent in each of the two perspectives, recognition is given to the strength of using both theoretical positions when structuring a comprehensive literacy acquisition curriculum. An integrated theoretical perspective therefore supports both explicit or direct teaching of phonics as a "system," and opportunities for implicit learning of whole language through "meaningful" whole language experiences (Botel, 1981; Botel & Seaver, 1984).

As yet, since we do not have a comprehensive "theory" of beginning writing, theoretical notions about the processes involved in learning to read seem to be the philosophical underpinnings of beginning writing programs. Such early writing programs, in the relatively few places where they exist as a stated concern, appear to reflect either "holistic," "atomistic," or "integrated" beliefs about written language acquisition. Holistic teachers tend to present writing informally, as a natural complement to the beginning reading program. They allow children to write spontaneously without initial regard for analytical parts of language or conventions. Other more traditional teachers believe in the necessity of a "bottom-up" foundation accomplished through formalized "methods," with a fractionated emphasis on parts: the teaching and directed practice of "learning sounds" and their respective symbols with the ultimate goal of joining these language parts to form words and sentences. Still other teachers present a combination of both methods by characteristically teaching subskills with whole language writing experiences in an integrated reading and writing literacy acquisition curriculum.

Prior to 1970 very few studies were directly concerned with the process of learning to write. Even fewer studies had actually observed young children in the process of learning to write. Gibson and Levin (1979) report that, historically, research into the area of literacy acquisition was somewhat behavioristically-oriented and curriculum-based, in contrast to the more current process-oriented and theory-based designs. Although such a perspective appears simplistic and may lead to overgeneralizations that infer one research method "pre-empts" the other (Botel, February 1984, personal communication about misconceived notions that curriculum-based research and theory-based research are mutually exclusive), the issue such dichotomizing addresses is the corpus of research whose concern more clearly focuses on developing curricula for the teaching of reading and writing, rather than with inquiring into the initial learning of these processes. Inherent in such behavioristic inquiries is the underlying assumption that by some "magical" process, what is taught by teachers is causally related to what will be learned by the student. Emig (1981) notes: "That teachers teach and children learn no one will deny. But to believe that children learn because teachers teach and only when teachers explicitly teach is to engage in magical thinking . . . from a developmental point of view" (p. 21).

Since about 1975, the trend has been toward an interest in the introspection of the learner (Flower & Hayes, 1977; Emig, 1971), as well as in the observation of the development of writing as a process (Graves, 1973, 1975, 1982, 1983; Harste et al., 1981; Gundlach, 1981, 1982; Dyson, 1981, 1983). Research in the specific area of beginning writing seems to be a somewhat recent and emerging area of interest, which steadily contributes to our understanding of the beginning writing experience. Movement toward theory-based research with a focus on the process of learning, as well as the child as an active constructor of the meaning of his learning, seems to be a characteristic of present studies in the field of beginning writing (Chomsky, 1970, 1971; Read, 1971, 1975; Clay, 1975; Graves, 1982; Dyson, 1981; Ferreiro & Teberosky, 1982; Ferreiro, 1978, 1984, in press (a), in press (b); Harste et al., 1981; Whiteman & Hall, 1981; King & Rentel, 1979; 1981; Gundlach, 1981, 1982; Bissex, 1980).

A RESEARCH PROJECT: LEARNING TO WRITE IN KINDERGARTEN

The Pilot Study

My own inquiry into the beginning writing process began with a series of observations in five kindergarten classrooms. The purpose of these initial observation was to docu-

ment variation in beginning writing programs in three northeastern public schools and
two private schools, where mixed ethnic groupings were the norm. The kindergarten
settings I observed included both inner-city and suburban classrooms of varying
socioeconomic levels.

It was during these five initial observations that I first noticed that kindergarten
teachers in the five classrooms I observed followed one of two programs of beginning
writing instruction. The first type of program was curriculum-based, in which the
teacher would select "the program" and the children were directed to "copy" a printed
model. In these classrooms, there appeared to be an implicit assumption that such practice would somehow automatically teach children [to learn] to write (i.e., "magical
thinking," Emig, 1981). The second type of beginning writing program was one that
was more process-oriented and child-centered, with the teacher encouraging the children to "self-direct" their own writing via spontaneous printing (i.e., invented and unconventional spellings). In such programs, because teachers expected children to direct
their own writing, the copying of print was an individual choice.

In classrooms where teacher-oriented "copying"was the mode for the beginning
writer, models of print were provided by experience charts, print around the room,
and/or worksheets. The stated expectation for such copying was for the child to reproduce the model. By contrast, in classrooms where "spontaneous printing" was the
mode—whereby children were encouraged to "just write" or "make up words" during
writing activities—a different philosophy and structure of teacher control existed. Such
programs were characterized by a generalized child-centered teacher style, which incor-
porated an explicit sensitivity and respect for the child's inherent knowledge as a beginning writer. This respect and sensitivity was then operationalized by skillful teacher
facilitation of the child's personal self-direction and efforts. Although help was given by
the teacher when requested via appropriate use of direct teaching, more generally the
child was expected to construct the meaning of "writing" through a cognitive and social
interaction within the context (i.e., with the other beginning writers at the writing
table). In essence, the written products of the self-directed writers were constructed
jointly, with the children helping each other to build and make meaning of a written
language system.

A striking difference in the children in these two contrasting programs was evident
at the end of the kindergarten year and merited further explorations: a discrepancy became apparent in the levels of conceptualization about writing, as well as in the independent performance of the "copiers" and the "spontaneous writers." The spontaneous
writers who directed their own writing seemed to flourish as beginning writers; they
were quite able to produce a simple sentence via invented spellings. Some of these children could even produce several sentences that began to resemble the coherent structure
of connected discourse. Conversely, the directed "copiers" displayed an observable level
of frustration and anxiety when asked to write without benefit of a printed model. A
common response to a request such as "Write something you like," was "I don't know
how to write," or simply "I can't." After months of using "copying" as a style and
writing method, these children had difficulty generating spontaneous print. While
other variables in these directed "copier" classrooms undoubtedly had an effect on the

performance differences, it was clear that the "copiers" had become dependent on "copying." The children were doing little more than passively mimicking a model. In fact, the copying activities were more like handwriting practice than a developmental writing experience which would include active problem-solving techniques.

There is further evidence of the passive role of "copiers" in the content of the talk that co-occurred with the writing during the copying experience. Children who were copying print either generated little or no language, or engaged in conversations that were unrelated to the print they were copying. It was as if they were not cognitively or personally connected to the activity in which they were engaged. In contrast, the spontaneous writers, who directed their own writing experiences, generated talk that was coordinated with the task, suggesting an active relationship between oral and written language during written language learning.

This oral language evidence suggests the need for further exploration of beginning writing approaches. Apparently, certain forms of teacher-directed beginning writing techniques (i.e., directed copying of an external printed model), are not in the child's best "active learning" interest. One explanation might be that certain kinds of directed "copying" activities put the child's innate writing potential (i.e., the goal for generative and creative expression) in a temporary holding position. Furthermore, writing programs that use copying activities exclusively as a beginning writing technique may incorrectly or erroneously reframe the child's expectations about writing during what may turn out to be an extremely sensitive period of written language development, as judged by the performance levels of 5-year-olds who are given opportunities to write spontaneously in kindergarten (see Blazer, 1984).

The Second Study

The differences between the affect of the children with regard to writing, in the five classrooms, led to a second observational study where the focus was on one of the beginning writing approaches—spontaneous writing. The purpose of this study was to explore how children who direct their own beginning writing experience learn to write. I chose to conduct a second study in one of the five schools documented in the pilot study. My choice was a classroom in a large private school in New Jersey, where a "spontaneous" writing program had been in existence for more than 10 years. In this classroom the foundation of the writing program was a writing table, where children were free to write anything they chose during a morning activity period. In general, three to six children would sit together, simultaneously talking and writing for about 20 to 30 minutes, jointly constructing written products. In the role of participant-observer, I positioned myself at the writing table one day per week over a 5-month period and collected both oral and written language sample as they were used in the construction of written products. By becoming a participant-observer during beginning writing activities, I was able to document three aspects of the beginning writing process:

1. The individual products themselves and their history of development.
2. The individual developmental patterns that could be identified by considering the products of a given child over time.

3.   The more general social and developmental patterns that emerge when studying the collected products of several children.

The focus of this study became the beginning writing processes, as characterized by the oral and written language used in the construction of written products. My goal was to explore the social and psychological aspects of writing acquisition, as well as the relationships between speaking and writing, and what these two language modes can tell us about the developmental patterns of beginning writers.

During my observation at the writing table, it became clear that an investigation of the talk and activities of beginning writers is critical to any reliable understanding of interpretation of the final written product: the social and cognitive interactions during beginning writing actually are the processes that create the product. One particularly important insight that emerged from this study was the recognition that every initial written product that is spontaneously generated has a history of development. Only limited information can be gleaned from examining the product of a beginning writer without observing the social context and the sociocognitive interactions that were the history of the product.

Four other relationships emerged from the time spent at the writing table:

1.   A regular relationship could be documented between talking and writing in spontaneous writers. The talk generated was specific to the writing task, either giving meaning to the written product or used as a means of facilitating print (i.e., the oral sounding of letters simultaneously with the writing of the symbol for the sound).[1]

2.   A group characteristic of the "talker-writers" became clear. They were "constructors," actively engaged in reinventing the conventional writing system by hypothesizing about the print being generated. The self-directed beginning writers engaged in problem-solving behaviors (i.e., hypothesizing, guessing, risk taking, etc.), and, in general, operated in an epistemological manner.[2]

3.   There was apparent accelerated development of the more vocal "talker-writers" within the larger group of spontaneous writers. It appeared that the more oral language used in conjunction with writing, the more accomplished the child became as a beginning writer. The children who spoke more demonstrated greater facility to match a phonetic sound orally with the appropriate written symbol. They became facile with invented spellings and could produce simple sentences at the end of the kindergarten year. Some of the early "talker-writers" could even write stories by the end of the year. It appeared that oral language that accompanied beginning writing acted as a parallel support to the initial learning of written language, and fostered its development during a particular stage.

---

[1] This phenomenon supports Dyson's (1981) work which identified a similar role of oral language in beginning writing.

[2] This phenomenon supports the work of Harste, Burke, and Woodward (1981) identifying "process universals" in beginning writers, and the work of Ferriero on constructive written language learning (1978, 1984).

4.   There was a definite reduction in the amount of talk generated during writing by the more "advanced" writers at the end of the school year.[3] It seemed that after children had attained a certain level of conceptualization about the sound-symbol relationship and had had enough practice using oral language as a support for beginning writing, talk became egocentric and finally went inward, disappearing as an observable manifestation of the cognitive processing.[4] At the same time, such "advanced" beginning writers seemed less dependent on the social context to mediate and facilitate the generation of print. In fact, the often complained about the noise, and asked to be allowed to write in the school library during whole class writing activities.

THE MAJOR STUDY

The emergence of the four relationships just described led to an in-depth study designed to explore a variety of questions about beginning writing processes. Critical to this investigation was an ethnographic methodology which enabled a focus on these relationships between oral and written language in the beginning writer. I conducted a one-year study, from September to June, in a kindergarten classroom where children directed their own initial writing experiences. The classroom I chose was philosophically enriched as far as teacher attitudes toward the 5-year-olds' ability to write. I therefore expected to see an accelerated process which facilitated maximum development of writing in kindergarten.

The Setting

The major study was conducted in a small, private kindergarten in a southern New Jersey school. This classroom would best be characterized as a "literate environment" where a positive and enriched interaction existed between the teachers and the children in regard to literacy acquisition. Besides an environmentally rich display of print, any literacy-related behaviors were met with explicit teacher approval, as well as a consistently supportive affect. In fact, written products were often received exuberantly by the teachers, and at times even accompanied by a hug and a kiss. Love and affection were part of the kindergarten environment.

The physical setting provided an abundant array of print: posters, bulletin boards, a daily calender, and weather chart area, a work chart with children's names and their

---

[3] The designation of "advanced" for a beginning writer is his or her ability to generate more than one sentence, cohesive in content, as in connected discourse.

[4] This looks as if it may be one of the ways in which a transition occurs, signaling the development of inner speech that becomes focused when writing. (Note: inner speech is defined as a plane that exists between external speech and actual thought.) "Inner speech is a kind of thought connected with words but not embodied in words" (Vygotsky, 1962):

"In inner speech words die as they bring forth thought. Inner speech is to a large extent thinking in pure meanings. It is a dynamic, shifting, unstable thing, fluttering between word and thought . . . . Every sentence that we say in real life has some kind of subtext, a thought hidden behind it . . . . Just as one sentence may express different thoughts, thought may be expressed in different sentences" (p. 149).

jobs, alphabetic letter displays, word displays, book area, and so on. In addition, a context for writing practice was provided via a permanent corner designated "The Writing Center." This area was supplied with paper, markers, and pencils. The center was available as an option during a one-hour play period (i.e., "playtime"), which was a scheduled choice period every morning. Children who visited the writing area during this time were encouraged to talk with other children at the writing center and jointly construct their written products by helping each other. A second context for writing in this classroom was during "whole class writing activities." At these writing times children sat at their assigned seats (a small table of four or five children), and paper and pencils would be passed out with an accompanying directive given "to write." During both of these writing-practice contexts the teacher and the teaching assistant circulated within the room, making themselves available for help or answers to specific questions. For example, although they encouraged the children to self-direct their writing activities (i.e., "Sound it out, say the sound and then write it"), they did help with spelling when a child asked for direct assistance (i.e., "I want the real spelling").

The pedagogical philosophy in the room was one of support for children's initiative, as well as for their own inherent problem-solving ability. The teacher clearly stated her role as one of facilitator of the learning process and was able to successfully structure the literacy activities into an open-ended and flexible framework. This educational philosophy allowed for child-centered learning in a variety of areas, and was based on child-stated needs, interests, and individual variation. The selection of this school for the major study was based on the supportive administrative and teacher philosophy in regard to literacy acquisition as a kindergarten concern.

The class grouping was ethnically and socioeconomically mixed, with 25 children, 16 girls, and nine boys, comprising the kindergarten roster. The children ranged in age from 4.10 to 5.8 years at the beginning of the school year. Family SES ranged from working class to professional, in ratio of about 3:1, with 23 of the 25 children coming from two-paycheck households. This private kindergarten was chosen by many families because a full-day program was offered, with an additional provision for extended day care for working parents.

The Method
An ethonographic perspective uses a variety of techniques for collecting data. Some of the methods being used in this study to collect data and written child language included:

1. Interviews, both informal and structured, of children, parents and teachers, about beginning writing.
2. Transcriptions of audio-recordings at the writing table and during whole class activities.
3. A collection of written products, documented and filed individually and cross-filed according to joint writing event.
4. Observations recorded in daily field notes, documenting activities related to literacy acquisition (i.e., drawing, reading, dramatizations, oral story-telling, etc.).

5. Daily topical summaries from field notes.
6. A photographic documentation to aid in the annotation of the historical development of the writing program.

For the purposes of this chapter, two kinds of oral language data are analyzed. The first kind of data is structured interviews, drawn from what children say about writing when they begin to write. These data will be used to assess what children know about writing as they begin to write. The second kind of data are the transcriptions of an interaction between beginning writers, during a self-directed whole class writing activity. These data will be used to analyze the nature of the relationships between speaking and writing during beginning writing experiences. (As stated previously, two contexts for writing existed in this classroom: writing during "playtime" as an optional choice and writing during a "whole class writing activity," which was not a choice. Only a "whole class writing" context will be presented in this chapter).

The data to be presented are intended to demonstrate how the beginning writer uses his knowledge about writing, as well as his oral language competence and confidence in the development of writing skills, and in support of a correlation between knowledge and performance in beginning writers (see Blazer, 1984). These two kinds of oral language data are used to see how the two language modes, speaking and writing, complement, support, and move the child forward in the process of learning to write. These two sources of oral language data are additionally useful to inquiries on early writing because they illuminate the creative process of the individual product. Thereby, the beginning product, as well as the process, may be viewed from a developmental perspective.[5]

Procedure: The Interviews

The first interview was designed to elicit oral descriptions about writing from the 5-year-old's point of view. Structured ethnographic interviews were used to find out what children know about writing when the enter their first formalized literacy setting (i.e., the schoolroom). Based on their willingness to talk to me, 16 of the 25 children were interviewed (eight boys, eight girls). In total, four periodic interviews were conducted throughout the year with these same 16 children, in order to document their changing conceptualizations about writing.

A primary methodological concern when interviewing children is the importance of establishing rapport, in order to insure cooperation and reliable responses. Thus, it wasn't until late October, after I had spent five weeks as a visitor to the classroom getting to know the children, that I conducted the first set of interviews. In the beginning of the year the teacher introduced me to the children as a teacher who likes to watch children write. I established my role as participant-observerr by seating myself at the writing table during "playtime." The interviews were conducted in the library, with just the child and myself present, and lasted about 15 minutes.

---

[5] See Blazer (1984) for a third level of data analysis performed on written products.

In order to have a conversational point of departure for the interview, I spoke about a contemporary cult figure of the middle-class youngster during the previous summer (1982)—E.T., the extraterrestrial from the movie of the same name. (I had been alerted to the status E.T. had in the Kindergarten culture by the variety of E.T. artifacts brought into the classroom by the children—trading cards, posters, buttons, shirts, and so on—as well as the children's early ability to write E.T. on their written products.) I first asked the child if he or she had seen the movie. In fact, 15 of the 16 children had. After a brief conversation about E.T., I asked questions that centered around a theme of E.T. arriving in the kindergarten classroom, wanting to know what the children were doing when they held pencils in their hands and made marks on papers. The questions E.T. might ask were structured to include:

1. What is writing?
2. What is drawing?
3. Is writing the same as drawing?
4. What is good writing?
5. What is bad writing?
6. What is good drawing?
7. What is bad drawing?
8. Why do people write?
9. Why do you write?
10. What do you write at home (school)?[6]
11. What is a letter?
12. What is a word?
13. What is a sentence?

(For interview schedule, including questions and answers, see Appendix A at end of chapter; for developmental interview data, see Blazer, 1984.)

In total, 25 hours of audio-recorded child interviews were transcribed onto approximately 300 typewritten pages, representing 76 child interviews that were conducted at four intervals during the school year. An analysis of the initial interview data showed that within this group of children, there were several different levels of conceptualizations about writing. In other words, no single descriptive profile could characterize the beginning writer's initial conceptualizations about writing. In addition, the initial knowledge that is variable across the children in a given classroom does not seem to be related to age or sex difference. This variation in initial knowledge may be explained by differences in cognitive and linguistic development, as well as the role of previous home and school experiences. Because of these differences, one cannot predict what a child knows about writing when he or she enters kindergarten.

In order to analyze the children's responses to the interview questions, I devised a three-point rating scale, so that I might categorize varying conceptual levels of children's understanding about writing. The assignment of one point represented minimal

---

[6] Several of these questions were taken from Y. Goodman and B. Altwerger, "Child's Concepts of Written Language and Pictorial Representation" task-sheet, University of Arizona, 1981.

knowledge, two points represented moderate knowledge, and three points indicated some kind of exceptional or abstract knowledge. Four categories of knowledge emerged after an analysis of the responses at each level. These categories suggested four different kinds of knowledge about writing: affective (related to the child's feelings about print), concrete (related to the actual form or graphic display of print), constructive (related to the communicative function and meaning of writing), and creative (related to imaginative and abstract use of print).[7]

The first level of clear conceptualization about writing fell into an affective category, characterized by "feeling" responses. For example, in reply to the question, "What is writing?" some children answered, "Something you give people, or make people, to make them happy." Several more examples of this level of understanding are the following selected affective responses:

Question: Why do people write?
Paul: Because they feel like it.
Ryan: Because they want to.
Anna: Because they like to.
Liz: Because they want to give things to people.

The second level of responses fell into a category of literal and concrete knowledge about writing. This level was characterized by figural and graphic knowledge, with reference to tools, mechanics, or the physical display of the figural form. Some examples of concrete and literal knowledge follow.

Question: What is writing?
Mandy: Something you do with a pencil.
Paul: When you make a P and a L . . . like in Paul, that's writing.
Denny: Making letters.
Question: What is drawing?
Paul: Make a face with two eyes and a nose and a mouth.
Denny: Drawing? . . . when you make pictures.

The third level of initial writing knowledge may be termed "constructive" knowledge. The most distinctive feature of this level response is that children describe writing as if it were a function (i.e., that product becomes deemphasized and the majority of responses are spent making meaning of the process). Several other features of construc-

---

[7] A zero rating was assigned to a first, undetermined category of responses, characterized by the statement "I don't know," or a nonverbal shrug of the shoulders. When such a response occurred, there appeared to be a uniformity across questions. In general, children who said they didn't know what writing was also did not know what the difference was between writing and drawing, or why people write. The zero level for these responses is not meant to mislead the reader into interpreting this as a valueless response. Rather, it is meant to be interpreted as arbitrary because little analysis seems justifiable, given the variety of affective factors that could be related to the "I don't know" statement (i.e., child's discomfort with the researcher or the questioning procedure; child's lack of experience with being asked to verbalize about conceptual questions).

tive knowledge about the writing process are: insight into purpose and use of writing; recognition of written language as a communication tool; construction of a personal meaning for writing; and an awareness of a relationship between oral and written language (i.e., "writing is a kind of talk written down"). This level can be characterized by the use of meaning-making responses, indicating active problem solving by the learner (i.e., hypothesis testing, risk taking, making inferences, evaluating) or an abstract understanding of the relationship between talking and writing. Some examples of such kinds of responses are:

Question: What is writing?
   Tessa: When you push words and sentences together to say something. It's kind of talk that is written down.
   Mitch: Just making words and sentences to tell people things that live far away.

Question: What is drawing?
   Mitch: Making pictures . . . like in business, you may have to if you are a carpenter . . . draw pictures to explain things.

Question: What is good writing?
Jonethan: Doing you words right and trying to spell.
   Mitch: Writing that is interesting . . . like about nice things that happen to you. (Note: This could also be categorized as a fourth level, creative response, because it infers a control of the content).

Question: What is bad writing?
Jonethan: When you really don't write anything.
   Mitch: Writing that is not very interesting . . . like "Dear Mitch, will you write to me, love so and so . . . "
              (Blazer: Why is that bad?)
              Because you don't have anything to tell. (Note: Here again Mitch's knowledge may more likely be categorized as creative because of an awareness that the content may be altered and controlled).

Question: Why do people write?
Jonethan: To write letters to people, to write things, to write the news, and to write what happened.
   Mitch: To tell people things.

Question: Why do you write?
Jonethan: So I can send letters to people . . . and to keep them for me to read when I get bigger.
   Mitch: To tell my grandparents how do they feel and how I am feeling.

The fourth level of knowledge about writing appears to be somewhat more abstract and may be accompanied by a creative response. Although this was infrequently a response made by a beginning writer, such a response seemed to indicate that an awareness had developed in regard to the variability of communicative content. This response was distinctive in that it was characterized by the knowledge that content can be controlled. On this level a kind of abstract knowledge was indicated by a reference, explicit or implicit, to the use of imagination and its role in communication of ideas. Attention to forms and processes at this level give way to the creative potential of written forms. Two examples of this level response will be given.

> Question: Is drawing the same as writing?
> Mitch: Same, because you use your imagination for both.
>   (Blazer: What is imagination?)
> Mitch: Just thinking of things that you don't know . . . you don't know it for sure, but you think it's a certain way . . . it doesn't matter if you think it the wrong way or right way in your imagination.

An example of a creative response that indicated a kind of theorizing or the emergence of a philosophical perspective, was not given at the initial interview screening. About midyear, however, Janet's interview responses and written products began to illustrate this kind of abstract thinking about writing.

> Question: What is writing?
> Janet: (repeats question) What is writing? (pauses) Writing is writing.
>   (Blazer: (looks puzzled) But what *is* writing?)
> Janet: (pauses) What is love? Love is love. Writing is writing (smiles).

One possible way of viewing the developmental nature of the initial knowledge that children bring to their first kindergarten writing experiences is on a continuum, where a relationship could be charted between conceptual levels of understanding and active use of written language as a communication tool. Each level could then be represented in a more detailed way on its own continuum, characterizing the complexity of development at individual levels (see Figure 2).

Although these developmental categories seemed to cut across different interview questions thereby suggesting a uniformity of individual conceptualizations about writing, there was some movement between consecutive levels, in both directions. In other words, although there was a consistency within individual children in regard to their level of response, it appeared quite natural for children to respond within consecutive categories (i.e., one and two, or two and three, or three and four) for different questions. On the other hand, it was rare to find any example of a child skipping categories—as in a mixing of level zero or one response on some questions with a level three response to other questions. This finding is supported by Ferriero's work (1978), which demonstrated general developmental patterns. In this study of early perception of print, a similar phenomenon was observed. Of the child subjects interviewed about print, 90% presented either a single category or "contiguous category" response, representing their conceptualizations about writing (p. 35). Ferriero claimed that these "contiguous category responses" strongly suggest a developmental line where the sequence is

Figure 2. Developmental conceptual levels and use of writing as a communication tool in beginning writers in kindergarten.

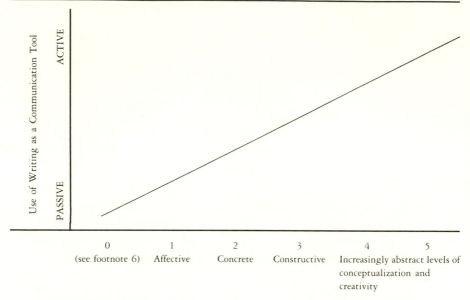

developmentally ordered (i.e., where each step is necessary in order to teach the next one)" (p. 35). Such findings demonstrate a consistency about what individual children know about writing, as well as the existence of an initial conceptualization about written language.

This pattern of general consistency of conceptual levels was confirmed in my research, during three subsequent interviews. These later interviews, when analyzed in conjunction with other observational data, continued to support the presence of a developmental sequence that was orderly and characterized by a gradual forward movement toward increasingly active cognitive processing (i.e., movement toward problem solving) and more knowledge. For example, children who were grouped at level one at the beginning of the year, in general, were giving mostly level two and three responses by the end of the year.

After further analysis of the frequency and distribution of children's initial interview responses in regard to "writing," several generalizations emerged about the children in this single kindergarten classroom:

1. Twelve out of the 16 children interviewed demonstrated concrete and constructive initial levels of knowledge about writing during the beginning part of the kindergarten year.

2. Fifteen out of the 16 children interviewed demonstrated concrete levels of understanding about drawing (i.e., "drawing is making pictures").

3. There seemed to be a relationship between drawing and writing in the conceptualizations of beginning writers.

a. The literal understanding of drawing as "making pictures" seemed to provide the experiential framework for parallel literal conceptualization about writing as "making letters" (for those children who demonstrated a concrete level of knowledge about writing).

b. Concrete concepts about good writing seemed to evolve from children's knowledge about drawing. Child knowledge about good drawing, as defined by conventions for neatness, staying in the lines (i.e., as in coloring books), and not doing sloppy or messy work, and so on, seemed to carry over to writing definitions, creating an initial structure about good writing.

c. The majority of children in this study entered kindergarten with concrete, literal, or figurative knowledge about writing, specifically in regard to its graphic form. These conceptualizations may have had their inception in earlier experiences and concepts about drawing.[8]

4. Children enter school with various levels of understanding regarding functions (i.e., the social factors) and reasons (i.e., the psychological factors) for writing. These levels are analogous to their definitions of "writing." For example, if a child displays a constructive level of understanding about writing, it can be expected that his response to functions and reasons for writing will be equally sophisticated for a beginning writer. However, it is interesting to note that regardless of the 5-year-old's level of sophistication in regard to why other people write, his or her personal rationale for his or her own writing, in the very beginning stages (i.e., before they can produce print that is meaningful) is overwhelmingly an affective one: they write because they like to. This leads one to suggest that in the beginning, writing seems to be related to the child's affective experiential enjoyment of other expressive and communicative symbolic forms, as in the use of gesture, play, games, and drawing.[9]

5. An observable relationship existed between childrens' use of oral language about writing and their beginning writing products. Those children who orally demonstrated concrete or constructive knowledge about writing could generate meaning in a written form via print. For example, such a child might attempt an unconventional spelling and show the teacher, saying the word or making the statement "Look what I wrote." Conversely, those children who orally said they didn't know what writing was, or gave an affective level response, tended not to be able to write anything other than their name or a memorized word during the first part of the school year. Such children consistently used writing time to draw or practice single letters or letter strings. After such activities they would come up to the teacher to "show" their picture, or if they wrote would ask "What did I write" or "Does this say anything?" In sum, it appeared that there was a strong relationship between what a child said about writing and his actual written product.[10]

---

[8] See Vygotsky's (1978) discussion on the "Prehistory of Written Language," pp. 105–120.

[9] Same as the above.

[10] See Blazer (1984) for a discussion of the relationships between talking and writing, and the written product.

Audio-recorded Talk During Writing Activities

Data collection during writing times focused on the childrens' use of oral language in conjunction with the writing task. In order to establish a baseline for early writing processes to be used for comparison with data collected at later times, an initial data collection phase was conducted during the first few weeks of school. It was during this period that all the children in the study classroom were given opportunities to write. More specifically, during prescribed "whole class writing experiences," paper would be passed but, pencils stood available in cans in the center of each small table, and a simple directive would be given to the children to "write, just write anything you would like."[11] To collect the spoken language, tape recorders were placed at each table during these prescribed writing activities, so that all of the child language could be collected. In addition, observational notes were kept of the interactions at one of the five writing tables, so that nonlinguistic context could also be integrated with the oral and written data. Later, the recordings were transcribed and, where appropriate, coordinated with the observational notes. Next, this annotated transcription was aligned with the child's written product, so that the developmental history of each product would be ready for analysis.

In total, 25 hours of audio-recorded child talk were logged as collected, representing about 125 joint writing episodes, 54 of which were whole class writing activities. After analyzing the product through its oral and written history, it became evident that both the speaking and the writing were creating an interactive feedback system that functioned to organize the beginning writing event. This same speaking-writing system, when looked at over time became useful for demonstrating the developmental process inherent in learning to write.

The analysis that follows is based on data collected during these initial data collection procedures and serves to present a number of important linguistic and social behaviors that the beginning writer needs to integrate and coordinate in order to learn to write. Two levels of these linguistic and social interactions are important to discuss. First, on a primary level, are the intra-individual "talking-writing" interactions that occur *within* the child as he writes. Such egocentric talking and writing relationships represent the internal linguistic resources and problem-solving abilities the child brings to the writing situation. On this level the child directly uses oral language to support his writing. On a secondary level[12] are the interactional talking and writing relationships that are external and interpersonal. They exist *between* individual children. Such talking and writing interactions not only represent linguistic and problem-solving resources that children bring to and share during the writing event, but add the child's

---

[11] Unfortunately, we were not aware of the linguistic ambiguity we were presenting with the directive, "Just write." Although "just write" was meant to encourage practice and choice, the children may have interpreted it as an exclusive instruction, perhaps fostering some of the negotiations and clarifications that became part of this activity. "Negotiation" however, has been identified as the first "process universal" in the beginning writing process by Harste et al. (1981).

[12] Secondary, because without internal linguistic resources, a child could not participate in a writing event.

level and use of social resources, necessary as an element of beginning writing growth. In sum, the child actually seems to be operating on three levels of oral language competence simultaneously, to support and make meaning out of the beginning writing event: first, his *intra-individual* use of language to support his writing; second, his social and *interactional* use of language, characterized by a sharing of his resources with other children who are part of the beginning writing event; and third, his use of language, problem solving and social resources in a *receptive* manner, so that he may draw from other children's resources. This integration of resources and interactional levels may ultimately be the process that facilitates growth and understanding of the beginning writing event.[13]

The transcription selected for analysis in this chapter (see Appendix B) has been chosen to illustrate the dimensions of the intra- and inter-individual interactions that operate as components of the beginning writing event. It will be shown that these interactions are systematic and logical, and serve to organize various oral and written language relationships (within the beginning writing event) into a predictable shape or form. The speaking and writing relationships that are present in the beginning writer seem to organize the writing episode into three orderly stages or processes of beginning writing development. These three stages which ultimately serve to shape the beginning writing event may be summarized as follows: first, the clarifications and negotiations *within* and *between* the writers before the writing task; second, the intra-individual coordination of the talking and writing during the actual writing event; and third, the inter-individual sharing, comparing, and evaluating of the written products by the joint group of writers, signaling the end of the writing event. What follows will be a detailed description and analysis of children's language, as it organizes their beginning writing experiences into a beginning writing event.

THE ROLE OF ORAL LANGUAGE IN THE BEGINNING WRITING EVENT

Excerpt 1: Clarification of Directions and Negotiations about the Writing Task (see Appendix B, Excerpt 1)

This excerpt illustrates the relationships between talking and writing that exist inter-individually during beginning writing experiences. Very often during the first few weeks of school, when the children were told to write, they asked if that meant they could draw if they didn't know how to write. A definite lack of clarity about the differences between writing and drawing was evident during these times. The teacher consistently answered that they could do whatever they liked, but they should try to write "just a little bit." Even though they had teacher permission to draw, there was a social pressure from some of the children who knew how to write, to write. It was common at the beginning of such activities to hear the initial negotiations between the children who were opting to draw, and those children who were more knowledgeable about writ-

---

[13] See Blazer (1984) for a discussion of theoretical interpretations.

ing and therefore literally interpreting the directive "just write" to mean you may only write (Appendix B, lines 3–30). Notice (lines 23–30) how Janet and Mandy insist that Joanie cannot just draw. Her drawing will be acceptable only if she writes too. Although she maintains her ground initially and appears just to be drawing a figure of a man, later in the activity (Excerpt 2), the social context, which consists of everyone else writing, seems to inspire or demand a writing effort on her part.

Lines 1–30 also illustrate the varying developmental levels of written language knowledge that underlie the child-child interactions which begin the writing activity. Information collected during the initial interviews regarding children's initial conceptualizations (i.e., affective, concrete, constructive, and creative knowledge) are used heuristically to interpret the interaction that provided the clarification/negotiation prewriting structure of the beginning writing event.

Denny.   Examination of Denny's responses to the questions in the first interview revealed a definite movement toward concrete and literal levels of initial knowledge about writing. This helps to explain his immediate concrete cognitive reaction whereby he repeats the teacher directions (line 3) and his second literal and figural interpretation that to write means "You are not allowed to draw" (line 8). The social context then became a resource for organizing the writing activity when Denny asked another child to confirm his own interpretations (lines 9–11). Throughout the activity, Denny used the social context interactively as part of his writing process.

Ryan.   Ryan's response to Denny, "Draw pictures and write, both" (line 12) reflected a combination of his "affective level" of cognitive processing and a personal style of not taking strong positions in social interactions. In an "affective" conceptual mode, Ryan usually enjoyed using writing time for the purpose of drawing. He had often stated during writing activities that he "makes letters for people I like, to make them happy." These folded letters were often pictures or colorings, without any writing. His initial conception of writing as revealed in the first interview, was "drawings with some names on it." In response to why people write, he replied, "to give people things." In the transcribed portion he was actually solving the dilemma by authorizing what he understood writing to be: "First draw pictures and then put a name or letters on it." (This was the response given by Ryan to the first interview question, "What is writing?") Ryan most often worked by himself, usually interjecting conversations that was characteristically egocentric. Notice in line 19, the only time Ryan interjected without solicitation, he maintained a position of avoiding the interpretative social and linguistic issues of what the teacher expects, and instead directed the writing of his own name.

Joanie.   Joanie (line 14), like Ryan, tried to negotiate for both because she too preferred to draw. In fact, during the first few weeks of school, Joanie had not done any spontaneous writing that was self-directed or of an invented or unconventional genre. She entered school with a writing repertoire of three memorized words—"cat, dog, kitten"—and her name. She wrote these same three words on all her papers when she was pressured to write. At the beginning of the year she seemed to have little interest in the active self-direction of generative writing. Her initial interview revealed an undetermined level of knowledge about writing, as more than half of her responses were, "I don't know." When the child-child interactions from lines 24–30 determined the instruction to be "You have to write," Joanie actually refused, continuing to draw without even writing her name, as the teacher had requested.

Note in the next excerpt that Joanie is the only child who initiated talk that was not related to what she was doing (lines 40–44). She does not actually turn over her paper to write until line 54, when every other child at the table had become involved with coordinating their talk with their writing. This phenomenon seems to be an observable example of the critical nature of the social context as a mediator in the beginning writing process. In this case, the social context was enticing, supporting, and perhaps, at this point, indirectly pressuring Joanie to push toward and actually function at a higher and more abstract cognitive level of written language processing (See Vygotsky's "zone of proximal development," 1978).

Janet.   Janet, who first interacts on line 24, seemed least in need of clarifying or negotiating the directive. She interjected with perhaps the highest level of certainty and clarity, "You don't just draw, you write too." This lesser need to participate in the beginning interaction was predictable according to her high constructive and sometimes creative conceptualizations about writing, as revealed by her meaning making and sometimes abstract responses to the initial interview questions. Janet feels comfortable problem solving herself, by hypothesizing and risk-taking (see Excerpt 2), independent of the children who are at lower conceptual levels. Janet was confident about writing and able to self-direct her writing behaviors. Her product revealed mostly print, accompanied by a few related drawings. Janet entered kindergarten as one of the most advanced beginning writers because of her oral and written language facility.

Excerpt 2: The Relationship Between Talking and Writing: Talk is Coordinated with Task (see Appendix B for transcription)

This excerpt illustrates the relationship between talking and writing that exists both intra- and inter-individually in the beginning writer. At this stage, the child's oral language can be seen as a kind of a printout of the thought processes she or he is using to support the generation of print. The evidence for this guiding and supportive role of language is the written product itself (see Figure 3). The oral language creates the developmental history of the written product: performance is guided by oral language in beginning writers.

When viewed alongside the transcribed oral language, a direct correspondence is evident. This supportive relationship between the talk and the writing suggests that the child is thinking out loud, using oral language to work through the new learning. This coordination of talking and writing appears to be representative of the more abstract relationship between language and thought that exists in the more mature language user (Vygotsky, 1962) and more specifically in the mature writer. Of course, in the

Figure 3.   Written products, November 1, 1982

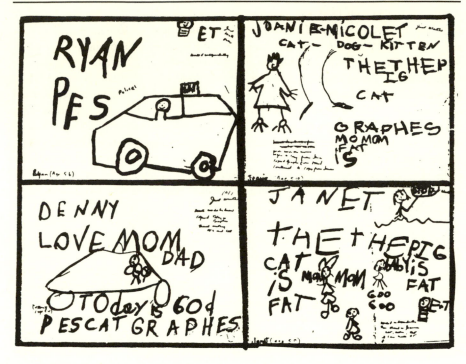

mature writer the relationship between language, thought, and writing becomes far more complex and therefore less direct.

This excerpt further demonstrates the difficulty in analytically distinguishing between cognitive and social processes during a social interaction. The difficulty in separating out the complex processes within the interaction is demonstrated as Ryan announces what he is going to write, and then begins to approximate the spelling (lines 31–34). Although Ryan is talking egocentrically about what he is doing, without a clearly marked addressee, Denny is sitting next to him and is listening attentively. Minutes later, Denny begins to sound out the same word using the same letters, and reinvents Ryan's invented spelling of "police" (i.e., P—E—S, lines 48–49; see Figure 3). Mandy also follows the talking and writing lead, and announces that she knows how to spell a name which she had previously memorized (line 45). She proceeds to say each letter and follows her verbalization with writing (line 47). Joanie next follows Mandy's letter calling and writing with a word she had memorized (lines 55 and 59–60). Between the Mandy-Joanie interaction, Janet interjects at her more actively constructive level, hypothesizing and taking risks regarding the sound-symbol relationship of the word "kitten."

This type of analysis of interactions at the writing table is an illustration of the integration of social and cognitive interactions that occur during learning in a natural setting. Such an illustration leads me to believe that the "element" of learning to write is a kind of joint sociocognitive transaction. During the joint writing activity, learning to write seems to be *within* the intra-individual interactions of the social and cognitive processes and *between* the participant interactions and the social context. The "how" part of the beginning writing process therefore seems to reside in the connections and relationships between social and cognitive factors, represented by the beginning writer's use of two communicative modes—talking and writing—which are supporting each other.

Excerpt 3: Comparing, Sharing, and/or Evaluating: The Validation Process (See appendix B)

The first half of this excerpt illustrates the way self-directed writers naturally copy print in their environment as a beginning writing strategy and style. The distinctive feature of self-directed "copying" is that when elected, both the print and the mode are self-chosen. In other words, rather than explicitly being directed to "copy," it appears as a natural alternative when participating in self-directed writing. In most cases, "copying" is a commonly chosen mode at earlier levels of conceptualizations about writing, and is usually not accompanied by the writer's comprehension (as indicated at this beginning stage by the ability to read what has been written). A speculation about the infrequency of copying at the higher constructive levels is that since such levels also include some ability to read, writing time gives the beginner a chance to actively practice some of the sounds they have begun to reflect upon and master receptively. Characteristic of children at constructive levels is the preference to write spontaneously, rather than to copy. In essence, they have more independent and active written language power than children who choose to copy. Note that Janet reads what Denny has written (line 69) but does not copy "graphs" onto her paper, whereas Joanie and Mandy, at lower conceptual levels, do (see Figure 3).

More importantly in relation to the writing "process," the first half of this excerpt represents an instance of the way children begin to share and compare their product via a "look at my paper" or "look at what I wrote" statement (line 67). In this case, since "copying" was the strategy used by some of the children to generate print, it became the vehicle for the third process of sharing, comparing, and/or evaluating. This final validation process served as a signal that the writing event will soon come to an end. It is interesting to note the social dynamics that underlie the evaluative process and end this particular writing event. Such dynamics are represented by the last several lines of this excerpt (74–81), and reveal a metalevel of the writing event: observable social dynamics and stratifications appear to be a social element in the organization of the beginning writing event. In this case, the issue of copying is being used to make rules in order to provide the criterion by which the early product may be evaluated: while it is acceptable to copy print around the room (albeit an admission to a lower level of cognitive processing and not respected by the constructive level writers), it is not acceptable to copy from another child's paper (i.e., Denny, line 77) unless specific permission has been granted by the originator (lines 80–81). Here the social context again directly mediates and interacts with the cognitive processing, continuing to structure the beginning writing event.

There are definite, observable patterns that emerged during this study in regard to social stratifications according to levels of literacy attained. Literacy appeared to be a necessary but not sufficient condition for leadership in the kindergarten classroom. Again, social and symbolic relationships interacted, and a centralization of power in the kindergarten classroom was amassed by the most literate and socially sophisticated children.[14]

CONCLUSIONS

This study, with a focus on the child as informant, used the child's oral language as a primary data source to examine the social and linguistic processes by which children develop as writers during the kindergarten year. If one believes that the beginning writing experience depends on a relationship between oral and written language and the social context, then what the child says *about* writing and what the child says *while* writing provide two critical levels of metalinguistic data about the beginning writing process.

Beginning writing develops in the context of many different kinds of relationships, both social and symbolic, and is facilitated by the child's social and cognitive processes, within given social contexts. Writing is a socially, as well as a psychologically constructed achievement. Viewed from such an interactive perspective, the development of writing occurs within social and symbolic relationships. It is these relationships that are

---

[14] For further analysis of the social networks and issues of patterns of leadership with literacy see Blazer, B., "The Social Consequences of Being a Writer in Kindergarten" (in preparation).

the source of information that will ultimately inform us about the processes of literacy acquisition. Investigation grounded in such joint relationships, between symbolic systems and social contexts (i.e., between talking and writing, drawing and writing, reading and writing, playing and writing, etc.), will provide the fertile domain for future study on the beginning writing process, with the larger goal of increased understanding about the process of literacy acquisition. [15]

One major finding of this research is that children enter kindergarten with varying degrees of knowledge about writing and the writing process. In fact, individual variation is the norm in kindergarten groups, due to differences in developmental, linguistic, educational, and sociocultural backgrounds. A heuristic has been created whereby children may be asked conceptual questions about writing, in order that their knowledge may be identified and viewed developmentally. This heuristic enables the child's knowledge to be categorized according to increasing degrees of activity in constructing meaning about writing. These levels of knowledge may be described by patterns of behaviors, moving from "affective" to "concrete," from "concrete" to "constructive," and from "constructive" to "creative" responses. Such categories of responses have been described herein.

A second finding is a demonstrable relationship between speaking and writing that is evident from the beginning writer's behaviors. During the early stages of using written language, the role of oral language is one of support and facilitation: the child's talk is coordinated with and guides his or her written efforts. Furthermore, children who write spontaneously and self-direct their activities within small groups, where social interaction via talking is encouraged, seem to flourish and progress as beginning writers during the kindergarten year. About 75% of the children in this study who were given free writing time to actively make their own meaning of the written code were able to write in simple sentences by the end of the school year. Approximately 50% were able to compose short stories of four to eight sentences by the close of the kindergarten year.

A third finding is the identification of three processes that form the beginning writing event, indicating that oral language helps to organize and structure the beginning writing experience. These three processes represent the relationships and interactions between social and symbolic systems which move the beginning writer through an activity which becomes the beginning writing event. It is here that we can see the development of rules of writing and writing conventions, as well as the social procedures that become part of accomplishing the task. Three processes have been identified: clarification, coordination, and evaluation. These processes tend to shape the writing episode and may be described as follows: first, through clarification and negotiation among beginning writers, rules and values about writing emerge (both social and symbolic), creating boundaries for beginning writers that help them to achieve the writing task; second, childrens' use of oral language during writing both anticipates and becomes coordinated with the writing process, acting to facilitate the actual mechanics and successful achievement of the task; and third, through the validation process of

---

[15] See Blazer (1984, chap. 6) for a summary of interactions *between* and *within* social and symbolic relationships that creates the beginning writing process.

sharing, comparing, and evaluating, the written product becomes completed and the writing event comes to an end. When these three processes are given the time to occur sequentially they form a predictable shape—the beginning writing event.

This study has direct implications for the development of writing programs in kindergarten. Since 5-year-olds come to school with competence and confidence in their oral language, these strengths should be built on and used as a foundation for expanding communication. Opportunities for early and free writing practice time in kindergarten create contexts for confidence building in another language mode: written language. Observation of young writers in a variety of kindergarten environments suggests the necessity for planned opportunities that encourage children to self-direct their own spontaneous writing abilities, mobilizing their social and psychological oral language abilities via sounding, planning, questioning, explaining, hypothesizing, risk taking, negotiating, and so on.

Speaking has a special relationship with beginning writing because it is children's confidence and competence with their oral language that not only supports, but leads their passage into the acquisition of literacy. Additionally, it appears that when kids do connect talk and task as they did during spontaneous writing, multiple expressive systems become connected and work together to produce meaning and learning. By contrast, when children copied during the course of this study, such joint copying activities were accompanied by an oral language that was not related to the writing task, which perhaps might characterize disconnected expressive systems. The *absence* of an integrated speaking and writing relationship during beginning writing, where two modes are relevant to each other and to the learning, may represent a cognitive and/or personal disconnectedness with the activity at hand. If such premises are valid, it is possible that certain kinds of traditional beginning writing programs, which primarily employ copying-handwriting activities and practice, may not facilitate beginning writing. This study suggests that research into developmental differences due to methods used in beginning writing programs is critical at this time.

In sum, this research project suggests that writing should be able to begin without direct instruction or specific limits. It may be that just as oral language is learned in the context of speaking with others, writing may be the same kind of "natural" process if children are able to begin "naturally," that is, by using it, and creating the writing process as well as the written product from their own communicative strengths. Children's spontaneous written experiments should be recognized and encouraged as a natural curiosity that will grow and develop if given the time and space to do so. Kindergarten classrooms may be one of may contexts for initial writing experiences that should begin in such a manner.

In conclusion, the advancement of educational systems in the 1980s is characterized by a belief in the child as a leader of his learning. Educators and researchers alike are becoming increasingly aware that the child is a knowledgeable and skillful being, whose backgrounds, interests, needs, and levels of understanding differ and must be recognized. These inherent strengths and differences must additionally be made explicit if the child's competenccies are to be used generatively for the acquisition and development of new skills and knowledge. This study has addressed some of these current concerns, most specifically in regard to the creation of educational environments and contexts that will enhance and support maximum beginning writing experiences and development. This study also suggests that the time has come for us not only to listen and build on what children say about writing, but also to feel confident that encouraging their talk while they write will enhance and add meaning to their literacy acquisition and development. It may be that future research will show that free expression and development of different kinds and amounts of talk during writing play a critical role in written language growth and development. Written language does have an oral language that is at its base (Olson, 1977); let us call on the child's language and speaking-writing relationships to lead the way to the child's acquisition of literacy.

APPENDIX A: THE INTERVIEW SCHEDULE

These data are being presented in the spirit of ethnographic inquiry so that others may draw upon and reinterpret it as they wish. Because ethnographic methods of data collection and data analysis are deeply integrated, it is my hope that these data, if used, will be kept in the contextualized state in which they were developed and are being presented.

The following selected responses illustrate children's "initial levels of conceptualization" (i.e., underlying knowledge) about writing, at the beginning of the school year. At the beginning stages of analysis, the responses were loosely and tentatively ordered according to increasingly abstract conceptualization about writing as a communicative tool.

Question 1:	What is writing?
Joanie:	I don't know.
Ryan:	Something you make for people you like.
Paul:	When you make a P and a T . . . like in Peter, that's writing.
Denny:	Just making letters and stuff.
Jonethan:	It's words that you spell, you need words or you can't even say anything when you write.
Tessa:	It's when you push words together to say something. It's a kind of talk that is written down.
Mitch:	Just makin' words and sentences to tell people things that live far away.
Question 2:	What is drawing?
Paul:	Like you draw a bat and no words. Making a face with two eyes and a nose and a mouth and ears.
Joanie:	When you draw, you make something, like a person or something.
Denny:	Drawing . . . when you draw pictures.
Anna:	When you get a crayon and draw something.
Jonethan:	Drawing is pictures you can draw like an artist or something.
Mitch:	Makin' pictures . . . like in business, you may have to if you are a carpenter . . . draw house pictures to explain things.

Question 3:   Is drawing the same as writing?

Ryan: Well, yes, because you can write a little picture to give to people you like.

Paul: No. There is like no writing if you draw a face, or a spider or something.

Anna: No. 'Cause when you want to write somebody, you write something . . . but when you want to draw, you draw something.

Tessa: The same because for both you use pens and markers.

Brandy: The same because they are both writing that tells something.

Jonethan: Different because writing is words and drawing is just stuff you do for fun. Writing is something you sound out and drawing is a nice picture you could look at.

Janet: Writing is letters and words and drawing is, um, a picture.

Mitch: Same, because you use your imagination for both of them.
(Blazer: What's imagination?)
Just thinking of things that you don't know . . . you don't know it for sure but you think it's a certain way . . . it doesn't matter if you think it the wrong way or right way in your imagination.

Question 4:   What is good writing?

Joanie: I don't know.

Ryan: No scribble scrabble on it and no messing up.

Paul: It is the one where I don't get out of the lines. It's also when you take your time and use a lot of different colors.

Denny: Good writing is going in the lines in writing . . . careful in the lines. You touch the line and then you go down.

Janet: Good writing is something when you make it neat.

Lizzie: When you write letters . . . I mean when you write things.

Jonethan: Doing your words right and trying to spell.

Mitch: Writing that is interesting . . . like about nice things that happen to you.

Question 5:   What is bad writing?

Paul: Well . . . without different colors. Like if you use black, that is not real good colors . . . orange or red are better.

Ryan: Scribble scrabble and messing things up.

Denny: Bad writing is when you go you of the lines.

Janet: You don't make it neat.

Joanie: Curse words.

Lizzie: When you don't really write anything.

Mitch: Writing that is not very interesting . . . like "Dear Mitch, will you write to me, Love so and so."
(Blazer: Why is that bad?)
Because you don't have anything to tell. Also long writing is nice.

Question 6:   What is good drawing?
Joanie: I don't know.
Paul: You use all different colors.
Brandy: You can make a little birdie, draw a house.
Ryan: Like good pictures, like a horse or truck.
Lizzie: When you make pictures.
Tessa: You are not drawing sloppy.
Janet: When you draw nice and neat, like slowly.
Holly: When you make it good and you stay in the lines.
Mitch: Making pictures that are nice.

Question 7:   What is bad drawing?
Paul: Everything in the same color.
Denny, Ryan: Scribble, scrabble.
Lizzie: When you don't make nice pictures.
Tessa: Sloppy.
Mitch: Messy pictures.

Question 8:   Why do people write?
Brandy: I don't know.
Paul: Because they feel like it.
Denny: Because they want to.
Lizzie: Because they want to give people things.
Marty: 'Cause sometimes they want to mail it to somebody.
Jeremy: So if they live far away they can write to someone . . . they could like
               mail it. Just as if mailing instead of telling them, going over, or talk-
               ing to them over the phone.
Jonethan: To write letters to people, to write things, to write the news, and to write
               what happened.
Mitch: To tell people things.

Question 9:   Why do you write?
Anna, Joanie: Because I like to. Because it's fun.
Ryan: Because I like to . . . it's so much easy and funner than scribble scrabble.
Paul: Because I feel like it, doing hard work for the teacher, Mom, or Dad . . .
               I like to do that.
Denny: 'Cause I feel like it.
Lizzie: To give people things.
Janet, Tessa, Brandy: So people can write back to me.
Jonethan: So I can send letters to people . . . and to keep them for me to read when
               I get bigger.
Mitch: To tell my grandparents how do they feel and how I am feeling.

Question 11:   What is a letter?
Question 12:   What is a word?
Question 13:   What is a sentence?

There was an overwhelming consistency in the responses to these questions. For the most part, children in the beginning of the kindergarten year could not describe these terms; the most counted response was "I don't know." Interestingly, more than half of the children responded to the question "What's a letter?" with the more concrete referent . . . the letter form (i.e., "like a Dear Mom, Love Lizzie . . . letter?"). Most of the children in this age group appeared not to have yet developed the concept of an alphabetical letter as "a sign," and seemed to know little about "words," and even less about "a sentence." As children became more familiar with reading readiness worksheets that offered phonics (i.e., sound and symbol practice), and continued to practice writing at the writing table, they slowly (toward midyear) began to understand the concept of a letter as "a sign" (see Clay, sign feature, 1975). Shortly after internalizing the "sign concept" and easily defining "a letter" as "an A . . . or a Z" or "things that you push together to spell," correct responses to probes like "what's a word?" and "what's a sentence?" quickly followed. Analysis of the endterm interview data supported the finding that more than three-fourths of the children, in this kindergarten classroom, were able to correctly define "a letter," "a word," and "a sentence" by June of the kindergarten year. Such an understanding seemed to be facilitated by the children's own interest and motivation for "conventions" (i.e., spelling, punctuation, and specifically "leaving spaces so people can read it"). It is the belief of the teachers and myself that this understanding was a "natural" development of the positive experiences children had during the year in this classroom with reading and literacy acquisition, and more specifically with their epistemological experiences at the writing table.

APPENDIX B: TRANSCRIPTION OF THE WRITING EVENT

This beginning writing event took place in the kindergarten year about the same time as the initial child interviews, and lasted for about 15 minutes.

Excerpt 1

Theme: Clarification of directions and negotiations of the writing task.

1	Teacher:	This morning I want to take a few minutes . . . I want
2		you to just write.
3	Denny:	Write, write, write, write . . .
4	Teacher:	Oh, first you have to put your name . . .
5	Child:	(calls out from another table) Write anything?
6	Teacher:	Yes, just enjoy yourselves.
7	Denny:	You can write anything . . . you are not allowed to draw,

8		you are not allowed to draw . . . write.
9		Didn't you hear her say write or not write?
10		What do you say (looking at Ryan, sitting next to him,
11		and waiting for an answer)?
12	Ryan:	Draw pictures and write, both . . .
13	Denny:	You don't have to do both.
14	Joanie:	You are supposed to draw and write.
15	Mandy:	She said you are supposed to just write.
16	Joanie:	I just asked, she said write and you could draw, so
17		I'm gonna make a little . . . my Mom taught me how to draw
18		something (begins to draw).
19	Ryan:	But the most important thing is to write your name . . . your
20		name (begins to write his name on the top of his paper).
21	Joanie:	My Mom taught me how to draw something (continues drawing).
22	Denny:	(to Joanie) Oh yeah . . . you forgot your name.
23	Mandy:	(to Joanie) Well you are not supposed to just draw.
24	Janet:	Nuh uh (shaking her head) . . . you don't just draw . . . you
25		write too (emphatically).
26	Mandy:	Yeah, you write.
27	Joanie:	Well, I'm not going to write anything.
28	Mandy:	You have to.
29	Joanie:	I don't have to (continues drawing, no longer listening).
30	Mandy:	Yes you do.

Excerpt 2

Theme: Talking-writing event begins. Talk is coordinated with task as children actively construct meaning of writing.

31	Ryan:	I'm gonna write police, P, E. Egypt begins with E (writes PE).
32		Police, S, S, S, S, E, E, S.
33		PO LICE (breaks up word into syllables)
34		E, S (writes S) says or reads) POLICE

35	Joanie:	My Mom teached me how to draw (begins drawing).
36	Denny:	Ho, ho, you spelled police, right?
37	Ryan:	(Busy coloring) I'm coloring this [the police car] grey
38		because it has to be like metal.
39	Denny:	Not real metal.
40	Joanie:	I have a motorcycle.
41	Denny:	Who has a motorcycle in the basement, raise their hands.
42	Joanie:	My brother is gettin' a hundred. [I think she means HONDA.]
43	Denny:	I have a motorcycle.
44	Joanie:	Don't you have a hundred? My brother does.
45	Mandy:	(to Janet) I know how to spell your sister's name . . .
46		H O L L Y (says each letter name).
47		(Writes HOLLY) Holly, that's how you spell it.
48	Denny:	P E S, police . . . I spelled it.
49		That's how you spell police (to Ryan)?
50	Joanie:	(To Mandy, looking at the writing HOLLY) That's how you
51		make L's?
52	Mandy:	I didn't put a tail on it (adds lower horizontal line
53		to form capital).
54	Joanie:	(Turns over her paper, after finishing a drawing)
55		You know how to spell kitten?
56	Janet:	Kitten, I think it's C.
57	Mandy:	C O L E (says each letter name).
58	Janet:	C O
59	Joanie:	(interrupts) K I T T E N (says each letter name)
60		Kitten!
61	Janet:	Yeah, kitten, kitten (apparently reading Joanie's writing).
62	Denny:	Here's cat (writes CA).
63	Mandy:	Uh, uh . . . you are supposed to put a T at the end.

64	Joanie:	C A T (says each letter name) cat.
65	Denny:	C A T, that's how you spell cat. Are you sure?
66	Joanie:	I'm positive. Ask the teacher.

Excerpt 3 (lines 69–81)
Theme: Sharing, comparing/evaluation of product.

67	Denny:	Look what I copied off of the word board over there
68		(points to word graphs on his paper).
69	Janet:	Oh, that's graphs.
70	Mandy, Joanie:	(Start copying graphs—"graphs" spelled on board "graphes"—saying each letter as
71		they look up at the board, and then copying it.
72		Sounding of letters coordinated with writing.)
73	Ryan:	(As he is coloring) I'm making her have a red sweater.
74	Janet:	Yeah, Joanie's going to copy off me and she's allowed,
75		you're not.
76	Mandy:	I can copy off of your paper if I want to.
77	Denny:	You can't copy off of anybody's paper.
78	Janet:	Well, Joanie asked me (seems to be a friendly gesture
79		if person asks before copying).
80	Mandy:	Can I copy off of your paper, please?
81	Janet:	Um . . . yes.

REFERENCES

Bissex, G. D. (1980). *GNYS AT WRK: A child learns to write and read.* Cambridge: Harvard University Press.

Blazer, Bonita B. (1984). *The development of writing in kindergarten: Speaking and writing relationships.* (Doctoral dissertation, University of Pennsylvania).

Botel, M. (1981). *A Pennsylvania comprehensive reading/communication arts plan.* Harrisburg, PA: Department of Education of The Commonwealth of Pennsylvania.

Botel, M., & Seaver, J. T. (1984). *Phonics revisited: Toward an integrated methodology.* Unpublished manuscript.

Chomsky, Carol. (1970). Reading, writing and phonology. *Harvard Educational Review, 40,* 287–309.

Chomsky, Carol. (1971). Write first, read later. *Childhood Education,* 296–299.

Clay, Marie. (1975). *What did I write?* London: Heinemann.

Dyson, A. Haas. (1981). *A case study examination of the role of oral language in the writing processes of kindergarten-ers*. (Doctoral dissertation, The University of Texas at Austin).

Dyson, A Haas. (1983). The role of oral language in early writing processes. *Research in the Teaching of English*, *17*, 1–30.

Emig, Janet. (1971). The composing process of twelfth grade writers. Urbana, IL: National Council of Teachers of English.

Emig, Janet. (1981). Non-magical thinking: Presenting writing developmentally in schools. In C. Fredericksen & H. Domenic (Eds.), *Writing: The nature, development, and teaching of written communication* (Vol. 2) Hillsdale, NJ: Erlbaum.

Ferriero, E. (1978). What is written in a written sentence? A developmental answer. *Journal of Education*, *160*, 25–39.

Ferriero, E. (1984). The underlying logic of literacy development. In H. Goelman, A. Oberg, & F. Smith (Eds.), *Awakening to literacy*. Exeter, NH: Heinemann.

Ferriero, E. (in press-a). Literacy development: A psychogenetic perspective. In D. Olson (Ed.), *Literacy, language, and learning*. NY: Cambridge University Press.

Ferriero, E. (in press-b). The interplay between information and assimilation in beginning literacy. In W. Teale & E Sulzby (Eds.), *Emergent literacy*. Norwood, NJ: Ablex.

Ferriero, E., & Teberosky, A. (1982). *Literacy before schooling*. Exeter, NH: Heinemann.

Flower, L. S., & Hayes, J. R. (1977). Problem solving strategies and the writing process. *College English, 39*, 4, 449–461.

Gibson, Eleanor, & Levin, H. (1979). *The psychology of reading*. Cambridge, MA: MIT Press.

Gleitman, Lila R., & Rozin, Paul. (1973a). Teaching reading by use of a syllabary. *Reading Research Quarterly, 8*, 447–483.

Gleitman, Lila R., & Rozin, Paul. (1973b). Phoenician go home? *Reading Research Quarterly, 8*, 494–501.

Goodman, K. S. (1967). Reading: A psycholinguistic guessing game. *Journal of the Reading Specialist, 4*, 126–135.

Goodman, K. S. (1973). The 13th easy way to make learning to read difficult: A reaction to Gleitman and Rozin. *Reading Research Quarterly, 8*, 484–493.

Goodman, K., & Goodman, Y. (1979). Learning to read is natural. In L. Resnick & P. Weaver (Eds.), *Theory and practice of early reading*. Hillsdale, NJ: Lawrence Erlbaum.

Goodman, K., Goodman, Y., & Altwerger, B. (1981). *A study of the development of literacy in preschool children*. Center for Research and Development: University of Arizona.

Graves, Donald. (1973). Children's writing: Research directions and hypotheses based upon examination of the writing processes of seven year old children. (Doctoral dissertation, State University of New York at Buffalo).

Graves, Donald. (1975). An examination of the writing processes of seven year old children. *Research in the Teaching of English, 9*, 227–242.

Graves, Donald. (1982). Patterns of child control of the writing process. In R. D. Walshe (Ed.), *Donald Graves in Australia—Children want to write*. Roseberry, NSW, Australia: Primary English Teaching Association.

Graves, Donald. (1983). *Writing: Teachers and children at work*. Exeter, NH: Heinemann.

Gundlach, R. (1981). On the nature and development of children's writing. In C. H. Frederiksen & J. F. Dominic (Eds.), *Writing: The nature, development, and teaching of written communication* (Vol. 2). Hillsdale, NJ: Erlbaum.

Gundlach, R. (1982). Children as writers: The beginnings of learning to write. In M. Nystrand (Ed.), *What writers know: The language, process, and structure of written discourse*. New York: Academic Press.

Harste, J. C., Burke, C. L., & Woodward, V. A. (1981). *Children, their language and world: Initial encounters with print*. Final Report to NIE-G-79-0132. Indiana University: Bloomington, Indiana.

Hill, M. W. (1978). Look, I can write: Children's print awareness from a socio-psycholinguistic perspective. (Doctoral dissertation, Indiana University).

King, Martha L., & Rentel, Victor. (1979). Toward a theory of early writing development. *Research in the Teaching of English, 13*, 243–253.

King, M. L., Rentel, V. M., Pappas, C. C., Pettegrew, B. S., & Zutell, J. B. (1981). How children learn to write: A longitudinal study. NIE Grant no. G-79-0137 and G-79-0039.

LaBerge, D., & Samuels, S. J. (1976). Toward a theory of automatic information processing. In H. Singer & R. Ruddell (Eds.), *Theoretical models and processes of reading* (2nd ed.). Newark, DE: International Reading Association.

McCall, J., & Simmons, J. L. (1969). *Issues in participant-observation*. Reading, MA: Addison-Wesley.

Olson, David. (1977). From utterance to text: The bias of language in speech and writing. *Harvard Educational Review. 47*. 257–281.

Piaget, J. (1972). *Psychology and epistemology*. London: Penguin Books.

Piaget, J., & Inhelder, B. (1969). *The psychology of the child*. New York: Basic Books.

Read, C. (1971). Preschool children's knowledge of English phonology. *Harvard Educational Review. 41*. 1–34.

Read, C. (1975). *Children's categorization of speech sounds in English*. (Tech. Report 197). Urbana, IL: NCTE.

Read, C. (1980). What children know about language: Three examples. *Language Arts. 57*. 144–148.

Rozin, Paul, & Gleitman, Leila R. (1977). The structure and acquisition of reading II: The reading process and acquisition of the alphabetic principle. In A. S. Reber & D. L. Scarborough (Ed.), *Toward a psychology of reading*. Hillsdale, NJ: Erlbaum.

Shatzman, L., & Strauss, A. (1973). *Field research*. Englewood Cliffs, NJ: Prentice-Hall.

Slobin, Dan. (1979). *Psycholinguistics* (2nd ed.). Scott Foresman.

Smith, Frank. (1977). Making sense of reading and reading instruction. *Harvard Educational Review. 47*. 386–395.

Smith, Frank. (1978). *Understanding reading: A psycholinguistic analysis of reading and learning to read*. New York: Holt, Rinehart, and Winston.

Smith, Frank. (1982, October). *Creative achievement of literacy*. Paper presented at University of Victoria Symposium, Vancouver, Canada.

Spiro, Rand J. (1980). Constructive processes in prose comprehension. In R. J. Spiro, B. Bruce, & W. F. Brewer (Eds.), *Theoretical issues in reading comprehension*. Hillsdale, NJ: Erlbaum.

Vygotsky, L. S. (1962). *Thought and language*. (Edited and translated by E. Hanfman & G. Vakar). Cambridge: MIT Press.

Vygotsky, L. S. (1978). *Mind in society: The development of higher psychological processes*. (Edited by M. Cole, V. J. Steiner, S. Scribner, & E. Souberman). Cambridge: Harvard University Press.

Whiteman, Marcia F. (1980). What can we learn from writing research? *Theory Into Practice. 19*. 150–156.

Whiteman, Marcia, & Hall, William. (1981). Introduction. In M. Whiteman (Ed.), *Writing: The nature. development. and teaching of written communication* (Vol. 1). Hillsdale, NJ: Erlbaum.

Zalusky, Vilora Lyn. (1982). Relationships: What did I write? What did I draw? In W. Frawley (Ed.), *Proceedings of the Delaware Language Symposium III on Language Studies*. New York: Plenum Press.

6

Six Authors in Search of an Audience

Deborah Braig

University of Pennsylvania

INTRODUCTION

In his play, *Six Characters in Search of an Author,* Pirandello suggested that there are unwritten dramas implied in people's lives which permit the characters to search for an author to fulfill their drama. An analogy could be made to the young writer. Graves (1982) contended that, by the end of the first grade and the beginning of the second grade, children's writing reflects representational play created for themselves as well as communication produced for others. As young writers become more concerned about the audience and the audience's understanding, they place more emphasis on the conventions of text. Children become more critical of their work as they perceive writing to be a message having some permanence and therefore available for others to view. During this time the young author may be in search of a responsive audience to help develop the specific strategies demanded by written language use. Young students need help in accessing the strategies of writing to a specific "someone." Just as Pirandello's characters searched for an author to fulfill the unwritten dramas of their lives, young writers may be ready to respond to a real audience in order to fulfill the undeveloped potential of their written language competence. A communication dyad in writing may be an important means of assisting young writers to discover the pragmatics of writing for an audience. One form that this might take would be dialogue journal writing between student and teacher.

Jana Staton (1982) has defined dialogue journal writing as an instance of the natural and functional use of writing by students and teachers. The student writes to the teacher and the teacher responds in writing. Staton examined the dialogue journal writing of older elementary school children in fifth and sixth grades where this writing represented a developmental link between the children's competence in oral conversation and their emerging competence in written language. This form of writing in journals was seen as a bridge between informal conversation and the traditional essay writing in school. Dialogue journals provide opportunities for the student writer to internalize the perspective of the audience since the teacher's questions and comments may serve to model how an audience thinks and reacts to written communication. Staton observed that dialogue journal writing meets the essential conditions for any communication event: writers are responsible for their own topics; there is a concrete situation and functional relationship between writer and audience; the audience interacts or responds to messages in some immediate way. Dialogue journal writing between *young* children (first and second graders) and their teacher may provide a forum for the authors' developing abilities as they seek an audience, a place to have an explicit and ongoing relationship with an audience. The communicative strategies that help in the development of oral language may, through this form of writing, be of assistance to the beginning writers in the development of their written language. Each mode can serve to support and enrich the growth of the other.

This chapter reports research which examined the role of dialogue journal writing of young authors (ages six to eight) with an emphasis on "audience awareness." The concept of "audience awareness" is widely used in composing research and is commonly defined as the author's concern for the reader's understanding of the written text. Britton (1975) stated that growth in a sense of audience is an important dimension of the development in writing ability. He defined this sense of audience as "the ability to make adjustments and choices in writing which take account of the audience for whom the writing is intended." Rhetoricians claim that this awareness of audience contributes to the effectiveness of the discourse. Britton went further and observed that "adjustment to audience is inherent in the social contract of all language use." From this perspective, both written and oral language make demands on the language user. Speakers and writers, as well as listeners and readers, must learn the language system in order to communicate with others. In our culture effective communication in writing requires topic focus, elaboration, and a sense of audience (Staton, 1982). The emphasis in my research was supported by two constructs:

1. Dialogue journal writing may be an important link between oral language competence and written competence: an oral and written language support system where assisted informal writing occurs before independent formal writing as in oral language development.

2. "Audience awareness," an essential element in written communication, may develop and diversify within the structure of dialogue journal writing because of the oral language supports within the dialogue journal design: a dialogic relationship between writer and known audience which provides interaction and feedback between participants.

As pointed out in Staton's work, young children learn linguistic symbols gradually within complex communicative transactions. Perhaps if the early writing experiences of children were to be given a real communicative function in the form of dialogue journals, then the writing might be altered structurally—the concept that function facilitates the acquisition of form. In the particular instance of dialogue journal writing, several possibilities exist for the various *functions* of written language to facilitate the diverse *forms* of written language. In speech, sustained and coherent dialogues develop through monitoring by the participants. Speakers produce requests, comments, questions, and so on, with the expectation of some acknowledgement. Listeners become speakers and learn to respond appropriately through talk exchanges. Dialogue journals provide diverse written functions such as questioning, commenting, describing, and reflecting. If young children see purposes for these written functions, because they are part of children's exchanges and because of shared mutual control of topics, then children may develop the ability to produce appropriate written forms. Within the complex communicative transactions of dialogue journal writing, young writers might gradually learn the conventionalized forms of written language used to represent personal intentions and feelings to others.

Thus there is suggested the possibility that growth in written communicative competence may be, at least in part, a function of the type of written experiences and the number of encounters with functional written experiences shared by young authors. The stage is set: the conversational strategies of oral language are to supply the potential script; dialogue journals will be the carefully selected props in the language setting; and the ensuing drama is intended to allow young authors to develop and project a sense of audience in writing.

DESIGN AND PROCEDURES OF THE STUDY

The research presented in this chapter represents part of the data from a nine-month study which was conducted during the school year 1982–1983. A total of 17 children and one teacher/researcher participated in this ethnographic study which examined the audience awareness characteristics in the dialogue journal writing of children ages six, seven, and eight. The purpose of the research was to observe young children's writing in order to learn about the concept of "audience awareness" within the specific context of dialogue journals. The children's written products in the journals, as well as what they said about writing in taped interviews and conferences, were examined to provide instances of behaviors which indicated "audience awareness" strategies used by the young writers. In other words, did the authors demonstrate in their writinng that they had made choices which took into account the needs of their intended audience? Further, did the children's "talk about writing" in interviews and conferences show that they had specifically intended to meet the various needs of their audience?

The site of the study was a large elementary school in the Philadelphia public school system where I served as the reading specialist. It is a desegregated school in a working class neighborhood. The school boundaries include two communities: the immediate neighborhood surrounding the school and a housing project eight blocks away. Approximately 40% of the children come from homes where parents receive some form of welfare assistance. This percentage entitled the school to receive federal money in Chapter I (formerly Title I) programs during the school year 1982–1983.

The six young writers who are highlighted in this chapter were part of the larger study of 17 children whose individual teachers had requested assistance from me as the reading specialist. The children discussed here are representative of the larger study with respect to age, sex, and reading ability. Table 1 provides profiles of the six children reported on in this chapter.

At the beginning of the year the children referred to me by classroom teachers for special reading instruction were divided into two groups, a morning group and an afternoon group. The groups met with me each day for 45 minutes in the reading room, an office-sized space set up as a mini-classroom. The teacher's desk and bookcases framed the room, giving front stage to a rectangular wooden table in the center of the room

Table 1.   Student Profiles

Pseudonym	Grade	Age[1]	Sex	Race	Referral Reason[2]
Clifford	2	6.10	M	B	I
Joseph	2	7.7	M	W	II
Michael	2	7.1	M	W	III
Rebecca	2	7.1	F	W	II
Sandy	2	7.3	F	W	II
Sharonne	2	6.10	F	B	III

[1]Age: years and months when child entered study.
[2]Referral reason: I = above grade level in reading and above class average;
II = at grade level in reading but above class average; III = below grade level
in reading (individual problems).

which accommodated about eight people. The children and I sat around the table. The activities of two of the five days of each week involved language arts programs geared to the children's individual needs. On each of the remaining three days the children wrote in their journals at the beginning of the period. The writing would typically last about 15 to 20 minutes. The children began writing at the same time; as each finished he or she would select a book to read until all of the journal entries had been completed. The remainder of the three writing periods was devoted to other language arts activities.

DATA COLLECTION AND ANALYSIS

The data base for research reported on in this chapter included the dialogue journal samples from October through January, transcribed notes from the initial writing interview when children were asked the same questions about the writing process (see Appendix A for writing interview questions), transcribed notes from taped individual conferences when children were asked individual questions about their specific writing, and researcher field notes taken during the dialogue journal writing periods.

Since an important construct of this research centered on using oral language strategies for bridging the gap between conversational speech and informal writing, it seemed appropriate to adapt an oral language heuristic to analyze "audience awareness" in writing. Keenan and Schieffelin's (1976) notion of "recipient design," which had drawn from the work of Sacks and Schegloff (1974), provided a way to examine young children's utterances. Children's communicative competence was considered within the framework of good or poor "recipient design." While "audience awareness" is a more inclusive concept which can take account of the audience's understanding of and interest in a text, the concept of "recipient design" provided a focus for describing the relationship between writer and audience in dialogue journals. The following outline adapted "recipient design" in children's utterances to children's writing. The roles of speaker/listener were changed to those of writer/audience. In order for any communication to have good "recipient design" (as aspect of audience awareness), these four requirements must be met:

1. The writer must secure the attention of the audience. (The form of dialogue journals provides for this, since teacher and student interact in a specified one-to-one manner.)

2. The audience must receive a minimally comprehensible message from the writer. (This requires that the topic be presented clearly enough for the audience to be able to understand and to collaborate; the visual world of text requires that the writer produce printing that is readable and that the writer conform to conventions of print in a minimal fashion.)

3. The given information—new information contract (Clark and Haviland, 1977) requires that the writer refer to individuals, objects, and events in such a way that the audience can identify the referent. (The writer is required to make choices about the audience's background knowledge in order to decide what to write and how to write it. Dialogue journals allow for clarification requests if information given is not sufficient.)

4. The writer must identify the discourse topic proposition. (The writer must focus on the relevant topic or clearly mark that a new topic is being introduced.)

"Recepient design" provided the beginning of a structured analysis of the children's written documents and interview data. It is my position that young authors who demonstrated good recepient design would also be providing evidence that they were accommodating their writing to meet the needs of their intended audience.

SIX AUTHORS

The following profiles serve as a glimpse of six dialogue journal authors. The children were selected as a representative sample of the larger study with respect to age, sex, and reading ability. When asked to write to a real audience who would respond to each entry in writing, the children presented and recorded their developing ideas. From an examination of the dialogue journals and from an analysis of the "talk about writing," it seemed that these children shaped their own thoughts and feelings as a function of this special form of writing. In addition, they demonstrated individual development in writing styles which revealed a concern for the audience's understanding.

Author 1: Rebecca: "I will explain it like this"
During the first interview Rebecca defined writing as being "like something that you do when you want to write a letter or something." It was clear to her that you write letters *to* people, but her stated reasons for writing did not include concern for the reader's understanding. Rather, she said that she would write letters and notes to her mother because she loved her and that people write letters "because they feel like it." While the stated purpose for writing letters was affective, Rebecca was aware that writing was directed to a specific, real audience. In contrast, when asked whom she would draw for, she emphatically stated: "Myself." During this writing interview good writing (of stories and letters) was discussed within the framework of handwriting; when asked why she judged writing as good, Rebecca replied: "It's good printing." On the basis of these

interview data I expected that Rebecca would be a journal writer concerned with producing good printing and with initiating topics of personal interest.

In the early journal entries it became apparent that Rebecca's self-assessment of her writing was accurate, although by no means a projection of her potential. She had been able to think about and talk about her own writing process: her printing was carefully accomplished and her choice of topics in the journal was on a personal level directed to me:[1]

Ex. R–1 (11–9)[2]
You are as / sweet as can / be. You are like / sugar to me. / Roses are like / you and I / love you. / Violets are / lovelbe like you / and so are / roses.

Rebecca's entries were comprehensible to me and allowed me to collaborate with her on topics which she chose. Within continuous discourse over several turns I was the "referent." Rebecca requested background information that later supplied topics for her writing. She was exploring with the generation of information. Since I responded to her questions and her comments, the dialogue journal represented a way for her to secure data from me:

Ex. R–2 (11–12)
How old are / you? / plese, plese, plese / write back. / When is / your birthday./ plese write / back. / Did you have / a husband / before I met / you. plese tell /me.

Although Rebecca controlled the topics, we shared the question-answer format mutually supplying needed details. In our joint attempts at communicating and generating ideas we alternated as reader and writer. During the first weeks of writing Rebecca responded to my entries with details and reasons:

Ex. R–3 (11–16)
You get better / every day / becose you / are nice and / that's all /and you are /very, very, / very nice too / and that's / why I rote / you get better /every day.

She also introduced topics about herself and her family, supplying details and comments without my probing for more information:

Ex. R–4 (11–22)
My dad/s / birthday was / Oct. 8, 1982 and /he is 36 now. / He is a old / man./ I'm not done. / (She finished writing the next day.)

Rebecca's ability to give details about referents, to explain the topics of focus, and to relate specifically to the audience's communicative needs increased over time. The fol-

---

[1] The children's spelling, capitalization, and punctuation were preserved in all examples from the journals. A slash (/) indicates line boundaries.
[2] The date indicates the day on which the journal entry was made.

lowing entry represented a return to the comments about me as well as the introduction of a new topic which was of interest to her:

Ex. R–5 (12–1)

I think you / have nice hand / writeing. / Are teacher / writes lines /all over the/ blackboard / becouse the / class gets so / noisy she has / to make them. / You whare / nice julare.

When I wrote back to her that I did not understand exactly what she meant about her teacher and the blackboard (clarification request), Rebecca made a valiant attempt to assist me in comprehending her text. She understood my topic and she supplied details to assist in my understanding of the specific event:

Ex. R–6 (12–8)

I will explain / it like this. / One day / the teacher / was working /with a raeding / group and / the class / got so noisy when / they were / at the book / case she / told the class /that they / cound't go to / the book / case / any more / now do you /understand? / Thank you / for telling / me that I / worte some / nice things.

The importance of accurate comprehension of the printed word was not only my concern. Rebecca was able to deal with her problem in comprehending a particular entry by implying that I sharpen my own audience awareness skills. My writing did not clearly identify the referent and she made a clarification request. Example R–7 illustrated the reciprocal nature of journal writing—writer becomes reader:

Ex. R–7 (12–21)

Which / parent do / you meen? / Ones 36 and / ones 32. My / Dad is 36 and /my moms 32

In requesting clarity from me Rebecca was careful to supply all of the details needed to make her statement comprehensible.

This young writer took a serious approach to the dialogue journal. She worked hard and became adept at using every language tool at hand. The journal served as a spelling aid and as an idea bank for writing. During a writing conference held in December Rebecca searched through her journal looking for the correct spelling of a word. When I asked her how she knew that the particular word was there, she said: "Because I remember you wrote something." Her facility with topic building over several turns became a source of ideas for topics in writing. The following conversation which took place during the same writing conference illustrated how journals assisted in topic generation:

Ex. R–8

T:[3]   What gave you the idea to write about your bedroom and your sister's bedroom?

---

[3] T = Teacher

R: I asked you what color your bedroom was and you answered me so I
      thought I would tell you what *my* bedroom was like and my sister's.

As a function of her written interactions with me, Rebecca began to think about her
own writing and her own thinking. In the following series of written turns from the
journal, she offered an explanation that was not clear to me. Rebecca considered the
difficulty of my question, and over successive turns she stayed on topic and finally gave a
convincing personal appraisal:

Ex. R–9 (1–21, 1–25, 1–28)

R: I did not / ask him if / he meet / to hute me / but I think / he meet it.
      /Love, Rebecca

T: Don't you think it's better to find out if he meant it? That way you might
      still be friends.

R: I know he meant / it because we /where playing. / Love, Rebecca

T: How could you know it just because you were playing? I don't understand
      that.

R: I don't / like a kid / named Jennfr. / you asked / a head quoaien. / Love
      Rebecca

T: It was a hard question. But I just want you to think about it and try to
      answer.

R: I will tell / you from the /beging. / I was taking / to my friend / Laura and
      / John was / running /behnd me / and he pushed me. / That's how / I
      know / that he meet / it and that's / that. / Love Rebecca

Rebecca's final entry reflected temporal sequence, cause-effect, and certainly a conclusion. It was a concerted attempt to aid in my understanding of her experience. Rebecca
began as a writer who expressed her reactions and feelings. The beginning journal
entries illustrated good recepient design: her messages were comprehensible to me and
her writing showed evidence of her ability to identify referents and to focus on the topic
of immediate concern. Rebecca expanded her writing style to include the ability to provide an explanation which was supported with details (Ex. R–6, "I will explain it like
this.") and to present an argument with confidence (Ex. R–9, "That's how I know . . .
and that's that.").

Author 2: Clifford: "What I mean is . . . "
Clifford, the youngest second-grader in the dialogue journal groups, manifested some
confusion when he talked about writing and drawing during our first interview. In discussing writing he said: "When you draw stuff . . . it's like when you make a house."
He defined drawing as "When you make, like castles and you make sand bottles." His
expanded view of drawing included "I draw words and I draw math." During this interview it appeared that Clifford could not linguistically distinguish the different symbol
systems involved in pictorial representation and letter, word, or number representation.
However, when asked directly to tell the difference between writing and drawing he

demonstrated understanding: "When you write that means you just make stories and when you draw . . . make pictures like houses, hotels." Clifford knew the difference between writing and drawing but had trouble talking about it. His response to why people write offered a possible explanation of the interweaving of drawing and writing. He suggested that, "People write because it's like exercise for your fingers and hands." The physical task of printing was exacting for this six-year-old. From my observations of his printing process I would speculate that "drawing" words was an effective description of what he was doing at this stage.

When asked to whom he wrote Clifford, like Rebecca, said that he wrote to a specific individual: "My mom, my mom and dad, and my sisters." Letters were written for affective reasons: "Because they want, if you're sad, they wanta make you happy." This stated purpose for writing letters was apparent in the first journal entry to me:

> Ex. C–1 (10–27)
>
> I like you family. / I like doing work / with you and / you help me /learn. and you / help me write / good. that's why / I like uou / XOXO ** A + A + XO

Clifford was beginning to develop a style of supplying reasons and details in his writing, but during the first days of journal writing his entries were not made in direct response to my questions or comments. He made an effort to identify referents, but Clifford did not focus on the topics that I chose. He negotiated the terms of our interactions in writing; he would read my entries and initiate his own topics. On two successive days I requested clarification about drawings that he had added to his writing. When he finally responded, the answer was explicit:

> Ex. C–2 (11–2)
>
> ABOUT THE SINS / THIS MEANS XXOO / kiss hug AND / THE ohters /mean YOUR good / XOXO**A + XO

Clifford had given me the information that I needed and, interestingly, he changed my reference to "drawing" to "signs," which was a more accurate description of the symbols.

In his writing throughout the next month Clifford participated in topic building by identifying referents and by focusing on the topics of interest to both of us. He established a pattern of reading my entries, focusing on my topic, and then initiating his own topics. He expressed this pattern to me in a writing conference in December: "I just read yours and if it's an answer (question) put the answer on the book and then when I do that I think of something else that I haven't wrote." Clifford explained further: "I answered your question, than I wrote what I wanted to write, and I thought of what you wrote to me." The following entry illustrated that Clifford was able to describe his writing process in the journal. In Example C–3 his first sentence was an answer to my question; his second and third sentences were topics of his choice:

> Ex. C–3 (11–19)
>
> What i mean / is that i didn't / mess up 1 /letter. / your the great great Reading / Teacher. / I'll try to / ask my mother / to let me / right a story / to you. /XOX A +

By late November Clifford demonstrated that he could reflect on his own writing (Ex. C–4), and that he made some assumptions about my thinking (Ex. C–5).

Ex. C–4 (11–24)
I no where / I skipped the / letters. / (He had omitted words.)

When asked what he thought about the omitted words, he wrote:

Ex. C–5 (11–30)
I just leave it. / you know what / I wrote! / you do good / work. / is your work /like HOMEWORK. /

Clifford had made a decision about my ability to understand his entry, and he was correct. The omitted words were predictable within the context that he had created. This conclusion was further supported by his responses during a writing conference. When asked why he reread the journal (which he often did), Clifford answered, "If I skipped any letter or messed up. Because after I finished, I read it again and I knew that I was alright." This was not a young writer who composed with the tacit assumption that he would be understood. Instead, Clifford showed that careful thought went into his writing to a known audience.

For Clifford the journal was a place to satisfy his urge to tell. Since he was an extremely verbal young man who received many complaints from family and school members about his noisy manner, it did not surprise me that the journal was not used as a way to elicit information as it was by Rebecca. Instead, the reader-audience became an attentive listener for him:

Ex. C—6 (1–2)
$\frac{\frac{32}{14}}{\frac{23}{59}}$
I like school / becouse We learn / Math like this $\frac{32}{14}$ $\frac{23}{59}$ I like home / becau se I get /a lot of exciting / things. I like /it here because / I learn vowels a stuff. / I like the Dukes / of Hazzard. / and the Benny Hill show. /and I like soccer / footbal basketball / like Sixers / baseball resling /and boxing. /

Example C–6 demonstrated good recepient design in Clifford's writing; his message was comprehensible to me and the topic (what he likes) was identified. His writing style included a concern for my understanding of the referents by using graphics, by providing reasons, and by giving examples. The journal was a way for Clifford to talk in writing. He used the journal writing to serve functions for him *and* he attended to the needs of his audience.

Author 3: Sandy: "I'll tell you more"

During the initial writing conference it became apparent that Sandy knew that print could do many things. In response to my question she defined writing in affective terms: "Writing is something that you like to do when, sometimes you *like* to do writing, sometimes you *have* to do writing." When asked what she wrote at home Sandy talked about personal letter writing. In answering why she wrote letters she said: "Because Desiree is my cousin and I love her very much even though she's only five years old. And I write to Anthony, he's my other cousin, Desiree's brother." However, she went beyond the affective purposes of writing and revealed an awareness of writing as an alternative communication channel, and she demonstrated an awareness of the permanence of writing which could transcend geographic separation: "Because some people can't talk and if they can write that's the best thing for them to do and people write because if somebody is far away you can't just go up and talk to them." Along with the other children Sandy shared the common concern about the physical appearance of writing—the neatness of the printing. When she talked about "publishing" and "making sense" Sandy was dealing with writing in the real world and writing as the transmission of understanding. According to her a writer is good, "If they like publish books and I looked through them and I said, 'Boy, these are good books.' I'd write to that person and I'd say, 'You're a good writer and I would wait for him or her to put . . . answer me." In contrast a bad writer used "just bad words, he doesn't know what to put. I just mean, like he says, 'I love you, good night, good bye, good morning.' *It doesn't make sense."* Sandy's diversified approach was apparent in a self-appraisal of her own writing. When asked if her writing were good she replied: "That comes to what I did. I did some sloppy work and I did some good work so I don't know what I am."

During the beginning days of dialogue journal writing Sandy wrote in a direct style which demonstrated a concern for her audience. The journal entries illustrated good recepient design; her written messages were comprehensible to me. She also included drawings with some of the written entries. The drawings were usually afterthoughts accompanied by some verbal comments which indicated she was making sure that I understood her writing. The drawings seemed to be a way for Sandy to make certain that the referents were identified clearly. She initiated her own topics (Ex. S–1, a) and she focused on my requests for information (Ex. S–1, b):

Ex. S–1 (11–3, 11–5)

a.   I hoop you / have a / lovely day.

b.   I like / to read. I like / to play. I like / to draw / and I like /to rit. I like /to play Pac-Man

Sandy explored other functions of journal writing. Her third entry took the form of a strong position about animals:

Ex. S–2 (11–5)
anamils have / just a nof / rit as you / do to live.

The journal was also a means of requesting information from me:

Ex. S–3 (11–12)
I love you. / I hopp you / have a lovly / afternoon. / Do you love /your parent's /I love / myn.

Sandy's response to my answer demonstrated sensitive and inferential thinking:

Ex. S–4 (11–15
sory I don't / no your parents / and now / I never will. / I am sory /that there /not liveing. / you are to / I bet. / SORY. / I LOVE YOU. /

Example S—4 fulfilled the requirements of good recepient design: the message was comprehensible, the audience was able to identify the referents, and the writer focused on the topic of concern. Sandy's writing also supplied evidence that a larger concept of audience awareness was developing. As the intended audience I can speak to the fact that her writing had a powerful affective tone. Her written message illustrated a concern for her audience in cognitive and affective ways.

Requests for information continued and Sandy began to include directions for how I should answer. The format guaranteed comprehensible answers for her:

Ex. S–5 (12–6, 1–3)

    a.   wats you / nieces / babys name. / right it down here.

    b.   Did you / have / a / Happy / New / Year. / circle the one / you had. /no yes

Sandy's journal writing developed with rich detail demonstrating good recepient design. The particular social context of the journal interactions provided a forum for Sandy's emerging ideas which was evident in the following written turns:

Ex. S–6 (1–5, 1–6, 1–10)

    T: Write to me about something that is very important to you.

    S: hers on / reading. / another is / writing. / and another / is loveing. / toys. /and I / like / Christmas. / I like / lots of /things. / I would like / to be a /star in / conserts.

    T: These were fine ideas. I am especially interested in your wish to be a star. Tell me more.

    S: I'll tell you more. / I like being / part of / the reading /sycle. I'm / also interested / in the moon. / I like the sun / to but I like / the moon more. / I'm interested / in the world / to. it is very / interesting.

    T: This was an exciting note. Please write to me about why you think the world is interesting! I am anxious to read about your ideas.

    S: I think the world / is nice becuase / there is lots / of things to do. / school is nice. / jobs are nice. / skating is nice.

Sandy seemed pushed beyond her years in taking such a sophisticated world view. At this point, however, the moon and sun are on an equal par with skating. An important issue was the role that dialogue journal interactions played in the developing conceptualizations of this student. Ideas must be explored before the process of encoding can occur. Journal writing was providing the support for Sandy to encode her developing thoughts and feelings and was allowing for the development of her individual writing style. The conceptualization and writing processes were maturing and diversifying within the mental exercise required as author, audience, and text interacted in this personal way.

Author 4: Michael: "Cause you wouldn't know what I meant"
Michael was an energetic child who considered school, and in particular writing, to be hard work. During the first interview he described writing as "something, like if you're

at school, right, and you're doing your work, you're writing." The "work" factor seemed to create a dislike for writing. When asked if he liked to write he said, "No, because it's not enough to do . . . you write, write, write, write all day." His view of the writing process was task-oriented and he evaluated writing by its physical appearance. Good writing was described as "like you got lines, right, you have to write right on the lines and you write on the lines, that's good writing." Michael did understand the relationship of author, audience, and text: "People write stories so the other people can read them." He explained that people write letters because "Letters, well like, if you live in New Jersey and somebody lives in Philadelphia, you send them a letter and they read it." Michael also stated an understanding of purpose with respect to the intended audience. When asked about drawing that he did in school he replied: "Today we did some with Miss C." When I rephrased the comment indicating that he drew for Miss C., he corrected me: "No, today we did it *with* Miss C." "For" and "with" were perceived differently.

From the first entry Michael's journal style revolved around asking me questions:

Ex. M–1 (11–4)

    can we /havf ssr / (gloss: sustained silent reading) Love, Michael

His next entry in the journal included an example as if to help clarify or emphasize the referent:

Ex. M–2 (11–5)

    Can we have gams. / Like this gam / monkey puzzles. /

During the first month of writing in the journal Michael took my requests for additional information lightly. His messages were comprehensible to me and he demonstrated concern for identifying the referents in his writing, but he often ignored my topic focus. Michael would read my comments, sometimes orally question me about them, and then introduce a new topic in his writing. He demonstrated more interest in word play than in details for his reader:

Ex. M–3 (11–10, 11–29)

    a. can we do our own thing. / (Transformation of a sentence on a poster)
    b. I had a Ball. / (Meaning 'fun') ⊖

By early December Michael directly expressed concern for my understanding of his writing by seeking the correct spelling for words. When this was not possible he invented his own abbreviations:

Ex. M–4 (12–8)

    Is it going to / rin tomr? / Did you dr. you /home. /

Example M–4 included many drawings of Christmas decorations including one of Santa Claus wearing a sweater with the abbreviation S. C. In a writing conference about this journal entry Michael explained why he had drawn the illustrations with his writing: "Cause you wouldn't know what I meant." Pointing to "dr." he said: "This is 'decorate,' but I can't write it that good. It's a other abbreviation, 'decorate.' " By December he began leaving spaces between ideas as a beginning attempt at paragraphing. The spaces marked for me that a new topic was being introduced. Michael would focus on my topic by answering or responding to my writing and he would then initiate his own topics. Variations of this pattern developed with all of the children in the study.

By midyear details and explanations which aided in my understanding began to appear in Michael's writing without a direct probe from me:

Ex. M–5 (1–3)
A list of my think / i got for Christ / mas. Atre and Dain / Micke that's all, /Miss B.

And then in a burst Michael demonstrated a keen awareness of how to transfer his written message to me:

Ex. M–6 (1–10)
All about me /and you. / My name is M.J.D. / My baithday is S / ept. 21 I well be / 8 years old. / How old are you. / Chor the one. / 30 34 40 45 29 / 6 22 26 35/ 21 52 49 33 / if you are not one / of then put a x on / the one you are / the closet to. /

Not only had he provided me with details and directions for the transfer of information, but he had done so in a very explicit manner. I was to circle the age if it were my exact age. Michael made careful provision to ensure accuracy by deciding on an 'x' to indicate approximate age. Example M–6 illustrated good recepient design by providing detailed and explicit referents which focused on the topic. This attention to the audience's needs was also evident in Michael's oral comments when he expressed concern for my understanding and explained why he had devised abbreviations and graphic illustrations. Michael voiced a reason for why people write: "People write stories so people can read them." Both implicitly and explicitly he added to this formula that it was important for his reader to know what he meant. He wrote for me so that I could read it; naturally, it should make sense to me. To this end Michael used his available language knowledge in the transfer of ideas from author to audience.

Author 5: Joseph: "Like people write, cause they like to"
Joseph was a young man of few words. He was not a shy child, but he expressed himself in a succinct style of speech. In the initial interview he defined writing as "Like people write." He told me that he wrote stories for himself: "Because I like to." The reason that he gave for why people write was: "Cause they *like* to." He expressed the opinion that people write to others "Cause they love people." Joseph was aware of the relationship between audience and author in the form of personal correspondence. At this stage of development letter writing served affective needs: he said that he wrote to his mother "Because I love her." The evaluation of writing was based on its physical appearance. Good writing was described as "If somebody is a artist."

Joey, as he preferred to be called, embodied his portrait of a writer. He printed carefully with an artistic flair, almost like drawing. In his first journal entry he expressed positive feelings about me and included symbols of affection. This early style of writing was direct and simple:

Ex. J–1 (10–26)
    You are a nice / teacher. You are / a very — very nice / teacher. From Joey
/XOXOXOXOXOXOXO /

His beginning response to my written comments were short and to the point:

Ex. J–2 (11–2)
    Because I realy-/realy like you. / I play with / my little car. /

My requests for additional information were met in a minimal fashion. Joey's messages were comprehensible to me and he did focus on the current topics in the discourse, but he provided little detail to assure the identification of his referents:

Ex. J–3 (11–3)
    It runs very fast. / It gos very fast. /

While the other children's writing developed with detail, seemingly aimed at increasing my understanding, Joey seemed intent on convincing me of his point of view:

Ex. J–4 (11–5)
    I really do / like it. / I really do. / I'm not kidding. /

He demonstrated a concern for his audience in a manner that was different from the other children. That was not to say that his writing lacked details. When I requested that he write to me about something that he liked, he wrote:

Ex. J–5 (11–24)
    I do like a / Huffy. a / Huffy is a Bike. /

Joey answered the question and provided me with the needed background information. If he were speculating that I had no knowledge of a "Huffy," he was correct. This entry provided evidence that Joey was concerned that I could identify the referent in his writing. The second sentence in Example J–5 made the difference in my comprehension of his text.

In January, after approximately three months of writing, Joey expanded his functional use of the journal by discussing feelings and concerns. When asked what bothered him, he wrote:

Ex. J–6 (1–11)
    When me and my sister / fight. and what makes / me happy is when / me and my sister / don't fight. What / makes me the happyist is / when we don't have /them problems.

His succinct style prevailed. The following written turns illustrated that Joey's attempts to aid in my understanding were based on achieving clarity:

Ex. J–7 (1–18, 1–19, 1–25)

J: Now that my /sister is sick *she* / and *I* won't *have* to *fight*. /
T: Why is that Joey?
J: I just don't fight with / my sister when / she is sick. /
T: Could you explain why?
J: When she is sick / we don't fight. When / she is not sick we /fight. / Love,
     Joey

I was seeking details and reasons while Joey was intent on my understanding the basics of his topic—they didn't fight when his sister was sick.

During the beginning months of journal writing Joey answered my questions and responded to my comments. By midyear he expanded his use of the journal by initiating his own topics, thereby taking more control of his writing. The following entry illustrated how he separated the topics in his journal as a form of paragraphing:

Ex. J–8 (2–4)
Now that I am gron up / now I can get all of /
the toys that I want. /
The Special Question: /
I like the name "Joey"
Happy Birthday to you /
Happy Birthday to you /
Happy Birthday Dear Ms. / Braig Happy
Birthday/ to you.

Example J–8 gave evidence of good recepient design in Joey's writing. The journal entry was divided graphically with the use of lines into three separate units. He began his writing by focusing on my topic from the previous entry. Next, he reintroduced an old topic by clearly identifying the referent using my words, "The Special Question." Finally, he introduced a new topic and directed it to me. Joey knew that it was my birthday and he wrote a personal note to me in a song format. His sense of audience developed in a diversified and individual manner. Joey provided understandable discourse for his audience and in the process seemed to discover that writing could serve many functions for him.

Author 6: Sharonne: "This is privet so don't tell ane one this"

Sharonne was a pleasant, outgoing child who seemed interested in most things. During our first interview she defined and evaluated writing in terms of its physical features: "Writing is when people draw, like, when they write things and they don't go past the lines. Oh good writing, I know what good writing is. Good writing is when you write something and you don't go past the lines or you don't just write your name up top." Her stated reasons for writing were affective: "People write because when they . . . like when you write to your mom and your father. Like, 'cause I love my mom." Story writing seemed to be a self-directed activity which was not necessarily written for communication with others. Sharonne told me: "I write stories when nobody's home and I can get my paper and stuff." Writing letters *to* someone took on a very different framework: "I write to my brother. He's only five years old. He can't read that good so I write things that he can read." Sharonne already had a differentiated notion of writing directed to someone and of writing as a personal representation, perhaps similar to drawing. In talking with me about her writing to her brother Sharonne demonstrated a concern for the audience by directing attention to the kind of language that seemed appropriate.

During the first month of journal writing Sharonne used the journal as a way to elicit information from me. Her purposes for writing seemed social and informational:

Ex. Sh–1 (11–3, 11–10)

    a.   Hi Ms B / hol you ding / you read in / we work / is im funny. /

    b.   What do you know about / papel. /What do you / know about / anmls./ do you have a son? /

She responded to my direct questions by offering reasons and details which made her messages comprehensible to me:

Ex. Sh–2 (11–7, 12–8)

    a.   The only wuy / I love ssr is / because / I love / you

    b.   Toys r fun and / funny to. / In you get them / from sana if you / r good if you / is bad you / wouldin get no / toy. /

Sharonne also used illustrations to aid in my understanding of her writing. Several entries included drawings of people with appropriate dialogue. The illustrations served the purpose of identifying and clarifying the referents since the drawings were directly related to the meaning of the text.

About the fifth week of writing the questioning abruptly stopped and Sharonne began to use the journal as a means to inform me of her thoughts and feelings on many subjects:

Ex. Sh–3 (12–17)

    I love surprise / when peple give / me giets / I like suprise / becaus / when I get/ surprise I get / happy It is nice of / you to be a / special teacher /and to have a /special class. / Today we are a / little noise. / maybe we is / noise but we /still love you / Ms. B.

This young writer negotiated the terms of the dialogue journal interactions as she controlled the topics that we pursued. However, she also developed a sense of supplying me with the needed information for identifying referents which would aid in my understanding of her writing:

Ex. Sh–4 (1–14, 1–19, 1–20)

    a.   I like to came / here a lot. / The only wi / I like to came /here is that / I can lren / something / in I can / make new / friends. /

b. So far I love / to come here / in I like to / work in I / like doing /things for / you that is / wi.

c. I learned a lot / here. I /learned that / I love you. /Will I learned / that you / loves me to /and what you / did for me. /

Sharonne used the dialogue journal for a variety of functions. It was a resource for her to gather information by soliciting my opinions, but it was also a place for her to explore her own developing ideas. She demonstrated expanding uses of writing which served to assist in our mutual understanding. In addition, she made some dramatic changes in her use of language. The first journal entry, Example S–5, sounded very much like written down speech:

Ex. Sh–5 (11–3)
    is im funny /

This language use changed after two months of journal writing to a style which sounded much more like conventionalized text:

Ex. Sh–6 (1–7)
    This is privet / so don't tell / ane one this. /What if / someone likes / you and you / don't like / him or her / what would you / do? /

Sharonne's dialogue journal writing showed a development of a writing style that increased in its effectiveness to communicate ideas and feelings to the audience. Her written messages were comprehensible to me and demonstrated good recepient design. From the beginning of the year she had little difficulty in identifying the referents and focusing on the relevant topics in the written discourse. However, the power of the ideas and emotions expressed in her writing could not be described in linguistic terms only. If audience awareness is a characteristic of writing that can be demonstrated by how effectively the author touches the reader through the use of written language, then Sharonne had developed into an audience-sensitive young author.

SUMMARY AND CONCLUSIONS

This chapter began with a loose analogy between Pirandello's characters in search of an author and young writers in search of an audience. It was with poetic license that Pirandello assigned the explicit motivation for his characters declaring knowledge of the implied drama in their lives. It was with theoretical license that I pursued this analogy with the six-, seven-, and eight-year-old writer. On the basis of this research using dialogue journals I take the position that young writers are not explicitly searching for a specific audience; more realistically, young writers are implicitly in need of a nonevaluative reader to provide an answer to the question: "Why write?" All of the children discussed in this chapter began with some view of writing as a personal representational language mode. The many communicative functions that writing served developed later. If, as children move from representational to communicative uses of written language, they see no relevant purpose for writing, then what expectation can be made for the growth of their writing process?

Gundlach (1979) raised an important issue in the development of the writing process of the young child: an important dimension of learning to write is learning the uses of written language. He proposed a dynamic model of the activity of writing as a series of relationships that the writer has with subject, composition, and reader.

An important influence on the development of these relationships is the particular use that writing serves. The specific function, as well as the ability of the individual writer, would influence how the key relationships would be negotiated. The use or function of writing determines an author's emphasis on the subject, the composition, or the reader. It was Gundlach's position that writing was not an efficient means of communication for the young child, except in personal correspondence. It was this exception that I chose to examine. My research emphasized the relationship between the writer and the reader engaged in dialogue journal correspondence and the influence that child-determined uses of written language had on the developing process. Ultimately the writer must balance all three relationships for effective communication, but the beginning writer needs the interactive and social nature of the journal as a support system in order to make connections between oral and written language strategies.

The children discussed in this chapter shared some common perceptions about writing. At first it was a physical task that required some dexterity. The boys and girls were in agreement that good writing should "look right." After just a few months of writing they were in agreement that writing should "sound right" and that the audience should be able to understand it. The children's beginning journal entries were similar to their oral language use in informal situations. The writing was social and chatty as they made positive remarks about me seemingly following a polite conversational model. It did not take long for their writing to demonstrate individual styles as writing began to serve many functions for them. The young writers used their journals to recreate experiences, to express strong feelings, and to ask questions in order to obtain information from me. Eventually the journals came to be viewed as a place to record and to retrieve ideas and language conventions. When these young authors realized the potential of the permanence of writing, they used their journals as resources to check past information, to get correct spellings, to refresh their memories about previous ideas, and to assist in generating new topics for writing. The interactive nature of the writing between adult and child provided a stimulus for the young writers to reflect on their language and their thinking as they responded to their adult audience. It seemed to provide motivation and opportunity to rehearse their future behavior as an adult writer. The children would "try on" adult, text-like language. However, the acquisition and sequence of development of written language uses in the journals varied from child to child. Each

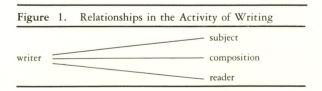

Figure 1.   Relationships in the Activity of Writing

young author responded to the audience in a unique way. The personal needs and experiences of each writer determined the course of events in the development of dialogue journal writing. Despite the individual styles of the learning and writing that emerged the young authors did share some similarities: oral language conversational strategies provided rich written dialogue and the journals served as successful props in encouraging and supporting written discourse.

The dialogue journal writing of these children could be considered within Harste's (1981) framework of literacy process universals: textual intent, negotiability, language use to fine-tune language, and risk taking. Each writer demonstrated growth in these areas. There was the expectation that language be meaningful since the writers created their own texts. The expectation that writing be meaningful to them transferred to the expectation that writing be meaningful to the reader. Without evaluative constraints the children became adept at negotiating language use in the interpretation and transmission of meaning between writer and audience. Each child used language to fine-tune language. It was this intermingling of language resources (speaking, listening, reading, writing) that made it impossible to provide the exact locus of the writing growth. I suggest that dialogue journal writing be viewed as one part of this involved equation. Finally, Harste's risk-taking component was considered along with the affective features of the writing examined in this research. The young writers indulged in hypothesis testing of syntax and semantics. As the children became secure with putting their ideas on paper they became willing to explore new language uses and to deal with sensitive subject matter.

The affective factors of dialogue journal writing, both for teacher and student, were powerful. As the participant observer in this study I was delighted by the cognitive development of the children as demonstrated in their writing and I was enormously touched by the emotional bond that developed between each child and me. Young writers need to be supported and encouraged so that their written language uses will mature and diversify. The social and interactive nature of the journal writing provides a richly individualized forum for the novice writer. If one goal of a literate society is to produce proficient and independent readers and writers, then researchers and educators will have to join hands to help young students make connections between known and unexplored language uses.

The young authors in this research developed a sense of audience in their writing which included the communicative framework of "recepient design" and the larger framework of affective and reflective responses to the audience. A complete analysis of this year-long project included a system of categories which provided a way to examine children's writing and their "talk about writing" (see Braig, 1984). The dialogue journal was selected for this study as a specific context for exploring the concept of audience awareness in writing. Within this journal context the young writers demonstrated the ability to respond in diverse ways to a known audience over time. Their "talk about writing" supplied support for the fact that the children intended to meet the needs of their audience. The dialogue journal format seemed to facilitate the children's writing development and their ability to talk about writing with respect to audience. Journals provided topic choice and feedback, major characteristics of oral language, which encouraged and supported the children's diverse uses of written language. In the process of attending to their audience the young writers learned the personal functions that writing could serve for them. Six authors had searched for and had found an audience in the written exchanges of dialogue journals.

APPENDIX A: WRITING INTERVIEW QUESTIONS

What is writing?
Why do people write?
What do you write? (at home, at school)
Why do you write? (at home, at school)
To whom do you write? (at home, at school)
What do you do when you write?

What is good writing?
What is a good writer? What does a good writer do?
What is bad writing?
What is a bad writer? What does a bad writer do?
What kind of writing is this? (Children were shown a handwritten story)
What kind of writing is this? (children were shown a handwritten letter)

Why do people write stories?
When do you write stories? To whom?
Why do people write letters?
When do you write letters? To whom?

Are you a good or bad writer? Why?
Do you like to write? Why?

What is a drawing?
Why do people draw?
Do you draw? (at home, at school)
Why do you draw? For whom?

What is a good drawing?
What makes it a good drawing?
What is a bad drawing?
What makes it a bad?

Are your drawings good or bad? Why?
Do you like to draw? Why?

REFERENCES

Braig, D. (1984). Six authors in search of an audience: Dialogue journal writing of second graders. *Dissertation Abstracts International, 45,* O5 A. (University Microfilms No. 84-17, 269)

Britton, J. (1975). *The development of writing abilities.* London: Macmillan.

Britton, J. (1978). The composing processes and the functions of writing. In C. Cooper & L. Odell (Eds.), *Research on composing: Points of departure.* Champaign, IL: National Council of Teachers of English.

Clark, H., & Haviland, S. (1977). Comprehension and the given-new contract. In R. O. Freedle (Ed.), *Discourse production and comprehension.* Norwood, NJ: Ablex.

Graves, D. (1979). *Growth and development of first grade writers.* Paper presented at Canadian Council of Teachers of English annual meeting, Ottawa, Canada.

Graves, D. (1982). Patterns of child control of the writing process. In R. D. Walshe (Ed.), *Donald Graves in Australia.* Exeter, NH: Heinemann.

Gundlach, R. (1979). The ontogenesis of the writer's sense of audience. In L. Brown & M. Steinmann (Eds.), *Rhetoric 78: Proceedings of theory into rhetoric.* Minneapolis: University of Minnesota.

Gundlach, R. (1982). Children as writers. In M. Nystrand (Ed.), *What writers know: The language and structure of written discourse.* New York: Academic Press.

Harste, J. C., Burke, C., & Woodward, V. (1981). *Children, their language and world: Initial encounters with print.* Bloomington: Indiana University.

Keenan, E., & Schieffelin, B. (1976). Topic as a discourse notion: A study of topic in the conversations of children and adults. In C. Li (Ed.), *Subject and topic.* New York: Academic Press.

Sacks, H., & Schegloff, E. A. (1974). Two preferences in the organization of reference to persons in conversation and their interaction. In R. J. Wilson (Ed.), *Ethnomethodology: Labeling, theory and deviant behavior.* London: Routledge and Kegan Paul.

Staton, J. (1981). *It's just not gonna come down in one little sentence: A study of discourse in dialogue journal writing.* Paper presented at the annual meeting of the American Education Research Association, Los Angeles.

Staton, J. (1982). *Analysis of dialogue journal writing as a communicative event, Vol. I.* Final report to NIE, Grant G-08-0122.

Staton, J., Shuy, R., & Kreeft, J. (1982). *Analysis of dialogue journal writing as a communicative event, Vol. II.* Final report to NIE, Grant G-80-0122.

7

Teacher/Child Collaboration as Oral Preparation for Literacy[1]

Sarah Michaels
Courtney B. Cazden
Harvard Graduate School of Education

Increasingly, our urban schools serve an ethnically diverse population of children. A disproportionate number of minority children consistently perform below grade level on standardized tests of literacy skills, even when attending schools with a good reputation. We suggest that in spite of their exposure to what appears to be the same classroom environment, these children are not participating equally in key classroom activities in which basic literacy skills are learned and practiced. In research begun in Berkeley and then continued in the Boston area, we find increasing evidence that discourse patterns related to ethnic background affect the quality of teacher/child collaboration in ways that, cumulatively, deny certain children access to key learning opportunities in the classroom.

COLLABORATIVE EXCHANGES

It is widely recognized that learning is not a simple transfer of knowledge from one individual (the teacher) to another (the student). Rather, learning is mediated through complex interactive and interpretive processes, and whether learning takes place is a function of the way an activity is structured, and the amount and quality of contact, instruction, and practice.

Considerable evidence has accumulated from research in the last 10 years that when a child's home-based interactive style differs from the teacher's style and expectations, interaction between teacher and child is often disharmonious and not conducive to effective help by the teacher or learning by the child. (See Philips, 1972, for an early report; Au, 1980, for the most detailed analysis; and Cazden, Carrasco, Maldonado-Guzman, & Erickson, 1980, for a summary of such research in bilingual settings.)

The research reported here continues this tradition, but focused specifically on

[1] This work was supported by grants from NIE (#G–78–0082, 1978–1980) and the Spencer Foundation (1981–1982). We thank the teachers—Mrs. T., Mrs. J., Ms. W., and Mr. J.—and their children, for making this study possible.

teacher/child collaborative exchanges in literacy-related classroom activities. By "collaborative exchanges," or more simply "collaboration," we mean connected stretches of discourse in which, jointly, teacher and child develop an elaborated set of ideas on a particular topic—as for example in giving a narrative account, summarizing information, describing an object, providing evidence, or giving an argument. This kind of collaborative exchange occurs in classroom activities such as small group reading lessons, individual writing conferences, and oral discourse activities such as "sharing time" (also known as "show and tell").

The pattern we are interested in can be characterized as follows: the child says something (often in response to a teacher's question), is again queried by the teacher, and then provides more new information as elaboration. Two examples of this kind of collaborative exchange follow. Both exchanges occurred during a small group reading lesson in a second-grade classroom. The story being discussed was about an early space flight in which two monkeys were sent up in a rocket. The lesson took place on the same day as a space shuttle launch.

Example #1

T: OK Janine, what about this rocket ride? Is this the one that the astronauts are going to be taking today? Is it the same kind? (Janine shakes head "no.") How is it different?

J: Monkeys are in it.

T: Monkeys are in it. What will be in the rocket that's going up today? The space shuttle.

J: Astronauts.

T: There'll be astronauts instead of monkeys. Good. OK. (45-second interlude during which three children working at their seats are reprimanded for talking and another child is helped in finding a book.) OK, are we all looking at page 129?

C's: Yes.

T: And Janine has just told us that the difference between today's space shuttle and this rocket ride was what, Janine? (four-second pause) Who's going up today, and who went up in this story?

→J: Astronauts.

→T: Tell me about that.

→J: The astronauts went up today.

→T: A:nd in thi:s story—(said as if speaking for Janine, telling her how to continue: colon indicates elongated vowel)

→J: In this story the monkeys went up.

T: OK very good. Monkeys went up instead.

Example #2

T: OK, can you tell us about their coming back to earth? Tell us about that part. How do
          they do it? How do they get back? (Three-second pause) They're way out there in
          space, traveling at a very high speed. Paul, how do they get back?

→P: They used their parachute. They went down into the water.

→T: Tell me more about that. You mean they put a parachute on the monkeys?

→P: They used the parachute on the, on the rocket and went, went down into the water.

T: Very good.

Two features of the exchanges indicated by arrows are notable. First, the child's expan-
sion is a result of interaction with another speaker who provides an interactive slot and
thematic focus for new information that clarifies or elaborates. Thus through a sequence
of questions and answers, teacher and child together construct a single, expanded
message. Secondly, this kind of exchange gives the child practice at being lexically explicit and packing progressively more new information into a single syntactic unit.
(Compare Paul's original two sentence turn—"They used their parachute. They went
down into the water."—with his elaborated and syntactically more complex single
sentence—"They used the parachute on the rocket and went down into the water" (correcting for dysfluency). The Scollons, calling these collaborative sequences "vertical
constructions," suggest that "in the decontextualized and constant pushing for
upgrading of new information in utterances, caregivers are preparing the child for the
patterns of discourse characteristic of literacy" (Scollon & Scollon, 1982).

Collins (1983) has looked at similar exchanges in the comprehension segments of
high and low group reading lessons and found that the quality of teacher/child collaboration is linked to progress in reading achievement scores. Using a formal measure of
the syntactic, semantic, and pragmatic relationships across child/teacher utterance
pairs—which he terms "teacher uptake"—, he is able to document that teachers incorporate or make use of high group children's ideas in their succeeding questions
significantly more often than with low group children. With low group children, there
are more occurrences of "pragmatic misfires," broken or mistaken anaphoric chains, or
no incorporation whatsoever of a child's contribution in the teacher's following questions.

SHARING TIME AS A SITE FOR STUDYING TEACHER/CHILD
COLLABORATION

"Sharing Time" (or "Circle Time," "Show and Tell," etc.) is a common speech event in
early elementary school classrooms which typically generates a great deal of connected
talk from children—as they tell about some past event or describe an object brought
from home—as well as attempts from teachers to collaborate with children about their
topic. In the School/Home Ethnography Project, carried out in Berkeley (1978–80),

Sharing Time (henceforth ST) was first identified as a "key situation" in which children had unequal access to important literacy-related experiences. The teacher in the Berkeley classroom participated actively at ST, asking questions and making comments to help children clarify, structure, and expand their discourse. The model of a "good" ST turn that was implicit in this teacher's questions seemed to be based on adult notions of literate discourse (Tannen, 1982, 1984; Chafe, 1982; Keenan & Bennett, 1977). Through the teacher's questions, children were encouraged to be clear and precise, and to put all the information the teacher felt the audience needed into words, rather than relying on shared background knowledge or contextual cues to communicate part of the intended message (Scollon & Scollon, 1981). ST in this classroom could thus be considered a kind of "oral preparation for literacy."

But not all of the children gained equal access to this kind of help. The teacher collaborated more successfully with some children than with others at ST, depending on the degree to which the teacher and child started out sharing a set of discourse conventions and interpretive strategies. As a result, some children got more practice and informal instruction in producing expanded, literate-style narratives than did others (Michaels, 1981).

Thus ST was a recurring activity in which children either did or did not receive literacy-related instructional help. It has also proved to be a strategic research site for studying not only variation in children's oral discourse patterns but variation in teacher/child collaboration as well. A study of this one activity, an ordinary activity in classrooms across the country, thus became a window on the larger problem of equity in education.[2]

But just how common was this kind of ST, and how common was this finding of differential treatment? In order to examine the generality of these findings, we replicated the single-site Berkeley study in four primary classrooms in the Boston area. In what follows, we will summarize the findings of the Berkeley and Boston-area ST studies, focusing on the influence of ethnic differences in discourse style on teacher/child collaboration.

THE BERKELEY ST STUDY

The Berkeley study was conducted in a racially-mixed first-grade classroom taught by Mrs. J., a white teacher. The list gives general characteristics of this classroom per-

---

[2] In spite of the importance of ST as a research site, both in itself and as an example of differential treatment more generally, there are relatively few studies of ST in the research literature. We know of only Hahn (1948), Lazarus (1981), Dorr-Bremme (1982), and Wilcox (1982). The Hahn study is a description of the content and form of ST accounts, as compared to the same children's performance in a one-on-one interview with the experimenter; Lazarus describes variation in children's participation as one teacher changed ST into more of a group discussion; Dorr-Bremme describes variations in ST between subsequent years in one teacher's classroom; Wilcox compares ST in an upper-middle-class and a working-class school; but none documents differential treatment in a single classroom.

taining to ST. (The children's styles and the terms "topic centered" and "topic associating" are explained below.)

Number of children: 30
    14 white
    15 black
    1 Asian
ST norms, rights, and obligations:
    Teacher selected sharers, and freely
    interjected comments and questions
    while a child was sharing.
    Topic latitude: wide (except no sharing about TV or movies)
Children's preferred ST styles:
    white children: topic centered
    black children: topic associating

ST, as conducted in this classroom, was a daily classroom activity in which children were called upon by Mrs. J to give a formal description of an object, or narrative account of an important past event to the entire class. All the children used a special and highly marked intonation contour, and formulaic beginnings such as *Yesterday*—which served to mark their talk as "ST talk." These ST narratives differed from conversationally-embedded narratives in several ways: the teacher held the floor for the speaker; the narrator did not have to tie the story to previous discourse topics; the teacher collaborated with the child speakers by interjecting questions, comments, and reactions, and had the final word on what counted as an appropriate ST topic. ST turns had both a monologic (child-structured) component and a dialogic component in which the teacher, through collaborative exchanges, helped the child focus, clarify, and expand his or her discourse. Close analysis of the tapes and transcriptions of the Berkeley ST turns provide strong evidence of differences among the children—both in the monologue part of their turns, and in the success of the teacher/child collaborative dialogues (Michaels & Cook-Gumperz, 1979; Michaels, 1981; Michaels & Collins, 1984).

Briefly, in this classroom, the discourse of the white children tended to be tightly organized around a single topic with a high degree of cohesion, and lexically explicit referential, temporal, and spatial relationships. There was a marked beginning, middle, and end, with no shifts in time or place. This style, which we refer to as "topic-centered," seemed to match the teacher's own style and expectations. With these children she was very successful at picking up on the child's topic and expanding on it through her questions and comments. With a shared sense of topic, teacher and child were often able to develop an account of an object or event that was more complex and lexically explicit than the spontaneous utterances the child initially produced without the teacher's help.

The black children, by contrast, were more likely to tell narratives consisting of a series of implicitly associated personal anecdotes, often involving shifts in time, location, and key characters, with no explicit statement of an overall theme or point. This kind of discourse, which we refer to as "topic associating," is often difficult to follow for those who, like the teacher, expect the narrative to focus on a single event or object. The teacher often perceived these narratives as having no beginning, middle, or end, and hence, no point at all. Detailed linguistic analyses of the tapes indicates that topic shifts are, in fact, signaled prosodically. But the teacher, on the spot, was unable to recognize the structure or focus of the discourse, and simply assumed the child was just "rambling on." Her attempts at collaboration were often mistimed, stopping the child mid-clause. Moreover, her questions were often thematically inappropriate and seemed to interrupt the child's train of thought rather than collaborate with it. The teacher sometimes even used a kind of confrontational (rather than collaborative) strategy with these children, cutting them short and urging them to talk about "important things" or "one thing only." The following ST turn with Deena and Mrs. J is an example of this.[3]

Example #3

Deena: I went to the beach Sunday / and to McDonald's /
         and to the park / and I got this for my birthday / (holds up purse)
         my mother bought it for me / and I had two dollars
         for my birthday / and I put it in here / and I went
         to where my friend / named GiGi / I went over to
         my grandmother's house with her / and she was on
         my back / and I / and we was walkin' around /
         by my house / and she was HEA:VY //
         She⌈was in the sixth or seventh grade//
T: ⌊OK I'm going to stop you // I want you to talk
         about things that are really really very important //
         That's important to you but can you tell us things
         that are sort of different? // Can you do that? //

Discussion: Deena begins with explicit physical and temporal grounding but then appears to move fluidly from topic to topic—activities on Sunday, a birthday present, playing with a friend. The lack of any lexicalized markers other than "and" between topics makes the discourse difficult to follow thematically, for someone expecting "topic-centered" narrative accounts. Deena seems to be rambling on from one event to

---

[3] For the sake of readability, we have deleted most intonation markings from these transcripts. However, the following symbols are used: "/" indicates partial closure, akin to a comma (signaling "more to come"); "//" indicates full closure, akin to a period; vowel lengthening is indicated with ":" after the elongated syllable; "[" indicates simultaneous speech; capitalized letters indicate extra loudness; ". . ." indicates a brief pause. In those cases where intonation (i.e., change in pitch) is marked, the following symbols are used: "\" low fall; "\" high fall; "/" low rise; "/" high rise;"–" level tone; "|"a stressed syllable; "⌐" a shift to a high pitch register; "⌐" a shift to a low pitch register (both applying to the entire intonational phrase).

the next, which makes it sound as if she were simply free associating, with no important point to make. However, it is not that the topics, per se, are inherently trivial. Taken separately, any one of these topics would have counted as a highly appropriate ST topic. Deena's problem is more one of discourse form, than of discourse content.

Topical shifts are indicated prosodically through emphasis and vowel elongation on key words which introduce a new theme (on "Sunday," "birthday," and "friend"). Moreover, she uses exaggerated emphasis and lengthening on the word "heavy," which suggests that she is building to the main "point" of her narrative. Just at this point, however, she is interrupted by the teacher and told to "talk about things that are really, really very important." Deena's conclusive point, which the teacher misses, was the fact that she was able to carry her friend—fully twice her age—around on her back, quite a feat considering that Deena was a particularly tiny first grader.

It is worth noting that one year and four months after this ST turn was recorded, Deena, now a second-grader, was asked in an informal interview (with Michaels) what she thought about ST in the first grade. She said, "Sharing time got on my nerves. She was always interruptin' me, sayin' 'that's not important enough' and I hadn't hardly started talkin'!" Taken together, these two ST records highlight indirectly (a) the importance of oral discourse skills in school activities and (2) the effect of ethnic differences in discourse style on classroom interaction. As Deena's comment suggests, the teacher's notion of what sounds important may be quite different from the child's. In cases where teacher and child do not share the same ethnic or communicative background, there can be subtle but systematic differences in the way talk is interpreted and evaluated. In these cases, the teacher may inadvertantly interrupt or fail to see the point of what the child is saying. Over time this can lead to consistent patterns of differential treatment or negative evaluation of the child's abilities.

Research in this one Berkeley classroom suggested several general hypotheses which formed the basis of the expanded ST study in the Boston area:

1.   To the extent that children get practice clarifying, expanding, and focusing their discourse to meet a teacher's implicit literate notions about how information should be organized and lexicalized, collaborative exchanges at ST may serve to bridge the gap between children's home-based oral discourse competence and the more literate discourse strategies valued in school and required in written communication. In this sense, successful collaboration at sharing time serves as an oral preparation for literacy in the way that earlier parent-child dialogues in educated middle-class families have been shown to do (Scollon & Scollon, 1981).

2.   Successful collaboration is more likely to occur if teacher and child share a set of narrative strategies, expectations, and a sense of topic. Where teacher and child do not share a set of discourse strategies, the teacher—despite the best educational intentions—may be unable to build on what the child already knows, or may misassess the child's skills and needs altogether.

3.   Differences in children's narrative strategies as well as the relative success of teacher/child collaboration correlates with children's ethnic background. In this one

classroom at least, black children received less help and thus less practice constructing a literate-sounding oral narrative. In this sense, they were being denied access to instruction in important literacy-related skills.

THE BOSTON-AREA STUDY

During 1981–82, we replicated the single site Berkeley study in a larger number of classrooms to test the generality of its findings. The research was conducted in four primary classrooms (one first, one second, and two combined first/second grades) in two Boston-area school districts. The teachers selected for the study met the following criteria:

all had excellent reputations in their schools and districts
all were interested in participating in this project and volunteered for it
all valued oral language activities in their classrooms
all had ethnically mixed groups of children
as a group, they were themselves an ethnically mixed group of teachers: one black and three white.

ST was a recurring event in each of these classrooms. We tape-recorded the activity on a systematic basis, approximately once a week through the academic year, with periodic breaks for school vacations, transcription, and analysis. To supplement our observations and recordings, interviews were conducted with both teachers and children in each classroom to elicit their perceptions of the goals of ST and their expectations about what counts as "good" ST talk.

In each of the four classrooms, ST had a somewhat different organizational format, which influenced the kind of talk that occurred, the kind of collaboration generated among participants, as well as what counted as "good" sharing time talk. Table 1 gives the significant dimensions of variation among these four classrooms.

The most notable contrast across these four classrooms had to do with whether the activity is student-run or teacher-run—that is, the contrast between Classroom D and the others. Where the children participated without the help (or presence) of the teacher (as in Classroom D), contrasts emerged with respect to the preferred narrative styles of black and white children, corroborating the Berkeley "topic-centered"/"topic associating" contrast. However, the children in this class appeared to appreciate multiple ST styles, as evidenced by audience attention and peer judgments elicited in interviews. Nonetheless, the children were critical judges, and some children were considered better sharers than others, independent of their preferred ST style of presentation (see Michaels & Foster, 1985, for a description and analysis of this "kid-run" ST).

Where teachers led sharing time (as in Classrooms A, B, C), their expectations and evaluative criteria for what counts as "good" sharing prevailed and competence became narrowly defined. In each of these three classrooms fundamental consistencies emerged, generalizing the principal findings of the Berkeley study, both with respect to ethnic differences in children's narrative styles and teachers' differential treatment of children.

Table 1.   Significant Dimensions of ST Variation in Four Boston-Area Classrooms

Grade level	Classroom A Second	Classroom B First	Classroom C First/Second	Classroom D First/Second
No. of children	16	26	23	28
No. of white	11	22	12	19
No. of black	4	2	8	7
No. of others	1	2	3	2
Ethnicity of teacher	white	white	white	black
Sharing Time Norms, Rights, & Obligations: Local name	sharing time	morning meeting	circle time	sharing time
Frequency	daily	daily	daily	daily
Event Type	teacher-led ST	teacher-led ST,	teacher-led ST, as prewriting event	child-led ST (teacher absent)
Who selects sharers?	child-leader	teacher	child-leader	child-leader
Topic latitude	wide	wide	often predesig- nated topic	wide
Participation of teacher	freely interjects questions and comments	freely interjects questions and com- ments	freely interjects questions and com- ments	— (teacher absent)
Participation of audience	children can com- ment but rarely do so	children can ask two questions; sharer selects C's	children can com- ment	children question and comment
Frequent sharers' preferred ST styles: Black children:	topic associating	topic associating	topic associating	topic associating
White children:	topic-centered	topic-centered	topic-centered	topic-centered

*While we have referred to the ethnicity of participants as "black," "white," or "other," we assume that a person's ethnic identity is a complex function of many factors in addition to race, such as socioeconomic status, religion, community background, and so on. We further assume that one's ethnic identity develops out of long-term patterns of association and communication and hence is reflected in one's use of language and one's interactive style. In the ethnic category "other" are included five Asian children, two Hispanic children, one immigrant Russian child, and one Hopi Indian child. At this nt we do not know enough about sys- tematic differences in these children's communicative styles to say anything general about differences among these groups.

We will describe these patterns in Classrooms A and B, where the children were permitted to talk at length on a topic of their own choice.[4]

Classroom A

ST in this classroom was a daily activity in which children were called upon (by a child-leader) to give an account of some past or future event, or talk about an object brought

---

[4] In Classroom C, ST often served as a prewriting event. On these occasions, the teacher selected the topic to be discussed (e.g., "an animal I'd like to be or have"), and the children's language was restricted to a sentence or two. On occasions when children were permitted to talk at length on a topic of their own choice, we found patterns similar to those noted in Classrooms A and B, whereby the teacher collaborated more successfully with some children than with others, and evidenced difficulty with children who used an episodic narrative style.

from home. The teacher, Ms. W, played a pivotal role as listener/responder, addressing questions and comments to the child-sharing or to the audience at large, trying to help the child clarify and expand his or her discourse, or to link the child's personal topic to more general classroom themes or experiences.

All the children marked ST as a unique speech event through the use of a formulaic intonation pattern which clearly marked their discourse as "ST talk." This "sharing intonation" (henceforth SI) was an integral feature of their discourse and occurred in no other classroom speech activity. The intonation contour, in its most pronounced form, was a high-rising tone with vowel elongation, stretching over the last word or two of a tone group (an unbroken intonational phrase), resulting in sharp pitch modulations, and a slowed rhythmic tempo. The accompanying utterance was often a syntactically complete independent clause where an adult would more likely use falling intonation. The following ST turn illustrates the melodic contour of ST intonation.

Example #4

1	Sandy:	Um . . . tomorrow / my sister's gonna have her birthday party: /
2		it's gonna be at the Arlington Boys' Club /
3		'cuz they have a swimming poo:l /
4		and we're gonna rent it /
5		'n . . so we can use it /
6		and . . and . . . there's gonna be a lot of . . people /
7		and so my sister /
8		we're gonna have . . b-be able to use the game roo:m /
9		and . . my mom said . . . she left all her bathing suits /
10		down the Cape / so she's gonna have to go buy one /
11		and my mom said / um . . . um . . it's a heating swimming pool /
12		and she'll be in there a:ll / . .ₗa:ll da:y //

Rising arrows indicate the SI contour. As the transcript indicates, SI does not accompany each tone group. It does however segment the text into a series of information units of varying complexity, ranging from a single word, "tomorrow," in a single tone group, to the larger, syntactically complex information unit "and . . . my mom said /. . .she left all her bathing suits / down the Cape / so she's gonna have to go buy one/" (containing four minor tone groups, each ending in a rising tone).

In this classroom, black and white children used the same stylized rise at sharing time. There were, however, ethnic differences with respect to how extensively this marked contour was used and where it occurred in the narrative account. SI accounted for over 60% of the tonal contours in white children's narratives and was used by some white children in over 80% of all tone groups, often in its most exaggerated form. This stylized rise was generally found marking off information units throughout the account with no falling tones occurring until the closing (as was the case above). In contrast, SI contours accounted for only 37% of the tones in black children ST accounts and in longer turns (of a half-minute or more) the contour was likely to be used at the beginning, then fall away, replaced by contoured or falling tones, and then resume at various places in the story.

Related to these differences in intonation were contrasts with respect to black and white children's preferred strategies for structuring a narrative account, confirming the Berkeley findings. The example above is representative of the "topic-centered" style used predominantly by the white children, accounting for 96% of the white children's turns. As noted in the Berkeley findings, this is tightly structured discourse on a single topic, with lexically explicit referential, temporal, and spatial relationships. The ST turn above, for example, evidences a high degree of lexical cohesion through nominal and anaphoric chains ("swimming pool," "rent it," "use it," "heating swimming pool"). In addition, there is a high degree of thematic cohesion in that key nominals relate to a familiar cultural institution and its sponsored activities (Boys' Club," "swimming pool," "game room," "bathing suits," etc.). Thematic progression is achieved through consistent topicalization of key nominals (e.g., "birthday party" in line 1 becomes "it's" in line 2; "Arlington Boys' Club" in line 2 becomes "they" in line 3, and so on). The discourse also evidences internal patterning of segments, punctuated syntactically by units of "and . . . so," with SI contours throughout the account until the closing which is marked by lowered pitch and falling tones.

Characteristically in this classroom, topic-centered turns began with temporal grounding ("tomorrow"), a statement of the focus ("my sister's birthday party"), and some indication of spatial grounding ("the Arlington Boys' Club"). This information was made salient through tone grouping and pausing, highlighted prosodically with marked SI, and generally appeared in the first four tone groups. This patterned format accounted for approximately 92% of all topic-centered turns. Several other examples of this formatted opening follow:

> Carl: welL / last night
>   my father /
>   he was at work /
> Jerry: well when I slep' over my mother's /
>   the ca:t /
>   in the middle of the night she w- /
>   she went under the covers /
> Sandy: last year /
>   my mother and father /
>   well they went to Portugal /
>   and uh they brought us back a lot of presents /

What followed this orientation was some sort of elaboration on the topic (which provided complicating action, or additional descriptive information), with no major shifts in temporal orientation or thematic focus. SI intonation marked continuity, signaling "more to come" (and did indeed, in most cases, ward off comments from the teacher), and then led directly to a punch line sort of resolution, signaled by markedly lowered pitch and falling tones.

SI for these children served to highlight key orienting information and mark thematic continuity prosodically. These stylized tonal contours served as a melodic structure for the child in organizing a narrative account. At the same time, they served as a reliable interpretive guide for the listener—provided the listener had certain conventionalized expectations about SI narrative structure, that is, was expecting orienting information at the beginning and brief thematic elaboration leading quickly to a resolution. As it turned out, this conventionalized format closely matched Ms. W's expectations for ST accounts expressed both in interviews and in her questions asking for temporal clarity and spatial grounding when that information was not explicitly provided. With children who used this style, Ms. W was very successful at picking up on the child's topic and extending it through questions and comments. She thus was able to build on these children's narrative intentions, and help them lexicalize unclear referents ("You said your father went up in a green thing. What's that?") and clarify temporal ordering of events and points of confusion.

In contrast, only 34% of the black children's ST turns could be characterized as topic-centered (and only 27% of the black girls' turns). These children were more likely to tell narratives using what Michaels (1981) called a "topic associating" style and which we have come to call "episodic" (Cazden, Michaels, & Tabors, 1985). Their ST discourse often consisted of a series of implicitly associated anecdotal segments or episodes. Temporal orientation, location, and focus often shifted across episodes, but the episodes themselves were linked thematically to a particular topical event or theme. Linguistic analysis of these turns has shown that segmental shifts were signaled prosodically through shifts in pitch contouring and tempo, often accompanied by a formulaic time marker. *Yesterday, last night, tomorrow* could occur more than once in the same turn, each time accompanied with stylized SI. While these shifts were signaled prosodically, this kind of discourse was consistently difficult for the teacher to follow and build upon. These turns were often perceived by the teacher as confusing or lacking a point. The structure was there, however, if one were expecting and listening for multiple segments. One such story follows:

Example #5

Leona: on George Washington's birthday /
          I'm goin' / ice: / my grandmother /
          we never um / haven't seen her since a long ti:me /
          and / . . . and she lives right (n) nea:r u:s /
          and / . . . she: / and she's gonna /
          I'm gonna spend the night over her house /
          and / . . . every weekend / she comes to take me /
          like on Saturdays and Sundays / awa:y / from ho:me /
          and I spend the night over her house /

and one day I spoi:̄led her di:nner /↗
. . . um and we was having um / we was / um
'she ˌpaid ten dollars /
and I got <u>eggs</u> /̂ . . . and 'stuff /
and I ˌdidn't ˌeven ˌeatˌanything //

Leona begins with a temporal indicator and a future tense orientation, using SI tempo and contours. She marks the end of this segment with increased tempo in line 6. "I'm gonna spend the night over her house." The second segment begins with a shift in temporal perspective—from the future to the iterative—with a resumption of SI tempo and continued SI contours. This segment ends with increased tempo in line 9, a lexical and prosodic repetition of line 6 "spend the night over her house." Played side by side, these two phrases are indistinguishable, an implicit signal of the association across these segments. What they have in common is the fact that on both the holiday and the weekend, Leona spends the night at her grandmother's. The third segment shifts to a particular occasion, and shifts focus to dinner, rounding the story out to a close, again highlighting the relationship with her grandmother by recounting an episode in which there was a breach in the relationship. The closing is marked with staccato rhythm and falling tones.

Two things about this story are notable. One is that temporal markers with SI contouring recur at the beginning of each segment. In topic-centered accounts, there is generally one temporal indicator per turn. In topic associating accounts, there is an average of 3.9 temporal indicators, ranging from 2 to 8. Secondly, and this is even more obvious in some of the longer topic associating turns, SI is used not to mark continuity, but to highlight discontinuity, marking the separation of narrative segments and a shift in temporal orientation, location, or focus.

It it worth noting that in this classroom both Leona and Sandy were selected by their classmates as "star sharers." Nonetheless, Ms. W had consistent problems collaborating with Leona. Turns were marked by asynchronous exchanges and frequent probes as to who did what when, often seeming to derail the child's presentation. In interviews, the teacher described Leona as a "tall tale teller" because of her very long and complex sharing time accounts, and because, in response to the teacher's challenges about the "facts," she would on occasion contradict herself. Ms. W noted that many of these turns left her wondering who did what when, and that she found it "hard to make connections."[5]

---

[5] We want to underscore the fact that we get very similar responses to the black children's narratives when we play tapes of them to teachers, graduate students, and other audiences. White middle-class adults uniformly comment on the "rambling" quality of the texts. Much more disturbingly, some go further and infer from the texts that the child speaker is mentally "slow." For example, one reading specialist, engaged full time in the diagnosis of children's problems, said immediately after hearing one of Leona's longer ST turns, "She has no sense of time. This is a very slow child." After we played this ST turn several times, and pointed out Leona's recurrent use of particular prosodic cues to segment the story into distinct episodes, the audience began to appreciate the complexity of Leona's story and several teachers commented on her skill as a story teller. (We are indebted to New, 1982, for a detailed analysis of this ST turn.)

Classroom B

"Morning meeting" took place every morning in this classroom and, once a week, children were encouraged to bring in objects to talk about. On the other mornings, Mr. J suggested a topic for discussion, or simply let the children tell something of interest. During "object" sharing time, Mr. J opened the activity saying, "OK, who has something to share?" Children who wanted to talk raised their hands and Mr. J called on one child to begin. From that point on, he simply went around the circle, calling on children who raised their hand, in round-robin fashion, and even occasionally took a turn himself. He responded freely to the sharer, during or after the child's monologue, with questions, comments, or embedded instructional sequences (e.g., illustrating on a map where Texas is, following a child's account of a trip to Texas). After Mr. J's questions and comments, the children listening were allowed to ask two questions of the sharer, and the child sharing selected the two questioners. The format for other morning meeting sessions varied, depending on the topic, but in all cases children were encouraged to talk at some length on a particular topic, and Mr. J responded freely, interjecting questions and comments. In what follows, data from both object-sharing time and other morning meeting sessions will be discussed.

Of the 26 children in this classroom, only two were black. One rarely shared; the other, Kenan, shared frequently. Kenan's narrative accounts were relatively short (compared to the longer narratives more commonly told by black girls in all the other classrooms). Nonetheless, this child also used an episodic style, whereby concrete personal anecdotes were linked together to highlight a particular theme or event. The narratives of this child were markedly different from the narratives told by the white children in this classroom who tended to focus on a single event, even in giving complex accounts of a trip or car accident. The following narratives on the same topic, given during the very same morning meeting, exemplify this contrast in styles.

Example #6

1	Joe:	Um. . . I walked to school / and I was freezing //
2		all the wind was blowing on my face //
3		. . . and I was freezing and /
4		I was. . . fine up here and on my um. . . my shirt and stuff /
5		but my feet and my um. . . hands / were freezing //
6		so. . . I was walking to school with cold hands //
7	T:	What was the coldest part of you / coming to school today? //
8	?:	Hands //
9	T:	Hands? // What was the coldest part of you? //(unintelligible)
10	Joe:	(chuckles)
11	T:	What was the coldest part of you? //

12   Joe: My face //

13   T: Your face? // Why do you think? //

14   Joe: Because my face wasn't covered //

This narrative was told by a white child. It is a simple descriptive account of feeling cold while walking to school on a particularly cold January morning. Thematic development is achieved through a kind of thesis, antithesis, synthesis structure; it consists of a complex statement of the theme "I was freezing" (lines 1–3), qualification (line 4), and resolution, involving a restatement of the theme incorporating elaboration (lines 5–6). Marked prosodic emphasis with falling intonation on key content words signals the progression of the "freezing" theme ("freezing"—three times—"feet," "hands," "cold hands"). After the child stopped on a low falling tone which sounded final, Mr. J asked several questions which elicited more information on the same theme—that the child's face was the coldest part of his body because it wasn't covered.

The second narrative was told by the one black child who shared regularly in this classroom. This narrative is also an account about a bitterly cold morning (in fact, told during the same morning meeting session) but the theme is developed quite differently.

Example #7

Cold Morning 2

1   Kenan: Well / . . . when my mother called / to my room / she says /

2   it's school / a:nd / when we went out to the bus stop / and /

3   T: Daniel waita minute // Daniel / leave //

4   Kenan: See / it was so cold that my head start hurtin'

5   and it was free:zin' to death / and it was cold there /

6   and my face start hurtin'/my chin / and my whole face was cold /

7   my ha:nds were cold / my gloves were not . . um . . um /

8   wa:rm enou:gh / and / my coat wasn't warm enough / my pa:nts /

9   and my shoe:s were / nothin' / no-NOTHIN' was /

10   Kenan: then. . when we came to school / me and Menaka /

11   we were out there / then. . um / me and him /

12   we were gonna pretend like we. . froze / and. . . well

13   (3 second pause)

14   T: You were waiting outside for the bell to ring? //

15   Kenan: Mhm //

16   T: Instead of waiting in the cafeteria? //

17	Kenan:	We were getting ready to go inside the cafeteria /
18		but ⌐
19	T:	└ Oh you got there / just as the bell was ringing? //
20	Kenan:	Mmm /
21	T:	OK //

There are several distinct episodes in this narrative, each shifting place and key participants, and each marked off by a lexical and prosodic formula ("well," "see," "then"
with sustained level tones, in lines 1, 4, and 10. The narrative begins with a brief
anecdote set at home with the child's mother saying, "it's school." Such a beginning,
with an anecdote about a close family member, is a feature we have noted in many black
children's narratives. In the next segment, the setting shifts (presumably to the bus
stop). Here the "cold" theme is developed through a parallel prosodic and lexical altera-
tion between body parts being cold and hurting ("head," "face," "chin," "hands") and
items of clothing not being warm enough ("gloves," "coat," "pants," "shoes"). Prosodically, each body part noun and reference to cold is marked as salient, with emphatic
falling intonation. This is followed by a shift to a slower tempo, lower pitch, and more
level tones as items of clothing are mentioned. A kind of "listing" rhythm is established
(through stress and vowel elongation) and much of the attributional information is left
implicit ("My coat wasn't warm enough / my pa:nts / and my shoe:s / nothin' / no-
NOTHIN' was /"). In the third segment, the setting shifts to the school yard and the
child highlights the "cold" theme implicitly, through an anecdote about pretending
"like we fro:ze" with another child from the classroom. In line 12, the child says
"well," a cue that another segment was to follow. After a three-second pause, Mr. J
begins to ask questions about why the child was waiting outside for the bell to ring,
rather than in the cafeteria. This line of questions relates only to the last episode and
only peripherally to the child's overall theme. Moreover, on the basis of the child's common use of "well" to begin a narrative segment, it appears likely that he had more to say
when the teacher began to ask questions. Note also that the question in line 19 interrupts the child's utterance in line 18 ("but. . . "). In short, Mr. J did not build fully on
the child's narrative intentions and may even have unintentionally cut him short.

Teacher/child collaboration in these two examples is illustrative of subtle differences
in teachers' ways of "tuning in" to children's accounts and asking questions, both with
respect to content and timing. As isolated examples, such differences would be
insignificant. However, these two examples are indicative of stable patterns of differential response. In this classroom, we have eight good-quality recordings of the black
child, Kenan, at ST. In five of the eight cases, there is a complete absence of collaboration following the child's account, something that occurs very infrequently with white
children. In the remaining three occasions where there is attempted collaboration, there
are two cases of confusion (with recycled questions), one case of misinterpretation of the
child's intent, and two cases (as in the one cited above) where the teacher initiates questions before the child seems to be finished. Cumulatively, these patterns of problematic
collaboration or no collaboration whatsoever serve to exclude the child sharer from the
practice and help that ST can provide.

SHARING TIME REPLICATION—GENERAL CONCLUSIONS

Our analysis of ST in these four classrooms has replicated the major findings of the single-site Berkeley study. First, we have seen fundamental patterns across the Berkeley and Boston teachers in the way they respond, on the spot, to children's oral narratives. With remarkable consistency, they try to help children clarify and organize their discourse, according to their own expectations about what a well-formed, coherent story sounds like—expectations that seem to be shaped by adult notions of literate discourse.

Second, just as consistently, we find that this help is more effective with some children than with others, thus replicating the most important and troublesome of the Berkeley findings. Third, in spite of the smaller number of black children in each of the Boston-area classrooms, patterns across these classrooms suggest that problematic collaboration with urban black children is a widespread phenomenon, not just an unfortunate fact about one classroom. (Because the one black teacher in our sample turned out to be the teacher who organized ST solely for child participation, we have no information on the effect of teacher ethnicity.)

Along with these confirmations of the Berkeley findings, one notable difference emerged. These Boston-area teachers rarely used the confrontational strategies used by the Berkeley teacher. Children were rarely overtly cut short, or explicitly asked to talk differently. On only two occasions did we observe that a dialect feature was "corrected" by the teacher, and this was not at ST. One explanation for this difference may be our selection of teachers who particularly valued ST activities in their classrooms. These teachers were highly cooperative listeners and responders, and accepting of superficial dialect variations among their children. Nonetheless, while more blatant forms of differential treatment did not occur, consistent (albeit subtler) patterns of unsuccessful collaboration were still present. These findings are all the more striking in light of the fact that in the Boston study, we actively sought out highly effective, concerned teachers, hoping to document and learn from successful teachers' techniques. The fact that even excellent teachers have difficulties collaborating with their black children suggests that we cannot simply write off these problems as due to incompetence or lack of good will. Moreover, these problems cannot be attributed to a specific type of ST format, or the instructional approach of any one particular teacher. It appears that this is a more general problem, stemming from a mismatch between teacher and child's narrative strategies and use of prosody that, over time, results in differential amounts of practice and instruction for children in organizing information according to a literate model.

THE ETHNIC BASIS FOR DECREASED COLLABORATION

There are serious limitations to our naturalistic data base on ethnic differences, especially with respect to the problem of differential treatment. We feel confident of statements about ethnic differences in children's narrative style, because very similar features of black narratives—child and adult—have been described by others. In an ethnographic study of a poor black South Carolina community referred to as Trackton, Heath describes the stories of young black children:

> Trackton children must be aggressive in inserting their stories into an ongoing stream of discourse. . . . The content ranges widely, and there is "truth" only in the universals of human experiences. . . Trackton stories often have no point—no obvious beginning or ending; they go on as long as the audience enjoys and tolerates the storyteller's entertainment. (1982, p.68)

And the black scholar Geneva Smitherman, in her book *Talkin and Testifyin*. writes:

> Black English speakers will render their general, abstract observations about life, love, people in the form of concrete narrative. . . This meandering away from the "point" takes the listener on episodic journeys and over tributary rhetorical routes, but like the flow of nature's rivers and streams, it all eventually leads back to the source. Though highly applauded by blacks, this narrative linguistic style is exasperating to whites who wish you'd be direct and hurry up and get to the point. (1977, pp. 147-8)

From this kind of evidence, it seems likely that black children's ST narratives fall within a highly developed narrative tradition and that these children are approximating a well-formed adult standard.[6] But the relationship between these stylistic differences and teacher's differential treatment is much less conclusive. With the exception of the Berkeley classroom, the number of black children in each classroom is small; each child is responded to by only one teacher; we have no black teacher/child collaboration, and even if we did, we could not observe a black and white teacher responding to the same ST narrative.

In order to document more conclusively the ethnic basis for the decreased collaboration and instructional help, we conducted a small experiment in which mimicked versions of children's topic-centered and topic-associating turns were played to black and white adult informants, all students at the Harvard Graduate School of Education. These mimicked versions maintained the child's rhythm and intonation contours, while changing Black Dialect grammatical features to Standard English, and obvious social class indicators (such as "down the Cape") to neutral ones (such as "at the beach"). The adult informants were asked to comment on the well-formedness of the story, and make evaluative statements as to the probable academic success of the child telling the story.

The results of this study showed that black and white adults responded differentially to topic associating narratives. White adults were more likely to find these stories hard

---

[6] Why children continue to tell episodic ST narratives in spite of teachers' difficulties with them, even after years of practice at ST, is not clear. Several possible explanations can be suggested. (a) Black children may be able to tell simpler, topic-centered narratives but simply prefer not to. (b) Their own narrative style may be reinforced at home and in the neighborhood and be quite resistant to change. (c) Finally, it may be that the teacher's standards and concerns for ST narratives are not expressed in a way that is helpful to children at ST, so that the children may not be fully aware of what the teacher wants.

to follow, or bad stories, and they were more likely to infer that the child telling the story was a low-achieving student. Black adults were more likely to evaluate positively both topic associating and topic-centered stories—noticing differences, but seeming to appreciate both.

Because the sample sizes of black and white adults are small (seven white and five black subjects) and only five ST stories were played, we have not done statistical analyses of the results. However, the differences are striking and consistent. In order to illustrate these differences qualitatively, we will summarize the responses to one topic-associating story—Leona's grandmother story (Example #5, analyzed in detail on p. 20). The story repeated below, with all Black Dialect grammatical features changed to Standard English, is the mimicked version played to subjects. (Grammatical changes are underlined.)

Example #5

> Leona: on George Washington's birthday /
> I'm goin' / ice: / my gra:ndmother /
> we never um / haven't seen her since a long ti:me /
> and / . . . and she lives right (n) nea:r u:s /
> and / . . . she: / and she's gonna /
> I'm gonna spend the night over her house /
> and / . . . every weekend / she comes to take me /
> like on Saturdays and Sundays / awa:y from ho:me /
> and I spend the night over her house /
> and one day I spoi:led her di:nner /
> . . . um and we were having um / we were / um
> she paid ten dollars /
> and I got eggs / . . . and stuff /
> and I didn't even eat anything //

In responding to the mimicked version of Leona's grandmother story, white adults' responses were uniformly negative, with comments such as: "Terrible story; incoherent." "Hard to follow." "Mixed up." "Not a story at all in the sense of describing something that happened." "Doesn't connect." "This kid hops from one thing to the next." When asked to make a judgment about this child's probable academic standing, they without exception rated her below children who told topic-centered accounts, saying for example, "This child might have trouble reading if she doesn't understand what constitutes a story." Some referred to "language problems" affecting school achievement, and others suggested that "family problems" or "emotional problems" might hold this child back.

Black adults reacted very differently, finding the story well-formed, easy to understand, and interesting, "with lots of detail and description." Three selected it as the best story of the five they had heard. All five commented on "shifts," "associations," or the "nonlinear" quality of the story, but none appeared to be thrown by this. Two of the informants explicitly expanded on what the child meant, saying that the holiday is just like the weekend because there's no school and it's an occasion when she gets to visit her grandmother—the implicit point here being that her grandmother is an important figure in her life. One subject commented that if you didn't make this inference, you missed the entire point of the story (which was the case with the white adults). In addition, all but one of the black adults rated the child as highly verbal, very bright, or successful in school. One adult commented on her "good language skills" which should provide "good language experience for writing." The differences between the black and white adults' evaluation of this child as a student are especially striking given that the informants had only the ST narrative to go on, and had no way of knowing whether the story had been told by a black or white child (as all surface dialect features had been changed to Standard English).[7]

Taken together, our ST classroom data and this pilot experimental study suggest that it is harder to hear and appreciate the structure in discourse if it is not the kind of structure you are expecting or are attuned to. This problem must be considered from the perspective of schools as institutions required to track and evaluate children. ST activities are generally set up—as in Boston classrooms A, B, and C—so that the teacher's expectations and evaluative criteria prevail. In order to be considered competent, children must conform to the teacher's implicit expectations as to how information should be organized, developed, and presented. And if teachers fail to hear the structure or logic in a child's discourse, they are naturally inclined (as we all are) to assume it isn't there; that the talk is rambling, unplanned, or incoherent. Such negative judgments and the academic inferences that often follow can serve to exclude children from the time and engagement with the teacher they need, and may also serve to rationalize tracking policies and the "poor scores" of low-achieving students.

BEYOND SHARING TIME

ST is an activity in which children are allowed to talk at length, and exchanges between the teacher and an individual child are often lengthy as well. Hence the problem of differential treatment is relatively easy to observe and talk about. But do similar processes take place in other classroom speech events in which teacher/child collaboration in the clarification and elaboration of ideas may be even more important for literacy development? Because so many classroom activities are, like ST, mediated by conversational exchanges, we hypothesize that similar problems would be present in other contexts where teachers and children attempt to collaborate in the joint development of a coherent message.

Literacy-related activities in which this occurs include teacher/child writing conferences and the comprehension segments of small group reading lessons. Each of these

---

[7] After this was written, Cazden spent four months in New Zealand and elicited reactions to the same experimental tape from three all-white ("Pakeha") groups of education faculty and graduate students, and speech therapists. The responses were generally very similar to those of white informants at Harvard: Leona's grandmother story (5) was considered very hard to follow. However, one white teacher evaluated it as our black informants had done. In her words, it was "the best in terms of rich description of grandparent as well as a twist of humor."

activities requires fine-tuned listening and on-the-spot responding. Participants must be able to predict likely length and structure of ongoing talk, follow a line of argument, and correctly fill in implicit information so that their contributions will be heard as thematically relevant, appropriately timed, and structured so as to sound coherent and to the point (Gumperz, Kaltman, & O'Connor, 1979).

Interestingly, in a large study of children's functional language competence at the Center for Applied Linguistics, it was found that being relevant, or what Peg Griffin calls "speaking topically," was the criterion that differentiated most sharply between children considered more and less competent by their classroom teachers (reported in Cazden et al., 1977). We suggest that "speaking topically" is an interpretive judgment based both on what the child actually says, and on whether the child's talk meets the teacher's expectations for how discourse should be sequenced and structured. In our work on ST narratives, we find that some children explicitly lexicalize thematic connections, so that topic shifts "sound" relevant, while other children signal shifts implicitly through the use of prosodic cues. And where relevance is easy for teachers to hear, they are more likely to provide effective help, through collaborative expansions.

There is suggestive evidence that the quality of collaborative exchanges in other classroom activities does influence children's participation and educational success. Collins' work (1983) focuses on differential treatment in high and low reading groups in urban second- and third-grade classrooms. He has found that teacher/child collaboration is significantly better in high group lessons than in low group lessons, a difference that persists over time (and thus is independent of reading level) and that occurs regardless of the instructional approach used by the teacher. He argues that this is one of the key factors which explains why high group children make proportionally greater gains in reading than their low group counterparts in these classrooms. Additional suggestive evidence comes from our own exploratory taping of other classroom activities (along side our ST research), including small group reading lessons—as in examples 1 and 2 above). We have found in preliminary analyses of these recordings that problems in teacher/child collaboration, reminiscent of those we found in ST, do occur. And we find that instances of markedly unsuccessful teacher/child exchanges, while relatively rare, are more likely to involve minority students.

On the basis of this preliminary but suggestive evidence, it is important to identify other key discourse activities in which literacy skills are directly or indirectly taught and practiced, and test hypotheses about ethnic or subgroup differences in discourse style that, over time, could contribute to adverse educational outcomes. In these activities, we must look systematically at the distribution of collaborative exchanges as well as patterns of differential treatment, both with respect to ongoing interaction and with respect to the evaluation of children's performance. Finally, and this is the most important task of all, we must work closely with teachers to develop ways of making these findings useful to them.

We do not mean to suggest that improving teacher/child collaboration in oral language situations like ST or even reading group instruction can be a panacea for minority children's depressed academic achievement. But we do believe from these analyses that improving teacher/child collaboration can increase these children's opportunities to learn by increasing their access to the kind of quality instruction that they need and that teachers intend to provide. If these extended discourse activities are truly key situations influencing children's access to literacy instruction, then in the service of equity and improved educational practice, we must try to understand and improve conversational engagement and collaboration between teachers and children of all backgrounds.

REFERENCES

Au, K. H. (1980). Participation structures in a reading lesson with Hawaiian children: Analysis of a culturally appropriate instructional event. *Anthropology & Education Quarterly*, (2), 91–115.

Cazden, C. B., Bond, J. T., Epstein, A. S., Matz, R. D., & Savignon, S. I. (1977). Language assessment: Where, what and how. *Anthropology and Education Quarterly*, 8, 83–91.

Cazden, C. B., Carrasco, R., Maldonado-Guzman, A. A., & Erickson F. (1980). The contribution of ethnographic research to bicultural bilingual education. In J. Alatis (Ed.), *Current issues in bilingual education*. Georgetown University Round Table on Language and Linguistics. Washington, D.C.: Georgetown University Press.

Cazden, C. B., Michaels, S., & Tabors, P. (1985). Spontaneous repairs in sharing time narratives: The intersection of metalinguistic awareness, speech event and narrative style. In S. W. Freedman (Ed.), *The acquisition of written language: Revision and response*. Norwood, NJ: Ablex.

Chafe, W. (1982). Integration and involvement in speaking. Writing and oral literature. In D. Tannen (Ed.), *Spoken and written discourse*. Norwood, NJ: Ablex.

Collins, J. (1983). A linguistic perspective on minority education: Discourse analysis and early literacy. Unpublished doctoral dissertation, University of California, Berkeley.

Dorr-Bremme, D. (1982). Behaving and making sense: Creating social organization in the classroom. Unpublished doctoral dissertation, Harvard University, Boston, MA.

Gumperz, J. J., Kaltman, H., & M. O'Connor. (1979). *Thematic cohesion in spoken and written discourse*. Unpublished manuscript, University of California, Berkeley.

Hahn, E. (1948). An analysis of the content and form of the speech of first grade children. *Quarterly Journal of Speech*, 34, 361–366.

Heath, S.B. (1982). What no bedtime story means. *Language in Society*, 11, 49–76.

Keenan, E., & Bennett, T. (Eds.) (1977). *Discourse across time and space*. Southern California Occasional Papers in Linguistics, #5. Department of Linguistics, University of Southern California, Los Angeles.

Lazarus, P. (1981). Kindergarten children's communicative competence: An ethnographic study. Unpublished doctoral dissertation. University of New Mexico, Albuquerque, N.M.

Michaels, S. (1981). "Sharing Time": Children's narrative style and differential access to literacy. *Language in Society*, 10, 423–442.

Michaels, S., & Collins, J. (1984). Oral discourse styles: Classroom interaction and the acquisition of literacy. In D. Tannen (Ed.), *Coherence in spoken and written discourse*. Norwood, NJ: Ablex.

Michaels, S., & Cook-Gumperz, J. (1979). A study of sharing time with first grade students: Discourse narratives in the classroom. *Proceedings of the Fifth Annual Meetings of the Berkeley Linguistics Society*.

Michaels, S., & Foster, M. (1985). Peer-peer learning: Evidence from a kid-run sharing time. In A. Jaggar & M. Smith-Burke, (Eds.), *Kid watching: Observing the language learner*. International Reading Association and National Council of Teachers of English.

New, C. (1982, March 21). *Sharing time as a teacher-directed speech event*. Paper presented at the University of Pennsylvania Ethnography Forum, Philadelphia, PA.

Philips, S. (1972). Participant structures and communicative competence: Warm Springs children in community and classroom. In C. Cazden, V. John, & D. Hymes. (Eds.), *Functions of language in the classroom*. New York: Teachers College Press.

Scollon, R., & Scollon, S. B. K. (1981). *Narrative, literacy, and face in interethnic communication*. Norwood, NJ: Ablex.

Scollon, R., & Scollon, S. B. K. (1984). Cooking it up and boiling it down: Abstracts in Athabaskan children's story retellings. In D. Tannen (Ed.), *Coherence in spoken and written discourse*. Norwood, NJ: Ablex.

Smitherman, G. (1977). *Talkin' and testifyin': The language of black America*. Boston: Houghton Mifflin.

Tannen, D. (Ed.) (1982). *Spoken and written discourse: Exploring orality and literacy*. Norwood, NJ: Ablex.

Tannen, D. (Ed.) (1984). *Coherence in spoken and written discourse*. Norwood, NJ: Ablex.

Wilcox, K. (1982). Differential socialization in the classroom: Implications for equal opportunity. In G. Spindler (Ed.), *Doing the ethnography of schooling: Educational anthropology in action*. New York: Holt, Rinehart & Winston.

8

Sub-rosa Literacy: Peers, Play, and Ownership in Literacy Acquisition*

Perry Gilmore

University of Alaska-Fairbanks

INTRODUCTION

Too often the limitations of traditional language and literacy assessment techniques restrict our knowledge about what children are capable of doing with written and oral language. By observing natural language behavior in a variety of contexts, we see dramatic demonstrations of abilities often unseen and unimagined in formal school or testing situations. Recent ethnographic research which examines language and literacy use in context, rather than focusing on elicitation, interview and testing data, has provided new insights into the literacy competencies of pre-school and school aged children. Examples of this work are presented in this volume and offer a unique perspective on the acquisition and development of literacy. Through this approach, which relies on observation of naturally occurring behavior and non-intervention techniques, we discover that we had often underestimated the oral and written communicative abilities of the participants.

Two related aspects of language need to be considered in the study of children's linguistic and literacy development and ability. The first is the discovery of examples of children's competencies in a range of communicative abilities and oral and written performances. The second is an understanding of the children's interpretations of what oral and written language does and what it means in their social world. Issues of language competence cannot be understood apart from the social world of which they are an integral part.

Children's play forms and peer social interactions often provide an unusually rich mode of expression for displays of language and literacy competence as well as for displays of culture and social relationships (see for example Kirshenblatt-Gimblett, 1979; Bauman, 1982). Caillois (1961) has suggested as much in his assertion "Tell me what you play and I shall tell you who you are." In this chapter I will present examples

---

* The research reported here was supported by grants from the National Institute of Education to Dell H. Hymes, Principal Investigator 1979–81 and to David M. Smith, Principal Investigator 1981–82 (University of Pennsylvania). I am grateful to both these individuals for the support and comments they offered throughout the course of the study.

A shorter version of this chapter was presented as an invited paper at the Symposium "Speaking, Literacy and Speaking About Literacy" American Educational Research Association, Montreal 1983.

of peer social interaction and play I observed during a 3-year literacy research project which contrasted language and literacy-related skills identified and described within school culture with those skills practiced in peer contexts (see Gilmore, 1982, 1983, 1985, and forthcoming for further discussion).

The study was part of a larger research project conducted in a black, low-income neighborhood in Philadelphia. The school in which the observations were conducted had an all-black student population and an equal proportion of black and white faculty. It characterized itself as a traditional back-to-basics institution and had an excellent reputation in the city. Although most of the students in the observed classes were identified as skill deficient, observations, to the contrary, indicated that the students were skill proficient. The examination of these language behaviors shows that the school's assessment of their language and literacy skills was inadequate because it did not consider the cultural organization of student performances.

In the following discussion, literacy skills, identified and defined by school culture, will be contrasted with literacy skills practiced within the domain of peer culture and play. "Sub-rosa" literacy and literacy-related skills, those skills owned and demonstrated in peer contexts, are examined with regard to the language competencies they display and the symbolic meanings they represent. Both oral and written genres of verbal expression will be considered. They will include girls' performances of a distinctive genre of street rhymes, locally referred to as "steps," and boys' participation in group literacy activities when playing the game Dungeons and Dragons.

TALKING ISN'T VERBAL EXPRESSION: LANGUAGE AND LITERACY IN CLASSROOM CONTEXTS

Classroom interaction seems to have two lines of activity. There is one line, organized and orchestrated by the teacher, who writes schedules on the board, gives assignments, gives rewards and punishments, and the like. These activities are foregrounded, public, and dominant. Interferences in their flow are thwarted, suppressed and punished. It is at this level that labels usually are given for what is happening in the classroom—we're doing math, reading, checking homework, and the like. A second line of activity is the peer social interaction that is maintained through such channels as covert talk and secret notes. It's content is meant for peers, not adults.

Teachers usually perceive the second line of activity as irregular side events to one main level of interaction, the one they control. An observer may listen to and see the steady stream of interaction among the students, ways of being in tune with one another, that teachers mostly glimpse only briefly at moments when they emerge inappropriately. The two lines of activity are more clearly marked as distinct in traditional classrooms.

Contexts and settings are not necessarily a matter of physical location but can frequently be a matter of situations within a physical setting. Within a classroom where expectations are that the teacher is supervising formal learning activities, frequently interactions occur with an altogether different frame. Participation structures (Philips,

1972) and roles vary within the same physical dimensions of the setting, creating altogether different kinds of interactions, organized and reorganized for different purposes.

For example, though instructional sequences such as Mehan (1979) depicts, composed of *initiation, reply, and evaluation* segments, do represent the "lesson" it is misleading to think that such a model characterizes the general nature of the discourse going on in the class setting. The lesson talk may be indeed more foregrounded, but it is certainly not the only talk taking place. Multiple discourse contexts and corresponding participation structures can be identified within the same classroom occurring simultaneously at any given time.

When teachers in traditional classrooms refer to "verbal expression" most frequently they are identifying the student language (written or oral) which is framed in the lesson context. This language "counts" in school as part of a set of skills associated with language arts and literacy. When teachers in traditional classrooms refer to "talk," however, they are identifying something quite different. Most often they are commenting on student language that is seen as interfering with lesson discourse and smooth classroom procedure. Comments on report cards are evaluative statements which reflect these two categories of language use. It isn't difficult to interpret the different meanings conveyed by such statements as: "He has excellent verbal expression." or "He is always talking in class."

"Talkers! Against the wall!" was not an unusual command to hear from a teacher in the hall or a supervisor of the cafeteria. Often the simple referent "talker" is used to label misbehaving children. Students know that "talking" is equated with misbehaving. An awareness of that knowledge can be heard in the following comment written by a fourth grader in a self-marking assignment at report card time:

> I have problems in behavior. I don't know why I talk a lot but I want to be different so I won't talk a lot. I'm not going to talk that much now and I will always be quiet and that's a promise.

This statement accompanied the grade she gave herself in behavior, which was a C.

Another fourth-grade girl, after being told to stand against the wall at lunch time because she was talking, returned to her classroom and wrote the following statement on the chalkboard in very large, bold and sprawling print:

> God gave me a mouth, and I'm going to use it whenever I want.

In both written statements the students made no spelling or punctuation errors.

The link between oral and written language in schools is strong, though the scholarly literature in related disciplines suggests otherwise. For example, Gumperz and Cook-Gumperz (1981) suggest that especially in minority black communities and generally in the home, children operate within an oral tradition and, in school, where formal learning takes place, the primary channel is in a literate tradition. Heath (1982) suggests an alternative view:

> There is little or no validity to the time honored dichotomy of "the literate tradition" and "the oral tradition." Cultural diversities in the uses of writing, reading

and their links to speaking provide not a dichotomy, but multiple-faceted continua in which oral and written language structures and functions intersect in a wide variety of ways. (p. 2)

My own observations indicate that schools primarily teach, practice, and test reading and writing skills in oral ways. Consider the very beginnings of reading instruction, where emphasizing phonics, teachers repeatedly ask students to orally produce words that begin with the same sound as "bat," or a word that rhymes with "race," et al. Comprehension is also most commonly taught or at least quizzed orally. Finally consider that few report card marks are given in the lower elementary school grades based on numerous written tests. Progress is usually monitored and evaluated in the oral interactions of teachers with their students.

When teachers in the study site were asked what some of their students' problems in literacy were, their own answers usually covered a range of language behaviors which included both oral and written performance. Often the statements were such that it was not possible to tell whether teachers were themselves distinguishing the two. For example, teachers might say that students have trouble with syllabification, rhyming and medial blends. All of these are word analysis skills which are practiced and tested both orally and in writing. They might say that the students cannot identify main ideas. This comprehension skill is most frequently practiced and tested orally in reading groups.

The distinction for teachers seems less to be between oral and written modes than it is between sanctioned and non-sanctioned modes. Most teachers were quick to say that students don't write. Observations of students in and out of school show that kids write all the time. But what they write does not get sanctioned, because it is outside the domain of school. Just as talking was distinguished quite clearly from verbal expression, 'tellers' are clearly distinguished from writing. "Tellers" are what this particular group of students labeled the notes they secretively passed to each other. The notes, which were usually passed sub-rosa, under the desks, stood in striking contrast to the written work done for the teachers on top of the desks. The "tellers" were full of evidence of literacy competencies the students were often described as not having evidenced in their 'top of the desk' activities. Tellers were a common channel for communication in a context where silence was expected. One only had to observe the skillful writing, tearing, folding, and cooperative passing performed while continually looking up to monitor the teacher's attention, to know how well practiced and private this channel of communication was.

One student I observed chose a silent pause in a math lesson to tear, too loudly, a message out of her tablet. The child looked up guiltily. The teacher whose back was turned, at the sound of the tear turned, looked at her sternly and said, "After school!" No further explanation was needed. They both knew a rule had been broken, as did the others in the class who silently were witness to the event.

With both the talking and the writing described here, the content of the communication was not meant for adult authorities. Peer audiences were addressed. Peer related issues were often the topics. These sub-rosa language and literacy activities indicated alignments, peer alignments. As a result they did not 'count' as language or literacy skills. They were not seen as corresponding with institutionally recognized norms of literacy instruction.

The remaining discussion will focus on two literacy related events in which peer groups engaged regularly. The first sub-rosa literacy event to be examined, "steps," was a wide-spread, popular activity for girl peer groups in the study site. The second activity observed in the study site was a less widely practiced but most noticeable game called Dungeons and Dragons played primarily in boy peer groups.

By examining features of these two events, some key issues concerning literacy competence as well as the social meanings of literacy and instruction will be detailed.

Steps

I first noticed steps early in the spring of my first year of fieldwork. Girls would almost burst out of the hall at recess on to the playground, form lines and begin "doin steps." "Steps" are a distinctive genre of street rhymes which seems to have grown out of the tradition of drills and cheers. The performance involves chorally chanted rhymes punctuated with foot steps and hand claps which set up a background rhythm. It is performed by groups of girls and consistent with tradition in children's folklore, it is full of taboo breaking and sexual innuendo in both the verbal and non-verbal modes of its performance. The dances were striking. The chants full of verbal virtuosity. But they were "nasty." They were seen as defiant. They were seen as part of black street repertoire. They were seen as representing "deteriorating attitudes." And they were banned from the school.

When studying children's peer group culture in different ethnic and racial groups all over the world not only the "playful whimsical and artful aspects" emerge but also the "aggressive, obscene, scatological, anti-authoritarian and inversive elements" (see Bauman, 1982). Peer culture folklore is often representative of counter-culture values.

Often teachers would comment that their students lacked necessary literacy skills. They were concerned that students had skill deficiencies in word analysis skills, for example they would say—"my students can't rhyme, do syllabification, or identify initial and medial blends." They were concerned that their students lacked comprehension skills; for example students couldn't identify main ideas, develop narrative themes, recognize semantic differences in homonyms and the like. Finally, teachers were concerned that their students lacked the necessary "good citizenship" skills required for school literacy instruction; teachers would say, for example, they can't listen to or cooperate with each other, they can't get organized or work in groups.

With these teacher concerns in mind let us take a closer look at the performance of one very popular step, "Mississippi." Five versions are presented in Figure 1.

The step, "Mississippi," is performed in a variety of ways, each version having its own choreography and rhythm to accompany and accent the verbal alternations. Each version has as its core the spelling of the word Mississippi. These variations include description of and metaphorical references to the letters and on-going narratives which play with the letters as beginnings of utterances.

Figure 1.   Mississippi

(1) M I SS I SS I PP I	A straight spelling, reciting each letter in rhythmic patterned clusters—the most concrete literate form of the rhyme.

(2) M I CROOKED LETTER CROOKED LETTER I CROOKED LETTER CROOKED LETTER I HUMP BACK HUMP BACK I	A spelling which includes description of, or metaphorical reference to the physical features of some of the letters. In this version the "crooked letter" represents an *s* and the "hump back" a *p*. The children sometimes refer to the entire genre of steps as "Kookelater (crooked letter) Dances."

(3) M for the money I if ya give it to me S sock it (to me) S sock it (to me) I if I buy it from ya S sock it S sock it I if I take it from ya P pump it P push it I : : : :	This version is often followed by version #2 above with a smooth transition. The spelling uses the letters of *Mississippi* to produce the first word of each line in an on-going narrative.

(4) Hey _____ (name) _____ , yo You wanted on the phone Who is it? Your nigger. I bet he wants my lips, my tits, my butt, my smut, My CROOKED LETTER CROOKED LETTER I	A controversial narrative which is only punctuated with parts of the spelling. The play with narrative rather than the orthography dominates the verbal content. The "crooked letter" by its position in a series of "wants" takes on an ambiguous sexual meaning especially as the letter is being adorned in dance.

(5) Hey, Deedee, yo Spell Mississippi Spell Mississippi right now You take my hands up high You take my feet down low I cross my legs with that gigolo If you don't like that Throw it in the trash And then I'm bustin out With that Jordache Look in the sky With that Calvin Klein I'm gonna lay in the dirt With that Sergi ert (Sergio Valente) I'm gonna bust a balloon With that Sassoon Gonna be ready With that Teddy I'm gonna be on the rail with that Vanderbail With the is-M is-I CROOKED LETTER CROOKED LETTER I	This version of *Mississippi* was performed by fewer individuals and was viewed as an accomplished recitation by peers. The jeans' theme made it a favored version of the narrative performance.

The performance of "Mississippi" is an intersection of visual and verbal codes, using the body dramatically as an iconic sign for the letters. The most prominent, noticeable and controversial dance movement is the formation of the letter *s* or "crooked letter." The transformation of the body into the letter *s* is demonstrated in a limbo-like dancing movement with one arm forming a crook at the shoulder. It is not uncommon to find an elementary school teacher asking students to make their bodies shape a letter as part of reading instruction. Yet although the steppers successfully perform such bodily letter representation, it is interpreted negatively. By using sexual innuendo and other markers of ownership in verbal context and body idiom, they have created interpretive frames that signal to any onlooker, that if, indeed, this is a literacy related performance it belongs to the children and not to the adults who ordinarily teach them rhymes, syllables, homonyms, spelling, reading comprehension, good citizenship skills, and the like.

A common phrase that girls will utter as they first step out of the line to perform is "Gimme room." Indeed not only do they ask for "room" but they are expected to take it. Having your own style within the conventions and boundaries of the performance is expected and valued. Each girl does the performance with some embellishments and markers of individuality. The degree of oral composing varies, but performers who are creative are recognized for their virtuosity and often are designated as "captains" who organize and instruct the others.

While teachers and parents had heard and seen the steps performed enough to notice and ban it, most had never really listened to it enough to be aware of the general content. Rather, they were aware of isolated signal words and phrases that were considered too sexual or improper. Although the chanting was in a broadcast mode it is interesting that the words were obfuscated by the melodic prosody. Once the "sirens" lured a listener in, the taboo words would be heard with assaulting clarity.

The behavior belongs primarily to the transitional period between childhood and adolescence. When older girls did perform they considerably modified the sexual movements. And so, though the movements and theme were *sexual,* the mode and key were clearly playful.

Finally, as a symbolic expressive form the performance of "Mississippi" can be examined as a mock "instructional routine." In many ways the routine sounds like what one might expect in a school classroom. Directions are called to an individual to spell a word—Mississippi, a difficult word to spell at that. Yet there are several aspects of the instruction that seem to break with expected norms of speech and politeness and with predictable co-occurrence rules of classrooms.

First instead of a single teacher's voice, the entire group of steppers chant the request in loud chorus. This is the reverse of the stereotypic model of an individual teacher request followed by an entire class's choral response. The request itself has marked characteristics that counter expectations of what a classrooom teacher would say.

Hey, (Wendy).
Spell Mississippi. Spell Mississippi, right now!

The request sounds more like a challenge or a dare. The use of the word "hey" is informal, usually considered inappropriate for school, and has a slightly threatening quality—as if one is being "called out" rather than "called on." Further, there is an impatient tone to the demand as a result of the quick repetition "Spell Mississippi" and the conclusion "right now." It has been pointed out that teachers tend to use politeness forms frequently to modify the power and control they have. These forms soften acts of instruction that might be interpreted as face-threatening to students (see Cazden, 1979). The teacher request in "Mississippi" seems to do exactly the opposite. Politeness forms are absent and the face-threatening nature is intensified.

As mentioned, the stepper who is called on to perform the spelling task usually utters a quick phrase like "gimme room" or "no sweat" as she jumps forward out of the line to begin her routine. These utterances indicate the stepper's willingness to take on the dare and the stepper's confidence that the performance is fully within the range of her competencies. Thus the instructional routine sets up an aggressive and suspicious teacher command and a student stepper who takes on the challenge with a sexual swagger and obvious confidence about her spelling prowess.

A spelling exercise, ordinarily practiced in the classroom is transformed through linguistic play and dance with a marked shift in ownership. By reframing the instructional exchange the literacy-related behaviors are recontextualized—taken from the school's mode of literacy instruction and made a part of the children's own world. Interpretive frames are created that signal to onlookers that this particular performance of literacy-related behaviors does not belong to or count for school.

The syncopation of this spelling lesson allows children, as subordinates, to mock school instruction. In much the same way skits and jokes can present concrete formulations of an abstract cultural symbol, the images conveyed in the "Mississippi" performance can be seen as containing interpretations of the children's symbolic constructions of their own social portraits of the dynamics of schooling.

Thus the message conveyed by these students through the performance of "Mississippi" can seem quite a poignant one. It is not merely defiant. It can easily be seen as face-saving, a way of maintaining dignity through collective autonomy when confronted with the school's undermining doubt in their ability. At the end of "Mississippi" the entire group does the spelling performance in a striking flourish, declaring for all to see, their excellence as literate spellers, dancers and as kids.

Dungeons and Dragons

There is a widely accepted assumption in the literature in literary criticism and in the literature on reading comprehension that narrative prose is simpler to read and to write than expository prose. Very basically speaking narrative usually refers to a story whereas exposition is descriptive and informational text. A concern with developing flexible readers, that is, readers who can adjust their reading performance to the demands of various genres (e.g., poetry, fiction, exposition), has been a dominant theme in curriculum development and instruction in language arts for the last decade.

Calfee (1981) has asserted that:

Even first graders can comprehend stories, but by the time they leave third grade, they need to be able to comprehend other kinds of texts better than they do. The ability to handle expository text structures comes less from everyday experience and more from formal education. (p. 43)

The assumption here is that expository text is more decontextualized and therefore is more characteristic of formal learning and associated with higher level cognitive and abstract skills acquired in school contexts.

But first consider that it is very difficult to find pure representations of literacy genres in text. Most narratives contain a significant amount of exposition and similarly characteristic features of narrative are often found in expository text. In the real world of literature, genre lines are crossed with predictable regularity.

Further observations conducted in out-of-school contexts in my study show a very high incidence of expository text in informal use by preschoolers on up through adolescence. Most often observed as high interest reading material for preschoolers other than story books (i.e., narrative text) were books about pre-historic monsters, cars, trucks, and machines, science, wildlife, and dictionary alphabet books. Older school age children often read sports cards, magazines, newspapers (especially sports, comics, ads, movie and TV listings), catalogues, model directions, and the like. It was interesting to note that expository text was favored by boys generally. In fact, in the study site readers, who declared themselves non-readers (that is, they say they don't read, or read very much), read regularly, but they read almost exclusively expository prose rather than fiction narratives (see Robinson, 1982).

The examples of expository text in Figure 2 are not taken from a formal school lesson. They are excerpts from a game many boys actively play around the middle school years (grades 6–8). Although originally designed and written for college age individuals, the game in the past few years has been discovered by a rapidly growing population of much younger boys. Most prominent are groups and clubs of primarily preadolescent boys who meet regularly to play Dungeons and Dragons or D&D. Though some girls do play, it is primarily an activity for boys. Those who played in the study site generally were introduced to the game as a result of exposure to it from other more middle class and racially mixed communities. Boys who went to magnet schools outside the immediate community brought it back to siblings, other family members and neighborhood friends. The game itself requires a great deal of reading and there are a large assortment of books, manuals, guides, cyclopedias, and modules available. The expense of these literacy materials has no doubt kept it a more middle class indulgence. A widely held assumption by adults who know of the game is that it is for "gifted kids." However, none of the children whom I observed in the study site ever suggested that when discussing it with me. When asked if kids who can't read very well can play, the answer was that it doesn't matter because "the dungeon master helps them." The role of the dungeon master is to lead players through various adventures, consulting reference books to enhance the game.

One 13-year-old boy in the study site described his role as Dungeon Master in the following way:

I have to lead (the players) through the dungeon. And every evil character they meet—I'm the mind of the character. (The game) involves dice, little books and dungeons. Dungeons is where they try to find gold. The dice determines the moves, the hits and the strikes. I read the books to reference evil characters and

Figure 2. A page from *Dungeon Masters Guide* (Gary Gygax, TSR Games, 1979); reproduced by permission.

COMBAT (MISSILE DISCHARGE)

Missiles from giants are approximately 1' in diameter, as are those from small catapults. Those from large catapults (and trebuchets) are approximately 2' in diameter.

See also **GRENADE-LIKE MISSILES** and **Special "To Hit" Bonuses.**

Strength Bonus Considerations: The strength bonus for hitting and damage does not apply to missiles unless the character so entitled specifically takes steps to equip himself or herself with special weapons to take advantage of the additional strength. This will result in the weapon having an additional chance to hit and do the additional damage as well. In no event will it add to the effective range of the character's weapon. Thus, the character will employ a heavier missile or a more powerful bow and heavier arrows or larger sling missiles to gain the advantage of strength. To do so, he or she must obtain the special weapon or weapons, and this is within the realm of your adjudication as DM as to where and how it will be obtained, and how much cost will be involved.

Dexterity Penalty And Bonus Considerations: The *Dexterity Attacking Adjustment* is for missile firing considerations when initiative is considered. It adjusts the initiative die roll for the concerned individual only. Thus, it may well allow the concerned individual to discharge a missile prior to the opponent's attack even though the opponent has gained the initiative otherwise or vice versa. More important, this factor also gives the individual a "to hit" penalty or bonus when discharging a missile at an opponent.

Special Note Regarding Giant And Machine Missiles:

When giants hurl boulders or any of the various siege machines (ballistae, catapults, etc.) fire missiles, target characters do not gain dexterity bonus considerations to armor class when "to hit" computations are made. Consider this as follows: Character A has an armor class rating of –2, but as dexterity accounts for 2 of these factors, AC rating drops to 0 if a giant is hurling rocks at the character or if some machine is discharging missiles at him or her.

Missile Fire Cover And Concealment Adjustments:

Adjust the armor class of the target creature as follows if cover (hard substances which protect) or concealment (soft substances which screen) exists:

TARGET HAS ABOUT	ARMOR CLASS BONUS
25% cover	+ 2
50% cover	+ 4
75% cover	+ 7
90% cover	+ 10
25% concealment	+ 1
50% concealment	+ 2
75% concealment	+ 3
90% concealment	+ 4

25% is cover or concealment to the knees, or part of the left or right side of the body screened; it might also be a target which is seen for only three-quarters of a round. Men on a walled parapet would typically be 25% covered. 50% cover or concealment equals protection or screening to the waist, half of one side of the body, or being seen for only half the round. Figures in thick brush would be at least 50% concealed; men on a castle wall with embrasures and merlons would be at least 50% covered. Shuttered embrasures and narrow windows would provide 75% cover, while arrow slits offer 90% cover.

For the effect of cover on magic, see **SPELL CASTING DURING MELEE, Effect of Cover on Spells and Spell-like Powers.**

GRENADE-LIKE MISSILES: BOULDERS AND CONTAINERS OF ACID, HOLY/UNHOLY WATER, OIL, POISON

Hurling various containers of liquid is a common tactic in dungeon adventures in particular. For game purposes it is necessary to make certain assumptions regarding all such missiles.

COMBAT (MISSILE DISCHARGE)

Size:
Acid —	½ pint (8 oz.)	
Holy/Unholy Water —	¼ pint (4 oz.)	
Oil —	1 pint (16 oz.)	
Poison —	¼ pint (4 oz.)	

Effect:

Liquid Contents	Area of Effect	Splash	Damage From a Direct Hit
—acid	1' diameter	1 h.p.	2-8 h.p.
—holy/unholy water	1' diameter	2 h.p.	2-7 h.p.
—oil, alight	3' diameter	1-3 h.p.*	2-12 h.p. + 1-6 h.p.**
—poison	1' diameter	special	special

* Flaming oil splashed on a creature will burn for 1-3 segments, causing 1 hit point of damage per segment.

** Direct hit with flaming oil causes 2-12 hit points of damage the first round, and 1-6 additional hit points of damage the second round, but then burns out.

Range: The range of all such container missiles is 3". Beyond 1" is medium, and beyond 2" is long (–2 and –5 "to hit" respectively).

Hits: When the die roll indicates the missile has hit, then it is necessary to roll again to see if the container shatters or not — use the BLOW, CRUSHING column on the **ITEM SAVING THROW MATRIX** —unless special procedures were taken to weaken the container, i.e. the container was specially scored, it is particularly fragile, etc. Damage occurs only if the container breaks, except with regard to oil which must be alight (flaming) to cause damage. If oil has been specially prepared by insertion of a rag into the opening of the container (or wrapped around the neck of the container) and set afire prior to hurling, it will burst into flame when the container breaks upon target impact; otherwise, a torch or other means of causing combustion must be brought into contact with the oil.

Poison special is dependent upon whether or not the poison is a contact poison or if the container was hurled into the ingestive or respiratory orifice on the target creature. In the latter case, breakage is not necessary if the container was unstoppered; if stoppered check saving throw for breakage using the BLOW, NORMAL column on the **ITEM SAVING THROW MATRIX.**

Splash Hits: All creatures within three feet of the impact and breaking point of the container missile must save versus poison or be splashed with the contents of the shattered container.

Boulders: Boulders, for game purposes, are considered to be 1' in diameter for giants, 2' in diameter for siege engines. Range and damage specifications for siege machines are given in the appropriate section. (See **MONSTER MANUAL** for giants' abilities.)

A dropped boulder (or any heavy weight) will do damage as follows: each 14 lbs. of weight will inflict one point of damage per foot of distance dropped between 10' and 60' (distances above 60' are treated as 60'). Alternately, each 14 lbs. of weight will inflict a flat 1-6 hit points of damage.

Misses: If the "to hit" die roll indicates a miss, roll 1d6 and 1d8. The d6 indicates the **distance in feet** the missile was off target. (If the target was large, simply compute the distance from the appropriate portion of the target, i.e. the character aims at a section of the floor which is 1' square, and miss distance is measured from the appropriate edge as explained below.) The d8 indicates the **direction** in which the distance in feet of the miss is measured:

1 = long right	5 = short left
2 = right	6 = left
3 = short right	7 = long left
4 = short (before)	8 = long (over)

At short range you may optionally use d4 to determine distance off target, but then use d8 for long range distance determination. If the missile is hurled at a plane such as a wall, read long as high, short as low, measuring up the wall and then along the ceiling or down and then along the floor.

Lighting Oil: If a torch is used to attempt to light spilled oil, use above procedures for misses, as it still could land in the puddle of oil or oil covered what is in the room itself. For the characters there's certain characteristics they need to have. OK, I take three six-sided dice. The highest they can score is eighteen, and the higher the better. And there's six or seven characteristics they need to have. OK, on the side of a loose leaf paper they have these initials: D—dexterity. That shows the speed and agility of a person. Uhh, C—for constitution. That's their strength and endurance. S—for strength, W for wisdom and CH—for charisma, that's how good they are/do their courage.

(The book) describes the character. Well, these, what I've just explained, go on separate pieces of paper, the characters' names and their hit points and armor class. Now hit points is (sic) when that particular person has been hit. OK, by a sword or anything. You take away so many hit points to show their damage or wounds and the lowest hit points you can get is negative ten on the integer scale and that shows the person is dead...(from interview conducted by Andrea Robinson, 1981)

A significant irony here is that the population who regularly play this literacy fantasy game corresponds with a population which has been depicted as contributing the literacy drop-off rate: that is, intermediate grade age males. Whether successful in classrooms in school or not, these young males rush home to get their school work done so they can play D&D (often much more challenging reading than their school assignments). Students will get to school early, organize themselves at lunch (assigning roles for buying, etc.) so that they have enough free time to play. Many hours of individual reading and preparing written character and dungeon descriptions often precede the actual group play. Some players keep detailed logs and journals to record their character life histories over periods of several months to several years. Saturday afternoon might be set aside to tutor a new player in one particular aspect of the game—such as how to use "psionics." D&D, though replete with skills demands of literacy and math comparable to school assignments, belongs to peer culture and is seen as fun, and not part of school skills repertoire. In the days of back-to-basics and fill-in-the-blank instruction, Dungeons and Dragons represents a literacy explosion in rich factual knowledge, vocabulary, spelling, graph, and chart reading, cross referencing, and original creativity. Challenging exposition text provides both the substance and the procedure for the players who weave complex and fanciful narratives around the structured themes. It raises a serious question for educators when a population which performs poorly in reading in a school context enthusiastically and voluntarily engages in more demanding, highly technical literacy texts for fun with friends.

Consider the skill demands required for comprehending the expository D&D text in Figure 2. The reader is expected to demonstrate competence with a highly technical and complex lexicon, considerably more advanced than a sixth-grade basal reader vocabulary. D&D readers must interpret charts, graphs, and highly detailed information. Directions frequently require cross-referencing skills in the various guides, manuals, and handbooks used by the players. It is interesting to note that the D&D text itself does not look like a conventional notion of high interest text for 9–12-year-olds. The print is small, margins minimal, tables and graphs prominent, and illustrations limited. The general message conveyed by the visual image of the page is that it contains highly technical informational text which is difficult to read.

Like "steps" for girls, D&D for boys is a pronouncement of literacy and language prowess, but in a counter-culture event. Like steps, D&D is also controversial—full of violence, and religious and sexual taboos.

In many communities it has been labelled satanic, occult, or just plain addictive. Like steps, D&D is marked as peer-owned by obfuscated language. With steps, syncopation and melodic prosody were devices used to obscure the meaning of what was publically chanted. The extensive technical lexicon of Dungeons and Dragons marks it as a distinct and unintelligible jargon which outsiders cannot easily comprehend.

In much the same way the steppers take on the challenge to spell Mississippi with an air of defiant virtuosity, the D&D players express a similar defiance of the school's assumption about their skill limitations. The text of D&D itself conveys the clear message that these players are capable of comprehending complex, technical expository prose.

Like steppers acknowledge peer virtuosity by selecting skilled performers as captains, D&D players defer to their Dungeon Masters as instructional leaders. Unlike the competitive school model (e.g., see Labov, 1982; Henry, 1963), in these peer situations, singling out experts means that they become available as exploitable resources for the entire group.

While most reading and language arts curricula break literacy skills down into discrete hierarchies of subskills and assume learners must work through the skill sets systematically and linearly, D&D players approach and succeed in their literacy task demands in a much more organic and holistic manner. They jump into the game totally and moves are perfected as they go. But most important, they are not alone. Learning D&D with friends is a perfect example of peer teaching and learning. Reminiscent of Vygotsky's zone of proximal development (1978) the learners are guided through new problem solving experiences in supportive, interactive syncrony. They learn pragmatically as the need arises in the game. In my observations of D&D, I have never heard a comment like, "He'll never learn this" or "You're so slow." The pedagogy of the game begins with a belief in the ability of each player.

That expository text is harder to comprehend than narrative text is part of the tradition of literary criticism and part of the lore of curriculum. However the ethnographic observations conducted during this study demonstrate clearly that the difficulty of text has very little to do with the established literary genres of exposition or narrative. The children's folk categories of genre have much more to do with ownership than readability formulas or conventional genres labels. D&D belongs to peers; it is very difficult for adults to follow and learn, tedious to read and remember. Kids find it fun and exciting. Genre as conventional curriculum and instruction theory uses it is hardly useful as an explanation for reading difficulty.

The sub-rosa literacy events, steps and D&D, provide vivid examples of student competencies in a range of oral and written performances. Ironically these are precisely the literacy skills schools have identified as deficiencies in the same population. I do not offer these demonstrations of competencies in peer contexts to suggest that curriculum projects in schools incorporate street rhymes or fantasy adventure games. Though some attempts to do so have been instructionally effective, most such efforts are weakened by the simple act of transforming children's folklore into acceptable school material. The very nature of the clean up requires the removal of all the anti-authoritarian, obscene, and inversive elements which characterized it as part of children's peer culture in the first place. Once it is neutered, colonized, and socially controlled by the school it is, in fact, no longer children's folklore (see, for example, Cazden, 1982; Sutton-Smith, 1982).

I do offer these examples of sub-rosa literacy skills because there are several profound messages conveyed by these performances which are dramatic pronouncements of the individuals' language and literacy abilities. These events carry serious social and educational reminders. Successful and respectful assessment and instruction must be responsive to what children are capable of doing with language across various social contexts; not only in formal classroom or test performances. Too often teachers say that students can't rather then students won't. The former implies a skill deficiency; the latter an issue of social control (see Smith, forthcoming for further discussion). Consider, for example, that the teachers in the study discussed here regularly said that their students couldn't perform certain word analysis skills, comprehension skills and citizenship skills, though observations of the students' participation in both steps and D&D demonstrated otherwise. What were the instructional effects of these false assessments and underlying assumptions about skill deficiencies? If a teacher assumed a student couldn't rhyme or count syllables, the instructional approach taken in the classroom often focused on repeated practice and drill in that particular skill area. Consider that even successful performance in such skills instruction, from the teacher's point of view, reflected no new learning on the part of the students. These low expectations foster low achievement.

When examining children's literacy and language development, if only performances within instructional contexts are examined, we tend to be measuring the degree of student acceptance of or resistance to the school's values rather than measuring their oral and written language abilities. By confusing the two areas we make little progress in ameliorating the circumstances of either one.

The implications for classroom instruction are simple. Both the D&D players and the steppers have been urging us to listen to the plea to "Gimme room." They are all asking for room to be seen, trusted, and evaluated as skilled language users—as individuals who have the right to instructional circumstances where respect, pride and ownership are the central features of learning. Recent attention to school reform has frequently pointed to the need to raise teacher expectations of student performance. There is a danger that this laudable goal can easily backfire. If student abilities are understood with the conventional myopia pervasive in education, then raising teacher expectations may be nothing more than increasing teacher demands for more useless drill and meaningless instruction. Literacy assessment has too often meant closing doors rather than opening them.

Instead, teacher expectations should be raised through an awareness that students are capable of doing more with language when they are given the room and respect to do so. This awareness develops easily—by listening to students and coming to understand who they are and what they need. In repeated chants, the steppers advise all who are willing to hear that, given the room they need, they are more than able to master the skills.

One final stepping rhyme presents a student self-evaluation which seems to sum up the underlying educational implications for both the steppers and D&D players discussed here. Dawn is asking for, and deserves a chance. She speaks for all our children.

> My name is Dawn—yeah!
> And I'm a Scorpio—yeah!
> And I can do it—yeah!
> Ain't nothin' to it—whooh!

REFERENCES

Bauman, R. (1982). Ethnography of children's folklore. In P. Gilmore & A. Glatthorn (Eds.), *Children in and out of school*. Washington, DC: Center for Applied Linguistics.

Caillois, R. (1961). *Man play and games*. New York: The Free Press.

Calfee, R.C. et al. (1981). *Designing reading instruction for cultural minorities: The case of the Kamahameha early education program*. Cambridge, MA: Graduate School of Education, Harvard University.

Cazden, C. (1979). Language in education: Variation in the teacher-talk register. In *Language in public life*. Washington, DC: 30th Annual Georgetown University Round Table.

Cazden, C. (1982). Four comments. In P. Gilmore & A. Glatthorn (Eds.), *Children in and out of school*. Washington, DC: Center for Applied Linguistics.

Gilmore, P. (1982). *Gimme room: A cultural approach to the study of attitudes and admission to literacy*. Unpublished doctoral dissertation, University of Pennsylvania.

Gilmore, P. (1983). Spelling mississippi: Recontextualizing a literacy-related speech event. *Anthropology and Educational Quarterly, 14*, 235–255.

Gilmore, P. (1985). Silence and sulking: Emotional displays in the classroom. In D. Tannen & M. Saville-Troike (Eds.), *Perspectives on silence*. Norwood NJ: Ablex.

Gilmore, P. (forthcoming). Sulking, stepping and tracking: The effects of attitude assessment on access to literacy In D. Bloome (Ed.), *Literacy, language, and schooling*. Norwood, NJ: Ablex.

Gumperz, J., & J. Cook-Gumperz. (1981). From oral to written culture: The transition to literacy. In M.F. Whiteman (Ed.), *Writing: The nature, development and teaching of written communication*: Vol. 1. Hillsdale, NJ: Erlbaum.

Heath, S. (1982). What no bedtime story means. *Language in Society, 11*, 49–77.

Henry, J. (1963). Golden rule days: American schoolrooms. In *Culture against man*. New York: Random House.

Kirshenblatt-Gimblett, B. (1979). *Speech play*. Philadelphia: University of Pennsylvania Press.

Labov, W. (1982). Competing value systems in the inner-city schools. In P. Gilmore & A. Glatthorn (Eds.), *Children in and out of school*. Washington, DC: Center for Applied Linguistics.

Mehan, H. (1979). *Learning lessons: The social organization of classroom behavior*. Cambridge, MA: Harvard University Press.

Philips, S. (1972). Participant structures and communicative competence: Warm Springs children in community and classroom. In C.B. Cazden, V. John, & D. Hymes (Eds.), *Functions of language in the classroom*. New York: Teachers College Press.

Robinson, A. (1982). Observations in the environment and lifestyles of a declared non-reader and two declared readers. In *Using literacy outside of school: An ethnographic investigation*. David M. Smith, Principal Investigator, University of Pennsylvania. Report to National Institute of Education.

Smith, D.M. (forthcoming). *Explorations in the culture of literacy*. Norwood, NJ: Ablex.

Sutton-Smith, B. (1982). Play theory of the rich and for the poor. In P. Gilmore & A. Glatthorn (Eds.), *Children in and out of school*. Washington, DC: Center for Applied Linguistics.

Vygotsky, L.S. (1978). *Mind in society*. (M. Cole, V. John-Steiner, S. Scribner, & E. Souberman, Eds.). Cambridge: Harvard University Press.

PART III

School Comes Home: What Can Parents Do?

9

Parents As Teachers:
Observations of Low-Income Parents and
Children in a Homework-like Task*

Jean Chandler
Diane Argyris
Wendy S. Barnes
Irene F. Goodman
Catherine E. Snow
Harvard Graduate School of Education

Low-income, working-class children in the United States are much more likely than middle-class children to fail to achieve adequate levels of literacy, as defined by grade-level norms. Furthermore, the differences between middle- and working-class children increase as the children continue through school, becoming especially serious at grade 4 and above when the ability to read complex material in order to acquire new information becomes crucial to school success (National Assessment of Educational Progress, 1981). A task of major importance to researchers and educators is to explain why working-class children experience such risk of failure at literacy development.

To many, the fact that there are social class differences in literacy achievement suggests that the cause is to be found in the home or in some aspect of the relationship between home and school. One claim that has been made concerning the source of some children's difficulty with literacy achievement is the discontinuity between home and school. The work of Au and Jordan (1981) and Philips (1972) on the experience of discontinuity by children of cultural minorities provides a context for such a claim. Some, like Heath (1982a, 1982b, 1983) have extended this model to poor white and black rural children. In this chapter we will present data from our study of 31 low-income families from various ethnic groups living in an urban setting in the northeastern United States in order to show that the discontinuity hypothesis does not hold for our population.

---

* This research was funded by NIE, Grant #G–80–0086. We gratefully acknowledge their support.

HOME-SCHOOL DISCONTINUITY

Ethnographic studies of the uses of literacy in low-income homes demonstrate that low-income and minority children experience a tremendous discontinuity between home and school in (a) the functions of literacy, (b) the functions of language, and (c) the nature of typical teaching/learning experiences, and suggest furthermore that these discontinuities may explain the children's failure at school.

Functions of Literacy

A number of ethnographers have pointed out that the uses to which literacy is put vary widely in different communities. Shirley Brice Heath (1983) studied three Southeastern communities: Roadville, a poor rural white community; Trackton, a poor rural black community; and Maintown, a middle-class white community. Varenne, Hamid-Buglione, McDermot and Morrison (1982), after conducting an ethnographic study of 12 families of low socioeconomic status in a borough of New York, reported extensive case studies of two families. Scollon and Scollon (1981) compared the acquisition of literacy by Athabaskan children to the acquisition of literacy by their daughter.

In the lower-class communities studied by both Heath and by Varenne et al., children experienced general and specific discontinuities. Overall, for these children, the print used at home had an immediate function. Things were rarely written for their own sake; print was utilized for specific extrinsic purposes. Most of the contexts for reading for these children were tied to the immediate tasks of everyday life; in Heath's distinction, they did not learn to read as much as they read to learn (1980).

Varenne et al. (1982) and Heath (1980) independently identified specific functions of literacy. Activities which call for literacy included (a) household activities such as directions for operating gadgets, recipes, and so on; (b) keeping up a social network, such as exchanging letters, notes, and greeting cards; (c) communications for social institutions, such as notices from school, tax returns, insurance policies; (d) marketplace shopping, which included reading and comparing labels and prices, ingredients, and so on (Varenne et al., 1982).

Reading is crucial to all of these activities, and writing to some. All these exercises of literacy, however, constituted a means to an end; they were not particularly valued in and of themselves. Thus, as Heath (1980, 1983) points out, children from Trackton and Roadville were unfamiliar with the need to focus on reading and writing as ends in and of themselves, as school tasks require them to do.

Communicative rules around reading and writing differ as well. The reading of a letter in Trackton, for instance, became a collaborative effort, involving decoding unclear words, gathering information and spontaneous storytelling inspired by the material in the letter. Given this, one could predict that the structure of traditional reading groups, with their emphasis on turntaking and on reading exactly what is printed with no embellishments, would be a puzzling and remote task to Trackton children.

The Scollons (1981) have illustrated that the rules for the use of literacy in Fort Chippewan, Alberta differ radically from those of traditional schools, due to the close connection between literacy and religion in Fort Chippewan. Children were taught to respect the text, not to reproduce it in writing, to learn through repetition and chanting, and to see reading as the task of an adult rather than a child. One could predict that children raised in this tradition would be reluctant to write, would be puzzled by demands on the part of the adult that they read, and might be uncomfortable with questions, discussions, and interpretations of the text.

Functions of Language

Researchers have found discontinuities not only in the functions of literacy but also in the functions of language. Heath (1982b), for example, found that Roadville and Maintown children were very fluent in responding to a questioning strategy which could be labeled "didactic," information-oriented questions such as those that parents and teachers often ask their children either in order to teach them new concepts or to check their understanding of old ones. Thus, Roadville children and children from Maintown were familiar with labeling questions ("What color is that?") and questions which asked them to repeat something ("And what did the little goose say?"). They were used to answering questions to which the asker already knew the answer. Didactic questioning is one of the primary questioning strategies of teachers in both traditional and open classrooms (Edwards & Furlong, 1978).

To the Trackton children, however, these questions seemed strange and silly. "Ain't nobody can talk about things being theirselves," stated one frustrated third-grader (Heath, 1982b, p. 105). Instead, Trackton children were fluent in answering questions which called less for factual information and more for metaphorical or descriptive information. Comparison questions ("What's that like?"), almost never seen in white families, were frequent among the black families. Questions were used in Trackton as story-starters ("What happened to James' car?") and as invitations to defend oneself ("What's that on your face?") but in school, questions were never used to serve these purposes. Heath (1983), Jordan (1981), Michaels (1981) and the Scollons (1981) have all identified differences between narrative structures learned at home and those expected in school. Michaels, for instance, has described the way in which children who used a topic-changing rather than a topic-centered style during sharing time were negatively evaluated by their teacher. Heath (1983) found that essays of the fifth-grade Trackton children were full of drama, dialogue, and emotion, but were low on factual information that helped to set the stage for the reader by alerting him or her to a change of scene or chronology. The Roadville fifth-graders, on the other hand, were skilled at creating literate narratives with a beginning, middle, and end, but stopped at a factual account and added little of the drama or dialogue found in Trackton stories. Thus, Trackton children were at risk of being evaluated as having little of the most elementary decontextualizing skills; Roadville children were at risk of being evaluated as unimaginative.

Learning Styles

The research of Philips (1972, 1983) and Jordan (1981) illustrates that discontinuities between the school and the home in the area of learning styles may greatly inhibit certain children's literacy achievement. Jordan and Phillips have indicated that Warm

Springs Indian children and native Hawaiian children are accustomed to learning most culturally-valued competencies among peer groups, not in a one-on-one situation with adults.

The Hawaiian children are accustomed to being responsible for their own and others' learning; thus there is much "peer tutoring" in their everyday learning. They are typically responsible for tasks which contribute in important ways to the smooth running of their households, taking the role of teacher as well as learner with their peers (Jordan, 1981).

The native American children are socialized to learn tasks on their own (Philips, 1972, 1983). They are rarely verbally instructed by parents; instead, parents may demonstrate the task, whereupon the child will practice privately and not make her new accomplishment public until she is fairly certain she can perform competently. It is clear how these children may be inhibited by the conventions of classroom learning. Public practice, performing publicly before competence is achieved, and verbal instruction both violate the norms to which these children have been socialized.

Interventions to Reduce Discontinuity

Thus we see that functions of literacy, functions of language, and learning styles are three areas in which home-school discontinuities can put a child at risk for acquiring literacy skills. The suggestion that home-school discontinuities are responsible for low literacy achievement is supported by the success of various changes implemented in the classrooms. Most of the changes are in the direction of adapting the structure and/or curriculum of the classroom to be more congruent with the home, that is, creating a better home-school match by changing school practices.

For example, using the native Hawaiian collaborative "talk story" narrative form as a basis for reading instruction has improved the Hawaiian children's success at learning how to read (Au & Jordan, 1981). Furthermore, simply informing teachers that their didactic questions may be unfamiliar to some children and suggesting that they also use some of the more open-ended question forms familiar to black children can improve the children's functioning in the classroom (Heath, 1982a). The purest form of such an intervention involves providing a teacher who is a member of the children's own culture and who thus understands, appreciates, and responds appropriately to the children's language use, narrative style, and literacy practices. Erickson (1975) made a similar suggestion concerning guidance counselors.

Another form of intervention focuses on the home as the site for change. Such early enrichment programs as the parent-training project of Levenstein (1983) work to reduce home-school discontinuities by training parents in some of the techniques that teachers typically use—didactic questions, demands for display of knowledge, demands for lexical specificity, and so on. Such programs are especially effective in improving children's school success during the primary grades (Lazar & Darlington, 1982). Although the positive effect of such early home intervention programs has traditionally been presumed to be on children's cognitive capacities, it is as likely that they operate by reducing home-school discontinuity.

All of the above suggests that when teachers understand more about the home environment and when parents' behavior is more similar to behavior encountered in the school environment, teachers can make children's home-skills relevant to school success. If they can do this, as well as teach school skills as additions to and not replacements for home skills, the children's probability of becoming literate increases significantly. As is evident, most of the descriptive focus of the ethnographic research is on what families do in their natural context, apart from school, to facilitate learning and literacy. The prescriptive focus is on how teachers can modify their own behavior and the classroom contexts they create to resemble these home contexts.

Limitations on the Discontinuity Explanation

A number of questions about and objections to the discontinuity explanation can be raised. First, most of the data is based on cross-cultural, not subcultural, differences. The convincing descriptions of discontinuity between home and school present data on groups which show very different cultural patterns from "mainstream" North Americans. Native Hawaiians, North American Indians, and native Athabaskans participate in truly different cultures from middle-class North Americans, and it is not surprising that classrooms staffed by white, middle-class teachers in schools organized by white, middle-class administrators would constitute very unfamiliar environments for such children.

It is tempting to extend the discontinuity hypothesis to explain the poor achievement of working-class, low-income children in general on the assumption that class is the primary source of the discontinuity between home and school, especially given Heath's work on poor rural children and Michaels' (1981) on the home-school discontinuity in narrative style for urban black children. We would argue, however, that such an extension is unjustified—we need to look carefully at various groups of low-income children to determine whether their home experiences are indeed significantly discontinuous with their schooling. Conversely, it would also be useful to compare the home and school experience of middle-class children. Surely, on many points these children also are required to make a considerable adjustment to school practices (e.g., conforming to rules for turn-taking and for not talking at will, respecting adult authority, sharing toys and other desired objects); yet their literacy development is not impaired.

Secondly, as Gilmore and Smith (1982) point out, one problem with home-school discontinuity as an explanation for school failure is that it may well do an injustice to the children and to the parents: First, it does not give children much credit for being able to adjust to new environments. McDermott and Gospodinoff (1981), for example, have convincingly demonstrated that what looks likes a manifestation of cultural ignorance on the part of a Puerto Rican boy appears to be, upon closer examination, an extremely skillful way of getting the entire classroom to run in a way that is functional for him. Just as the discontinuity explanation assumes a deficit of knowldge on the part of children regarding school culture, it assumes a similar ignorance on the part of the parents. It is to this point that we address the findings in this chapter: Many of the parents we observed appeared to be quite skillful at creating a school-like environment at home when it was deemed appropriate.

Analysis of the data we collected from 31 low-income families living in an urban setting suggests that the parent-child interaction over a homework-like task is very similar to dyadic interaction between a teacher and a child in school and the implicit theories of teaching and learning held by parents and by teachers are very much the same. We will present the data supporting these conclusions below, after describing the sample and data collection procedures in greater detail.

PARTICIPANTS AND PROCEDURE

The participants in this study were 32 chilren from 31 families, selected from one urban school system to meet the following criteria: (a) The children were in grades 2, 4, or 6 at the start of the study; (b) they could be classed as somewhat below-average or somewhat above-average readers, as measured by scores on standardized tests in reading. (Classification was based on school records and teacher recommendation, supplemented by individually administered reading tests); (c) they were eligible for the free-lunch program at school, based on the family's per capita income.

Approximately half the children were male and half female. The 31 families included 6 American black families, 5 black families of Caribbean origin, 3 Hispanic families, 3 Irish-American families, 2 Portuguese-American families, and 12 white families of remote or mixed ethnicity. Parents' education ranged from third grade to graduate school. Over one-third of the mothers did not graduate from high school. Of these eleven, four women had attended grade school only. Another third of the mothers had graduated from high school. The remaining third had some college or technical school training. Only the one mother with a master's degree had graduated from college.

A wide range of data was collected on the families: The children kept time allocation diaries; various family members and the children's teachers were interviewed; the children were observed at school; and their reading, writing, and language skills were tested twice at one-year intervals (see Chall, Snow, Barnes, Chandler, Goodman, Hemphill, & Jacobs, 1982, for a complete report on data collection). In this chapter, while we will draw on data from the interviews of the mothers and teachers and from our observations of home and classroom interaction, we will rely primarily on our observations of parent-child interaction during a structured, homework-like task.

We had planned to observe parent-child interaction during naturally occurring homework tasks. However, this proved to be impractical for a number of reasons: Many of the second graders were assigned little homework, some children had time to do their homework at school or during an after-school program, in many families there was no set time to do homework, and parents helped with homework only when it was too hard or too long rather than on a regular basis. We found in our pilot home observations that waiting to see parent-child interaction over homework or any other literacy-related activity was impractial and inefficient for the researchers, considering that we had 31 families to observe. We therefore decided to use the task of filling out time allocation diaries of children's activities as a focal point around which to observe parent-child interaction during a school-type task. This diary task resembles homework in that the children had to read and follow a set of directions, recall and organize factual details, write them in a prescribed format, and return the diary to us. A further advantage of the diary task was that it allowed us to observe parent-child interaction unobtrusively, since the focus of attention was on the child's activities.

The diary-observation visit always included two researchers—one to explain and one to observe. The researcher who had had previous contact with the family asked the child and whichever parent was present to participate in the task of filling out the diary. This researcher explained that we wanted a diary of the child's activities for four consecutive weekdays. Each day's diary consisted of spaces in which to write what the child had done, where he or she was, and who he or she was with, as well as a checklist on which any activity engaged in during the day had to be checked off (see Figure 1 for diary form). This researcher asked the parent and child to fill in the diary together right then and there for the previous day's activities "so it would be clear how to do it." It was left

Figure 1.

Name_____ Day_____

Please write down everything you did from the time you got up until you went to bed. Put 'woke up' next to the time you woke up, and start from there. Try to fill it in before you go to bed, so you don't forget all the things you did. Please mail these to us when you have finished all four days.

Morning	What were you doing?	Where were you?	Who were you with? (mother, father, brother, sister, friend, adult friend, relative, by yourself)
6:00			
6:30			
7:00			
7:30			
8:00			
8:30			
9:00			
9:30			
10:00			
10:30			
11:00			
11:30			
12:00			
12:30			
1.00			

up to the parent and child who should do the actual writing. During this whole time, the second researcher—who had not previously met the families and knew nothing about them—served as observer. The observer took notes in the form of a running narrative of the entire interaction over the task, including as much verbatim transcription of parent and child speech as possible.

When the observer had completed narratives for all the families, she developed headings for organizing the notes in order to facilitate comparison between families and to do other data analyses. These headings were:

1. Activities in progress when we arrived
2. The setting
3. The role of participants
4. Participants' manner toward the task and toward each other
5. Other simultaneous activities
6. Questions
7. Off-task remarks
8. Problems with the task and their resolution
9. Other interaction over the task
10. Participants remarks about the task
11. Participants' remarks about other participants
12. Language other than English.

Because of scheduling problems and attrition, observation of the diary interaction could be carried out in only 26 families. Thus, though we present data from interviews with the parents and teachers of all the children, the number on whom direct observational data are available is somewhat smaller.

SETTING AND ROLE OF PARTICIPANTS

Virtually every family was receptive and friendly to us upon our arrival and during the diary task. We were typically treated as familiar guests, offered refreshments and chatted with, but most family members went on with their own activities after greeting us. We observed a variety of activities on our arrival, for example, eating dinner, watching television, playing with an Atari, mother returning from jogging. Television was a constant presence in many of the families. In five families it was left on during our visits but appeared to be a continuing distraction to the child in only one (even when the mother turned down the sound but left on the picture). Another child, a second grader, jumped up in the middle of filling out the diary to turn on the TV in another room. In all the other families either the TV was not on or else the mother turned off the set when we arrived, in preparation for the task at hand.

Siblings of 11 of the children were present during the task, but they were not necessarily a distraction. Although in four cases the children's friends were asked to leave until the task was completed, no siblings were sent out of the room. Younger siblings invariably wanted to get involved in the task and we usually offered them a piece of paper to write or draw on. In some instances, though, the sibling played more of a role in the task. For example, a younger sister of one of the children reminded her that they had made up songs during the day. In another family, the younger daughter helped her sister remember events while their mother took care of the baby. At one point, the two girls argued briefly about what time something had occurred during the day and appealed to their mother for a solution.

In 23 families, the mother was present with the child during the task; in two families, fathers helped the child; in one family both mother and father were present. From our interviews with parents, we know that for the two families in which the fathers helped during the diary task, the father helped with homework regularly as well. In another family, the mother gave responsibility to the interviewer to help the child with the diary; she did not usually help the child with homework either. The only fourth-grader whose mother wrote the diary for him must have done some of his homework for him too since she commented in the interview "I like his workbooks; I think they're fun to do." We felt that what we saw, in terms of who helped the child, how much and in what tone help was given, was representative of homework help in general in these families. The two families in which parent-child interaction during the task was negative and nonproductive, in our view, were marked by similarly negative interactions during our other visits to the household.

Also, what parents said in interviews about helping their children was consonant with what we saw them doing in interaction over this task. One mother said, "I work with the kids during the summer so they don't forget stuff" and another commented, "I go over new things with her once before she does her homework." One mother told us, "She asks for help with words sometimes. Just last week they found a decomposed body in the project, and she asked me what 'decomposed' meant." Another explained how she helped her child with homework:

> When she reads ancient history, she doesn't know the words and it puts her head into a whirlwind. So I make her read each sentence aloud to help keep track of things. Then I ask her to say what it meant in her own words.

NATURE OF THE PARENT-CHILD INTERACTION

There were many parallels between the dyadic interactions over homework-like tasks we observed at home and those which we saw in classrooms. Like dyadic interactions between a teacher (usually female) and an elementary school student in the context of a normal classroom with other students present, the interaction we observed in the homes was primarily between one parent (usually the mother) and one child, but with other family members present and involving themselves in various ways. This kind of adult-child dyadic interaction is only one kind of interaction which influences children's development of literacy and probably not the most frequent type either in the classrooms or the homes in our study. The norm in many classrooms is a teacher with a small or large group of students or children working independently. The norm in our families—all but two of which had more than one child—was for older children, as well as parents, to help younger children with homework, as we discovered from our interview data. Still, a parent helping a child, like a teacher working with one student, was common in our sample (according to interviews with parents) and can be, as our observational data demonstrate, an important source of literacy learning.

The interactions we saw between parents and children, like the exchanges we saw between teachers and students, were varied in tone and in the degree to which they were helpful in completing the task and in acquiring literacy skills. We saw a few instances of parent-child and teacher-student interaction during which the emotional tone was negative and little school-related learning seemed to be going on, but most of the parents and the teachers helped the children pleasantly and skillfully.

Like teachers, different parents had differing expectations of children who were the same age. One parent of a second-grade boy who was getting restless during the diary task asked us, "How long can you keep kids interested in this?" Another parent of a restless second-grade boy said to him confidently, "I told you it was gonna take an hour and I know you can do it." One sixth-grader's mother leaned across the table during the entire task giving her orders about what to write and where. The child wrote as quickly as possible, with the mother admonishing her to "write nice." In contrast, another sixth-grader wrote the diary alone while her mother answered the phone, talked to her son, helped her husband, and chatted with the interviewer.

Two parents didn't try to help their children fill out the diary because they felt that they themselves could not read or write English well enough. But four of the six parents who did not help clearly felt they did not need to; their fourth- and sixth-graders could do the task themselves.[1] In contrast to parents who gave no help at all, four parents actually wrote the diary for their children. Most of these parents presumably did so to spare their second-graders the frustration of having to write so much.

From the behavior of the remaining 16 parents we inferred theories of education which are quite similar to those of the teachers we observed. Parents seemed to help their children in three primary ways: (a) structuring the physical environment (including preparing the child physically) and the task itself; (b) motivating the child to do the task; and (c) helping the child with form and content. Many helped their children in all three ways, others in only one or two. The ways in which the parents helped the children are an indication of their implicit theories of education as well as of their child's needs.

The first way parents assisted was by structuring the environment and getting the child ready for the task. In order to do this, parents sometimes turned on lights, turned off radios and televisions, turned away visitors and phone callers, found seats and writing surfaces, and got pens or pencils. One mother told her older daughter to do the dishes and two cousins to go and play so that the focal child could concentrate on the task. Some also made sure that they themselves had their glasses on and that the child was warmly clothed, fed, and had clean hands. One mother asked the interviewer if her daughter could write in pencil since it would be "cleaner" in case she made a mistake; several others helped erase mistakes. Many parents pointed out where the child should

---

[1] The amount, rather than the nature, of the help parents gave their children was the main difference between our above- and below-average readers' interaction over the task.

write and made sure all the boxes were filled in. The mother of a girl who was having extra difficulty remembering what she had done on Friday asked if Thursday would be easier. In some cases, parents, mostly of older children, left it up to the child to "get ready" for the task.

A second theory of education embraced by parents as well as teachers was that children need to be motivated in order to complete the task. Parents tried in various ways to motivate their children. Some parents patted the child or rubbed his back during the task. Several parents expressed confidence that the child could do the task or expressed approval of the way that various parts had been done. When the child hesitated, a typical mother said, "That's right." Parents' reassurance and emotional support of their children often seemed important to task-orientation and completion. When one second-grader complained, looking at his mother, "I'll mess up on the d's and b's," she responded, "That's okay." Another mother reassured her child, "Don't worry, I'll help you." Several parents demonstrated pride in their children during the task. "He's so precise, this guy," "Spelling's his best subject," and "She does have good handrwriting, considering" were remarks made by three parents. The expressions of approval were not limited to the children's behavior during the diary task. One mother showed us a gift her daughter had made for her; another smiled proudly when a younger child showed us his brother's drawing.

Only in a few instances were motivating comments in a negative vein. One mother threatened to hit her sixth grader if she didn't "write nice"; another actually did slap her second-grade daughter when she started to walk out after continuous conflicts over the task. Aside from these two families in which the interaction was consistently negative, all the families we observed showed relatively little hostility toward one another during the diary task. Several parents made occasional deprecating comments about their children, such as "She plays dummy, the dunce" or "I don't like your attitude, kid." However, these were often said in a joking manner and seemed directed at motivating a change in the child's behavior rather than undermining the child's underlying capabilities.

A third way in which parents demonstrated their own theories of education was by helping with both form—especially spelling—and content of the diaries. Correct spelling evoked much parent help, correction, and comment. Many parents just spelled out words, some with explanations; for example: "road, r-o-a-d, not as in animal, r-o-a-d." Others also tried to help their children with spelling by suggesting strategies or supplying rules, such as "Sound it out" or "It rhymes with mouse" or "Double the p" or "Drop the e before adding ing," or "$Supper$ is like $Superman$ but with two p's." One parent told her child to look up how to spell a word in the dictionary so she would remember and not "embarrass" herself. Two mothers had to ask one of the researchers for help with spelling words like $supper$ and $dining$. A few parents accepted their children's invented spellings; one referred to his child's "creative spelling" and another said, "Okay, do it your own way."

Clearly, both parents and children believed that spelling was very important. One mother said, "I always thought good spelling came with the genes. I won all the spelling bees. My kids read, but they can't spell." Another berated her child, "Your spelling is getting worse; what's the matter with you? It's supposed to be getting better." Another said simply, "I don't believe this" when seeing how her child spelled a word. One mother offered excuses for her child's spelling by saying, "Summer's here and he forgot everything." Some children also made comments about their spelling. One fourth-grader said, "I'm smart in everything but spelling . . . I wish I could spell." A sixth-grader commented, "I forgot how to spell even easy words in the summer."

Handwriting was also important to some children and parents. An older child said, "I have to practice my handwriting; it's so gross." Several younger children commented on the difficulty they were having forming individual letters, one saying he had forgotten how to make *g's* and another saying, "I get my *b's* and *d's* mixed up." A mother commented to her fourth-grader, "You're getting sloppy."

The accuracy of the content of the diaries was of utmost importance to most parents and children. It was the reason for most of the suggestions, corrections, and discussions between parents and children. To elicit accurate content, parents often prompted the children with questions:

Mother:	When did you have supper?
Child:	5:15.
Mother:	Wait a minute. Write on this line, 'Ate supper or had supper.' When did you start your homework?
Child:	About 6.
Mother:	When did you finish?
Child:	Around 6:30. What do I write?
Mother:	'Finish homework.' What happened at 6:45?
Child:	Nothing.
Mother:	Nothing at all?
Child:	I was listening to the radio.
Mother:	Okay, then write 'listening to the radio'. Did you go out to play?
Child:	Yes.
Mother:	What time?
Child:	Around 3:15.
Mother:	You didn't write that down.

Other examples of "tutorial questions" in our field notes were:

Father:	Did you talk on the telephone yesterday?
Child:	No.
Father:	No? How many times did you call me to bring your clothes? Not once, three times.

and

Mother:	What time did you wake up?
	(Child wrote.)
Mother:	Who were you with?
	(Child wrote.)
Mother:	Who was in the room while you got dressed? Who else was in the room?

Some of these questions were to spur the child's memory since the parent didn't know the answer, but some were clearly didactic questions. In our observations, these tutorial questions were frequently used in both home and school and thus did not represent a source of discontinuity between home and school for these children as they did for the Trackton children Heath studied.

In the course of filling out the diaries with their children, several parents acceded to their children's versions when there were disagreements over what had really happened when, or with whom. Some of these instances happened when the child apparently convinced the parent that he or she was right; for example:

> Mother: You got up at 9.
> Child: First I got up at 7.
> Mother   (smiling): I'll mind my own business.

In other cases, the parent admitted he or she did not really know what the child had done, having not been there. An example of a typical comment by a mother to her child was, "You know better than I do; I was at work." For whatever reason, in both situations power was given to the child in doing the task. Even when the parent actually filled in the diary for the child, the parent always asked the child some questions about his or her activities and wrote what the child answered. The one fourth-grader (a below-average reader) whose mother wrote the diary for him corrected her account of his activities, saying that he had gone to the library before returning home.

CONTINUITIES BETWEEN HOME AND SCHOOL

Observational Data: What Parents and Children Did

Many of the specific behaviors, as well as the ideas that motivate these behaviors, exhibited by the low-income parents in interaction with their children were very similar to the behaviors and ideas of the children's teachers (see below). Like teachers, the parents were simultaneously teaching ways of structuring the environment and preparing oneself to do the task. They were displaying attitudes toward literacy tasks and toward their children which could transfer, usually positively, to other school-related situations. In several instances, parents instructed their children in ways which improved their children's literacy skills and were furthermore similar to the teaching strategies used by good teachers in classrooms, such as modeling problem-solving strategies.

There were many opportunities for school-like teaching and learning during the diary task. Several children, when reading the checklist, asked their parents what "scores," "errands," and "relatives" were, and some parents checked to see that their children knew the meaning of words. In the course of the task, some parents also introduced their children to the use of ditto marks, abbreviations, arrows, and carats. For example, one mother said, "You were outside playing ball. . . . Now put ditto marks because you didn't come in till 6." Helping with abbreviations, one mother suggested, "You can use 'sq.' for 'square' "; another mother asked her child what "MDC" stood for when the daughter wrote "went to MDC swimming pool."

In addition to vocabulary development, several parents aided their children in decontextualization, a skill Scollon and Scollon (1979, p. 14) emphasize as important for "essayist" literacy. For example, one mother said, "If you put 'Mrs. F,' they ain't gonna know who you're talking about." Another suggested, "Put 'brother' instead of 'Jimmy' because they won't know he's your brother."

Doing the diary task stimulated another child to relate his concrete activity to a larger and more general category: When filling out the checklist, he asked his mother, "Is going to the store an errand?. . . . If I watch a basketball game, is that sports?" One mother suggested to her second-grader who was laboriously writing "brushed teeth, washed face, put on pants" and so on, that he write simply "got ready for breakfast." Another mother said to her fourth-grade child, "It's all right to write it short like that—'in house, eating.'"

The following is one example of several instances of a parent helping her child reason:

> Mother: What time did you come back?
> Child: 4:30.
> Mother: How could you have been watching TV?
> Child: I watched the Pink Panther.
> Mother: When does that come on?
> Child: 4:30.
> Mother: So you probably came back about 4:15.

Parental attempts at organizing the task and using it for teaching were very similar to teachers' behavior in classrooms. Teachers too organize the physical environment, see that the child gets ready to do the task, and structure the task itself. Teachers try to motivate children to work by reassuring them, by expressing confidence or pride in them or approval of their work, and by conveying expectations and attitudes valuing literacy. Some also correct, reprimand, or even threaten. One teacher in our study said that she didn't feel she had taught anything if she hadn't screamed at the children. Many teachers spend a lot of time showing children how to do a particular task neatly and accurately; they emphasize correct spelling and form, as did the parents. They, like many of the parents in our study, often use tutorial questions to elicit the right answer. At the same time, however, they teach vocabulary and higher thinking skills, such as generalization, decontextualization, and logical reasoning, useful in literate activities. Thus the lower-income parents in our study were similar to the teachers in the ways they fostered the acquisition and development of literacy in the children. From the ways parents and teachers worked with children, we could infer their theories about education and we found them to be strikingly similar.

Interview Data: What Parents and Teachers Said

Parents' implicit views about education were apparent from their behavior during the homework-like task. However, we also collected data on parents' explicit beliefs about education from interviews. Comparing results from the parental interviews with those from teachers' interviews, we again found parents' and teachers' theories to be highly convergent. Parents were asked what they felt should be the most important goal for schools. One third thought it should be basic skills, and one third of fathers and one quarters of mothers felt it should be reading. Only a handful said that discipline or social contacts were most important.

When parents were asked what a good teacher was, far and away the most frequent response was "someone who is caring and conscientious, who gives extra time to her work." The second most frequent response was "one who treats children as individuals, who helps them out with problems." One mother put it in these words, "A good teacher is one who takes her time with each kid . . . [who doesn't] just throw the paper on the desk and say 'do it' . . . [who explains] stuff so the child can do it right." "A patient and understanding person" was also mentioned by several parents. Other responses included, "someone who helps the children make the honor roll" and who has a "soft voice," who is "not grouchy."

Regarding their idea of a "good student," the most frequent responses by parents had to do with effort and attendance; good conduct and attentiveness were also mentioned frequently, as were good grades. Learning new things, being smart and curious were not frequent responses for mothers.

We found teachers' attitudes to be similar to those of the parents in our study. In interviews, teachers were asked to describe individual children in their classes. Their conceptions of what makes a good student can be deduced from their responses. Themes of task orientation dominate the teachers' descriptions of the children. Teachers, like the mothers in our study, were overwhelmingly oriented toward behavioral characteristics in their descriptions of a good student. When teachers were asked what individual focal children were like in whole-group lessons, virtually none of their responses had to do with the content of the children's contributions or the level of the children's understanding. Instead, teachers gave descriptions like "disruptive," "daydreams," "quiet," "distractable," or "attentive."

Teachers' responses to questions about children's independent work similarly centered on behavior and task orientation. During independent work, teachers described the children as "needs prodding," "conscientious," "tries," "slow," "talks to friends," "sometimes does it, sometimes doesn't," or "works to get it done." Only two children's teachers mentioned their ability rather than their effort, citing "well-organized" and "poor penmanship" in describing their independent work.

When asked to describe focal children's reading problems, teachers mentioned "not very involved," "has trouble getting work done," "lacks self-confidence," and "careless, rushes." Mention of these motivational problems reflects the teachers' view that reading is getting assignments done. The most frequently cited problems with reading were "rushes to finish assignments" and "not very involved."

DISCUSSION

For the population of urban, ethnically diverse, low-income children we studied, failure in literacy acquisition does not seem to be accounted for by extreme discontinuity between home and school. The below-average as well as the above-average readers in our sample (see p. 176 above) came from homes where both the theories about learning and teaching school skills and the nature of interaction over school-like tasks were strikingly similar to what they experienced at school.[2]

It is not surprising that "discontinuity" does not characterize the home-school relationship for this population. Although low-income and working-class, the families in our sample were in no sense isolated from mainstream North American culture; in fact, they were very much a part of it. Many of them had very high educational and occupational aspirations for their children (see Chall et al., 1982), and few were very strongly identified with their ethnic or religious subgroups.

Furthermore, the schools which the children attended were quite firmly integrated into their neighborhood structures; they were not strange or distant institutions. Many of the parents in the sample had attended the same schools and knew the teachers and administrators personally. Many of the teachers grew up in the same neighborhoods where the children were now living and some had not moved out. The schools, like the neighborhoods and the teaching staff, have long been racially and ethnically heterogeneous. The kind of discontinuity that occurs when a child from a homogeneous and culturally distinct community goes to a school that is not community-based could not have been expected for our population.

CONCLUSION

From our work with children from this urban, ethnically heterogeneous, low-income population, we would emphasize the degree of continuity which many children, even those who are at risk for school failure, experience when moving from home to school or when bringing schoolwork home. We conclude that home-school discontinuity cannot explain the problems these children have in acquiring literacy.

Like McDermott and his colleagues (1984), we observed that interactions between parents and children around school-like tasks can be counterproductive to literacy acquistion, just as teacher-student interaction can be. However, we found that most of the low-income parents we observed could maintain a fairly positive emotional atmosphere during a homework-like task and many were able to provide their children with skilled teaching and task management. That is not to say that all of the children had learned high levels of literacy skills, nor that all had benefited equally from the family interaction; half the children in our sample were reading below grade level, and there was a wide range of reading achievement among the siblings in many of the sample families (see Barnes, 1984).

These conclusions leave us with the question of why low-income children experience greater risk of failure at learning to read. No doubt discontinuity between home and school and dysfunctional communication over learning tasks provide part of the answer for some of the children, but other sources of success and of failure must be sought in low-income children's home and school experiences.

---

[2] For an analysis of the relationship between parent-child interaction around this task and parents' education level, see Chandler (1982).

REFERENCES

Au, K., & Jordan, C. (1981). Teaching reading to Hawaiian children: Finding a culturally appropriate solution. In H. Treuba, G. Guthrie, & K. Au (Eds.), *Culture and the bilingual classroom: Studies in classroom ethnography*. Rawley, MA: Newbury House.

Barnes, W.S. (1984). *Sibling influences within family and school contexts*. Unpublished doctoral dissertation, Harvard University.

Chall, J., Snow, C., Barnes, W., Chandler, J., Goodman, I., Hemphill, L., & Jacobs, V. (1982). *Families and literacy: The contribution of out-of-school experiences to children's acquisition of literacy*. (Grant No. G-80-0086.) Washington, DC: National Institute of Education.

Chandler, J. (1982). The relationship between parents' educational level and parent-child interaction around a homework-like task. Unpublished manuscript.

Edwards, A.D., & Furlong, V.J. (1978). *The Language of teaching: Meaning in classroom interaction*. London: Heinemann.

Erickson, F. (1975). Gatekeeping and the melting pot: Interaction in counseling encounters. *Harvard Educational Review, 45*, 44-70.

Gilmore, P., & Smith, D.M. (1982). A retrospective discussion of the state of the art in ethnography in education. In P. Gilmore & A. Glatthorn (Eds.), *Children in and out of school*. Washington, DC: Center for Applied Linguistics.

Heath, S.B. (1980). The functions and uses of literacy. *Journal of Communication, 30*, 123-133.

Heath, S.B. (1982a). What no bedtime story means: Narrative skills at home and school. *Language in Society, 11*, 49-76.

Heath, S.B. (1982b). Questioning at home and at school: A comparative tudy. In G. Spindler (Ed.), *Doing ethnography of schooling: Educational anthropology in action*. New York: Holt, Rinehart and Winston.

Heath, S.B. (1983). *Ways with words: Language, life and work in communities and classrooms*. New York: Cambridge University Press.

Jordan, C. (1981). The selection of culturally compatible classroom practices. *Educational Perspectives, 20*, 16-19.

Lazar, I., & Darlington, R. (1982). Lasting effects of early education: A report from the consortium for longitudinal studies. *Monograph of the Society for Research in Child Development. 47* (2-3, Serial No. 195).

Levenstein, P. (1983). Implications of the transition period for early education. In R.M. Golinkoff (Ed.), *The transition from prelinguistic to linguistic communication*. Hillsdale, NJ: Erlbaum.

McDermott, R.P., Goldman, S., & Varenne, H. (1984). When school goes home: Some problems in the organization of homework. *Teacher's College Record, 85*, 381-409.

McDermott, R.P., & Gospodinoff, H. (1981). Social contexts for ethnic borders and school failure. In H. Treuba, G. Guthrie, & K. Au (Eds.), *Culture and the bilingual classroom: Studies in classroom ethnography*. Rawley, MA: Newbury House.

Michaels, S. (1981). Children's narrative styles and differential access to literacy. *Language in Society, 10*, 423-443.

National Assessment of Educational Progress. (1981). *Reading, thinking, writing: A report on the 1979-80 assessment*. Denver: NAEP.

Philips, S. (1972). Participation structures and communicative competence: Warm Springs children in community and classroom. In C.B. Cazden, V.P. John, & D. Hymes (Eds.), *Functions of language in the classroom*. New York: Teachers College Press.

Philips, S. (1983). *The invisible culture: Communication in classroom and community on the Warm Springs Indian reservation*. New York: Longman.

Scollon, R., & Scollon, S. (1979). *Linguistic convergence: An ethnography of speaking at Fort Chipewyan, Alberta*. New York: Academic Press.

Scollon, R., & Scollon S. (1981). *Narrative, literacy and face in interethnic communication*. Norwood, NJ: Ablex.

Varenne, H., Hamid-Buglione, V., McDermott, R.P., & Morrison, A. (1982). *I teach him everything he learned in school: The acquisition of literacy for learning and working in families* (Contract No. 400-79-0046). Washington, D C: National Institute of Education.

10

"Why" Sheila Can Read:
Structure and Indeterminacy in the
Reproduction of Familial Literacy*

Hervé Varenne
R. P. McDermott
Teachers College, Columbia University

If Nancy Hanks
    Came back as a ghost
    Seeking news
    Of what she loved most,
    She'd ask first
    "Where's my son?
    What's happened to Abe?
    What's he done?"

    "You wouldn't know
    About my son?
    Did he grow tall?
    Did he have fun?
    Did he learn to read?
    Did he get to town?
    Do you know his name?
    Did he get on?"

    Rosemary Benet (1962: 65)

The poem we use as an epigram says it all. Here is a mother worrying that her son will not learn to read, will not get on. We know that Nancy Hanks' son, Abraham Lincoln, did learn to read, got to town. He got on and we know his name. We instinc-

---

*This paper is based on research conducted as part of a contract project for the National Institute of Education (#R–400–79–0046). Complementary funding was provided by the Elbenwood Center for the Study of the Family as Educator at Teachers College, Columbia University. We acknowledge the contributions these institutions have made to our work. We also want to thank the persons who participated in the project, particularly the field workers (Vera Hamid-Buglione and Ann Morison) and Professor Hope Leichter.

tively agree that if he had not learned to read he would not have gotten on and we would not know his name. We recognize the proper anxiety of the mother.

The motherly (and fatherly) anxieties and the assumption of a linkage between reading and adult success are still with us. They are crucial elements in the cultural scripts that help us converse about careers in our societies. The vocabulary may have changed from what it was 100 years ago, but the concern is the same. We still fear that our children may not learn to read. Interestingly, Nancy Hanks is not made to ask "Did he go to school?" She asks "Did he learn to read?" It is well known that Lincoln did not attend the great schools and universities of his time. He gained his education on his own. And, in the great tradition of American self-sufficiency and personal agency, this seems particularly appropriate. We know that Lincoln's personal biography is exceptional and totally atypical. But we also want to say that he really did it on his own because of some powerful inner quality that made him struggle against the odds, and eventually, win. Nancy Hanks does not ask: "Were the political conditions in the United States such that he could get on?" She does not ask: "What happened to his friends? What were the conditions that made it happen that we do not know their names?"

The questions that Nancy Hanks does not ask are questions that most of us, as parents in America, do not often ask. They are questions that those who have been given the political duty of transforming a parental worry into a scientific search unfortunately do not ask often either. If "Johnny can't read," it is probably for the same kind of reason that allowed Abe to learn to read; there is something in him that prevents him from running as fast as the others. Thus most research in education has focused on individual differences, many of them considered inherent to the person. In some cases, researchers, like parents, suspect that something that happened to the child may have helped or hindered a successful school career. It might be some characteristics of the family, perhaps its income, or the educational level of the parents, or their drive. It might be some early experience that the child had had, a matter of sex, birth order, constitution of the family (is the father present?), and so on. In any event, it is assumed that these experiences are "acquired." They become the property of the child and make him a particular kind of person who then becomes the agent of his performance in school. Rarely, if ever, does an inquiry into what makes some children learn to read and others not force a look at the structure of the social system in which the children live. It is as if the proper anxiety that parents in America have about children and learning to read could only be dealt with as a question about a child—by asking "Why can't Johnny read?"

In this paper, we argue that a focus on why individual children in our study[1] "can" (Sheila) or "cannot" (Joe) read keeps educators from asking the most crucial question about the conditions of the practice of literacy in and out of school. In particular, such a focus prevents educators from wondering about the forces that make everyone ask why a

---

[1] The fuller report on this study is available (Varenne, Hamid-Buglione, McDermott, & Morison, 1982). Ann Morison's dissertation (1982) offers a solid account of fieldwork in Joe Kinney's family. Two other papers are also based on the study (Leichter, 1984; McDermott, Goldman, & Varenne, 1984).

child can or cannot read. Why do these questions about "can' or "cannot' make so much sense? They certainly do not make sense because of anything the child does. They make sense because of something "we"—as participants in the American institutional framework—do as we jointly create the institutional framework within which we must then act. Children do not learn in a vacuum, but an interest in "learning environments" should not simply lead to search for antecedents to a child's performance. Such an interest must also lead to search for what happens after the child has acted. It must lead to an investigation of the institutional consequences of different kinds of performances. It must also lead us to an investigation of the symbols that allow us to communicate about success and failure. In brief, we want to ask new questions and point to the kinds of answers made possible when the concern about our children is examined as a cultural and institutional fact.

We placed quote marks around "why" in the title to this paper to make visible its rhetorical power. In educational research, such "why's" are transparent. They have the property of focusing the inquiry away from the questioner onto the child. Simply to ask "why Sheila can read" does not force us to wonder what difference it makes that *she* can read (while Joe cannot), or how it became enough of a cultural focus that someone officially decided that she *can* read (while Joe can *not*). If we simply focused on Sheila's institutionalized, that is to say, measured reading skills, we could easily miss the difference between "knowing how to read" as an everyday life event embedded in other familial activities and "knowing how to read" as a school event. We could also easily miss the fact that families themselves are in the business of enforcing this "school" distinction. Even when the school is not particularly good to them, we want to argue, families *make* The School.[2] To focus on Sheila (or Joe) obscures the social forces that organize her reading into an institutional concern and a symbolically recognizable fact.

Above all, simply to ask "why Sheila can read" makes us lose sight of the fact that, from a systemic point of view, Sheila is not the issue even when we are interested in her fate. The issue is the culture that determines the framework within which, and the tools with which, she will make her fate. It is not irrelevant to Sheila that she lives in a culture that uses school failure to affirm individualism by differentiating persons through presumed substances that are given to them, for example, talent, intelligence, drive. From a cultural point of view, equality is the negative side of inequality; it is noninequality. American democracy must generate inequality so that it can display its

---

[2] By "The School' we mean a cultural system of political consequences, that is, a set of historically derived, comparatively arbitrary, interactionally constraining, discourse conventions used to deal with experience. These conventions can take the forms of traditional sayings, typical conversations, more or less ritualized performances, legitimately constructed consequences, and so on. When talking about "The School' we do not mean any particular school except in so far as all schools, and all families, must organize their daily life in terms of The School (and The Family).

own struggle against it.[3] These, we want to emphasize, are not "macro-" concerns that could be safely ignored when looking at the details of the everyday life of a child and her family. The work the two of us have been doing on reading lessons, and cooking clubs,[4] small towns and suburban high schools[5] have been attempts to demonstrate that institutional and cultural constraints are intimately lived. The reflexive constitution of inequality is essentially invisible to participants precisely because it is performed by all the people in the details of their everyday life, whether they struggle to "get ahead" or protest against the need to do so.

It is only with a cultural approach that we can understand how people live and learn their way through everyday life. The people in our study, like us, worry that their children will not succeed. Like us, they celebrate when their children succeed. They struggle to make such celebrations possible. Like us, they worry whether Sheila, five years from now, will not simply know how to read, but will know how to program a computer. They do not simply "value" education; they work at it and they criticize those who appear not to work at the education of their children. It is not enough to say that they "view" education in the same manner as "the school" views it. It is necessary to notice that, everyday, they pay for it, work at it, worry about it, and cherish what it might deliver. These acts are the behavioral consequences of the cultural structure.

Even as their biographies unfold before them, people's lives are "uncertain." They cannot rely on their past to determine their future. They must constantly build this future. But they cannot build *any* future. To understand the limits on their possible futures is to understand the "structure" of their lives. For Sheila and Joe, this means that, without work, they cannot be whatever they will be. It also means that the uncertainty is not radical; it is structured by the two relevant possibilities: success and failure.

At the heart of this paper are the practical acts performed to separate children into individuals with differential attributions of success and failure. We are particularly interested in the processes which prevent educators and researchers in education from articulating their role in the sorting of children as successful or not in such a way that it

---

[3] The underlying argument in this paragraph is a development of Dumont's argument about the specificity of American racism (1980). For Dumont, the peculiar character of the justification for racism ("Blacks are not fully human" or, in "modern" terms, "intelligence is a genetic matter") is dependent on the political implications of individualism and democracy: if "all men are created equal" and have "certain inalienable rights," then one must justify the alienation of rights on the grounds that the targeted group is not quite human. The best of America is structurally homologous to the worst. Our further argument is that democratic individualism must also generate a special kind of inequality in order to deal with differentiation: since class distinctions cannot be a matter of birth or religion, then it must be based on individual differences.

[4] McDermott and Gospodinoff (1979); Hood, McDermott, and Cole (1980).

[5] Varenne (1977, 1978, 1982, 1983).

can have political consequences. To address these issues we report on an ethnographic study of two children as they, their families, and communities weave literacy into their daily life. The next part of the paper introduces Sheila, Joe, and their parents. In order to make our argument about the relationship between structure and indeterminacy in the practice and reproduction of familial literacy, we focus on three kinds of literacy we found in Sheila and Joe's houses. First, we look at "familial" literacy, that is, literacy that is used in passing through the daily round of life at home. This is the literacy that does not reveal itself as a topic for evaluation. Second, we look at the symbolic power of "special" kinds of literacies in the families' lives. These are literacies that are highly marked symbolically—though again not as a topic of evaluation. As we show, the special language of medicine has a power over the lives of the people that is quite different from the power of their own language. While related to the language of the school, the language of medicine does not raise issues of school evaluation.

This brief look at various types of nonschool literacies leads us to a more detailed look at a third type, the type that we understand as controlled by The School, namely, homework. We examine this home-school interface initially in terms of what the families do not control, specifically, the cultural forms that make an activity "homework" rather than, say, "curing-an-ailing-child." We suggest how the family members involved in the homework hold each other accountable for maintaining the School frame. Then, we look at variations in the doing of homework to suggest how families can "differ" in what they control while still being controled by the school structure. We close the paper with some comments on the "coherence" of failure.

SHEILA AND JOE

In the shadow of cosmopolitan Manhattan, "Kingsland" is one of those areas of New York City that preserves the provincial atmosphere of a small town; narrow streets, low clapboard houses, and neighbors a parent can rely on to keep track of the little ones. It is a working class, white, ethnic enclave that is best understood in terms of its borders.[6] The area is small, and racially different people dwarf the neighborhood into defensiveness. Natives think of it as a great place to have lived, but each generation yearns to move on. The road to success and the road out are parallel and education is essential to both. Those who have made it have taken their degrees, moved to the suburbs, and return on holidays to visit the older generation.

Both Sheila Farrell (age 10 in 1981) and Joe Kinney (age 9) live in Kingsland. Both their families think of themselves as "Irish" and draw on Irish ancestors to make their case. This does not prevent them for dating and marrying "outside" their group. The Farrells and the Kinneys are inserted into their neighborhood in quite different ways. Mr. Farrell is a truck driver. Mrs. Farrell held various jobs until the birth of her second child. Now she stays at home, near the center of a large group of close kin: her parents

---

[6] See Susser (1982), Suttles (1972).

and six siblings who live in three nearby houses. At another extreme is Mrs. Kinney who is the only one of her siblings to have stayed on the block of their youth. She has been separated from Joe's father, a salesman, for two years. She must spend most of her day outside the neighborhood, as a clerk in a government bureaucracy. Her family circle is expanded only to her mother who takes care of the children from the time they get out of school to the time when she comes back from her work. At that point she is by herself with Joe and his sister.

Sheila and Joe do not know each other though they live only a few blocks from each other and go to the same Catholic school (in different grades). Neither of them is highly remarkable among the students of this school. They were chosen initially because their parents told us that Sheila was "doing well" while Joe was "not doing too well." We must emphasize that the contrast lies in the parents' evaluation. It is interesting as evidence that the parents are in the business of evaluation.[7] As a matter of fact, it soon became clear that the formal contrast (as "objective measures" could determine it) was not great. Initially, it is perhaps easier to characterize both children as "typical" preteenagers from a working class, American-ethnic neighborhood. This erases a lot of the differences that do exist between them and their parents. Even if they are not exceptional, Sheila and Joe are unique in the details of their lives. They are still interesting to us as tokens of a type.

FAMILIAL LITERACY

Both the Farrells and the Kinneys are literate in the broad sense that their literacy is not a practical problem in either family. They can read what they need to read to conduct the life to which they have been accustomed. This does not mean that all the members of each family have the same "amount" of literacy. There is much variation between individual members in formal level and actual use of education. Some people never read much more than the sports page of the newspaper. Others have gone to college. Some will prefer to have recipes explained to them by someone who has already made the dish rather than read it. Others will keep up extensive bulletin boards of familial events. Both families expect the children to possess an unspecified but rather well-bounded level of familial literacy. When Sheila is asked to turn the coffee machine on "PERK," she is fully expected to be able to read the switches and, of course, she can. Similarly, whatever the opinion Mrs. Kinney may have of her son's success in school, she too relies on Joe's literacy for the performance of a large number of familial tasks that require

---

[7] Of course, it is not simply that parents are in the business of evaluation. It is that we, as researchers into educational processes from a "teachers" college funded by a "national " institute of "education," set the parents to evaluate their children. The "criteria" for selection of the families, as these were set for us by our own context (the funding agency and a tradition of scholarship), were that some of the families to be studied had a child "doing well" and some others a child "not doing well." Initially we had to inquire of parents whether they had such children. It remains that the parents had no difficulty entering into a conversation about the relative merit of their children in school terms.

specific, though perhaps limited, acts of reading. Both Sheila and Joe possess all the literacy they need to participate in their families' life within the social structure of their community. Indeed, it seemed to us that they already had the literacy they needed to occupy the type of working-class occupations their parents held.

We are making here a general, though difficult, point. The literacy of the Farrells and the Kinneys is a systemic literacy, not a personal one. It is not one for which the members are accountable in the same way as one is accountable for one's literacy in a second- or third- grade classroom. One does not "fail" familial literacy. Indeed, everyday literacy is all but invisible in the family. It is embedded in other tasks such as getting the right thing at the store, writing a card to a relative, or letting the children know where everyone is with a note on the refrigerator door. At such times, literacy as such is not highlighted.

Typical of this "passing" quality of literacy is an incident that entered our field notes in some detail. The Farrell's baby had contracted conjunctivitis. After considerable consultation among the many women in the extended family, it was decided that the infection could be treated at home with some eye ointment Mrs. Farrell had in the medicine cabinet.

> Mrs. Farell brought out a small bottle of ointment on which was written "Ophthalmic Ointment." She proceeded to read the small print on the label to see if it contained the ingredients that she remembered are found usually in such medicines from her previous experience with conjunctivitis. She was not totally convinced. She turned to Vera [the fieldworker] and asked her opinion. Vera read the label, said that it was probably alright but that she did not feel comfortable taking chances with medicines. Mrs. Farrell agreed and turned to her husband, asking him to phone the pharmacy to ask the pharmacist's opinion. Mr. Farrell asked her why she didn't phone herself, to which she confessed she felt embarrassed. Mr. Farrell called the pharmacist and read aloud the information on the label. At almost every point of his explanation and reading, Mrs. Farrell interrupted to correct both his inaccuracies in pronunciation and in points of fact. He was visibly irritated, but nevertheless changed his words to accommodate her criticisms. Eventually, it was established that the ointment was the correct one.

This incident is paradigmatic of the kind of scenes in which literacy is used in such families as the Farrells and the Kinneys. Here is an event, a baby's sickness. One must perform a joint action to resolve it. Analytically, the process of resolution is a practical achievement through conversation. The position of the participants is not the same at the end of the sequence as it was at the beginning. Something has happened. What happened is the product of smaller-scale sequences which particular people, occupying particular positions, performed in particular ways that have a particular power over future sequences. However this improvisational process which creates—in the full sense of the term—a unique event is fully controlled by "what-is-always-already-there," namely the set of definitions and rules of relationship which organize who can do what, when, how, and with what kind of effect. This regulation is cybernetic in that it is controlled by the feedback which each participant receives as he makes a move, utters some words in conversation, and performs an act.[8]

Schematically, the analysis we are sketching here moves by step through a series of levels which it might be helpful to specify so as to make clear what we mean by an activity being "an issue" that is "highlighted" through the "institutional consequences" it may have.

1. Take a short behavioral string, e.g., "Mrs. Farrell proceeds to read the small print on the label."

2. Determine the properties of the conversation within which the string is embedded, e.g., "finding the right medicine for a baby."

3. Investigate the properties of the conversations within which the particular conversation we first observed might itself be embedded, e.g., "times when one can take care of medical emergencies without calling doctors," "loving motherhood," and so on.

The behavioral strings (words and other actions) at each level use strings of the lower level as a token of what they are themselves about. Like the message "this is play," or "this is a joke" (or "this is an example in scholarly paper". . .), each next higher level conversation frames a particular utterance and gives it a particular weight; if this is a joke, then we should laugh, and thus laughter, or the absence of laughter, is at issue. If this is curing-your-ailing-child, then the child should get cured. What is *not* at issue if the frame is "curing-your-ailing-child" is the relative fluent quality of your reading. No such conversation could end with an utterance like "Good! You get an A for being able to read the label. Now, let's do some math." This is what we mean when we say that formal competence is not at issue in the family, except of course at special times, like homework which we investigate presently.

Our focus on all behavior as relational should serve as an introduction to our concern for differentiating the structural from the indeterminate in familial literacy. Clearly, the eye infection is not something that can be handled asocially. In a family like the Farrells a large number of people must be involved. But even in more isolated conditions, we would see that it takes many people, and many conversations, to deal with something like an infection. In any event, the Farrells must deal with each other. They must deal with experts. They must deal with a drug company. With each other and with the experts, they communicate essentially through oral conversations. It is with the drug company that their exchange is purely literate, but the reading of the label is only a part of a wider sequence. It is not the focus of the sequence.

---

[8] The reference to cybernetics is a reference to Bateson (1972) and his approach to communication processes. Our work is a development of the ethnomethodological tradition as it is best represented by Garfinkel (1967) and those who have worked on natural conversation: Pittenger, Hockett, and Danehy (1960), Scheflen (1973), Sacks, Schegloff, and Jefferson (1974). Finally, our interest in the uncertainty inherent in the structuring of conversations in real time is triggered by our reading of Bakhtin (1981).

It is difficult to know how to understand this practical literacy. It is so embedded within other activities as to appear irrelevant to the main issues that interest us, the issues of "success" as measured by status mobility and the more principled issues of liberal "self-education" and radical "critical consciousness." The apparent ability to read the switch on a machine, a label on a tube of medicine, the New York Post, an announcement from school, an item on the familial bulletin board, or the legend behind a snapshot seems such a low level matter as to be outside what we need to understand.

We think otherwise. It is not that, on some abstract scale, such literacy is "important." It is rather that such literacy is a systemic part of the life of the families. It is sufficient familial literacy, but it is not the only literacy they have at their disposal. If we continued the "level" analysis introduced earlier, we would come to a set of conversations in which it would be relevant that the passing familial literacy about which we have been talking is *not* other kinds of literacy. This paper is such a conversation but the participants themselves, in certain interviews specifically framed by the interviewer as interviews "about" literacy, reveal that they had a certain awareness that there may be multiple literacies to which one may orient. The description of the other kinds of literacy systematically organized by other parts of life within the community remains one of our long-range goals; without such a description no-one can easily make statements about the acquisition of literacy by particular children or groups of children in school.

SPECIAL LITERACY

Let us look again briefly at the eye ointment episode. How do the participants use literacy in this conversation? Initially, it looks as if they were involved in a search for information. This may be the way they would talk about the turn to the label. But such a common sense statement would rob the moment of a special character. At one level, *all* the moves in the conversation could be understood as information-gathering strategies. While the overall task was the curing of the baby, the means were an examination of all available information so as not to have to visit the pediatrician, an expensive proposition which, hopefully, would not have to be resorted to. If we look at the impact of various moves over later moves, we may recognize that the information gained through reading the label has a different force than information gained through oral inquiry from one's peers. The label has an "interrupt" value. It stops the conversation, it decenters the personal experience of the participants, it redirects their search towards the expert (the pharmacist) who, himself, refers back to the literate text.

The fact that some information is "printed" is not what gives it a special character. It is important that the printing is not seen as being generated by the people themselves. It comes from somewhere else, from a realm of "experts" who speak to the ignorant in a special voice, using a special medium, a special syntax, special words, that is, a special, symbolically-marked rhetoric. The practice of literacy, in this perspective, is less a function of a special individual competence (which must, of course, also exist), but a moment in a social exchange. The drug company "speaks" to the Farrells. They "listen" to it. However indirectly, they are in relationship with the company. This relationship is structured in the sense that it is differentiated from the other relationships that they have with other people and institutions.

We want to go even further. The special character of medical literacy is something that the Farrells, the Kinneys, and the rest of us also, *personally perform.*

Although the Farrells could not easily produce a text that would look like a label on a tube of medicine, such a text—if they knew that it had been produced by someone like them—would not have the weight a text produced by the proper kinds of person would have; still it is imperative that they, themselves, move their conversations towards the reading of the label and then redirect their investigation to the expert who can give the last word. This giving of the last word to such experts in specific circumstances is something that the Farrells actually and practically do. Such literacy has a "sacred" character. The recourse to literacy is differentiated in its communicative note from the recourse to oral confirmation. Literacy is *special,* even when it is embedded within larger sequences. Literacy is expert. It cancels the oral. It takes the family outside of itself even though it is performed *by* the family.[9]

This remark will carry its full weight when we begin investigating the place of school literacy in the family's conversations. Yielding to the practical power of medical literacy is not something that individual family members, singly, see themselves doing. It is not something that one could easily change. Personal awareness of it as an inappropriate dependency, for example, would not lessen the *potential power* of this kind of medical literacy on further interactions. Medical literacy acquires its readers and doles out expertise almost regardless of the participants or their opinions. In our terms, medicine is an issue whenever human beings are ailing within the reach of our society. That the same can be said for school literacy offers us an important background against which to understand its social patterning.

HOMEWORK AND SCHOOL LITERACY

Familial, medical, and school literacies are three quite distinct social events. They are not simply different because they are produced by different collectivities of people ("family members," "medical personnel," or "teachers"). Rather fathers, mothers, and children can themselves practically produce, within their own conversations, the special symbolic acts that mark a performance as relevant to family, medicine, or education.

---

[9] A full analysis of the incident would investigate the role of oral conversation with the pharmacist and its own interrupt function. The Farrells' recourse to the pharmacist suggests that they do not trust their collective reading of the label. In a certain way, not only are they not competent to write the label, they are not absolutely competent to read it either in its contextual relevance. In other words, while all the participants in the scene, including perhaps Sheila, could "read" the label to satisfy the school, none had the power to "read" the label to cure a baby, which suggests the existence of a hierarchy of literacies and, through it, of a hierarchy of readers.

We only have room here to sketch an analysis and to offer a summary statement of its relevance. As part of the data collection, we videotaped the Farrells and the Kinneys as they performed for us "homework." In both cases the actual event which we taped was unique, if only because we were there with our machinery. Although both fieldworkers felt that what had been captured was somehow representative of their respective family's usual evening round, we prefer to treat the homework performances precisely *as* dramatic performances. Our analysis is not based on replication. We are not trying to answer the question of whether they do the same thing every night. We are taking up instead the question of how family members can put together a school literacy event. When called on by the local university to play school, more particularly to have the world watch them display their best homework performances, what do the families have to work with? What is the script they rely upon? Who are the *dramatis personae*? What will allow the intended audience to recognize them? These are the questions that drive us.

The taping was done is each case in the location where Sheila and Joe usually did their homework. The people involved (except for the fieldworkers) are the people who are "usually" involved, that is, they are the kind of people who "can" be involved (even though it is certain that all of them are not always actually so involved). In Sheila's case, this means that many people come within range when she does "her" homework: mother, father, sister, aunt with boyfriend, television, and so on. This list could be longer; the kitchen table where homework is done and the couch where it is checked are at the center of the Farrells' social network. Fewer people get involved in Joe Kinney's homework. This does not mean that he and his mother are by themselves: the sister, the grandmother, some friends and neighbors all have to be dealt with (not to mention, again, the television). From all accounts (the tapes, the fieldworkers' observations, interviews, and our general knowledge of homework in American families), homework is never an event that is radically separated from the family's life. There must be a careful involvement of the family and its social environment even to achieve what most people think of as homework, namely, times during which children do their homework "by themselves," "with no distractions." The very separation of the child is a social construction.

The often assumed separation of children from their families during homework highlights the social complexity of the homework performance. While the separation of the child is a social construction, it is so organized as to make society disappear. The appropriate dramatic representation of this separation must involve the creation of an empty physical space around the child, an absence of face-to-face interaction between the child and others during a certain time, a narrow focus by the child on a specific task, and so on. As performed, such moments are difficult to capture cinematographically in their social aspects. So we focused our analysis on the time when the parents "checked" the homework. This is a subroutine within the general definition of what homework is all about by being put in certain positions within the sequence. Teachers and schools disagree on the value of such "checking" and parents do not have much specific guidance about what it should consist of. Nonetheless, it is dealt with structurally as a "special" moment within the overall routine of the day. Separation and noninterruption are again at issue, but it is now the separation of the adult-child dyad rather than that of just the child.

In our families, dramatic separation was difficult to achieve. On the day we taped, Sheila did spend a half-hour "by herself" at the kitchen table. She was surrounded by much familial interaction, but she remained on its fringes. Similarly, Joe's sister was observed regularly doing her homework by herself. Joe, however, seems rarely to have been allowed this moment of solitude. His mother told us that if she (or her own mother) did not actively participate, Joe would not concentrate. In both families, the checking sequence was difficult to arrange. The successful separation of an adult from family life is almost impossible when that adult is the center of a large household (as Mrs. Farrell is) or when the adult is the only adult in the household (as Mrs. Kinney is).

While fully appropriate dramatic separation could not be achieved, the families did hold themselves accountable for it. They performed the structural markers of separation. The many people who entered the homework scene did it as either "help" or "distraction." But the homework always remained the homework *of the child* in every participant's speech. The Farrells, as they say it, do not do "their" homework: Sheila does *hers*. By now, this should cease being an obvious point. Strictly speaking, *everyone* in the family is doing homework. Sheila, however, is redundantly marked as being the focus by being put in certain positions within the sequence.

This becomes clearer if we think again of doing homework as a conversation among a great number of people for a long period of time. Thus, it is because Sheila is in school that the family must do homework. Without her-in-conversation-with-a-teacher, there would be no homework. In other words, the family does not generate homework. This was graphically represented to us when it so happened that the day we were to videotape Joe Kinney, the teacher, "for the first time in years" as we were told, had not "given" homework. As the kind of outsiders we were, we had the authority to ask the family to do make-believe homework, which they did. But it is clear that no homework would have been done that night had we not been there.

The presence of school in the family kitchen is apparent in the way members spotlight the child's performance. Even more striking is the fact that the specific talk that is generated as part of the homework scene is structured, as school talk is structured, to isolate individual competence displays. Such conversations follow a canonical progression that is the same as the sequences which represent the school to itself[10]: mother asks

---

[10] Here, as elsewhere in the paper, we are distinguishing between, on the one hand, the ensemble of the activities which can be performed in a certain settings among various people and, on the other hand the symbols that (a) define the setting as a certain type of setting and (b) define the subactivities which can be performed with the setting. Thus, within a "family" there are certain activities which are particularly "family-like" in that they are used as representation of the family as a special place within the possible places in the culture. "Loving" activities probably are such activities (Schneider, 1980). Within such settings, scenes like "homework" are themselves structurally differentiated. In school too, certain activities can be used to symbolize The School even though these activities are not all those that are actually performed there.

question, child answers, mother evaluates. This is a structure of the general form /Question-Answer- Evaluation/.[11] This canonical sequence can be performed in various ways. The evaluation can be dropped when the child is "right" and when a specific sequence is to be followed immediately by another. In all cases the sequence becomes more complex if the evaluation is negative. The child may question the mother's evaluation. The mother may simply reinstate the question or may give various kinds of hints. She may move on to a full "teaching" mode, restating a general rule, explaining how it applies, checking for an understanding of the principle, and so on. In any event, the position that the mother and child occupy are always asymmetrical; they cannot be exchanged. The child is the one who is accountable for the answer. The mother may check the answer in the book if she is not sure, but the child may not.[12]

The canonical progression can be thought of as a structure for a particular type of conversation where the conversational labor is divided differentially. What is particularly interesting about it is the way in which various sequences hierarchically nest into each other. In Figure 1 we offer a partial snapshot of the activities in terms of which we can begin to situate any moment of the homework situation.

The easy recognition and near ubiquity of application of our chart to homework scenes throughout the culture suggest that it captures many of the constraints on families when school comes home. Although family members have to perform the appropriate markers that constitute homework tasks as having been performed, the structural uniformity of the scenes indicates that the participants have little control over its organization. Whatever the families may think of the school, whatever the success of their children, whatever, indeed, the success of the families, all of them are accountable to the school and they behave accordingly. In other words, we have no evidence to suggest that there is any major gap between the family and the school on the subject of homework and, indeed, the structuring of education as a social interaction. They can fully participate in it.

VARIATIONS IN THE DOING OF SCHOOL AT HOME

The performance of the structural features which allow the family to recognize whether or not it is performing "homework" never prevents the joint performance of other features that can mark other structures. The family can be "itself" at the same time that it is "doing homework" in a traditional manner. Families are "free" to improvise around

---

[11] Mehan (1978). The conventions used here are the same as those used in Varenne (1983). They are derived from those used in structural linguistics to distinguish significant units in a system (/x/) and their realization in a particular context ([x]).

[12] This does not mean that the mother is not herself on the hot seat. Particularly in front of strangers, she can demonstrate embarrassment at both her own and her child's mistakes. We have a few cases of such demonstrations of embarrassment on our tapes and the literature is replete with accounts of the way parents are made responsible for the school failure of their children. These parents were aware of the extent to which they were on the spot. They knew they could be blamed for the failure of their children.

Figure 1.   Structural Replication of the School at Home

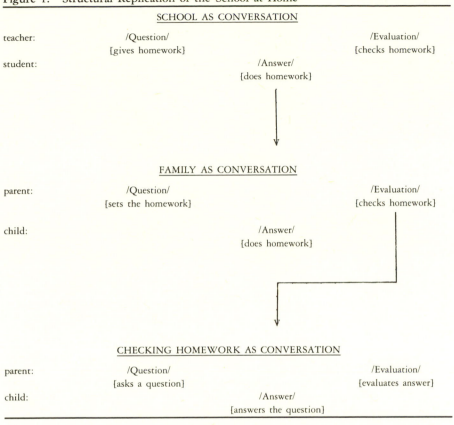

SCHOOL AS CONVERSATION

teacher: /Question/   /Evaluation/
                          [gives homework]   [checks homework]

student: /Answer/
                                              [does homework]

FAMILY AS CONVERSATION

parent: /Question/   /Evaluation/
                          [sets the homework]   [checks homework]

child: /Answer/
                                              [does homework]

CHECKING HOMEWORK AS CONVERSATION

parent: /Question/   /Evaluation/
                          [asks a question]   [evaluates answer]

child: /Answer/
                                            [answers the question]

the imposed theme particularly as it concerns the insertion of the school sequences within the families' own organization. In our main report, we deal with these variations in the doing of school under five main subheadings:

1. External sequencing (how the homework is organized with the other activities of the family).

2. Internal sequencing (how the various subroutines within the homework are organized).

3. The organization of intrusions (how the entry of nonhomework tasks are managed).

4. The identification of the participants during the sequence (what the participants imply about each other as they behave during the sequence).

5. The meta-identification of the participants (how the participants talk about each other in general texts outside of the sequence).

Given the limited space we have available here, we deal only with the first three subheadings. This is enough to suggest the direction of our analysis.

External Sequencing

The Farrells.   It is typical for Sheila to do her homework immediately upon her return from school. It is also typical for her mother to check it immediately after. There is no need for much prompting on the parents' part. Nobody is assigned to help her. Other participants are engaged in other activities. Even at the time of "checking" we still have all the participants engaged in a multitude of activities, but the performance of these other activities does not seem to slow down the homework process.

The Kinneys.   Homework, for Joe, is typically a two-stage affair. On most days, Joe first sits down to begin his homework under the supervision of his grandmother. According to all reports, this first stage is characterized by (a) a struggle between Joe and his grandmother about the need to perform the homework rather than to go out and play; and (b) the tendency of the grandmother to do parts of the homework for him, "sometimes in her own handrwiting," as Joe's mother told us. Joe generally wins this struggle and sets the scene for the second stage of the homework saga. After Joe and his mother return home, Mrs. Kinney begins to check what Joe had to do, and what he still has to do. This may last til late in the evening. The length of the procedure is partially the product of the fact that Mrs. Kinney, at the same time that she checks Joe's homework, must also prepare and eat her own meal, keep track of her daughter's activities, catch up with the children about their day, touch base with other members of her network, and so on.

Internal Sequencing

When we introduced the summary structural model of the homework conversation as a "special" event, we suggested that certain variations could be made on it. Obviously, these variations cannot modify the basic form of the conversation. It is possible, however, to expand the form. At one extreme, the family can initiate the homework sequence by insisting that the child does homework-like tasks even in the absence of school-initiated homework (as the Kinneys found themselves doing when we came to videotape them). It is also possible to do more than just "check" and acknowledge the mere act of having done the work. It is possible to evaluate it, something that both families did; they were interested in the child "getting it right." This evaluation itself can be varied. In particular, it is possible to go beyond pure "red-pencil" type evaluation into a full teaching sequence during which the child is made to rehearse the broken rule. Mrs. Farrell, for example, regularly asked Sheila questions that were less intended as right/wrong answers than they were intended to lead to the finding of the "right" answer. This variation can be treated as a subsequence within the "parent-checking" sequence, one that is activated by any "wrong" answer. The Kinneys did not get themselves into such subsequences.

Intrusions

Both the Farrells and the Kinneys cannot totally segment homework from other family activities even as they perform the markers that make homework "special" within these

Figure 2.

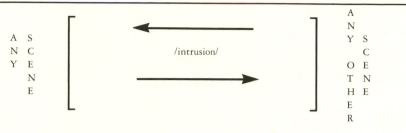

activities. This is a general fact of social life. Even the most specialized activities have to maintain their borders against each other. It is not just that a social group can perform several differentiated activities concurrently. It is also that the participants must some-how handle the motion back and forth from one activity to the other and that we can learn much by focusing on how they do it. Activities "intrude" on each other, so to speak. This situation may be diagrammed as in Figure 2.

To the extent that intrusions are concretely performed, social groups will organize this performance differently. Indeed, it is around the issue of the structuring of intru-sions that the Farrells and the Kinneys can be differentiated the most sharply.

The Farrells. In the scene which we use to demonstrate the peculiar style the Farrells use to deal with intrusions, we have Mr. and Mrs. Farrell, Sheila and the baby all checking Sheila's homework. The television, while passive, is on most of the time. "Watching television" is a differentiated activity and it is a possible source of intru-sions. We can see Mrs. Farrell and Sheila following what is happening as they lift their head from the workbook and stare at the screen. However, and typically, this moment only occurs when whoever is doing it is not "on" in the homework conversation. Nei-ther Mrs. Farrell nor Sheila watch the tube "in place of" doing what they were supposd "to do next" as far has homework is concerned; they watch only when they are not on immediate call (i.e., Mrs. Farrell watches when Sheila is answering, Sheila watches when her mother is reading in the workbook). Even the baby can be seen following the alternating focus between homework, television, and conversation.[13] For example, after it has been established that Sheila actually can do a little exercise in which she first made a mistake, she and her mother enter into a quick sequence of moves that can best be described, metaphorically, as the dance of a loving mother proudly reprimanding her daughter for a self-assurance and satisfaction that both know is grounded. The baby follows it carefully and, when it ends, turns to Sheila and laughs with her. Sheila recip-

---

[13] That a sixteen-month-old baby should participate in displaying the attentional structure of her family is not mysterious. It belongs with the capacity very young children have of producing intonationally proper "sentences" and conversational routines before they begin speaking in the more usual sense (M.C. Bateson, 1975). Similarly children position themselves relationally to reading long before they can actually decipher words (Taylor, 1983).

rocates and sings to the baby. In the meantime, the mother has returned to the home-work; even self-congratulation does not break the rhythm. Homework is maintained until its school-defined end, that is, until all the assigned exercises have been checked.

The Kinneys. The Kinneys also must perform the special markers of "home-work," and they too must deal with nonhomework intrusions into the special perform-ance. Food must be prepared and consumed. The telephone must be answered. Of such things is modern life made. The Farrells have taught us that such intrusions, *in them-selves*, need not fully "interrupt" the flow of any special activity. Interruptions are *made* by the family. Watching the Kinneys do their homework we see, for example, Mrs. Kinney, time and time again, ask Joe questions which he does not answer. She does not react to this silence. It is as if she had asked the question in such a way as to tell Joe that it did not count. Time and time again, we see Mrs. Kinney start a sequence, get Joe involved, and then abruptly drop it so that it does not develop. Quite often, there ap-pears to be a clear external cause to the interruption. For example, Mrs. Kinney asks a question, and then the telephone rings. She answers it. What would seem more natural than that she would forget what her question was? But it is on the subtler events that we rely in our argument that, perhaps, it is not quite "natural" for Mrs. Kinney not to complete sequences which she started. In contrast to members of the Farrell family who seemed always in tune with Sheila's homework, we see Mrs. Kinney and Joe often out of tune. When she notices his lack of attention to homework, it is often just at the mo-ment when we see him already turning back to his work. They are often hung between two activities in such a way that marks both as having been an "interruption" of the other.

Summary of Intrusions. In abstract terms, our argument is that "intrusions" are "empty" structures that gain their specific values only as a social group produces its own history. The following diagrams portrays the differential realization of "intrusions" as either "time-outs" in the Farrell house and as "interruptions" in the Kinney family. The difference between the two families is further emphasized by the presence of the teach-ing subroutine among the Farrells when the mother questions Sheila about the rule that she is supposed to be applying ("meta-questioning": "Mq"), and then supplies this rule if Sheila cannot produce it ("statement of rule": "Ru"), see Figure 3.

These are obviously not the only two ways of structuring intrusions. Furthermore, what ends up constituting the family in its (sub-)cultural specificity is the ensemble of the ways in which it has transformed what is given to it.

HOMEWORK IN THE ORGANIZATION OF FAMILY LIFE

The preceeding analyses may seem to have taken us far from the more general issue of understanding how families participate in reproducing their own literacy, and through this, the literacy of the whole society. But the interactional details protect us from fo-cusing on Joe or even his mother as the cause of his problem; the details call for an account of the connections between homework moments and the rest of the sequences that make up the culture. For example, given that Joe's sister is doing alright, we

Figure 3

	Farrell Homework				Kinney Homework		
	Qu		A		Qu		A
H	An	Mq	N	H	An		N
O S	Ev	An ←————————	Y	O S	Ev ←————————		Y
M C	Qu	Ru [time-out]		M C	Qu [interruption]		
E E	An		O S	E E	An		O S
W N	Ev		T C	W N	Ev		T C
O E	...	————————→	H E	O E	... ————————→		H E
R			E N	R			E N
K			R E	K			R E

might easily blame him for being, after all, "slow." Or we might blame his mother for not being able to organize an environment where he might blossom. But we feel that none of these diagnoses of the source of the trouble would provide an understanding of why it is that these matters of success and failure are in fact so important. Nor could we understand how they are performed, in the linear temporality of improvised everyday life. Even if Joe were dumb, he would still have to act dumb repeatedly, over many scenes, over a period of time. Even if his dumbness is only apparent and is the "product" of his relation with his mother (or with his teacher, father, sister, or with any combination of these), this production is not a single event that happened once mechanistically in Joe's history. It is something that must still be going on as it is constantly re-produced. In other words, it is not that, once upon a time, Mrs. Kinney did something to Joe which caused him to be slow. It is rather that, in history, a structure has developed that makes Joe redundantly act slowly. This structure is not Joe's personality, but it is not independent of him either. Like Joe, the structure is constantly on the verge of radical transformation.[14]

As we proceed in this analysis of stability-in-reproduction, we get back to an essentially "structuralist" position (in the "French" sense of structuralism). This structuralism is, however, carefully rephrased to take into account the ethnomethodological insights into the processual aspects of lived structures.[15] Doing

---

[14] Bakhtin's (1981) insistence on the centrifugal power of what is now referred to as "natural conversation" is something which we take to heart. No conversation is simply a mechanical "realization" of a structure. It is also a struggle with this structure. For a related insight, see Bourdieu (1977).

[15] While Saussure is mainly remembered these days as the straw linguist to criticize for statism and ignorance of the social aspects of language use, it should be noted that he specifically searched for a linguistics that was sociological. As for the issue of change, it should be noted that Saussure developed his structuralism as a method to understand his observations of linguistic change. His general statement about the epistemological status of "synchronic laws" (patterns or structures in our jargon) is particularly apt: "The synchronic law is general but not imperative. Doubtless it is imposed on individuals by the weight of collective usage. . . , but here I do not have in mind an obligation on the part of speakers. I mean that, *in language,* no force guarantees the maintenance of a regularity established on some point. . . The arrangement is precarious precisely because it is not imperative" (Saussure, 1966, p. 92, author's emphasis).

Conversely, while some who claim to belong to the ethnomethodological tradition specifically refute structuralist analyses, it has been emphasized that the work of Garfinkel (1967), for example, is in fact profoundly structuralist (Gonos, 1977).

homework is something that one has to create from scratch every day, in every sequence, subsequence, and utterance. The script itself is always loose, and it changes
from night to night and from year to year. The performance is always an improvisation.
Furthermore, as we showed at length, the script allows for a certain amount of freedom
so that families can imprint their own style upon it. It is clear, however, that there is a
script, a theme that is imposed. However fancy the improvisations can be, it is necessary constantly to come back to the theme.

We now want to focus on the constraints that define the themes. The most
significant ones are, of course, those which we identified in our analysis of what it is that
the families do not control. Let us now look at these constraints from the point of view
of their historical development. In the initial analysis, we defined the interactional
structures which could be realized in many different ways without transforming the
significance of the units. Given the extreme variation in form which homework could
take, it would seem difficult to recognize an utterance as "homework" if we did not
already know that it was homework.

The fundamental embeddedness of all behavior in contexts is a central property of
what we are dealing with and needs to be recognized so that we can understand some of
the more difficult consequences which interest us. While a full discussion would take us
too far, we want to mention that any single utterance (e.g., "what time is it?" or "it's
ten o'clock") only gains contextual sense when it is placed within an ensemble of other
utterances (e.g., "time to go!" or "good work, Joe!") which mark it as belonging to
different frames (e.g. everyday life, or elementary school).[16]

In real life, the signifying contexts are "always-already-there." Only in logic text-
books does one encounter single, unambiguous utterances. The contexts are predefined
by cues that are either being performed or have been previously performed with a clear
marking to the effect that the context established is valid for all further utterances until
notice is given that the scene is ended. Thus, in a scene originally marked as "homework," any utterance, or sequence, will be interpreted as homework, whether it is complete or not, whether it takes the canonical form or not. All this may appear confusing
in such an account as this one, but would rarely be so confusing in real life. There, we
always operate in terms of what has been called a "principle of cooperation."[17] The principle could also be understood as the principle of "Assumed Coherence" which could be
stated as: "all statements (including silence) are to be assumed to make sense in terms of
some context (within a set of contexts) which either has been predefined or is introduced
by the statement itself."

Homework, then, while it is continually being produced, is also an overarching
structure which transforms anything that happens within its purported boundaries into
homework (as either homework per se, or time-outs, or interruptions within it). Homework, in ths perspective is not so much characterized by what actually happens within it

---

[16] For the general point, see McDermott and Tylbor (1983). See also Bateson (1955) on the analytic implications of the message "this is play."

[17] Grice (1975, 1978). Garfinkel's (1967) experiments with trust and the routine grounds of everyday life
make many of the same points.

at any one time but rather by what differentiates it from the other activities which a family also enters in either before, after, or in parallel with it. It is only if we understand that this character of homework as a scene which is controlled down to the briefest utterances by an external set of features which establishes a coherence system for the interpretation of these utterances that we can understand the problems that confront our families, particularly the problem of failure.

THE COHERENCE OF FAILURE

Our analysis of the external features of homework which families do not control can be summarized in a statement to the effect that "homework" is a scene in which the knowledge particular individuals have of a topic is evaluated by someone else. Evaluation is a central aspect of homework. It is what makes it like school. School evaluation is the focused determination of the presence or absence of a piece of "knowledge." In other words, failure is a central possibility within evaluation. It is enough to remember that, in the canonical sequence /Question-Answer-Evaluation/, the Evaluation can be realized regularly as either "Right" or "Wrong." In fact it is the possibility of "Wrong" as a realization of Evaluation that makes tests necessary. Failure is the central condition of evaluation *even when one is doing well*. If failure were not possible, there would be no need for evaluation. And vice versa. To produce a statement that leads to another one to the effect that the first one was "wrong" is eminently coherent. Only exceptional persons are expected to "get it right" all the time. It is normal to get it wrong. In this sense, failure is not an interactional "problem." It is part of the normal, possible, progression of the scene. Finally, evaluation implies a "someone else" who controls it. And it implies an institutional framework within which it makes sense for more people to evaluate others on narrowly specified criteria.

But failure is, also, a massive problem of a different kind for the participants. It is, for all concerned, a-normal-event-that-should-not-happen-to-any-particular-person (it should only happen to somebody else). All concerned know that failure has massive consequences both in social and personal terms. It is in the great interest of the individuals directly concerned not to fail. To fail is to prove oneself dumb. It is to ensure a life history at the lowest rungs of the society. It is not surprising that individuals and their families should struggle. We saw how the Kinneys struggled. The problem is for us to understand how it is that the Kinneys, in spite of their constant struggles, in spite of the fact that they knew exactly what school expected of them and could perform, continued to produce something that was painful for all those involved.

The Kinneys, it will be remembered, receive feedback around homework from two sources. First, they suffer while doing homework. Second, they suffer when they find out what is the school's official evaluation of their homework: Joe is remaining below grade level. We could imagine that this should be enough to signal to them that they are doing something wrong and that they should change their operating procedures. Mrs. Kinney is aware that something must change. She does not like what her mother is doing with Joe. She is continually involved in "improving" the procedural aspects of doing homework (getting the right pencil, writing legibly, paying attention, working on a clean table, etc.). And yet, she has failed to engineer any improvement in Joe's relative competence. While we might have different opinions than hers as to what would make a difference in this competence, we believe that a focus on such "improvements" are not "solutions"; they are symptoms of the problem. Criticizing Mrs. Kinney's solutions and offering her others of the same order would only have the effect of underlining something which she is well aware of: she is failing homework, just as Joe is failing school. Comparing Mrs. Kinney to Mrs. Farrell would have the same effect. It would be unfair to all the Mrs. Kinneys of this world to say that she should do more of what Mrs. Farrell does (e.g., spend more of her energy rehearsing the principles of a school task rather than assuring herself that the "right" answer has been found). Her relative success would have to come at some other mother's expense: 50% of all parents will always have children below grade level as long as we define grade level as the average of the performances of all children in a grade.

The problem, for us, lies in the coherence of failure. Mrs. Kinney says of herself that she is "one who failed in school." That Joe should also fail is a cause for suffering, but it is not surprising. It is not incoherent as to what can happen to the people she knows. *It is so coherent, in fact, that she redundantly reproduces the very conditions that produce the failure.*

Let us summarize this argument as a conclusion to this paper.

We saw how, besides making failure interactionally coherent, homework also has the property of focusing this failure on the individual actions, the child first, and the supervising parent, second. If something is going wrong, it is the child that is to be "blamed." If this does not seem reasonable, the parent will be blamed. One might then blame the teacher and, perhaps, the particular school the child attends. What must be noticed is the way all these assignments of blame shift the focus away from the institution of scholastic evaluation back onto some individual unit. Thus, the Kinneys' experience of homework as a painful event does not lead to a critique of homework as such. It leads to a critique of *their own* way of doing homework. All the changes that they consider have the effect of leading them to more of what makes them suffer. Joe would like homework simply to go away—which would lead to a more radical type of failure (expulsion from the parochial school and placement in the remedial classes of a public school). Mrs. Kinney has focused on procedural matters: salvation, for her, is the more exact performance of those acts which make homework look more like homework as she believes the school wants her to do it (and as the school indeed suggests she should).

Given the spotlighting power of homework, we can understand that people should be blinded into seeing only themselves. We, as analysts, should not be so blinded. We must look at the spotlight itself, at the mechanisms that focus it, at the people who aim it and at the functions which it serves. When we do this we immediately lose sight of the individuals who seemed so important earlier. The School, as a cultural institution, that is, the system of political accountability that is imperative on *all* schools in America, is not designed to care about specific individuals except as ciphers to which scores must be attached. These scores must have the property of being high or low. They must have been attached during complex ritual sequences that are extremely well-specified. The exact performance of the ritual is the concern to which one is held accountable. A failure attributed during an improper ritual does not count.[18] If the ritual is not challenged, then the failure is coherent. It is sad for the failing person, but it is "normal." In other words, *who* fails is utterly irrelevant to The School (though not necessarily to Joe's, or Sheila's teachers, or any other teachers). Someone *must* fail, but it does not have to be Joe Kinney and his mother. Should *they* suddenly become successful, nothing would change for the system. There would simply be a minor recalibration of someone else's official evaluation: *that* person would now fail.

Finally, the irrelevance of failure as an event structurally tied to particular persons (rather than to some persons in general) also suggests that the "dumbness" which scholastic evaluations somehow uncovers is itself not the total personal event that it is made to be. School-evaluated dumbness is only relevant to school-controlled tasks. If we stand outside the school, suddenly dumbness and smartness cease to be relevant categories. As the need to evaluate disappears, so does the interactional coherence of the evaluation. Outside of homework, and schooling in general, Joe Kinney is not dumb and is not treated as such. Joe, like Sheila, fully possesses the literacy that is assigned to him in the family's everyday life. But this literacy is itself irrelevant to scholastic literacy since it is not performed within the appropriate ritual sequence. Joe and his mother are also extremely competent at the cultural performance of homework: they know what to do, they know the implications and consequences. They know when to suffer and who to blame for this suffering.

They practice this knowledge every single day. It is as deep a competence as the linguistic competence which they also have. They are not alienated from the school. What they do is not different in style or intent from what the school does. Indeed, what they do is a part of the total system of which the school is itself, in fact, but a small part. Without the Kinneys, and their "failure," the school could not be what it is. And so Joe Kinney, and millions like him, "fail." And so Sheila Farrell, and millions like her, "succeed."

REFERENCES

Bakhtin, M.M. (1981). *The dialogic imagination*. (C. Emerson and M. Holquist, Trans.). Austin: University of Texas Press.

Bateson, Gregory. (1955). The message 'This is play'. In B. Schaffner (Ed.), *Group processes: Transactions of the second conference*. New York: Josiah Macy, Jr. Foundation.

Bateson, Gregory. (1972). *Steps to an ecology of mind*. New York: Ballantine Books.

Bateson, Mary Catherine. (1975). Mother-infant exchanges: The epigenesis of conversational interaction. In D. Aaronson & R. Rieber (Eds.), *Developmental psycholinguistics and communication disorders*. Annals of the New York Academy of Sciences, Vol. 263. New York: The New York Academy of Sciences.

---

[18] Think, for example, of what happens when it can be shown that an S.A.T. question has not been scored properly. It is not enough that The School control a setting for evaluations that are particularly consequential to be considered appropriate. The School is a set of acts. It is a ritual that is efficacious only if it is performed exactly.

Benét, Rosemary, & Benét, Stephen. (1962). *A book of Americans.* New York: Holt, Rinehart and Winston. (Original work published 1933).

Bourdieu, Pierre. (1977). *Outline of a theory of practice.* (R. Nice, Trans.). Cambridge: Cambridge University Press.

Dumont, Louis. (1980). *Homo hierarchicus.* (rev. ed.) M. Sainsbury (Trans.). (Original work published 1961). Chicago: University of Chicago Press.

Garfinkel, Harold. (1967). *Studies in ethnomethodology.* Englewood Cliffs, NJ: Prentice-Hall.

Gonos, George. (1977). 'Situation' vs. 'frame': The 'interactionist' and the 'structuralist' analyses of everyday life. *American Sociological Review, 42.* 854–867.

Grice, H. Paul. (1975). Logic and conversation. In P. Cole & J. Morgan (Ed.), *Syntax and meaning.* New York: Academic Press.

Grice, H. Paul. (1978). Further notes on logic and conversation. In P. Cole (Ed.), *Syntax and semantics.* New York: Academic Press.

Hood, Lois, McDermott, R. P. & Cole, Michael. (1980). Let's *try* to make it a good day: Some not so simple ways. *Discourse Processes, 3.* 155–68.

Leichter, Hope. (1984). Families as environments for literacy. In H. Goelman, A. Oberg, & F. Smith (Eds.), *Awakening to literacy.* Exeter, NH: Heinemann.

McDermott, R.P., & Goldman, Shelley & Varenne, Hervé. (1984). When school goes home: Some problems in the organization of homework. *Teachers College Record. 85,* 391–409.

McDermott, R.P., & Gospodinoff, Kenneth. (1979). Social context for ethnic borders and school failure. In A. Wolfgang (Ed.), *Nonverbal behavior.* New York: Academic Press.

McDermott, Raymond P., & Tylbor, Henry. (1983). On the necessity of collusion in conversation. *Text, 3.* 277–297.

Mehan, Hugh. (1978). Structuring school structure. *Harvard Educational Review, 48.* 32–64.

Morison, Ann. (1982). *Getting reading and writing: A description of literacy learning patterns in three urban families.* Doctoral dissertation. Ann Arbor, MI: University Microfilms.

Pittenger, Robert, Hockett, C., & Danehy, J. (1960). *The first five minutes: A sample of microscopic analysis.* Ithaca, NY: Paul Martineau.

Sacks, Harvey, Schegloff, E., & Jefferson, G. (1974). A simplest systematics for the organization of turn-taking for conversation. *Language, 50,* 696–735.

Saussure, Ferdinand de. (1966). *Course in general linguistics.* (W. Baskin, Trans.) New York: McGraw-Hill.

Scheflen, Albert. (1973). *Communicational structure: Analysis of a psychotherapy transaction.* Bloomington, IN: Indiana University Press.

Schneider, David. (1980). *American kinship: A cultural account.* Chicago: University of Chicago Press. (Original work published 1968).

Susser, Ida. (1982). *Norman Street: Poverty and politics in an urban neighborhood.* Oxford: Oxford University Press.

Suttles, Gerald. (1972). *The social construction of communities.* Chicago: University of Chicago Press.

Taylor, Denny. (1983). *Family literacy: Young children learning to read and write.* Exeter, NH: Heinemann Educational Books.

Varenne, Hervé. (1977). *Americans together: Structured diversity in a midwestern town.* New York: Teachers College Press.

Varenne, Hervé. (1978). Culture as rhetoric: The patterning of the verbal interpretation of interaction between teachers and administrators in an American high school. *American Ethnologist, 5,* 635–650.

Varenne, Hervé. (1982). Jocks and freaks: The symbolic structure of the expression of social interaction among American senior high school students. In G. Spindler (Ed.), *Doing the ethnography of schooling.* New York: Holt, Rinehart and Winston.

Varenne, Hervé. (1983). *American school language: Culturally patterned conflicts in a suburban high school.* New York: Irvington Publishers.

Varenne, Hervé, Hamid-Buglione, Vera, McDermott, R.P., & Morison, Ann. (1982). 'I teach him everything he learns in school': The acquisition of literacy for learning in working class families.* New York: Teachers College, Columbia University, Elbenwood Center for the Study of the Family as Educator.

PART IV

Literacy Affects The Social Order

11

Literacy Instruction in a Samoan Village*

Alessandro Duranti
Pitzer College and University of Rome

Elinor Ochs
University of Southern California

INTRODUCTION

Literacy has been examined in many ways, particularly for the cognitive transformations it effects on acquirers in Western and non-Western societies. Major themes in this regard are the development of abstract reasoning and thought, the development of decentering—that is, the capacity to take the perspective of another—and the development of the ability to decontextualize one's language, all three interrelated topics (cf. Greenfield, 1972; Goody, 1977; Scribner & Cole, 1978).

* An earlier version of this paper was presented with an accompanying film at the Conference on Literacy and Linguistics, University of Southern California, Nov. 1981, and at Pitzer College, November 1981. We would like to thank the participants in both of those events for their stimulating questions and comments. We would also like to thank Peg Griffin for reading an earlier draft of this paper and providing helpful comments and inspiring criticism.

We are grateful to the people of the village of Falefaa, on the island of Upolu, in Western Samoa, for their patience and cooperation throughout our research project. Special thanks go to Rev. Fa'atau'oloa Mauala and his wife Sau'iluma for their kindness and for their willingness to understand our *paalagi's* views and needs.

We would also like to than the following institutions for sponsoring the research on which this paper is based: the National Science Foundation (Grant no. 53–482–2480—E. Ochs principal investigator), the Department of Anthropology, Research School of Pacific Studies, at the Australian National University (for postdoctoral fellowships to both authors in 1980–81), the Italian Consiglio Nazionale delle Ricerche (for A. Duranti's research), and the Gardner Howard Foundation (for a fellowship in 1982–83 to E. Ochs).

Transcription conventions. We have used traditional Samoan orthography with the exception of vowel length, which we have transcribed phonemically, that is, with a double (identical) vowel, rather than with a macron on a single vowel. The letter "g" stands for a velar nasal and the inverted apostrophe " ' " for a glottal stop.

For the transcripts of verbal interaction, we have used the conventions of Conversation Analysis, as presented in the Appendix in Sacks, Schegloff, and Jefferson (1974), with the exception of the hyphen, which has been used not only for truncated words, but also for indicating the process of separating words into syllables and single letters for teaching purposes.

Scribner and Cole (1978, 1981) have raised the issue of the relation of literacy to schooling, suggesting that many of the cognitive orientations discussed are consequences of the schooling experience rather than literacy per se. This suggestion has placed greater attention on uses of literacy and the ways in which literacy is instructed. Cognitive skills will depend on these two variables.

The focus of this paper is on literacy instruction. We will be examining the transmission of literacy in a traditional village in Western Samoa. Our point is simple, but one with far-reaching consequences: In the course of transmitting literacy skills, the instructor exposes and socializes children to new expectations surrounding the adult-child relationship and task accomplishment.

The role and behavior of adult and child in the class of events we might call "literacy classroom instructions" match that characteristic of many adult-child social interactions in Western middle class society (Heath, 1982). On the other hand, they do not match certain traditional Samoan beliefs, values, and social norms that underlie the relationship between adult and child. We posit that a global effect of literacy instruction is a change in the social identity of the child in Samoan society.

A more specific effect of literacy instruction concerns the notion of accomplishment or achievement. Instruction is organized in such a way that the child alone is pictured as having accomplished a particular task. While the instructor has assisted the child, his contribution is not acknowledged by participants within the interaction. In contrast, traditional tasks outside the classroom setting are not organized along these lines. Tasks are seen as cooperatively rather than individually accomplished. In this paper, we will consider differences in these two notions of accomplishment through comparison of the acts of acknowledging and praising in literacy instruction and in a variety of social contexts in daily Samoan life.

The consequences of exposing young Samoan children to Western patterns of adult-child interaction and task accomplishment are difficult to document but are as dramatic and pervasive as the other effects of literacy and formal schooling that have been considered. In transmitting literacy skills, the instructor transforms the way in which these children view themselves with respect to others. The particular emphasis on individual achievement in literacy instruction is compatible not only with Western notions of classroom achievement but with notions of economic achievement as well. We suggest that literacy instruction in this village provides the child with social and cultural knowledge necessary to participate in a Western-style economy: to obtain employment, carry out one's job, and be rewarded monetarily according to individual accomplishment.

This paper is organized in the following way: In the first section, we introduce the contexts of use of literacy and the basic features of the written materials used in literacy instruction (viz. Bible reading). In the next section, we describe the social organization of tasks and the concept of achievement in village settings outside the classroom. The following section analyzes the discourse patterns of literacy instruction. These patterns reveal attitudes, expectations, and values not characteristic of social interaction in other village settings. In particular, we focus on the child-centered nature of the verbal interaction and the orientation toward individual rather than collective achievement. In the final section, we summarize our findings and our perspective on the effects of literacy instruction.

The discussion presented in this paper is based on two field projects: a longitudinal study of language acquisition and socialization in a traditional village in Western Samoa carried out by Alessandro Duranti, Elinor Ochs, and Martha Platt in 1978–79; and a film documentary project carried out by Duranti and Ochs in the same community in the spring of 1981.

CONTEXTS AND SOURCES OF LITERACY IN A RURAL VILLAGE OF WESTERN SAMOA

In a rural village in Western Samoa, there are two main sources of written material in Samoan: (1) the Samoan version of the Bible, and (2) weekly newspapers that come from the capital, Apia. There are also a number of religious and educational publications put out, respectively, by various religious denominations and by the Education Depart-ment; the former are to be used within Church activities and the latter in the public schools. Texts for secondary education are in English.

In everyday life, we find writing used for a number of reasons and in a number of social contexts. The most common use is probably for listing names of people, espe-cially for the purpose of money collections and contributions, and fines to be paid to the village judiciary committees or to religious congregations. Writing is also used for cor-responding with relatives who have gone to work (or sometimes permanently live) over-seas, in New Zealand, in Australia, or in the United States.

There are also institutional records, for instance, church records kept by local pastors and priests who document dates of births, deaths, and special religious services for some particular family or group. Local hospitals also keep records of patients and treatments, births, deaths—it is worthwhile noticing that in the hospital records, people are listed under the name of the titled man (*matai*) who is the head of the extended family (see pp. 220-221) rather than alphabetically by individual names.

Within the household, with the exception of the above-mentioned family corre-spondence, and some secret books in which older men keep family geneologies and cere-monial greetings (*fa'alupega*)[1], writing is not a common activity.

Learning How To Read and Write
Much before the age for public education, at the age of 3 or 4, children are sent to the local pastor's school where they first learn the alphabet, Arabic and Roman numbers, and to recite a few passages from the Bible. With the help of an illustrated alphabet table (see Figure 1), young children recite the name of the letter and the name of the picture contained in the same box. Thus, for instance, they say aloud "a *ato*, e *elefane*, i

---

[1] There is a taboo, in fact, for anyone else but the one who wrote them to read these lists of names and ceremonial greetings. The violation of such a taboo is believed to cause misfortune or even death to the trans-gressor. Such a restriction reinforces (reflects?) the basic Samoan belief that one should learn from direct expe-rience, that is, from watching and listening to competent people.

Figure 1.   Literacy Instruction in Samoa

ipu," etc. for the vowels, and "fa *fanu,* ga *gata,* la *logo,* mo *moa,*" and so on for the consonants.

Given the age range of the pupils, the younger ones are immediately exposed to the more complex tasks and routines performed by the older children. They participate in such routines according to their competence. At first they may be able to perform only part of a given routine; as they mature, they perform in a more competent way, providing a model for younger and less experienced peers.

In Table 1 we have listed the words that correspond to the picture associated with each letter of the alphabet. For each word, we have listed their present spelling[2] and their actual careful pronunciation.

---

[2] As can be seen by comparing the "written" version of each word and its corresponding careful pronunciation, current educational publications in Western Samoa tend not to use glottal stops, despite the fact that the missionaries originally introduced a conventional sign for it, namely, the inverted apostrophe ('). This sign is used, although inconsistently, in the Samoan Bible and in newspaper articles.

Table 1.   Key to Figure 1

LETTER	WORD (as written)	WORD (as pronounced in reading)	GLOSS	
A	*ato*	?ato	'basket'	
E	*'elefane*	?elefane	'elephant'	(loan)
I	*ipu*	?ipu	'cup'	
O	*ofu*	?ofu	'dress'	
U	*uati*	wati	'watch'	(loan)
F	*fagu*	fagu	'bottle'	
G	*gata*	gata	'snake'	
L	*logo*	logo	'bell'	
M	*moa*	moa	'fowl'	
N	*nofoa*	nofoa	'chair'	
P	*pusi*	pusi	'cat'	(loan)
S	*solofanua*	solafanua	'horse'	
T	*taavale*	ta?avale	'car, truck'	
V	*vaa*	va?a	'boat, vessel'	
H*	*Herota*	herota	'herod'	(loan)
K*	*kirikiti*	kirikiti	'cricket'	(loan)
R*	*rapiti*	rapiti	'rabbit'	(loan)

*found only in loanwords).

There are several reasons for wanting to consider in some detail the alphabet table reproduced in Figure 1. It tells us some important things about literacy instruction in Samoa and it also confirms what is already known about literacy in other societies. We will focus on two aspects of the alphabet table: the Western orientation of its content (by "content" we mean both what is represented in the table and the particular way in which it is represented), and the conventions for transcribing Samoan sounds and words.

Western Orientation of the Alphabet Table.   Even without knowing much about Samoan culture, one can easily infer a Western orientation in the illustrated alphabet as shown in Figure 1. More generally, however, there is a clear preference for an imagery that evokes nontraditional settings, referents, and values. Out of the 17 pictures chosen to represent current Samoan words, none of them represent a "traditional" Samoan referent—"traditional" at last from an historical viewpoint: none of the pictures represents something that existed or was known to Samoans before contact with Europeans. This could have not been avoided for the last three letters (*h, k,* and *r*), which correspond to sounds introduced by Europeans for borrowed words: thus we find Herod, Samoan *Herota,* (from the Bible), cricket, Samoan *kirikiki,* and a rabbit, Samoan *rapiti.* What is striking, however, is that even for those words that could have been represented by an image of something "traditional" or familiar to a Samoan child, a corresponding less familiar object or artifact is chosen. This is the case, for instance, for the first picture on the top right corner, where, for the Samoan word *ato* 'basket' we find a kind of basket which is sold to tourists in the capital rather than the traditional basket used in everyday activities for carrying goods or collecting garbage. To represent *ipu* 'cup', we find a China cup rather than the traditional Polynesian cup, that is, half of a coconut shell. The dress, *ofu,* is an end-of-the-century British missionary's wife's dress (notice the short sleeves covering the shoulders, an unfitting feature for the hot and humid climate of Samoa). Finally, the picture of the boat, for the word *va'a,* is an ocean liner rather than the more familiar Samoan outrigger.[5]

These facts suggest that when a Samoan child is first exposed to literacy instructions he or she is taught something more than the alphabet. From the very first day of school, literacy is accompanied by an attention to a world of objects and values that either are removed from the immediate context of the child's everyday life or suggest Western alternatives within a range of possible choices that would include more traditional objects and values. We find reference to Western codes for dressing, Western products (viz. the bottle of "cola"), Western artifacts and technology (e.g. the sedan car rather than the more useful and familiar pick-up truck, the big ship rather than the outrigger). Finally, some of the words anticipate unknown characters (e.g. Herod, the snake—there are no such snakes in Samoa) soon to be encountered in the reading of the Holy Scriptures.

Features of the Literacy Register.   To illustrate the main feature of the sound system portrayed by written Samoan, let us take as an example the word that is used to illustrate the letter/sound *t,* namely, *ta'avale* 'car' but also 'truck' (literally 'rolling thing').

Especially where a village is located along a road, with trucks, buses, pick-ups, and cars passing by at all times of the day, the Samoan child must learn from his very first steps to watch for the often speeding motor vehicles. The word referring to 'car, truck' is thus often heard along and around the road, usually shouted as a warning to young children by older siblings or adult bystanders. *Va'ai ka'avale!* 'watch (for the) car/truck!' one hears, or simply *ka'avale!* 'car/truck!'. In these situations, the word is pronounced with a /k/ rather than with a /t/ (*ka'avale* instead of *ta'avale*). Such a difference between the way the word is written and read and the way it is pronounced in most of daily interaction reflects an important distinction between two sharply marked phonological registers.

In Samoan communities, these registers are called 'Good Speech' (*tautala lelei*) and 'Bad Speech' (*tautala leaga*). Figure 2 illustrates the differences between the two phonemic inventories.

As summarized in Figure 3, in 'Bad Speech' the alveolar segments /t/ and /n/ merge with the velar segments /k/ and /g/ respectively (N.B. Given that Samoan does not have a velar stop, we have here adopted the Samoan orthographic convention of using the

---

[5] In making these remarks, we are not suggesting that imported artifacts or concepts be considered "non-Samoan." We do take sedan cars, China cups, European dresses, clocks, and so on, to be part of contemporary Samoan culture and environment. We are simply pointing out that the choices made in illustrating the alphabet reflect a bias toward those elements of contemporary Samoan culture that are still overtly bound to Western lifestyle and values.

Figure 2. Phonemic Inventories of "Good Speech"
and "Bad Speech." (/g/ stands for a velar nasal)

"Good Speech:"					"Bad Speech":			
A) Consonants:								
P	t		k*	?	P		k	?
f,v s		l,r*			f,v s	l		
m	n		g	h*	m		g	
B) Vowels:								
		i		u				
		e	o					
		a						

*found only in loanwords.

letter g for representing a velar nasal—the voiceless velar segment replaces the voiced one in loanwords, for example, English *gallon* — Samoan *kalone*). Furthermore, /r/ and /l/ merge into /l/, and /h/ is often not realized in 'Bad Speech' or pronounced as a glottal stop.

As pointed out by Shore (1977, 1982), the contexts in which "good speech" predominates are strictly related to "imported" Western-oriented activities. Typically, such activities or interactions involve or presuppose the use of literacy. Thus, we find "Good Speech" used in writing, reading, school instruction, praying, singing, radio broadcasting, and talking to foreigners (who are prototypically seen as missionaries or teachers). 'Bad speech', on the other hand, is found in most of everyday spoken interaction, ranging over both formal (cf. also Duranti, 1981a, 1981b, 1983) and informal situations (cf. Ochs, 1982a, 1982b; Platt, 1982) (cf. Duranti, 1981a; Ochs, in press; and Shore, 1977, 1982 for a general discussion of the variation between the two registers).

Figure 3. Correspondences Between 'Good Speech'
and 'Bad Speech'

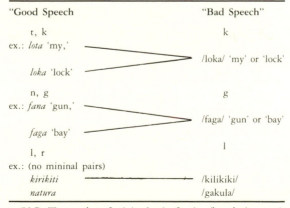

"Good Speech	"Bad Speech"
t, k	k
ex.: *lota* 'my,'	
	/loka/ 'my' or 'lock'
loka 'lock'	
n, g	g
ex.: *fana* 'gun,'	
	/faga/ 'gun' or 'bay'
faga 'bay'	
l, r	l
ex.: (no mininal pairs)	
kirikiti	/kilikiki/
natura	/gakula/

(N.B. The number of minimal pairs for the t/k and n/g oppositions is very low).

THE SOCIAL ORGANIZATION OF TASK ACCOMPLISHMENT
OUTSIDE THE CLASSROOM

We would like to focus now on one particular aspect of Samoan society and culture, namely, on the concept and practice of task achievement. To illustrate this concept, it is necessary to introduce certain aspects of Samoan social organization, specifically, its traditional stratified structure and collective responsibility for task accomplishment.

Social Stratification

Samoan society has been rightly characterized as "stratified" (cf. Sahlins, 1958), that is, as a society in which distinctions with respect to decision power and prestige are made not only in terms of the universal features of age, sex, and personal characteristics, but also, and crucially, according to the rank of particular "titles" that adult individuals may hold from a certain moment of their lives on, usually until their death. A very basic distinction is thus made in Samoan society between titled people, called *matai*, and untitled people or commoners, called *taulele'a*. A title is conferred to a person by a special session of the extended family (*'aaiga potopoto*) and gives its holder privileges and duties with respect to an extended family and to the village political structure. More specifically, a *matai* title gives its holder control over a plot of land and its products (taro, breadfruit, bananas, coconuts), decision power and responsibilities both within the family and in larger contexts, for example, village affairs. A *matai* title carries with it the right and duty to attend the meetings of the village council (*fono*), where important decisions are made and solutions to social dramas are negotiated among the most influential members of the community (cf. Duranti, 1981a).

Social stratification is seen in the division of labor within the family. Generally untitled men and women are the ones who cultivate food on family land, go out fishing, or nowadays work in the capital, and then bring the product of their labor back to be shared among all family members according to social status and the needs of the family at large. The highest ranking chief in the family generally has first rights to choose quality and amount of food; younger, lower status adults and children share what is left.

High rank is associated with stationary behavior, controlled, dignified (*mamalu*) posture (the term used to refer to the ceremony of installation of a title is *saofa'i*, the respect vocabulary word for 'to sit'). Low rank people instead are movable, run errands, carry objects or messages. The dichotomy between high rank-stationary and low rank-active is realized in many different ways, across all kinds of situations.

For example, when we observe people remodeling an old house, we see young untitled men of the family move long and heavy posts, while a much older woman is weaving new blinds with leaves from pandanas trees. Similarly, a young titled man and his wife may be supervising closely those carrying out the heavy labor, giving advice and directing children to help; in the meantime, the oldest man of the house and highest ranking orator in the compound sits silently in a nearby house, watching now and then the others working, while routinely making string from sennit (*'afa*). The string will be used to secure the new blinds and roofing to the house. Participation in this task, then, is differentiated according to social rank.

As this description suggests, more than activity level distinguishes relative status. Generally there is an expectation that low ranking persons will attend to and accommodate those of higher rank. The accommodation is at the same time mental and physical in the sense that lower ranking persons are expected to take the perspective of others to serve them.

At a very early age, young children are both explicitly and implicitly socialized into a disposition of attention and accomodation (Ochs, 1982b). Caregivers often hold and feed infants and toddlers so that they face outwards to others present. Chilren in the early stages of acquiring language are expected to notice activity of others and report on it to others. Further they are expected to speak intelligibly. Unintelligible utterances will generally not be unraveled by older persons present in the manner described for middle-class Western caregiver-child interaction (Ochs & Schieffelin, 1984). By the time children reach the age of three-and-a-half to four years, they will be asked to transmit orally lengthy messages to persons in other compounds. This task will demand of them competence in politeness conventions and respect vocabulary appropriate to the social status of the addressee.

Generally in carrying out these tasks, children are not praised or complimented. The child's accomodation to older persons is part of showing *fa'aaloalo* (respect), a crucial dimension of Samoan social life.

Collective Accomplishment: The Concept of *Taapua'i* ('Supporter')

Having briefly considered the organization of daily activities according to social rank and the socialization of children into such a system, we can start introducing a very important notion in Samoan culture, namely that of *taapua'i,* which can be translated as 'supporter' or 'sympathizer.'

In all kinds of daily activities, Samoans see other people as needing someone else to sympathize with them. Very rarely does a Samoan do something without someone next to him to provide recognition of his actions, attempts, or accomplishments. Whether building a house, singing a song, fixing a broken tool, or driving a car, Samoans know that they can usually count on the company of one or more sympathizers. The relationship between the actor and the supporter is truly reciprocal rather than unidirectional. When someone's work or accomplishment is valued and recognized by a suppoter, the supporter's "work" at recognizing the accomplishment is also recognized by the actor. This relationship is symbolically and routinely instantiated by the use of what we will call "a *maaloo* exchange." If the driver avoids a collision with another vehicle, the passengers will recognize his presence of mind with a *maaloo.* The driver will then acknowledge their support by answering with another *maaloo.*

The exchange goes as follows:

(1) (Context: driver does something that shows skill, presence of mind)

    Passenger(s):   *Maaloo le fa'auli!* 'Well done the steering!'
    Driver: *Maaloo le taapua'i!* 'Well done the support!'

If the driver is able to see a hole in the road and avoid it in time, the exchange might be as follows:

> Passenger(s):   *Maaloo le silasila!* 'Well done the looking!'
> Driver: *Maaloo le taapua'i!* 'Well done the support!'

This kind of routine is found in situations that at first appear more difficult to understand for a non-Samoan. Thus, as illustrated in (3), when a party of people who have been away on a trip returns home, those who stayed home welcome them with a *maaloo* greeting and those who just arrived reply with another *maaloo*:

(3)

> People at home: *Maaloo le malaga!* 'Well done the trip!'
> Travelers: *Maaloo le fa'amuli!* 'Well done the staying back!'

To understand this exchange, we must realize that in the Samoan view, the travelers' reply not only acknowledges the sympathy of those at home (some of whom might have worried about the outcomes of the trip), but also they recognize the fact that a trip is made into something valuable, deserving recognition, by the very fact that someone stayed home and did not go on the trip. The same is true for the exchange between the driver and the passengers. The driver is skillful to the extent to which his suppoters are willing to recognize his skills.

More generally, something is an accomplishment because of and through the recognition that others are willing to give it. Any accomplishment can then be seen as a joint product of both the actors and the supporters. In the Samoan view, if a performance went well it is the suppoters' merit as much as the performers. This is so true that if the performer receives a prize or some previously established compensation, he will have to share it with his supporters.

Concluding, the notion of 'supporter' and the *maaloo* routine reiterate the Samoan view of accomplishment as a collective and cooperative enterprise, in which the individual's competence is defined by his audience appreciation and his merit is framed within the merit of his group. Being skillful (*poto*) at something does not mean to stand out with respect to everyone else as much as to be able to create the conditions for a successful collective endeavour (cf. Mead, 1937). By sharing the products of his labor or his earnings (if any) with his supporters, a person gives goods back to those who gave him sympathy first.

LITERACY INSTRUCTION IN CLASSROOM SETTINGS

The Setting

As noted earlier, generally Samoan children first acquire literacy skills in a village pastor's school. They enter this school two to three years before entering the kindergarten class in the village public school. The classes meet in the late afternoon and many children of the congregation attend until their early teens. The interactions analyzed here are drawn from both pastor's and public schools, however our primary focus will be on literacy instruction in the pastor's school.

While the youngest children spend time learning the alphabet table, older children in the pastor's school concentrate on two important tasks: oral reading from the Bible and interpretation of Bible passages. The children typically sit cross-legged on mats, facing the instructor (the pastor, the pastor's wife, the pastor's assistant), who is also seated cross-legged on a separate mat, facing the children. Every child holds his Bible in his lap or places it on the mat in front of him. The lesson begins with Bible reading. In this part, each child reads one verse from the Bible, with the pastor's assistance (see example 4). Following this, the pastor questions the children concerning their understanding of the written material they have just read. Three stretches of classroom interaction between a pastor and his students illustrate the character of these events.

(4) Pastor's School: Reading Aloud (Context: A child reading aloud from the Bible misreads the word *faaliu* 'to turn towards'—spelled *faliu*—as *fa'aliliu* 'to translate'. Such a mistake is probably related to the fact that in the Bible the glottal stop (') is often left out and *fa'aliliu* could have been written *Faaliliu*)

1.	Child:	((* Error)) 'But Jesus translating to—'
2.	Pastor:	*Sipela le 'upu!* 'Spell the word!'
3.	(3.0)	
4.	Child:	*Fa-a-la-i-u.* 'F-a-l-i-u.' (N.B. the word is spelled with one *a*)
5.	Pastor:	*Ia. Le aa laa?* 'So. What is it then?'
6.	(6.0)	
7.	Child:	*'A 'ua fa'ai'u**. ((* Error)) 'But (he) ended.'
8.	Pastor:	*('A 'ua—)* (1.5) *Sipela le 'upu!* '(But he)—(1.5) Spell the word!'
9.	Child:	*Fa-a-la-i-u.* 'F-a-l-i-u.'
10.	(1.0	
11.	Pastor:	*Faa.* 'Faa,'
12.	Child:	*Fa'aliliu** (* Error) 'Translated'
13.	Pastor:	*Leo kele!* 'Speak loud!'
14.	Child:	*Fa'aliliu.* (* Error) 'Translated.'
15.	Pastor:	*'E lee se fa'aliliu! Fa'aliliu fa'afefea?* 'It's not 'translate'! How come translate?
16.		*Fa-a-la-i-u* 'F-a-l-i-u.'
17.	(4.5)	

18.	Pastor:	'*O le 'faa' ma le 'liu.' 'O le aa le 'upu?* 'Faa' and 'liu.' What is the word?'
19.	(2.0)	
20.	Child:	(Unclear)
21.	Pastor:	*Le aa?* 'What?'
22.	Child:	*Faaliu.* 'Turn.'
23.	Pastor:	*Faaliu. Le kele!* 'Turn. Speak loud!'
24.	(1.0)	
25.	Child:	'*A 'ua fa'al—faaliu Iesuu i—iaa te 'i—* 'But Jesus transl— turning to—
26.		*ia—iaa te 'i laatou 'ua fetalai (0.3) atu* 'up—upon them said'

(5) Pastor's School: Discussion of Herod

1.	Pastor:	'*O ai Herota?*' 'Who is Herod?'
2.	Teresa:	*Tupu.* 'King.'
3.	Pastor:	'*O le aa?*' 'It is what?'
4.	Teresa:	'*O le tupu.* '(He) is the king.'
5.	Pastor:	'*O le tupu. Lelei.* '(He) is the king. Good.'
6.		'*E iai se si e 'ese sana tali?*' 'Is there anyone else with a different answer?'
7.	Boy:	'*O le tagata lea na fia fasi fua iaa Iesuu.* 'The person who wanted to kill Jesus for no reason.'
8.	Pastor:	*Lelei fo'i.* 'Good also.'
9.		'*A 'o le aa lona—lona tofiga?* 'But what is his—his occupation?!'
10.		'*O le tupu aa,* 'The king, isn't he?'
11.		*Tupu lea saa—saa lee fiafia iaa Iesuu* '(The) king who did—didn't like Jesus'
12.		*ina 'ua fanau mai Iesuu* 'because Jesus was born'
13.		*ma 'ua folafola mai e tagata* 'and was proclaimed by the people'
14.		'*o ia 'o le tupu o tagata Iutaia aa,* '(that) he is the king of the Jews, right?'
15.		*saa—saa lee fiafia la iai* '(he) di—didn't like him then'
16.		'*ona 'o le manatu o Herota* 'because Herod's idea (was that)'

17.		*na 'o ia lava le tupu aa.* 'only he himself is the king, right?'
18.		*'e lee ai se si tagata e tatau* 'there is no other person (who) should'
19.		*ona—ona fai ma tupu* 'become king.'
20.		*Se'i vaganaa 'o ia lava.* 'Except he himself.'

(6) Pastor's School: Discussion of Barabbas

1.	Pastor:	. . . *Parapa saa fouvale i le—i le nu'u.* 'Barabbas had rioted in the—in the city'
2.		*Saa tele fo'i ana amio leaga na fai.* 'Many were the bad actions he had done.'
3.		*'Ona 'ave ai lea tu'u i le fale—,. . . .* 'so that (he) had been put in the pri—,. . . '
4.	Children:	*—puipui* '—son!'
5.	Pastor:	*Falepuipui!* 'Prison!'
6.		*Ia. 'O lona uiga 'a tu'u tagata* 'So. That is to say, if someone is put'
7.		*i le falepuipui 'o le aa le tagata legaa?* 'in a prison, what is that person?'
8.		*'O le paago—,. . . .* 'A priso—,. . . '
9.	Children:	*Paagota.** (* Error: the last *a* should be long, *aa*) 'Paagota.'
10.	Pastor:	((Correcting the pronunciation)) *PaagotAA!* 'Prisoner!'
11.		*Po 'o le paagota?'* 'What is a paagota?'

The Role of Literacy Instruction in Redefining Adult-Child Social Relationships

Examining the verbal interaction in these examples, we can see that the pastor/instructor enters into the activity of reading and interpreting at many points. Very much like contemporary Western pedagogues, the pastor in this village school grants permission to speak, selects topics, points out errors, correcting certain of them, and clarifies terms and passages.

Three constructions are heavily relied upon to introduce and clarify topics: *rhetorical questions* (Example (5), line 9), *test questions* (Example (5), line 1), and *incomplete sentence frames* (Example (6), lines 3 and 8). Rhetorical and test questions are similar in that, in both cases, the speaker knows a possible answer to the question posed. They are distinguished in that the rhetorical question is intended to be answered by the speaker, whereas the test question is intended to be answered by a selected addressee. The incomplete sentence frame functions as a question as well in that the instructor elicits through prosodic means missing information in a sentence he has initiated. Both the test question and incomplete sentence frame involve the instructor and student in the expression of an idea. The instructor provides the first part and the student the second part of the idea.

These pedagogical procedures are very familiar to the readership of this paper. These constructions and strategies parallel those found in classrooms following Western or European tradition of formal education (cf. Mehan, 1979; Philips, 1983). Indeed the parallel is not coincidental. The pastor's school is organized through the Christian church. Training in Western pedagogical techniques is provided to pastors and their spouses over a four-year period in a theological seminary.

The procedures characteristic of teachers in Western classrooms are extensions of practices of caregivers in Western middle-class households. In other words, *teacher talk* (Cazden, 1979; Coulthard, 1977) has something in common with middle-class caregiver speech to young children. In both situations, speakers simplify and clarify for the child (Ferguson, 1977). For example, rhetorical questions simplify a proposition by breaking it into two separate utterances. The child's attention is drawn to certain information (topic) in one utterance and then a predication (comment) concerning that information is made in a separate subsequent utterance (see Keenan & Schieffelin, 1976; Ochs, Schieffelin, & Platt, 1979; Scollon, 1976). Test questions and sentence frames simplify by helping the child to express an idea; typically caregivers/teachers produce the first part of the idea (topic) and the child completes the predication (comment) (Keenan, Schieffelin, & Platt, 1978; Greenfield & Smith, 1976). In Western middle-class societies, these procedures are part of a broader set of simplifying features that distinguish language addressed to young children from many other sociolinguistic situations. When a middle-class child enters the classroom, then, there is quite a lot of continuity with his or her early experiences in talking to adults.

In contrast, these features are not characteristic of traditional Samoan caregiver speech. *While these features reflect and express in middle-class society the expectation that adults should accomodate their language in relating to small children* (Ochs & Schieffelin, 1984), *the traditional Samoan expectation is the reverse—that children, not adults, should accomodate their behavior, including their speech* (Ochs, 1982b).

Samoan caregivers generally do not simplify their speech in addressing small children. Relevant to this discussion, they do not characteristically break down propositions into rhetorical questions and answers, nor do they jointly express propositions with children through test questions/answers and sentence frames/completions. As a rule, caregivers do not ask children questions to which they know the answers. For example, Samoan caregivers do not engage in labeling routines with small children, asking the child questions, such as 'What's this?', to which the caregiver knows the answer.

As noted earlier, in contrast to Western middle-class caregivers, Samoan caregivers place far greater responsibility for acquisition of knowledge with the child. Children are expected to watch and listen. Samoans say that the way to knowledge and power is to serve (i.e., attend).

When a three- or four-year-old Samoan child enters the classroom for literacy instruction, then, he or she participates in verbal interactions that differ in important ways from interactions with adults outside the classroom. *Most critically, in the classroom, the adult verbally accomodates (in terms of simplification and clarification) to the child to a greater extent than do adults outside this setting. In the classroom, the interactions are more child-centered; in other village settings, the interactions are more adult-centered.* The net result is a shift in social expectations surrounding the roles of adult and child.

The Role of Literacy Instruction in Redefining Task Accomplishment

In this section, we will consider how accomplishment or achievement is expressed in literacy instruction and contrast this with expectations outside the classroom setting. We will see that the notion of task accomplishment in the classroom further enhances the child-centered orientation of the interaction.

In the previous section, we have indicated ways in which the pastor/instructor facilitates the tasks of reading and comprehending written material. Examining the transcripts, we can see the achievement of these tasks has drawn on the efforts of both instructor and student. Indeed in certain cases the instructor and student together have produced the correct reading or missing information. Curiously, however, these accomplishments are not seen as cooperative in this social context. *Rather, tasks are treated as individually accomplished, specifically, as accomplished by a particular child.*

Support for this claim comes from the set of positive assessments—compliments or praises—that can mark the successful completion of particular tasks. Before proceeding with a comparison of complimenting/praising in and out of the classroom, we need to point out that, across societies, these forms of verbal behavior codify perspectives on task and achievement. Complimenting and praising can indicate *that* something has been accomplished, *what* has been accomplished, *who* has accomplished it, and *in what manner.* They are, then, good sources for understanding how members of a society conceptualize task. Where young children are involved, complimenting and praising socialize them into seeing task from a particular perspective or 'world view'.

We have noted earlier in this paper (pp. 221–222) that the successful accomplishment of tasks in day-to-day village life is often acknowledged through a verbal ritual—the *maaloo* exchange. Task accomplishment in the classroom is also associated with a verbal ritual. The successful completion of a task is often acknowledged by the instructor uttering praises such as *lelei* 'good' or *lelei tele* 'very good'. Example (5) illustrates two instances of this pattern. Lines 5 and 8 contain the assessment *lelei* 'good'. In these instances, the pastor praises two children for successfully answering a question. Below we provide another example of these assessments. Example (7) is drawn from the kindergarten/first grade class in the village public school. In this example the instructor acknowledges accomplishment through the predicates *lelei tele* 'very good' (lines 5, 10).

(7) Kindergarten/first grade class (Context: It is the second week of school. The teacher has just taken the class for a walk around the school yard. Once back in the classroom, she asks the pupils questions about what they have just seen.)

1.   Teacher: *Lima i luga lima i luga lima i luga!* 'Hands up hands up hands up!'

2.   *Si'i luga lima o le tagata* 'Raise a hand the person (who)'

3.   *e iloa ta'u mai se mea (iaa) te a'u!* 'can tell me something!'

4.   ((A boy raises his hand)).

5.   Teacher: *Lelei tele. "O ai fo'i le igoa laa?* 'Very good. What is the name there?'

6.   Boy: *Salani.* 'Salani.'

7.   Teacher: 'O ai? 'Who?'

8.   2 Girls: *Salagi.* 'Salagi.'

9.   Teacher: *Salagi tama lelei Salagi. Tu'u i luga Salagi.* 'Salagi good boy Salagi.
                                Stand up Salagi.

10   *Ta'u mai se mea na "e va'ai iai.* 'Tell (us) something you saw.'

11.   Salagi: *'Ulu!* 'Breadfruit(s)!'

12.   Teacher: *Lelei tele.* (Cont.) 'Very good.'

We turn now to a comparison of *maaloo* and *lelei* in the different social settings in which they are used. *Maaloo* is used pervasively in social situations outside the classroom setting; it is rarely used in the classroom. *Lelei* is used consistently in the speech of instructors in the course of literacy instruction; it is rarely used as a form of praise in social situations outside this setting.[4] In our discussion we will focus on one variable, the recipient of the compliment or praise (the one/ones who take(s) credit for the task accomplished.)

Comparing examples (1), (2), and (3) with examples (5) and (7), we can see that *maaloo* ("well done") and *lelei* ("good") have different conversational consequences. As noted earlier (pp. 221–222) *maaloo* is part of a verbal exchange. In conversation analysis terminology, the first utterance containing *maaloo* (*maaloo* #1: 'well done') is the first pair part of an adjacency pair and the second utterance containing *maaloo* (*maaloo* #2: 'and well done to you') is the second pair part (Sacks, Schegloff, & Jefferson, 1974). The important property is that once *maaloo* #1 is produced, there is a strong expectation that *maaloo* #2 will be produced.

Lelei ('good'), on the other hand, is not a first pair part of an exchange/adjacency pair. It is instead the last act of a three-part sequence, typical of classroom interaction, which Mehan (1979) called "Initiation-Reply-Evaluation." What is relevant for our discussion is that when the instructor acknowledges the child's achievement by uttering *lelei,* the child does not reciprocate and acknowledge the instructor's accomplishments in the so-

---

[4] Outside the classroom, *lelei* is used primarily to express agreement and conclude a topic, muck like the English *okay, sure, fine.* In these contexts, *lelei* is typically preceded by the particle *ia',* a boundary marker of discourse units, roughly corresponding to the English *well, so, then. Lelei* in the classroom also operates as a boundary marker, but performs a different speech act (praise rather than agreement). In addition, there are prosodic differences between the utterances in which *lelei* is used as a praise and those in which it is used as an agreement.

cial event at hand. The child does not say, for example, *Lelei fo'i* or *Lelei fo'i "oe* ('You did well too.'). In contrast to *maaloo, lelei* closes an interactional sequence.

Simply in terms of their sequential organization, *maaloo* and *lelei* reflect differences in giving credit for task accomplishment. When a speaker uses *maaloo*, credit is typically reciprocally given (two-directional.) When *lelei* is used, credit is unidirectional.

There are additional properties of *maaloo* that distinguish it from *lelei*. The *maaloo* exchange is not simply an exchange of compliments/praises. It expresses the idea that both parties to the *maaloo* exchange have contributed to the same task. As noted earlier, the initial expression of *maaloo* itself defines the speaker as a *taapua'i* 'supporter' and supporters should be given credit for accomplishing the task. Hence the speaker of *maaloo* #1 becomes the recipient of *maaloo* #2. The use of *lelei* apparently carries with it no such conditions. The instructor who uses *lelei* is not acknowledged by a child for his or her role in facilitating the achievement of literacy skills. Outside this setting, the same child told *maaloo* does *maaloo* back, acknowledging the contribution of others in achieving a goal.

Young Samoan children experience a type of secondary socialization in the course of becoming literate. They learn sociolinguistic norms that differ from those operating in family interactions within the village. In their primary socialization, they learn not to expect praises and compliments for carrying out directed tasks. Children are expcted to carry out these tasks for their elders and family. In their secondary socialization, they learn to expect recognition and positive assessments, given successful accomplishment of a task. In their primary socialization, Samoan children learn to consider tasks as cooperatively accomplished, as social products. In their secondary socialization, they learn to consider tasks as an individual's work and accomplishment.

This particular difference is not experienced by most western middle-class children entering school. These children are accustomed to praise (LeVine, 1980). Further, from infancy onwards, these children are socialized through language to see tasks as individually accomplished. They have experienced daily interactions in which jointly accomplished tasks of adult and child are evaluated by the adult as an accomplishment of the child (Ochs & Schieffelin, 1984). Adults provide the means for a child to accomplish a task, but then treat that task as the child's own achievement. Western middle-class caregivers repeat this pattern over and over in playing games, drawing, constructing (Bruner, 1975), putting away toys, telling a story jointly with their children. The behavior of teachers in contemporary Western classrooms is continuous in this sense with that of caregivers. In both cases, the adult does not take (or get) credit for her or his part in accomplishing a task; rather, the child is given full credit through unidirectional praising.

We can see from this description that the secondary socialization of Samoan children may extend beyond norms of classroom interaction. Samoan children may be acquiring certain attitudes that characterize Western middle-class relationships, including, most importantly economic relationships.

Rural Samoans acquire literacy skills primarily to be competent in reading the Bible and to be employable. The ability to read and write fluently is a requirement of most salaried jobs in the capital. But to participate successfully in the urban cash economy, a Samoan needs more than literacy skills in the strict sense of reading and writing. The urban economy is heavily influential by Western values. In particular, the urban economic system relies on the notion of individual accomplishment. This is what a salary represents. The salary symbolizes recognition and approval of an individual's achievements, that an individual has done what was expected (or more than expected) of him. The Western-style pedagogic procedures used in transmitting literacy skills prepare young children for the Western-style economy in which many will eventually participate. With a school certificate in hand, they have acquired (to some measure) *both* social and linguistic competence demanded in these economic contexts. However, secondary socialization may be superseded by primary socialization as long as the traditional social context stays unchanged. When the emigrant Samoan comes back to his village for a visit, he is expected to share his earnings with his family, friends, and *taapua'i*. The fruits of his labor are redistributed among those who helped him at some earlier time in his life or were thinking of him while away.

CONCLUSIONS

In a recent collection on literacy and historical change, Graff (1981, p. 258) has written: "Literacy's importance can not be understood in isolation, or in terms of self-advancement or skills; rather, its significance lies in its relation to the transmission of morals, discipline and social values." Graff and other social scientists (e.g., Galtung, 1981, Gintis, 1971) have argued that, in teaching literacy, educators have been simultaneously engaged in "the reshaping of character, behavior, morality and culture" (Graff, 1981, p. 257). Industrialists apparently recognized this activity long before social scientists and in the nineteenth century encouraged schools to promote values that are harmonious with economic productivity, for example, self-motivation, punctuality, regularity.

These observations are compatible with those of Scribner and Cole (1981). While the historians may ascribe more importance to social than to cognitive transformations (if such a distinction can be made), both perspectives indicate the importance of the *uses* of literacy. The consequences of literacy are related to the activities in which it is used in and outside the classroom. Children acquiring literacy are acquiring competence in these activities.

This paper has pursued this hypothesis in a somewhat different manner than has either the historian or the psychologist. It has proposed two important consequences of Samoan children's participation in literacy instruction activities and then has analyzed the discourse structure of these activities, relating specific uses of language and the sequential organization of discourse to attitudes, expectations, and values.

In particular, the paper has been concerned with the attitudes, expectations, and values surrounding the adult-child social relationship and the concept of task accomplishment. We have proposed that, in the classroom, adults (instructors) accomodate their behavior to children in conveying information. Such accomodation is not characteristic of adult-child verbal interactions outside the classroom. We can see this difference through a comparison of adult-child discourse in household and school settings (+/- test questions, +/- incomplete sentence frames, +/- rhetorical questions). We have also proposed that the discourse of literacy instruction reveals an orientation towards task accomplishment. We have focused on the structure of complimenting/praising and argued that in literacy instruction such speech acts are unidirectional, from instructor to child. Even though the instructor has participated in the task of reading and understanding, this participation is not verbally acknowledged by the child. In contrast, complimenting/praising in most other village settings is reciprocal. Achievement of a task is seen as a social product, dependent on the participation of different people carrying out different roles, including that of supporter.

Through such an examination, we come closer to understanding the effects of literacy and schooling on children. Children are socialized through participating in such verbal interactions into certain perspectives and values. The extent to which these children are affected depends on the extent of their education and the extent to which they continue to participate in village social life. Those who go on to secondary schools, and those who leave the village to work or study elsewhere are obviously affected more than others. For the majority of rural Samoans, the Western view of adult-child relationships and task accomplishment is restricted to particular settings, namely, school and work in the capital. This view coexists with more traditional views. Members of a Samoan village can shift their conduct and interpretative frame regarding children and tasks just as they can shift in and out of the literate register.

REFERENCES

Bruner, J.S. (1975). The ontogenesis of speech acts. *Journal of Child Language 2*, 1–21.

Cazden, C. (1979). *Language in education: Variation in the teacher-talk register.* Proceedings from the Third Annual Georgetown University Round Table on Languages and Linguistics, *Language in Public Life.* Washington, DC: Georgetown University Press.

Coulthard, M. (1977). *An introduction to discourse analysis.* London: Longman.

Duranti, A. (1981a). *The Samoan FONO: A sociolinguistic study.* Pacific Linguistics, Series B, vol. 80. Canberra: Department of Linguistics, R.S.Pac.S., The Australian National University.

Duranti, A. (1981b). Speechmaking and the organization of discourse in a Samoan *fono*. *The Journal of the Polynesian Society. 90.* 357–400.

Duranti, A. (1983). Samoan speechmaking across social events: One genre in and out of a *Fono*. *Language in Society, 12,* 1–22.

Ferguson, C.A. (1977). Baby talk as a simplified register. In C.E. Snow & C.A. Ferguson (Eds.), *Talking to children: Language input and acquisition.* Cambridge: Cambridge University Press.

Galtung, J. (1981). Literacy, education and schooling—For what? In H.J. Graff (Ed.), *Literacy and social development in the West.* Cambridge: Cambridge Unversity Press.

Gintis, H. (1971). Education, technology and the characteristics of worker productivity. *American Economic Review. 61,* 266–279.

Goody, J. (1977). *Domestication of the savage mind.* Cambridge: Cambridge University Press.

Graff, H.J. (1981). Literacy, jobs, and industrialization: The nineteen century. In H.J. Graff (Ed.), *Literacy and social development in the West.* Cambridge: Cambridge University Press.

Greenfield, P.M. (1972). Oral and written language: The consequences for cognitive development in Africa, the United States and England. *Language and Speech. 15,* 169–178.

Greenfield, P.M., & Smith, J.H. (1976). *The structure of communication in early language development.* New York: Academic Press.

Heath, S.B. (1982). What no bedtime story means: Narrative skills at home and school. *Language in Society*, *11*, 49–76.

Keenan, E.O., & Schieffelin, B. (1976). Topic as a discourse notion. In C.N. Li (Ed.), *Subject and topic*. New York: Academic Press.

Keenan, E.O., Schieffelin, B., & Platt, M. (1978). Questions of immediate concern. In E. Goody (Ed.), *Questions and politeness: Strategies in social interaction*. Cambridge: Cambridge University Press.

LeVine, R.A. (1980). Anthropology and child development. In *Anthropological perspectives on child development*. Special issue of *New Directions for Child Development*, *8*, 71–86.

Mead, M. (1937). The Samoans. In M. Mead (Ed.), *Cooperation and competition among primitive people*. Boston: Beacon Press.

Mehan, H. (1979) *Learning lessons: Social organization in the classroom*. Cambridge, MA: Harvard University Press.

Milner, G.B. (1966). *Samoan dictionary*. London: Oxford University Press.

Ochs, E. (1982a). Ergativity and word order in Samoan child language: A sociolinguistic study. *Language*, *58*, 646–671.

Ochs, E. (1982b). Talking to children in Western Samoa. *Language in Society*, *11*, 77–104.

Ochs, E. (in press). Variation and error: A sociolinguistic approach to language acquisition in Samoa. In D.I. Slobin (Ed.), *The cross-linguistic study of language acquisition*. Hillsdale, NJ: Erlbaum.

Ochs, E., & Schieffelin, B. (1984). Language acquisition and socialization: Three developmental stories and their implications. In R. Shweder & R. LeVine (Eds.), *Culture theory: Essays on mind, self, and emotion*. Cambridge: Cambridge University Press.

Ochs, E., Schieffelin, E., & Platt, M. (1979). Propositions across utterances and speakers. In E. Ochs & B. Schieffelin (Eds.), *Developmental pragmatics*. New York: Academic Press.

Philips, S.U. (1983). *The invisible culture: Communication in classroom and community on the Warm Springs Indian Reservation*. New York: Longman.

Platt, M. (1982). *Social and semantic dimensions of deictic verbs and particles in Samoan child language*. Unpublished doctoral dissertation. University of Southern California, Los Angeles.

Pawley, A. (1966). Samoan phrase-structure: The morphology-syntax of a Western Polynesian language. *Anthropological Linguistics*, *1*, 1–63.

Sacks, H., Schegloff, & Jefferson, G. (1974). A simplest systematics for the organization of turn-taking for conversation. *Language*, *50*, 696–735.

Sahlins, M.D. (1958). *Social stratification in Polynesia*. Seattle: University of Washington Press.

Scollon, R. (1976). *Conversations with a one year old*. Honolulu: University of Hawaii Press.

Scollon, R., & Scollon, S.B.K. (1981). *Narrative, literacy, and face in interethnic communication*. Norwood, NJ: Ablex.

Scribner, S., & Cole, M. (1978). Literacy without schooling: Testing for intellectual effects. *Harvard Educational Review*, *48*, 4.

Scribner, S., & Cole, M. (1981). *The psychology of literacy*. Cambridge, MA: Harvard University Press.

Shore, B. (1977). A Samoan theory of action: Social control and social order in a Polynesian paradox. University of Chicago dissertation.

Shore, B. (1982). *Sala'ilua: A Samoan mystery*. New York: Columbia University Press.

12

Studying Literacy In Morocco*

Daniel A. Wagner
Brinkley M. Messick
Jennifer Spratt
University of Pennsylvania

Vignette: At the Gas Station

It is a bright sunny April day as Si Mohamed drives the office car into the brand new Afriquia gas station in Berrechid, Morocco. When Allal, the gas station attendant, has filled the gas tank, Si Mohamed asks for a *facture* (receipt) for reimbursement. Allal rummages briefly through his leather money bag and carefully extracts a pad of blank *factures* and a blackened rubber stamp with the station's name and address. With a deep breath he exhales on the rubber stamp, moistening it slightly, and then presses it with deliberation into the *facture* paper. This small rubber stamp, like tens of thousands all over Morocco, serves as the guarantor of official literacy in Morocco. Allal, who cannot read or write, then hands the stamped paper to Si Mohamed, who fills in the date, amount of gas, and the price.

Mohamed and Allal have just engaged in a joint literacy act, which in some ways is representative of literacy not only in Morocco, but also in many parts of the world. For literacy is not possessed and understood only by a small elite, even in countries where a majority can neither read nor write. As this paper will show, literacy is a complex and culturally-mediated phenomenon which is only beginning to be understood.

* The research described in this chapter was undertaken in collaboration with the Faculté des Sciences de l'Education of Université Mohamed V (Rabat, Morocco). We gratefully acknowledge the help of several Moroccan faculty colleagues as well as our Moroccan field research assistants. Scott Paris, Elizabeth Moore, and Karen Seeley provided helpful input into the formulation of some of the ideas of this paper. The authors would also like to thank Caroline Bledsoe, Carole Edelsky, Dale Eickelman, Abdelkader Ezzaki, and the editors of this volume for their helpful criticism on earlier drafts of this paper. The material presented here is one part of the Morocco Literacy Project, which has been supported by funds from the National Institute of Education (G80–0182), the National Institutes of Health (HD–14898), and the Spencer Foundation. Portions of this chapter were also presented at the Annual Meetings of the American Anthropological Association, Chicago, November 1983. Requests for further information should be addressed to: Daniel A. Wagner, Graduate School of Education, University of Pennsylvania, Philadelphia, PA 19104.

INTRODUCTION

Morocco has been acquainted with literacy for over a thousand years, but the pattern of traditional literacy in Morocco may be characterized as "restricted" (Goody, 1968), since only a small, elite segment of the society was literate. In this century, however, the social distribution and culture of literacy have been transformed, first with the appearance of French, the colonial language, and second, with the establishment of a national school system from the time of Moroccan independence in 1956. For the first time, via a legal mandate requiring universal education, literacy is being extended to all segments of the population. Our current research is focused on the phenomenon of the spread of literacy to a nonelite, newly-educated stratum of a society which has had long contact with traditional religious literacy. Neither the old scholarly elite (*'ulama*) nor the French-speaking bourgeoisie will fall within the direct purview of this study, but both of these groups are, nevertheless, part of the general context for understanding the appearance of literacy among the lower-middle-class (or underclass) majority of Morocco's population.

Because of our interest in understanding the nature of literacy acquisition in children, a major concern is children's learning in the home and in school. Our sample population—selected from urban and rural field sites—includes about 370 boys and girls from four to eight years of age, and their families. It is drawn from Morocco's two indigenous spoken language groups, Moroccan colloquial Arabic and Berber. The sample is also divided according to the children's formal preschool experience—traditional (Quranic) or modern kindergarten or none—prior to entering the public primary school at about age seven. Comparing preschool experience is important, since the pedagogies of the traditional and modern schools are known to contrast in important ways which will be discussed later in this paper.

While we have generally restricted the field of inquiry to certain social strata and age groups, our chosen sample population still requires the consideration of a range of variables (such as the actual distribution of native language competences), for which there were virtually no hard data when the project began. This part of our interdisciplinary project is anchored in a variety of quantitatives measures of language, reading, and cognitive skills, supported by several other modes of investigation which will be described below. We begin by presenting further background material on Morocco which may help to situate the general hypotheses of the project. Following, in the second section, is a proposed general framework for studying literacy in complex societies such as Morocco.

LANGUAGE AND LITERACY IN MOROCCO

Three main languages—Arabic, Berber, and French—from three different language stocks—Semitic, Hamitic, and Indo-European—are found in Morocco. In addition, since Arabic is composed of different written and spoken versions, we may speak of a four-language context. For the purposes of this research, we have eliminated the French language from in-depth consideration in an effort to reduce the project scope. This decision is consistent with the socio-economic level of the population sample, since most of the children in our study are not directly exposed to instruction in French. Moroccan children in elite preschools and private primary schools may receive part or even all of their curriculum in French and their parents may also speak French at home, but this legacy of the colonial era is under pressure now from a national educational policy of Arabization. This policy, which involves the gradual, systematic replacement of instruction in French by instruction in Arabic at all levels of the national school system, is well underway in Morocco, and is complemented by a simultaneous policy of Moroccanization of the teacher corps (Hammoud, 1982).

From the perspective of this project, therefore, the language of literacy is 'standard,' or 'classical' Arabic (*fusha*).[1] This is the case whether a student comes from a colloquial Arabic (*derija*)- or Berber (*tamazight*)-speaking milieu. The Arabic alphabet has 28 letters and is written right to left. Since most of these letters change their figural form according to their place (beginning, middle, end) in the word, there are over 50 characters that the reader must recognize to use the Arabic script. Furthermore, Arabic, like Hebrew, makes use of diacritical marks or dots to distinguish between certain letters. As Feitelson (1980) has noted for Hebrew and for Arabic, multiple letter forms and diacritical marks are particularly susceptible to perpetual error by young children and unskilled readers. On the other hand, both Arabic and Hebrew have a strong built-in relationship between grapheme and phoneme (symbol and sound), which is often considered an advantage over the English alphabet in teaching beginning reading.

Moroccan children who begin learning to read in literary Arabic do so on a basis of oral competency in either colloquial Moroccan Arabic or Berber, or some combination of the two. Colloquial Arabic is not a written language but it is spoken by more than half of Morocco's population. An old alphabet (*Tifinagh*) exists for Berber, but it was mainly used for inscriptions, and it is not widely known or used in contemporary Morocco. On the rare occasions when Berber is transcribed, either the Arabic or French orthographies are used. Berber, in three dialectal forms, is spoken as a native language by perhaps half of the Moroccan population, though exact demographic statistics are not available. From what is known of the linguistic ecology of Morocco, it appears that the major concentration of colloquial Arabic monolinguals are found in the Atlantic plains and the major cities, while Berber monolinguals, who are thought to be predominantly women and young children, are located mostly in the mountain and desert regions. Most Berber-speaking men seem eventually to become bilingual in colloquial Arabic. There are, therefore, many more colloquial Arabic monolinguals than there are Berber monolinguals.

In the selection of our field sites we have chosen one location in a largely Arabic-speaking urban population (Marrakesh) and another in a largely Berber-speaking town (Al-Ksour)[2] in the Middle Atlas Mountains. One major area of interest of the project is

---

[1] "Standard" and "classical" Arabic may be considered as two written varieties. The "classical" variety is that of the ancient, religious, or formal texts, with the Quran as the penultimate example. Usually, "standard" Arabic is the modern written form taught in schools in Morocco and other Arabic-speaking countries. We thank A. Ezzaki for his clarification of this point.

[2] Al-Ksour is the pseudonym of a small town in the Middle Atlas mountains. All persons in this paper are real, but names have been changed to protect anonymity.

in contrasting how Arabic- and Berber-speaking children acquire literacy in literary (or standard) Arabic. It was hypothesized that the process of acquisition would be facilitated for colloquial Arabic-speaking children due to the kinship of their spoken language with literary Arabic (for more recent work in this area, see Badry, 1983).

Discovering a coherent emic definition of literacy for the population under study is another aim of our work in Morocco. The term "literacy" is obviously relative, and without knowing what it implies in a given population, it is difficult to assess how and whether literacy is used in that population. In some areas, for example, a man may be considered a "literate" Quranic scholar (*fqih*), because he has memorized the Quran, and can decode it orally and can write down Quranic verses without—as more than one *fqih* have admitted—actually comprehending the sense of what he has read and written. The term "literate" is most often expressed in colloquial Arabic as *qari'*, meaning "one who reads," but also "one who has studied" or "one who has gone to school." The same broadness of meaning occurs with the verb root of this word, *qara'a* ("to read") which is also used to mean "to study," and "to go to school": the semantic domains of literacy, reading, study, and formal schooling are all bound up together. Another common verb "to read" is *hafadh*—meaning more specifically "to memorize"; this semantic linkage seems to provide an emic rationale to many parents and teachers who believe memorization to be such a basic part of education. Whether these concepts are considered inseparable in actual practice in Morocco—denying the possibility of literacy without schooling or studying without reading, or reading without memorizing—is a question that requires an answer in order to understand and fairly assess what literacy means in Morocco.

Project Hypotheses

Some of the hypotheses of the project design have already been referred to above and others will be discussed more fully in the next section. Nonetheless, it is useful here to state briefly the main areas of project interest before continuing. In selecting our population subsamples, we have attempted to contrast several key variables within the overall contours of Moroccan literacy, within, of course, the selected socioeconomic level described earlier. One major contrast is between urban and rural environments, as we are interested in the potential effects of such factors as parental/family literacy, mass media, and availability of books across these different contexts. The subsamples are also paired into roughly equal numbers of boys and girls in order to look for gender-related differences in the socialization of literacy. International organizations, such as UNESCO, have noted a remarkable difference in literacy attainment between men and women in the Middle East (International Development Research Centre, 1979); whether this is due primarily to men's greater access to formal schooling or a combination of social factors is still an open question, but one we hope to address with the present data.

As mentioned above, we have selected samples of Berber monolingual children and colloquial Arabic monolingual children in order to compare reading achievement. Since the urban sample is composed entirely of Arabic speakers, this Arabic-Berber contrast is situated in the rural sample only. What we want to investigate here is a general instance of L_1 (for colloquial Arabic speakers) versus L_2 (for Berber speakers) reading acquisition, modified by the special language features of Moroccan society. Spoken Moroccan Arabic is formally an L_1 dialect, with significant vocabulary and grammar differences from the language of literacy instruction (i.e., standard Arabic). (See Badry, 1983; Sraieb, 1974, for further discussion of this distinction.) On the other hand, except for a limited number of loan words, Berber language is completely unrelated to standard Arabic, and offers, therefore, a classic example of L_2 reading acquisition.

Another major contrast concerns different instructional backgrounds among students. In both the urban and rural field sites we have selected samples of children who have attended Quranic schools for at least one year, as well as samples with children who have little or no preschool experience. In addition, in the urban field site we also selected samples of children who have been only to "modern" (i.e., non-Quranic) preschool. As mentioned earlier, we are interested in the effects of such diverse pedagogical environments on children's cognitive development and reading acquisition, studied primarily throgh an individually administered set of reading and cognitive tasks, adapted for and pilot-tested in Morocco.[3]

A final area of interest concerns the relationship of literacy acquisition to home environments. Represented generally in terms of urban versus rural sample contrasts, parental and family literacy will be primarily considered from data generated on parental survey questionnaires. Information about the literacy environment in the homes of our samples, including the educational background of parents and siblings, will eventually be compared with children's reading and cognitive performance. (For some preliminary empirical results, see Wagner, Spratt, & Snow, 1984.)

In sum, to study literacy in a complex multilingual, multiliterate and multiclass society, we have created a research design which attempts to capture some of the effects of this natural diversity. Even with a multitude of painstakingly constructed quantitative measures, much remains to be said about how literacy is embedded in the fabric of Moroccan social and cultural life. In the next section, we attempt to provide a framework for understanding the "culture" of literacy in Morocco, with the additional aim of providing a general model for studying literacy in other complex societies.

---

[3] The research of Scribner and Cole (1981) was devoted primarily to the question of whether (or how much) individual literacy skills affect individual cognitive development. Based on earlier, predominantly historical research (e.g., Goody & Watt, 1968; and Havelock, 1976) Scribner and Cole sought to disentangle the effects of literacy from other social factors (such as schooling and social class) on adult cognition in Liberia. The Morocco Literacy Project is focused on the question of how literacy is acquired and maintained in social context. In contrast to the Scribner-Cole interest in the cognitive consequences of literacy, we are interested in the cognitive and social "prerequisites" or correlates of literacy in Morocco. Thus, we focus on children's cognition and literacy acquisition in the home and school. Scribner and Cole mainly tested for adult cognitive skills, and attempted to correlate these with self-reported schooling histories. Our work with adults does not include cognitive testing for the parents of the children in our sample. Methodologically, however, we share with Scribner and Cole a strong commitment to ethnographic inquiry and experimentation as a basis for understanding literacy.

A FRAMEWORK FOR STUDYING LITERACY IN MOROCCO

Vignette: Taking the Bus

The impressive, newly-built Marrakech bus station has over 31 ticket counters for different bus lines and destinations. Numbered signs in Arabic and French quickly indicate, to
the literate, where they might but the desired ticket. Exit gates and individual bus quays
are also systematically numbered, and one can easily find a bus to Casablanca, following
the clearly marked signs: 'ligne Casablanca' ticket counter, exit gate no. 2, bus quay no.
10.

When Hammou stepped meekly into the bustling station, with the intention of
buying a ticket to Skhour des Rehamna to visit relatives, he came to the first window he
saw, and asked if the bus were going there. The Beni-Mellal ticket seller patiently instructed him where to go, pointing in the general direction of a row of counters to the left.
He was used to such requests. Hammou wandered a bit unsurely in the direction indicated, asking other travelers waiting in lines the same question, until he was rescued by a
man whose prime function at the station appeared to be guide and information-giver, who
shepherded him to the right counter. There, too, another man of unclear occupation,
lounging by the counter, asked Hammou where he planned to go, as he did the other
clients in the line, in a businesslike way.

Ticket in hand, Hammou asked again for directions to the waiting bus, and was offered
such information, even when he didn't ask, from the ticket-seller, from the doorman (who
guarded the exit to the quays against those without valid tickets), and from porters. Having found his bus, and finally settled into his seat, Hammou could survey his surround-
ings.

The inside front of the bus is adorned with the signs of the bus driver's tastes and
concerns. A gaudy cardboard hand of Fatima and a tiny sequinned slipper hang from the
rear-view mirror, and a phrase from the Quran is painted with a flourish in red above the
windshield for *baraka* or blessing. A smaller sign, painted less elegantly, admonishes the
passenger against smoking or spitting. A few faded postcards taped to the dashboard, and
a decal of a bathing beauty, complete the decor.

Next to him, Hammou found a Western-dressed, bespectacled young woman im-
mersed in a book. No doubt a Marrakech University student preparing for exams during a
weekend visit home. A handful of other people were reading too: three or four well-dressed
businessmen with Arabic and French newspapers, a teenage girl looking over a popular
cine-roman magazine (containing series of photographs from a film or television program,
with comic-book captions providing the dialogue); a young man studying his notebook
and a sheaf of stencils. But for the most part, the bus was filled with people chatting
amiably with their neighbors, sharing food, farmers discussing the weather and the year's
crop yield, women with nursing or sleeping babies, and others gazing pensively out the
window.

When Hammou noticed me (JS) reading beside him, he asked if I were a university
student. I nodded. "God help you," he said in Arabic, thinking I was Moroccan. "You
(the students) have the progress of our country in your hands." I had to smile in embarrassment as I held the illustrated cover of the Ian Fleming paperback out of his view.

This sketch of Hammou's adventure underlines several key factors in the culture of
literacy in Morocco. In many public situations, while reading skills might be advanta-

geous for efficient action, the need for them is commonly circumvented (to use Anzalone and McLaughlin's term [1983] in their discussion on The Gambia) by planned-for and equally acceptable recourses such as the presence of informal "verbal information guides" at the station. Secondly, the array of bus decor presents two very distinct uses of writing: the Quranic inscription was an aesthetic and comforting security measure, conferring *baraka* ('blessing') on the bus, while the notice of activity restrictions has a practical, though less spiritual purpose. Passengers reading on the bus were few, but some of the variety of reading materials available to them is represented: newspapers for information, notebooks and stencils for schoolwork, heavily illustrated magazines and comics for entertainment. And finally, the nonliterate Hammou's considerable respect for and appreciation of the powers of literacy is a testimony to the often-striking distinction between ideology and practice.

As has been noted by many others (e.g., Goody, 1968; Heath, 1980; Oxenham, 1982), literacy is a social, cultural, and political phenomenon that takes diverse forms in particular societies. For this reason, anthropologists and others concerned with the sociocultural dimensions of literacy have usually used ethnographic methods which have great explanatory power in specific situations and contexts, but often do not permit a more global analysis across contexts, domains, and levels in a complex society. With respect to Morocco, and perhaps more generally, we propose a three-part framework for approaching literacy in complex societies. First, under the rubric "Some Uses and Mediators of Literacy" we survey a range of societal structures and individual circumstances in which literacy plays a significant role. Second, what we term "Institutions of Transmission" refers primarily to school and home settings for the acquisition of literacy. Finally, we use the notion "Material Culture of Literacy" in connection with an historical inventory of the instruments and artifacts of literate activity. Throughout the following discussions, we continue our series of vignettes (based on life histories, ethnographic observations, and structured and unstructured interviews) which are intended to add contextual reality to the concept of literacy.

SOME USES AND MEDIATORS OF LITERACY

The present section focuses on the variety of situations in which literacy comes into play in traditional and contemporary Morocco, and how its use is mediated by individuals and institutions. Our in-depth observations of eight households in Al-Ksour range from a divorced Berber woman (often joined by her daughter and a friend with a grandson) to a family of eleven; and primary breadwinners including a migrant factory worker in France, a taxi driver, a woodcutter, a small-scale merchant, and a bathhouse owner. Through these observations, a set of literacy "domains" has emerged, providing a heuristic model useful for describing the literacy landscape of the social strata represented in this study. Five such general domains, which are often overlapping in everyday Moroccan life, have suggested themselves: household, school, religion, entertainment, and work. It is our view that the literacy uses, or even "needs", of such individuals and families in Morocco appear to vary more in frequency or degree than in the domain of literacy engaged. Most Moroccans are obliged to deal with the Moroccan government (i.e., literate) bureaucracy, but a civil servant's literacy needs are virtually daily, while a farmer's wife may require literacy only for registering her newborn son. In the same vein, a Quranic school teacher uses what we term religious literacy skills continually, but most Moroccans, as Muslims, make at least occasional use of such skills, even if only for the yearly Islamic festivals. This claim is not meant to imply that each individual accomplishes (or negotiates) such literacy needs in the same way. Thus, the Quranic school teacher, for example, may know several different ways (*tajwid*) of reciting the Quran as well as various commentaries or interpretations of the Quran itself. On the other hand, while many Moroccan men and women have memorized parts of the written Quran (considered here as a form of literacy acquisition) for the purpose of recitation or prayer, they may not actually be able to read the Quran with comprehension. Clearly, there are tremendous qualitative differences between these Quranic school teachers and the "average" Moroccan with some training in religious literacy.

In our ethnographic approach to literacy in Morocco, we have chosen the "literacy event" as the basic unit of observation. By literacy event we mean any activity which involves one or more of the following: reading (from decoding individual letters to reading for comprehension); writing (from copying in calligraphic style on a *luha* [see later description] to creative prose, to numerical calculations on a scrap of paper in a local market); manipulation of written materials or books with the intent to use them for some purpose; or any observed behavior or discussion that makes reference to reading, writing, or other activities in the material culture of literacy (discussed in more detail below). We have found, somewhat to our surprise, that most literacy events may be categorized as within the limited number of domains described earlier.

In this discussion, it is worthwhile to reconsider for a moment, the term "restricted" literacy (cf. Goody, 1968), which is sometimes used in a judgmental sense: there are the supposed "haves" and the "have-nots." This characterization of people of a given social level in terms of what they do not have (i.e., literacy) obscures the fact that such people do use literacy, even if indirectly (see Messick, 1983, for an example from North Yemen). People vary in their own literary skills, and those who are completely illiterate often have access to other, literate persons for their required needs. Historically, to be illiterate was not perceived with a negative stigma, although it can be in contemporary Morocco. In traditional Morocco, the demands literacy placed upon individuals were smaller, and there were individuals, institutions, and social mechanisms for satisfying these needs. Both "transmission" and "reception" of literate media were affected by a range of formal and informal mediators. These included public writers, on the one hand, and Quranic school teachers and educated neighbors and relatives, on the other. In large rural families it was common in traditional Morocco to select one of many sons to pursue the life of a *fqih*, while his brothers concerned themselves with cultivation or pastoralism and his sisters worked in the house or tent. A community *fqih* could handle a group's limited requirements connected with literacy. An important difference between then and now is one of ideology: literacy is now often perceived as an individual's personal need and right, whereas it once was something a person as a member of a group or neighborhood might accomplish indirectly. Historical and ethnographic data lead to the conclusion that in traditional times (up until perhaps the mid-twentieth century), Moroccans did not conceive of literacy as something that ought to pertain to every individual. Now, however, the ideology of personal literacy has gained a remarkably strong hold on public consciousness at all levels of Moroccan society. As one primary school teacher told us: "A person without literacy is like a soldier without bullets."

This does not mean, however, that traditional mediators of literacy are out of work, any more than popular or governmental ideology means that "illiteracy eradication" will soon be achieved. Accurate statistics on adult literacy in Morocco are unavailable, but based on figures of public education, it seems likely that considerably less than half the adult Moroccan population can read or write with fluency in any language. Traditional mediators of literacy, therefore, maintain a strong presence in contemporary Morocco, though their origins harken back to earlier centuries when only a handful of specialists accomplished the literacy needs for almost everyone else.

Among the important literacy mediators in Morocco are the several distinct professions of public writers. We are investigating the extent to which individuals rely on such writers, in addition to more informal appeal to neighbors, friends, and others. Moroccan society has an elaborate legal culture based upon written law, including both the Islamic *shari'a* or sacred law, and modern legislative law. In connection with a wide range of legal undertakings, formal written instruments are required. Examples are sale contracts for property transactions, marriage contracts, and inheritance documents, and those for rent, pawn, loan, partnership, and trusts. For the preparation of all such written instruments, an individual must go to a first type of public writer, the notary (*'adil*). Notaries have a long history in the Middle East (Tyan, 1959; Wakin, 1972) where they have served not only as the writers of legal documents but also as court witnesses. Notaries have been training in Islamic law and there are several published manuals which guide them in the correct formulation of the various document types; it is now required that they pass a government test before assuming notarial positions. In Marrakesh, notaries used to work out of shops in the marketplace, near the streets where private houses which doubled as judges' courts were located, but now the notaries of Marrakesh have been gathered together in buildings of the Ministry of Justice adjoining the courts. Notaries still write contracts and other documents longhand, use many of the old formulations, and sign in their distinctive, stylized manner. Whereas a document written by a general "public writer" requires registration in a municipal office to be considered binding and have any evidence value, a notarial document has the force of six witnesses. In many respects notaries who charge high fees serve the documentary needs of the bourgeois merchants and upper classes, who have property and estates to distribute and manage.

While notaries have always been a part of urban life in the Middle East and North Africa, "public writers" of a second, general variety did not emerge as a distinct profes-

sion in Marrakesh until late in the period of colonial rule. These men, who operate out
of marketplace stalls and who are not regulated by the government, provide services for
the popular classes. Their appearance on the scene is, perhaps, an indicator of expanding
literacy needs, espcially in less bourgeois segments of the population. In sharp contrast
to the notaries, who were and are highly educated in traditional, legalistic terms, these
public writers may have a very low level of formal education, and have only self-taught
expertise in legal matters. The public writers are further distinguished by the "modern"
character of their work: they frequently use typewriters (Arabic and French) to fill out
the ever-expanding variety of bureaucratic forms, write personal letters, and prepare the
most elementary of legal agreements. Compared with high status notaries, public writers rank low in public esteem, which is another sign of their link to the newly literate
lower stratum of Moroccan society.

A final type of public writer we have investigated is the *fqih* (meaning here, low-
level scholar, rather than the Quranic school teacher discussed in the next section) who
writes amulets and does astrological and numerological calculation for curing. As with
the notaries, this profession has a lengthy heritage in the Islamic world, and there exist
written reference manuals for guidance in providing services. But unlike the notaries,
whose place in Moroccan legal life seems secure even amidst contemporary societal
change, the traditional curative *fqih* is losing ground to a modern medical profession.
Such *fqih*s are nevertheless of interest for several reasons. First, their profession requires
a complex traditional understanding of the Arabic alphabet and its relation to numbers.
Second, as curers, these men tend to retain their popularity most with the lower classes,
our sample population. Third, curing and writing amulets was a traditional part-time
activity of Quranic school teachers. Fourth, *fqih*s who primarily specialized in curing
also provided general writing and reading services for people in their local neighborhoods. and, fifth, the principal textual material for amulets and other written cures was
the Quran itself.

Vignette: Medical Matters

Aisha, suffering from chronic arthritis, finally decided to take her problem to the *fgih*. Her
sister agreed to accompany her to Si Hariri's house one morning. Si Hariri is well known in
Al-Ksour as a Quranic school teacher, and also enjoys a reputation for his effective traditional remedies to common persistent ailments and domestic problems. He had gained his
knowledge of herbal recipes and amulet-writing from his own Quranic master, having requested such lessons in order that he might supplement the meager income he anticipated
in his career as a Quranic School teacher. Si Hariri's small library of the Quran, Hadith,
Shari'a, and Sheikh Kishk's theme-based collections of Quranic and Hadith quotations,
also includes two little yellow paperbacks, "*al-Kutub as-Safra*", the indispensible reference
books of the traditional healer.

He is well aware of the skepticism and disdain for his craft among modern doctors, the
Westernized younger generation, and many of his scholarly colleagues who disagree that
such activity is within the bounds of legitimate Islamic practice. He counters such disap-
proval with the proof that many have come to him after trying unsuccessfully the medicine
of modern doctors, and have found relief in his combination of herbal teas and applications

to fight the physical symptoms, and "writing" to exorcise the spirits that are causing the problem (*ar-riah*).

After listening patiently to Aisha's description of her symptoms, punctuated by her sister's vivid testimony, Si Hariri concluded that she was undoubtedly under the influence of spirits. He solemnly told her that he would have to prepare certain materials for this problem, and that she was to come back the next day. Upon her return, the *fqih* presented Aisha with three small packets wrapped in newspaper. The first two packets contained various herbs to be applied to the swollen joints and drunk in the form of herbal teas. The third packet held six pieces of notebook paper, one of them folded carefully into an inch-square "book" (*kitab*), as Si Hariri referred to it. It was an amulet, with a special inscription inside it, and was to be worn close to the patient's body, on a necklace or inside the belt, or under her pillow at night for a period of 10 days. The other five papers were each marked with letter-like but illegible scrawls in a watery brownish ink, a thinned version of the wool-based *smakh* used with the traditional *luha* or writing board. The patient was instructed to dunk one of the papers in slightly salted water, and rub it until the ink had been washed off. The water mixture must then be drunk, and some of it sprinkled on the affected areas and forehead, and the process repeated with the remaining papers each day, for a total of five days.

Across town, Zineba too was suffering from another flare-up of rheumatism in her wrists and ankles. She called her 16-year-old son Said to the drawer where inportant papers were kept, and requested that he find, read, and translate for her the medical prescriptions collected during visits to several doctors. When he reached the prescription written by a certain doctor from a neighboring town, she laid it aside, recalling that this remedy had once been particularly efficacious.

Paper in hand, Said set off for the pharmacy, with his mother's instructions to buy the particiular brands of pain killers and deep-heating rub specified in the prescription. When he returned home with the medicine, Zineba requested that Said read and translate the accompanying literature to her, so that she could follow the dosage and application instructions carefully. For Zineba, the idea of entrusting her medical matters to anyone but a modern medical doctor was unthinkable.

In these two scenes of women seeking health care, two very distinct uses of the written materials are observed. In the first, the writing—the amulet, the soaking papers—is itself the medicine; in the second, the prescription is saved as a record and is a means for procuring medicine, and the instructions provide information. The difference between an amulet and a prescription also serves to represent the extremes of traditional and modern thought grounded in literate usage. Produced by a *fqih* educated in astrology, numerology, and the old medical sciences, the amulet offers cure or protection via the power inherent in numbers and related letters, via the blessing of Quranic text, and by calling upon the action of spirits. Produced by a medical doctor trained in a European medical school, the modern prescription is anchored in a different tradition of medical thought. Here, traditional medicine and modern science use the power of the written word in completely different ways.

A second example of the extremes of traditional and modern material forms is the presentation of the Quranic text on television during Ramadan, the holy month of fasting. This modern communication medium, generally thought of as nonliterate in terms of the literacy requirements placed upon the viewer, now reaches the homes of Moroccans of all socioeconomic levels. Moroccan television is structured in its use of classical Arabic and French in newscasts and other programming, so that literate individuals have generally had more direct access. But the appearance of Quranic sections passing on the screen accompanied by an audio portion of chanted recitation, brings together the oldest and newest media, while at the same time places new demands on the home viewer.

A dimension of the overall spread of literacy requirements in Morocco concerns the functioning of governmental bureaucracies, the extension of public services, and the place of the post office. Candidates for every manner of employment must now present dossiers containing a range of public documentation, from birth certificates to a police form, in addition to diplomas and transcripts. The sophistication and variety of such documentation is barely a generation old. Older parents, especially in the lower social strata, have no record of birth, while for the younger generation, such documentation is mandatory. In addition, Morocco has instituted a national identity card and marriage and birth documentation (*hala madaniya*) for heads of families. As for public services, not only do piped water and electricity networks now reach into many rural areas, but the bill collection system is computerized, as it is for taxes on such personal items as televisions. The post office, following in the French tradition, is not only a center for mail, but also for telecommunications, and the receipt and sending of postal money orders which is a very important institution in Morocco.

This wide spectrum of modern governmental activity, all founded on the requirement of some degree of literacy, was introduced in the colonial period, but now reaches Moroccans in every social class. In a similar manner, the job market makes increasing literacy demands upon job seekers. Some categories of employment have expanded rapidly in recent years and demand high levels of literacy: for example, nurses, pharmacists, office workers, teachers, and banking staff. But beyond these obviously "literate" types of employment, literacy requirements have entered on the margins of many other jobs. In shops, for example, a clerk must be able to decode price and other product information on packaging, and merchants have to keep records of sales volume and inventories, as well as credit given to favored clients. Another example may be seen in literacy events at the taxi station in al-Ksour.

Vignette: A Taxi Driver

Aziz, a taxi driver between Al-Ksour and a neighboring town, awaited his *nuba* (turn-taking) as orchestrated by Moha the station master. Moha would register the arrival and departure, origin and destination of every taxi that rolled into his station, in a small spiral notebook. Depending on the day of the week, specific rules designed to give local and out-of-town drivers a fair share of the market, dictate which taxis may collect passengers at al-Ksour, and which may only discharge them. Referring to his notebook, Moha would usher the groups of waiting passengers to the taxis whose rightful turns had arrived.

Aziz looked foward to the days when the occasional Western traveler would share the ride, for then he could display and exercise his knowledge of spoken French. He had learned the language informally, while working with the French in the early 1950s, in a small commercial venture, after some exposure during his few years of primary school attendance. One was impressed by this simple country man's proficiency in the spoken language, and even more so when he carefully read aloud the written French instructions for installation and use of a newly-purchased fire extinguisher for the car.

Following the taxi-driver into his home, one finds that his literacy skills do not always meet the task at hand. During a heated argument with his son over a school notice, written in Arabic, about the boy's frequent absences from school, Aziz squinted hard over the note as though from poor eyesight. He then demanded that another son read it aloud to him: the man was literate in French but not in Arabic. His is an increasingly awkward position in the face of the government's present policy of "Arabization" of the language of literacy required in the public sector.

In homes, as a part of our observations of literacy events, we have witnessed, as above, different tasks that require varying levels of skill for which particular family members are recruited. Parents often depend on their literate children to read for them. In one family, for example, a teenage high school student was called upon to read the address written in an unfamiliar hand, on a letter incorrectly delivered to the house. His uncle, only partially literate, had examined it for a while but was unable to determine the mistake. This same elderly man, however, could decode numbers well enough to attend to his electric bills himself. Later, a female cousin visiting the family recruited the same high school student to write out an address for a friend. Returning to the "medical matters" vignette described earlier, it is also useful to note the role of mediators in the two events. At the traditional healer's, the client was accompanied by a family member for reasons of moral support and the dictates of propriety. Her own manipulation of the medicines, written and otherwise, did not require literacy skills; a good memory for oral instruction was the only requirement. In the second case, the son's mediation or participation in the event, through his interpretation of written materials, was crucial for the procurement and correct use of the medicines. Alone, Zineba would never have located the desired prescription or known how to use the drugs. Fortunately for Zineba, her formally-schooled son conveniently filled the gap between her own skills and the requirements of the situation. The impact on the family of this new pattern, with the child as literary mediator for the parent, will be discussed further in the section on Home Environment.

Institutions of Transmission

Schools.   For many centuries, schools have been the primary vehicle for the acquisition of literacy in Morocco. As indicated earlier, however, our chosen target population was generally nonschooled and illiterate. Nonetheless, although only a small, traditional elite was fully literate, there was, at all times, a trickle of upward literacy mobility from the lower urban stratum and from the rural areas. In addition, many males who would not go on to become literate did, nevertheless, receive some exposure to reading and writing through limited attendance at urban and rural Quranic schools, thus attaining a modest level of what we term religious literacy (cf. Wagner, 1983a, 1985).

Focusing on Quranic schools in the 1980s we find a combination of features inherited from the past mixed with contemporary innovations. In former times the Quranic school (*kuttab*) was the point of entry into education for young boys, while young girls were generally kept at home. Ideally, boys would stay in Quranic school for a number of years, attempting to memorize the entire Quran. In this sense the Quranic school was the stepping stone to the Islamic *madrasa*, the traditional institution of higher education (Wagner & Lotfi, 1980).

During the years of French colonial rule (1912–1956), this vast system of Muslim education was caught up in a succession of reforms, then went into decline with the rise of, first, the colonial and nationalist schools and, then, the national public school system. Quranic schools, with a few rural exceptions, now function as preschools since children who may attend for as long as three years are legally required to transfer to public primary schools at seven years of age. The Quranic schools also received attention in the form of a campaign called "Operation Quranic School," initiated by King Hassan II in 1968. Recalling the importance of Quranic schools in introducing the country's youth to the Quran and Islamic beliefs, the King charged the Ministry of Education with upgrading and standardizing Quranic instruction, and required all children to attend a preschool institution for at least two years. Due to these new laws, it is now common to find blackboards, class lists, and elementary arithmetic added to Quranic instruction, all of which constitute departures from the traditional style of the Quranic school. The two-year preschool attendance requirement also led to a tremendous growth in the number of children in the *kuttab*s, which now accept girls on an equal basis with boys, who were traditionally the exclusive clientele of these schools.

Old-style Quranic schools had no form of government regulation. They were essentially the private enterprise of individual *fgih*s, instructors who contracted for payment directly with students' parents or a village community, and who taught in a time-honored method handed down through the generations. *Fgih*s typically carried a single important credential: they themselves had memorized the Quran.

Quranic memorization is not merely committing a text to memory, however, for the Quran is understood by Muslims to be the actual Word of Allah. Memorization harkens back to a time when the Prophet, who was illiterate, reputedly received the Book orally from the Archangel Gabriel and recited it to his early companions who committed it to memory. It was not until some years following the Prophet's death that the Book was set down in writing (As-Said, 1975). Recitation of Quranic text is integral to Muslim prayer, and is important as well on many other ritual occasions. One who has memorized the Quran in its entirety is still highly respected and is considered to have a blessing or *baraka* as a "carrier" of the Quran (Eickelman, 1978). The act of memorization is, for many believers, the cornerstone of the faith, and a decline in memorization in contemporary times is considered indicative of the erosion of belief. Since the Quranic school is now often only a truncated, preschool version of the former institution in which young men could remain until they learned the whole text, there are few contemporary institutional means for accomplishing full memorization. Beyond their relatively brief exposure to it in Quranic school, students also study the Quran as a part of the curriculum of the modern preschool and primary schools, but spend only about 30 minutes to one hour daily on recitation.

Our classroom observations indicate that, while the typical present-day Quranic school and the modern preschool still differ widely in terms of frequency of activities, pedagogical styles, material culture, and general atmosphere, the traditional format of the old-style Quranic schools has been superseded by modernized pedagogy even in our rural site of Al-Ksour. Gone are the days of the wooden writing-board, the reed pen and burnt-wool ink, and the strictly Quranic textual material used in these schools. Such conditions generally exist these days only in the more remote mountain areas of the country, and in the few higher-level Quranic *madrasa*s still in operation (cf. Eickelman, 1983; Wagner & Lotfi, 1980). Today's Quranic schools make use of a blackboard, individual slates, and chalk for writing practice and easy corrections (as opposed to the painstaking washing and writing-surface preparations required for maintenance of the traditional wooden boards). Quranic school children are no longer expected to read and memorize the long Quranic passages, although chapter (*sura*) memorization and recitation still take place in the preschools through oral group recitations.

Aside from the practical difficulty inherent in the instruction of so sacred a text to restless young children who cannot be fully conscious of its religious value, there is the actual textual quality of the Quran itself. The language of the text is considered to be the finest example of pure classical Arabic, but as such it is remote from the children's practical linguistic world of spoken or written Arabic usage. In addition, the Quran is highly abstract, or even when concrete, metaphorical: it is, therefore, conceptually inaccessible as well. No effort at children's comprehension is traditionally associated with the initial rote acquisition of the text. Because of Islamic tradition, there are no visual aids in Quranic text and it is not age-graded. Also, being sacred, the text is immutable: there is, for example, no tactic of presenting vocabulary in other contexts to facilitate understanding, though the shorter passages (*sura*s) are presented first as they are thought to be easier for children to memorize.

Unlike in the past, these early aural-oral sessions of Quranic memorization are rarely buttressed by study of the written representation of the verses being learned or practiced. Presented on the classroom's blackboard, the content of decoding and writing lessons is usually limited instead to individual letters in all possible configurations, with short and long vowels and other diacritics, and embedded in single words. This written material is first repeated orally with the teacher or a student pointing out and modeling the pronunciation of the individual symbols, followed by rote in-unison chanting by the class and then individually. Finally, writing exercises on children's individual slates may entail copying a letter (or letters) from the blackboard. Thus, we see here an instance of "bottom-up" letter-to-blend-to-word, instruction techniques— similar to those in modern American classrooms—being used extensively in a setting where rote memorization techniques had once been the exclusive method.

Curricular content, too, is not as it once was, when the traditional Quranic school would concentrate entirely on study of Quranic texts. While memorization of shorter Quranic chapters remains a major thrust of Quranic education for the youngsters attending these schools, we have witnessed secular songs (including a National Tribute chant to King Hassan II and the Islamic Kingdom of Morocco), secular vocabulary to illustrate the configurations of letters in connected script, and basic arithmetic symbols and functions (including in one class visited, two-digit division problems), in both urban and rural Quranic schools. Even the inscription of the date at the top of the blackboard in more than one Quranic school used the Christian month and year instead of the Islamic calendar date.

Much of this diversification in teaching methods and content in the Quranic schools is the result of the aforementioned government campaign to standardize Quranic preschool education and the commonly-perceived need to prepare the child for primary school entrance by acquainting him with the types of activities and situations he will encounter there. To this end, periodic training sessions for Quranic school teachers, held in the primary schools in the area, describe newer teaching techniques in reading, writing, and arithmetic. Such sessions are infrequent, however, and some teachers choose not to attend them at all, but apparently none can escape the Ministry of Education's periodic (bi- or tri-yearly) inspections which rate the teacher's pedagogical style as either "modern" or "traditional," the condition and equipment of the classroom, and children's performance. It should be noted that this intervention by the government does not include financial support of any significance, a situation which creates considerable resentment among some Quranic teachers. The teacher himself, the school's materials, and sparse accomodations—usually a concrete-walled room that doubles as a community prayer room, a blackboard and chalk, and woven reed mats and a few low stools for sitting—are supported almost completely by contributions from the neighborhood, nominal customary fees from parents of attending children, and in some cases by a percentage of the collected revenue of the religious community, the *habus*.

The Quranic school classroom is still close and austere, with children required to sit still in one place for complete two-and-a-half to 3-hour sessions in somber rooms, but the legendary pitiless ogre, claimed by many adults to have severely traumatized them in their own childhood, has seldom been encountered among the teachers we have met during our research. In most cases present-day Quranic school teachers were themselves educated in the traditional way, with the wooden *luha*, hours of study from predawn to sunset, the master's ever-vigilant and far-reaching rod, even the permanent scars from a teacher's penchant for neck-pinching as a disciplinary measure. Despite their own experience in school, the teachers we have observed appear to have embraced the new methods and content as more practical for the children, and tend to use praise and nonthreatening correction methods to direct behavior, rather than the scare-tactics of old. The sternest measure witnessed to punish bad behavior was a harmless swat on the shoulder with a light-weight bamboo stick. While the observation situation itself might not be a typical one, and a teacher might not display his actual behavior in front of a foreign visitor, we also noticed that none of the children appeared to fear the *fqih*, but rather were generally uninhibited by the figure of the teacher. In several classrooms, a common reinforcement used by the teacher was to publicly acknowledge the good work of students, asking them to come to the head of the class to display their work, or praising them by name to the rest of the class.

Vignette: In the Kuttab

Si Gharoudi's *kuttab* in al-Ksour is a large but windowless room. The *fqih's* implements consist of a yard-square blackboard (*sebora*) affixed to a pillar, some chalk, a bit of sponge as an eraser, and his long pointing stick. There are no books to be seen, nor any decorations or visual aids on the walls. The children sit on worn reed mats and low wooden stools, and each has his own writing-slate, which may be nothing more than a plain slab of wood (not the carefully shaped and sanded *luha* of the past), or a scrap of sheet metal, painted black. A piece of chalk and a rag or sponge for erasing, replace the black ink (*smakh*) and white-wash (*selsal*) of the traditional Quranic school.

The morning class opens with the recitation of a memorized Quranic chapter (*sura*), first in unison and then by individual children. Work on a new *sura* then begins, a single verse (*aya*) per session. The *fqih* models the *aya* orally, and the children repeat, again in unison and then individually, until each member of the class can recite it to Si Gharoudi's satisfaction. The lesson continues with a more "modern" component, the presentation and drilling of an individual letter. In today's class the *fqih* writes the target letter on the blackboard in each of its positional configurations (initial, medial, final, and alone), with all the possible short- and long-vowel combinations, and as it appears in a few words. He models the decoding of each of these symbols, then calls on the children to repeat in a lengthy rote-learning session. Game-like recognition, decoding, and writing drills follow. Children are asked, for example, to point out on the blackboard a letter-vowel symbol on their individual slates from memory, and hold their slates up to the *fqih* for inspection. The morning session closes in the traditional manner, with the group recitation of another Quranic chapter, chanted in a pattern of three or four close-set tones. The afternoon session will also combine the strictly traditional methods and subject, with more modern ones, including a revision of the material presented in the morning, and a basic arithmetic lesson.

In the midst of modernization in the Quranic schools, there remain striking differences between these schools and the modern preschools (*rawd al-atfal*) available in larger towns and cities, run by the Entr'aide Nationale and the Youth and Sports ministries, and privately. Such modern preschools have sprung up across the country in recent years as a function of the 1968 law. Their teachers are predominantly women, while only a few women have now joined the formerly all-male ranks of Quranic school teachers.

Vignette: Lalla Zohra

Rising from the end of a cul-de-sac in the old *medina*, comes the singsong chanting of dozens of children. The visitor thinks he is approaching another of the ubiquitous Quranic schools of Marakech. He is surprised to be met at the door by Lalla Zohra, a vivacious woman of fifty dressed in European clothes. With henna reddening her silver hair, Lalla Zohra is the *mudira* or directress of one of the oldest—at 25 years—"modern" preschools in Marrakesh. The school is the first floor of her house, and the students, as she states openly, are "what Allah has given" her in the absence of natural children. Though not without a tinge of sadness, she fondly claims these 100 children as her own.

From her younger days helping the Resistance fighters against French colonialists to her recent pilgrimage to Mecca on her own, Lalla Zohra continually demonstrates a commitment and drive that Moroccan women are noted for in spite of various obstacles facing females in a Muslim society. Our arrival at her school naturally caused a fair amount of commotion. Lalla Zohra graciously served us mint tea and homemade cookies. Despite her position, she would later be found washing the tile floors, unable to pay a housekeeper to do this work for the school.

The teaching of reading—in Arabic and French—is a main goal of this preschool, which also gives extra classes for children "having trouble" in the public primary school. Lalla Zohra monitors this aspect of school pedagogy carefully, making small interventions when she thinks her young teachers could do something differently and better. Despite her wide experience, Lalla Zohra needs help in reading and writing Arabic herself, and is completely illiterate in French. How does one explain this apparent dichotomy in a woman who has been surrounded by literacy activity for a quarter-century? It appears that Lalla Zohra, like so many other "functional illiterates" manages to circumvent literacy requirements. While a literate ecology may promote literacy for those who are learning to read and write, little effect is seen on those who do not attempt to learn.

Unlike the single unadorned classroom of up to 75 students ranging in age from three to seven years and led by a lone Quranic school teacher, even the most modest kindergartens have separate age-graded classrooms, colorfully decorated with purchased and handmade teaching aids, student artwork, and other visual stimuli. The instructors have been formally trained for their work through pre-service programs lasting from six months to over a year or through frequent in-service meetings and occasional conferences, where child psychology and educational theory are studied and discussed, new teaching materials and techniques demonstrated, and ideas exchanged. A Quranic school teacher, in contrast, may be formally trained solely in the mastery of the Quran and perhaps in the Quranic sciences (cf. Eickelman, 1978).

With the children grouped according to age in separate classrooms and with separate teachers, the modern kindergarten teacher can concentrate on types and levels of activities deemed appropriate for the age group she is responsible for. The Quranic school teacher, on the other hand, delivers his daily fare of Quranic recitation, decoding, writing, and math instruction to a group of children ranging widely in age, receptiveness, and length of attention span. The modern kindergarten teacher also offers a greater variety of activities to her limited age-range class: oral expression and reading and writing

practice in Arabic and sometimes French; arithmetic; memorization and reciting of secular songs and perhaps an hour a week of Quranic material; but also handicrafts, drawing, painting, role-playing, and perceptual drills in the form of games such as card-
matching and puzzles.

The slate, chalk, and blackboard that comprise the sole reading and writing implements of the Quranic school, are supplemented in the modern preschool with pencils
and lined paper notebooks for writing practice, government-issue primers and
alphabet charts for reading materials, not to mention the use of clay sculpture, follow-
the-dots games, collages, and other games and artwork to encourage practice and
internalization of letter shapes. Shelves hold these materials when not in use, and large
round tables provide a working surface for the children.

Despite such material distance from the Quranic school, the methods used to present
and practice decoding and writing of letters, letter combinations, and words remain
similar to those witnessed in many Quranic school classrooms. A major difference, however, lies in the time spent and stress placed on these activities during the school day.
This holds true, for example, with respect to Quranic and secular text memorization (in
both cases, by rote repetition) and recitation. In the modern preschool setting, no more
than half an hour per morning or afternoon would be devoted to either of these activities, as the rest of the session would be taken up by crafts, oral expression (in dialectal
Arabic, not literary), instructional games, or math instruction; while in the Quranic
school at least twice that time would be spent on decoding and writing activities and
Quranic practice, and little or no time on other activities.

Home Environment. Our approach to the literacy-related features of the home
and family is informed by a group of recent publications in educational research concerned with out-of-school settings (e.g., Heath, 1983; Varenne & McDermott, Chapter
10, this volume). Two central questions predominate: As access to schooling and a
wider social distribution of literacy have begun to reach the Moroccan lower-middle-
class, are there resulting changes that occur in the domestic sphere? And, in this population of first-generation literates, what is the connection of the home environment to
literacy acquisition in children?

In order to gather such information about home and family life, we have employed
participant-observation ethnography in a small number of families (as mentioned
earlier) and have developed a parental survey which poses a range of questions of general
theoretical interest in as close to Moroccan terms as possible. The survey also attempts
to provide more quantitative information on issues generated from the ethnography.
These interviews, conducted with the families (usually the mother) of the children in
our population sample, are currently being analyzed.

In the Moroccan home, a related set of events appears to have transformed the relationship between literacy and the families in the lower stratum of Moroccan society.
The household is not only being exposed to outside literacy in new ways, it has also

become a major locus for educational learning and other literacy activities. While literacy cannot be assigned a simple causal role in the social changes occurring in Moroccan family structure, it seems nevertheless intimately related to those changes. Literacy is one factor—along with the demographic explosion, rapid urbanization, and fundamental economic change—that is playing a part in the reordering of the Moroccan family.

Within the family, the arrival of a new, younger generation of literate and schooled men and women has led to a "generation gap" between children and parents. At our targeted societal level, a first generation of literates must now relate to their parents who grew up in a world of "restricted" traditional literacy. In modern Morocco, where literacy counts in dealing with the structures of power in the wider society, children have partially reversed the old pattern of parent-child authority in the family. As we have seen in the previous section, it is the younger literate or biliterate (Arabic and French) generation who now provide access to new sources of information, through literacy skills which interpret the outside society for their less literate, nonliterate, or monoliterate (Arabic, Quranic Arabic, or French) parents. In this sense, one of the most significant discontinuities between home and school is located not simply in the relationship of the government public school to the private extended family, but within the family itself: between literate and nonliterate generations.

Even though they themselves were raised in a generation and a social class that did not have high literacy expectations, parents tend to have adjusted their nonliterate world views to the dictates of literacy in contemporary Morocco. Whether in an encouraging or threatening manner, Moroccan parents place a value on school achievement. Although they may not be able to help their children actively with schoolwork, many parents have internalized the new ideology of education and literacy. It is the generation in school which is experiencing the frustration of Morocco's pyramidal educational system, maintained by a high proportion of examination failure, and matched by a corresponding lack of job opportunities in the marketplace. It is perhaps ironic that in the parallel rise of literacy-related expectations and frustrations, it is generally illiterate parents who hold firmly to expectations while their literate children must live the frustrations. The parent's generation is at once more locked in tradition and more confident in the ideology of change.

Another example of change in the Moroccan family structure in which literacy and schools have played a part is in the area of gender roles. In former times in Morocco, a conception of differences in behavior and qualities of mind between girls and boys structured traditional child-rearing practices and had direct implications in the sphere of literacy. This old worldview, which rigidly distinguished the male/public and female/private/domestic domains, meant that boys went to Quranic school while girls learned domestic skills. Although the percentage of girls attending school in Morocco is still lower than that of boys (in relation to total numbers of school-aged children), especially in rural areas, the system of an exclusively male right to education has now been superseded by a policy of universal access. To the extent that literacy is a tool of power in the public realm, and to the extent that it "opens doors," it may be a vehicle for restructuring the gender-based division of labor both in the general society and within the family (see Lerner, 1958, for an early discussion of this question). Connected to the changing identity of women (and thus, also men) in Moroccan society and culture, is the gradual move toward more nuclear, rather than extended family living, and toward a higher divorce rate. Literacy, once the privilege or expectation of elite males, is now much more accessible to the men and women of Morocco's lower strata. (For more information on the changing roles of Moroccan women, see Davis, 1983; Dwyer, 1978; and Mernissi, 1975.)

For example, in pursuit of formal education and employment, a small but growing number of young unmarried single women are leaving their parental homes to live in school dormitories and rented rooms of regional centers. Such an event, virtually unheard of a generation ago and still without widespread sanction, challenges directly the traditional dictate that a girl must remain in the house of her parents until marriage. Now, many young unmarried female students and civil servants find themselves in a situation "without rules" or precedent to follow, and the effects of such novelty and liberty on the social structure of Morocco are still to be determined but may well be profound.

Homework is another new phenomenon, dating from the institution of the public school systems for the families of our socioeconomic level. In his examination of the Ibn Yusuf *madrasa* of the Marrakesh of the 1930s, Eickelman (1978) indicated the importance of informal peer group learning in the form of study sessions among Quranic school students outside the confines of the formal lesson. Just as there are observable analogues in the area of rote memorization between the pedagogies of the traditional Islamic *madrasa* and the contemporary, secular public schools, we find a similar continuity in peer learning, displaced, however, from the traditional Quranic school dormitory to the individual family dwelling.

Among the data recorded in family-based ethnography, homework figures importantly. Moroccan public school students study constantly, utilizing in their home efforts many of the strategies we have encountered earlier in connection with the schools. Memorization is the principal tactic for learning lessons, and oral recitation is the method by which the student checks his or her knowledge. In fact, although many contemporary Muslim educators trained in Western pedagogical methods consider rote memorization to be a debilitating remnant of an archaic system of instruction (cf. Wagner, 1982, 1983b; Wagner & Lotfi, 1983), memorization has been witnessed, throughout the higher levels of modern Moroccan school systems extending into the university, to be a central pedagogical principle and acquisition strategy. Comprehension appears to have an increased importance in students' conceptualization of their schoolwork, but, in practice, great reliance is still placed on memorization. To acquire a text—here secular classroom notes, not the sacred Quran—students repeat it aloud over and over, or, less frequently, read and reread it silently. Rote memorization of public school materials also occurs outside the house during the annual examination season in the late spring. At this time, students can be seen in serious concentration as they promenade singly in public gardens or stroll near street lamps in the evenings, eyes riveted to their open notebooks, lips mouthing the text. As it is in the West, school homework is becoming a central event in family politics in Morocco. Homework constitutes a new and important intrusion of the formerly public world of literacy into the once-bounded and private world of the family. Other intrusions, as for example the appearance of popular books, will be considered in the next section.

Material Culture of Literacy

This section represents a somewhat innovative approach to literacy from the point of view of its material culture. By material culture we refer to the technology and products of literacy in a given society: the instruments and physical means connected with literate activities (see also, Heath, 1980; Szwed, 1981). As has been our perspective thus far, we will attempt to convey a sense of how the material culture has changed through time and in relation to the overall shifts in the social distribution and ideology of literacy.

A literacy instrument that is at once the symbol of the Quranic school and its principal physical medium is the individual writing board mentioned earlier, the *luha*. In the traditional Quranic school each pupil had his personal *luha*, identified by the loop of colored string used to hang it on the wall in the schoolroom. *Luha*s were handmade by a small group of town craftsmen in several standard sizes, from a very small size intended for alphabet learners up to a large size, said to hold one-fourth of a *hizb* (the Quran text is subdivided into sixty *hizb*s). This larger size was, and in some areas still is, used by advanced Quranic students for the memorization and study of texts beyond the Quran itself (Wagner & Lotfi, 1980). On an advanced *luha*, for example, the lines of a grammar treatise are written widely spaced—this is the part to be memorized—and in between, at an angle, the teacher writes his commentary, which is not meant to be memorized. It is worth noting that this format of main text and commentary reproduced on the students' *luha* is the same as that found throughout Islamic manuscripts and published scholarly works: the main text is in the center, surrounded by the commentary in the margins.

In daily use, the *luha* is washed with a dissolved clay solution *(selsal)* that provides an off-white writing surface when it dries. The teacher either writes the material to be memorized in a traditional black ink on the student's board or corrects the student's effort. If, later in the day, the student is able to recite the text without looking at his *luha*, he will be permitted to wash the writing off and reapply a new white coat that will be ready the next day for a new body of text. Working from his own *luha*, each student proceeds at an individualized pace. In the old days, when a young male carried on with the Quran until he had memorized a significant portion of it, a special ceremony marked this achievement. Aside from the food and other preparations, which varied according to family wealth, the boy's *luha* figured prominently. For the occasion, it was elaborately decorated, often with floriated calligraphy or square *kufic* script, to symbolize an important intellectual event in the boy's life. Thus decorated, the *luha* came home for the first time, and was retired from use.

*Luha*s are still sold in the Marrakesh marketplace, but the buyers now come primarily from the rural areas. In town, the wooden *luha* has been nearly completely replaced by individual modern slates used with chalk or by a large blackboard *sebora* for the classroom, or both. Even the individual slate, although still referred to as *luha,* is differently conceived: it is for practice and is brought home with notebooks and readers. The blackboard at the front of the room is a material embodiment of a conceptual change in the organization of the Quranic school: the emphasis is on the group and lesson uniformity under ministry aegis, rather than, as with the traditional *luha,* a somewhat private, individualized endeavor.

We have also investigated the historical and comtemporary distribution of reading materials. This area of research concerns not only changes in the social distribution of such reading materials, but a transformation in the genre range of the materials themselves. We have interviewed a number of book dealers in Marrakesh, collecting oral histories of the profession from them. The types of books once available in booksellers' shops are quite different from the range found today. Thirty years ago the traditional spectrum of books included works on religion, Islamic law, Arabic grammar and letters, and history. In the 1920s there were only a few men selling books in Marrakesh, but it must be remembered that several centuries ago, during the great period of the Ibn Yusuf *madrasa,* there were numerous booksellers located around this old scholarly center.

Some of the traditional-style booksellers are still to be found in the poorer quarters of the old city *(medina)* of Marrakesh where our sample population lives. In other bookstores, however, located primarily in the new city, older Arabic genres are joined on the shelves by contemporary Arabic works, published either in the Levant or North Africa, and books in French and, to a lesser extent, in English and Spanish. These contemporary publications represent a new gamut of subject matter, both scholarly and popular. Some other bookstores stock only those books and supplies required by students in the primary and secondary schools. The expanded horizon of literate materials available ranges from novels (Western and Middle Eastern, in French and Arabic) to the sociology of Marx. In comparison with the traditional genres, these newly accessible titles represent a distinct development of secular reading interest. While books are quite expensive at *Gueliz* bookstores, there is now a flourishing street-vendor market in used books, located on the great central square *(jama'a l-fna)* of the old city. In addition to the regular vendors' stalls, at the beginning of the school year there is a lively trade in school books among student buyers and sellers.

Beyond the trade in books, which in both volume and genre are an indication of increased popular participation in reading, is another dimension of publishing: newspapers and magazines. As with the book trade, newspaper and magazine publication in Morocco has a history, but it is confined to the present century. The development of newspapers is closely tied to the country's modern political history. One interesting aspect of this complex subject is the role of newspapers as tools for communicating— nationalist views in the colonial period and government information now—to the general population. The effectiveness of newspapers is predicated upon the existence of a public that either reads or receives ideas through other literate individuals. Comparing early nationalist papers to present-day ones reveals a rise of popular interests which extend beyond purely political matters. Just as the book trade developed in a secular direction from a traditional specialization in "Islamic" subjects, so the newspapers went beyond politics, their initial *raison d'etre,* to include sports, cultural affairs, and world news. A parallel diversification is found in magazines, which include a variety of photostory publications that require little or no literate skills for appreciation. Campaign publicity is a third example of printed matter for literate and nonliterate consumption.

Vignette: Electioneering

Overnight, the city of Marrakesh had been swathed in multicolored sheets of paper— slapped in rows on walls, hanging from wires strung over passageways and avenues, festooning storefronts, in one case cleverly arranged to spell out the slogan "God, the State, and the King." On closer inspection, each sheet is seen to be printed with the photograph, name, and party platform details of a candidate for public office: the colorful scene announces not a carnival or holiday, but the campaign for coming local elections of city and regional representatives and other officeholders.

The variety of colors, apart from attracting attention, serves a very practical purpose for the largely nonliterate constituency. On election day itself, as explained by a knowledgeable though nonliterate mother of eight, voters are given a booklet of color-coded tickets, one for each candidate. Those who cannot read the name of their preferred candidate have only to match the color of the ticket with that of the candidate's posters, flyers, and election information booth, tear the ticket out, and place it in the voting box. As the multitude of candidates exceeds the number of available solid pastel colors for preparing stencils and posters, many candidates even have a two-color code scheme: lavendar with a yellow vertical stripe, sky blue with a green bar, gold with a brown one.

Even in rural areas, visual and oral politicking goes on during the pre-election period with a fury. Candidates and their supporters distribute flyers door-to-door and hold dinners to inform the public orally of their own platforms, but also to sling mud on the reputations and records of their rivals.

The literate and nonliterate public are thus both given the opportunity to inform themselves and to participate in the election process through this combination of written and oral information, photographs, and color-coding in the campaign and voting procedures. Parallel to but more pervasive than the elephant and donkey as visual symbols for the American voter, the color-coding system here described is a necessity, and an official recognition of the diversity in literacy levels of the Moroccan voting public.

The material quality of printed matter has also gone through a long evolution. Books are familiar objects, the physical embodiments of a lengthy literate tradition—at least in the experience of the lettered traditional elite. For the lower social stratum, the "literate tradition" was confined to the Quran, and this was an object not necessarily to be read but to be retained in the household for the *baraka* it holds as the "word" of Allah. In nonliterate families the Quran is often hung on the wall in a decorated bag.

In Morocco, as across the Islamic world, calligraphy is a traditional art, and the hand-copying of books on law, inheritance, grammar, and history was an important and meritorious scholarly activity. Manuscripts were preserved and transmitted in this fashion. Libraries of such hand-copied works were (and are) found in both the private collections of scholars and in the great mosque universities, such as the Qarawiyin in Fes ad the Ibn Yusuf *madrasa* in Marrakesh. Associated with this manual technology was the old craft of bookbinding, which made "Moroccan" leather famous worldwide.

A new technology—the printing press—became established under the French in the colonial period. The first presses in Marrakesh, for example, were owned by Europeans, but Moroccan employees received training. The Arabic printing industry was founded earlier and became far more important in Fes than in Marrakesh, where the first Moroccan "Islamic" printing press did not appear until 1933. Its founder had worked at one of the foreign-owned presses for a few years prior to establishing his own firm, and a document attesting to the Moroccan printer's proficiency still hangs on the firm's office wall. Next to that document in French is another in Arabic, written by a Marrakesh judge of the era, in the formulaic style of a diploma, certifying the printer's intellectual capacity in several areas.

As was the case elsewhere in the world, the technological shift from hand reproduction to mechanical reproduction of text in Morocco had important sociocultural implications. And these were bound up with concurrent changes in the social distribution of literate skills and new understandings about what kinds of subject matter could be transmitted through literate media.

Closely related to development in the printing and publishing of books were changes in the handling of individual legal documents. Here also a transition from handwritten script to other technologies of production and reproduction was made. The exception concerned the continued use of handwriting by the notarial profession, described earlier. It may be noted, however, that there is some political pressure to eliminate the notaries' monopoly by the introduction of standardized, printed document forms. In the work of the general public writers and that of bureaucracies, governmental and company, the typewriter has replaced the handwritten mode of text production. Although the typewriter did not become important in Morocco until late in the colonial period, one of its technological features, the production of copies by carbon paper, is already being replaced by the widespread use of photocopies.

We conclude this section with a brief comment about literacy "ambient" in a Moroccan urban environment. While we do not know how common such practices were in the colonial period, advertisements, posters, notices, banners announcing or celebrating a public event, graffiti, street signs and writing on storefronts are extremely common now in Marrakesh, and, to a lesser extent, in al-Ksour as well. These public writings are in Arabic or French, or both, and run the spectrum of usage from the most secular movie posters to official government announcements and nonofficial ones such as those witnessed during the election campaigns, to religious phrases from the Quran and other sources on banners in front of mosques during the month of fasting. To what extent individuals make use of such literacy available in the environment is still an open and interesting question. In the United States, where there is literacy attuned to children's interests on each box of cornflakes and virtually covering the urban landscape, a number of studies are beginning to demonstrate the importance of such literate ecologies (e.g., Ferreiro & Teberosky, 1982). In Morocco, and in other Third World countries, differences between rural and urban ambient literacy should provide fertile ground for studying possible effects.

These, then, are but a few examples of how one might begin to formulate a material culture of literacy. There is clearly a great deal of conceptual overlap between the present section and the previous two sections of this chapter, which only serves to illustrate, yet again, the degree to which literacy and the rest of Moroccan life are intertwined.

CONCLUSION

In this approach to studying literacy in Morocco we have endeavored to consider the phenomenon of literacy from several perspectives, and have addressed a number of dramatic changes occurring in the social and conceptual organization of literacy in Morocco. We began with a discussion of the spectrum of literacy usage and mediation in Morocco, and how it has changed over time, especially in the direction of secular and popular content and access. We then traced the evolution of Moroccan education from a characteristic "traditional" form, including Quranic schools and old-style *madrasa*s to a modern public system. In a like manner we have attempted to characterize developments within the institution of the Moroccan family. We also examined change through the concrete technology of literacy—its "material culture"—where several examples served to convey how, in a material sense as well, Moroccan literacy has shifted from a "traditional" to a "modern" form.

This ethnographic, social, and historical approach to studying literacy in Morocco is a key part of our multidisciplinary research. In addition, we are collecting quantitative data generated by reading and cognitive tests administered to young children, and derived from the sociological and attitudinal material in the interviews conducted with parents and teachers. The diverse levels of data collection we have embarked upon are designed to address a number of specific theoretical concerns summarized earlier as well as to shed light on the complex reality of Moroccan literacy.

Throughout this discussion we have emphasized the bounded nature of our inquiry. Our population is drawn from a particular level of Moroccan society where the widespread appearance of first-generation literacy is taking place. This entails a number of significant sociological features, such as a Moroccan generation gap in literacy. The appearance of first-generation literacy has occurred not only in societies where there has been no previous experience of literacy (e.g., Papua New Guinea; Scheiffelin & Cochran-Smith, 1984) but also in Morocco, part of one of the world's great literate civilizations. Even though adult literacy skills were not common at the socioeconomic level of our sample population, knowledge about literacy and access to it through formal and informal intermediaries was. Now, however, this society, once characterized by a pattern of "restricted" social distribution of both literate skills and literate usage, is moving steadily in the direction of generalized and popularized literacy.

To study literacy in Morocco is to discover that the concept of literacy itself may be defined by knowledge and belief as well as by the presence or absence of particular skills. How the former is related to the latter is a topic only beginning to be addressed (e.g., Wagner, in press). In addition, we must speak of literacies, rather than literacy, both in the sense of multiple languages and scripts, and in terms of multiple levels of skills, knowledge, and beliefs within each language and/or script domain. Thus, within a complex society, be it Morocco or the United States, literacy may be "mandated" by government authorities, but its acquisition and maintenance are surely dependent on the cultural beliefs, practices, and history within which it resides.

REFERENCES

Anzalone, S., & McLaughlin, S. (1983). Literacy for specific situations—A note to planners. Unpublished paper, Center for International Education, University of Massachusetts, Amherst.

As-Said, L. (1975). *The recited Koran: A history of the first recorded version.* Princeton, NJ: Darwin Press.

Badry, F. (1983). *Acquisition of lexical derivational rules in Moroccan Arabic: Implications for the development of Standard Arabic as a second language through literacy.* Unpublished Doctoral Dissertation, University of California, Berkeley.

Davis, S.S. (1983). *Patience and power: Women's lives in a Moroccan village.* Cambridge, MA: Schenckman.

Dwyer, D.H. (1978). *Images and self-images.* New York: Columbia University Press.

Eickelman, D.F. (1978). The art of memory: Islamic education and its social reproduction. *Comparative Studies in Society and History, 20,* 485–516.

Eickelman, D.F. (1983). Religion and trade in Western Morocco. *Research in Economic Anthropology, 5,* 335–348.

Feitelson, D. (1980). Relating instructional strategies to language idiosyncrasies in Hebrew. In J.F. Kavanaugh & R.L. Venezky (Eds.), *Orthography, reading, and dyslexia.* Baltimore: University Park Press.

Ferreiro, E., & Teberosky, A. (1982). *Literacy before schooling.* Exeter, NH: Heinemann.

Goody, J. (1968). *Literacy in traditional societies.* Cambridge: Cambridge University Press.

Goody, J., & Watt, I. (1968). The consequences of literacy. In J. Goody (Ed.), *Literacy in traditional societies.* Cambridge: Cambridge University Press.

Hammoud, Mohamed S. (1982). *Arabicization in Morocco: A case study in language planning and language policy attitudes.* Unpublished Doctoral Dissertation, University of Texas, Austin.

Havelock, E.A. (1976). *Origins of Western literacy.* Toronto: Ontario Institute for Studies in Education.

Heath, S. B. (1980, Winter). The functions and uses of literacy. *Journal of Communication, 30,* 123–133.

Heath, S. B. (1983). *Ways with words: Enthnography of communication, communities, and classrooms.* Cambridge: Cambridge University Press.

International Development Research Centre. (1979). *The world of literacy: Policy, research, and action.* Ottawa.

Lerner, D. (1958). *The passing of traditional society.* New York: Free Press.

Mernissi, F. (1975). *Beyond the veil: Male-female dynamics in a modern Muslim society.* Cambridge, MA: Schenckman.

Messick, B.M. (1983). Legal documents and the concept of "restricted" literacy in a traditional society. *International Journal of the Sociology of Language, 42,* 41–52.

Oxenham, J. (1982). *Literacy: Writing, reading, and social organization.* London: Routledge & Kegan Paul.

Schieffelin, B.B., & Cochran-Smith M. (1984). Learning to read culturally. In H. Goelman, A. Oberg, & F. Smith (Eds.), *Awakening to literacy.* Exeter, NH: Heinemann.

Scribner, S., & Cole, M. (1981). *The psychology of literacy.* Cambridge: Harvard University Press.

Sraieb,N. (1974). *Colonisation, decolonisation et enseignement: l'exemple tunisien.* Tunis: Institut National des Sciences de l'Education.

Szwed, J.F. (1981). The ethnography of literacy. In M.F. Whiteman (Ed.), *Writing: The nature, development, and teaching of written communication, Vol. 1.* Hillsdale, NJ: Erlbaum.

Tyan, E. (1959). *Le notariat.* Harissa, Lebanon: St. Paul.

Wagner, D.A. (1982). Quranic pedagogy in modern Morocco. In L.L. Adler (Ed.), *Cross-cultural research at issue.* New York: Academic Press.

Wagner, D.A. (1983a). Indigenous education and literacy in the third world. In D. A. Wagner (Ed.), *Child development and international development: Research-policy interfaces.* San Francisco: Jossey-Bass.

Wagner, D.A. (1983b). Rediscovering "rote": Some cognitive and pedagogical preliminaries. In S. Irvine & J. W. Berry (Eds.), *Human assessment and cultural factors.* New York: Plenum.

Wagner, D.A. (1985). Islamic education: Traditional pedagogy and contemporary change. In T. Husen & T. N. Postlethwaite (Eds.), *International encyclopedia of education: research and studies.* New York: Pergamon Press.

Wagner, D.A. (in press). When literacy isn't reading (and vice-versa). In M.E. Wrolstad & D.F. Fisher (Eds.), *Towards a new understanding of literacy.* New York: Praeger.

Wagner, D.A., & Lotfi, A. (1980). Traditional Islamic education in Morocco: Sociohistorical and psychological perspectives. *Comparative Education Review, 24,* 238–251.

Wagner, D. A., & Lotfi, A. (1983). Learning to read by "rote." *International Journal of the Sociology of Language, 42,* 111–121.

Wagner, D.A., Spratt, J., & Snow, L. (1984, April). *Reading acquisition in Morocco: Comparative issues in reading, cognition, and metacognition.* Paper presented at the Annual Meetings of the American Educational Research Association, New Orleans.

Wakin, J. (1972). *The function of documents in Islamic law.* Albany, NY: State University of New York Press.

13

The Anthropology of Literacy Acquisition*

David M. Smith
University of Pennsylvania

INTRODUCTION

The recent economic recession has not only witnessed the closing of a number of mills and factories but portends rather serious social changes. For many of those thrown out of work their unemployment promises to be more than a temporary inconvenience. Among the experts there seems to be a growing consensus that we are being faced with a serious restructuring of our economic base. Some of the basic industry, which appeared to form the unbreakable backbone of the American economy, is gone forever.

The new unemployed are not the barely employable fringe—minorities, young people, and women. They are increasingly the highly unionized and consequently highly paid, blue-collar middle class. For many the only hope of good reemployment lies in the new high-tech industries. As attempts are made, however, to facilitate these career changes, employers are finding—to their surprise—that many of these ex-blue-collar workers are "functionally illiterate." They are unable to read or write well enough to do the necessary paper work for the job transfers or to take advantage of proferred training opportunities.

These new illiterates, far from being the poor and nonmainstream, include those who constituted the very essence of the American dream come true and, in many cases, the basic constituency for politicians decrying the waste of resources upon those who were unwilling to help themselves by learning to read and write, among other things. Until the recent economic upheavals, for steel mill or auto factory production workers, limited reading and writing ability apparently was not a serious economic handicap. The discovery of this widespread illiteracy challenges some of our easy assumptions about the causal relationship between poverty, exclusion from the mainstream, and the other ills frequently laid to illiteracy.

* Some of the material in this article was prepared for the panel. "Cultural, Social, Economic and Political Effects of Non-Reading," organized by Professor Clementine Pugh for the American Orthopsychiatric Association Annual Meeting, Boston, April 1983, and also for a hearing conducted by The Mayor's Commission on Literacy, Philadelphia, June 15, 1983. Special thanks to Dell Hymes whose thoughtful comments on an early draft of this paper contributed substantially to its present shape. Much of the research reported here was supported by NIE under Grants #G–80–0002 and #G–81–0035.

That the traditional equations, that is, that illiteracy is the cause of poverty and exclusion from the good things of society, are of questionable accuracy should come as no surprise to an anthropology shaped by work in our own society and especially in education. The traditional "holism" of anthropology, its concern for the entire range of factors interacting in a single situation, calls attention to the complexity of forces affecting educational outcomes.

Two requirements of ethnographic research—participant-observation and the discovery of what situations mean to those within them—lead one to expect to find that the meaning of a situation may be different to different participants, and not necessarily at all what it had seemed from the outside. Moreover, close observation of social life almost inevitably leads one beyond broad categories, such as "illiteracy," to individuals and process. The persons grouped together by a label may have various sources and meanings in their lives. And when one traces such meanings and sources, as good ethnography does, a trait of social competence such as "functional illiteracy" no longer seems adequate as a starting point. It may seem as much a product and a symptom as a root cause. It may seem unlikely to be a trait that can be changed in isolation. It may seem unlikely to be something that, once changed, will inevitably entail a predicted set of consequences.

Explicating this view and the implications it holds for an understanding of literacy and illiteracy is the concern of this paper.

THE POPULAR VIEW OF ILLITERACY

That illiteracy is a major problem in the country today is a matter of consensus. Surveys, results of standardized testing in our schools, and even the latest national census all testify to the fact that large numbers of our population cannot read beyond the "fifth-grade level." Leaders of industry, commerce, and business publicly decry the waste of human resources when employees, usually minorities or women, cannot advance beyond entry-level positions. The report of The National Commission on Excellence in Education (1983) eloquently sums up—both in its tone and its conclusions—the concern about illiteracy:

> Some 23 million Americans are functionally illiterate by the simplest tests of everyday reading, writing, and comprehension.
>
> About 13% of all 17-year-olds in the United States can be considered functionally illiterate. Functional illiteracy among minority youth may run as high as 40%.

This apparent limited ability to read or write is perceived as a serious problem because it correlates with a number of other social facts. A disproportionate number of these illiterates are poor, are little-schooled, are un- or underemployed, find themselves in trouble with the law, and have difficulty in making use of important social institutions such as medicine, law, and the government. Furthermore, these are the same members of society who are the major recipients of government social services, welfare, Medicaid, subsidized remedial educational programs, and food stamps.

Advocates of these latter programs and of government expenditures to support them can point to numbers of cases where they have made real differences in people's lives. Additionally, the recent cuts in these government-funded remedial services have witnessed a coincidental increase in the numbers of the unemployed needy. It becomes easy, therefore, to infer a whole series of causal relationships. Illiteracy, seen by many a result of poor schooling, becomes a primary cause of the unemployment—and of other social ills—and reductions in government spending for remedial programs an exacerbating cause.

With the problem so perceived and the causes so clearly apparent, it follows that solutions would not be long in coming. Indeed, the present attention has spawned a welter of proposed answers to the illiteracy problem. For the most part, these have two things in common. They see the problem as located in the individual who needs to be changed, to becoming more skilled, and they see the remedy to be technological.

What is needed, we hear repeatedly, in one form or another, is a way to teach literacy. The details of the plans may vary. One will emphasize pedagogy, one materials, another instilling motivation, and still another training teachers—or some particular mix of all these elements. Success is measured almost exclusively by gains in the skill levels of students and this usually is measured by some paper-and-pencil test of competence. Some of these approaches are able to demonstrate gain on the part of individuals, and even in some cases, dramatic improvements in self-esteem and the quality of life. There is little evidence, however, that we are far on the way to seriously resolving the issue.[1] Indeed, if the Commission on Excellency's report is any indication, the situation is becoming increasingly serious.

AN ANTHROPOLOGICAL VIEW

While not promising necessarily easier solutions to the illiteracy issue, the perspective of anthropology leads to a rather different understanding of it, an understanding that can be of great practical value. In the following discussion I will consider briefly each of the three areas delineated above—the nature of the problem, the question of causality, and the ingredients of a solution—implicitly contrasting the popular and the anthropological approaches. In anticipation of this discussion a comment on the anthropological perspective and its concommitant assumptions is necessary.

---

[1] Advocates would undoubtedly argue that their problem is a lack of resources. Additional resources could perhaps increase the number of individual gains. It is not clear, however, that such efforts could resolve the entire problem. Perry Gilmore (personal communication) has pointed out, for example, what appears to be an irony to many of these successes. The most successful programs are those that restrict attention to students who have attained more than a fifth-grade ability and in some Philadelphia programs no one who scores below the seventh grade level is admitted. There is a sense in which these programs are not addressing reading problems. If a person has reached the fifth grade level of competence, he or she has already "cracked the system." What is lacking, and thus problematic, is more than likely self-confidence or the presence of a life context supporting the growth of facility in the skills already present.

The anthropology represented in this paper uses a data base provided by ethnography. Ethnography is an approach to inquiry whose primary heuristic is culture, that is, it seeks the explanation for behavior in the sets of understandings unconsciously shared by members of a society or social group. It is inductive and holistic, with participant-observation its primary research method. As a research paradigm it falls toward the left on the phenomenological-positivistic axis. An important goal of ethnography is to discover the meanings of phenomena (events, behaviors, artifacts) to members of a society.

Being inductive, ethnographers typically do not start out with fixed hypotheses as to what these meanings will be or experimental designs by which to test them. (This does not mean, as ethnographers are often accused of claiming, that they start without preconceptions.) They must indeed reckon with the biases resulting from their own enculturation. Furthermore, past experience and the accumulated knowledge of a particular research site may provide considerable orientation to it.

Ethnography's commitment to holism imparts a particularly important role to context in inquiry. In its simplest form, the commitment to holism is a recognition that meaning will ultimately only be explicated in an understanding of the larger context or the whole of which a particular phenomenon is a part. Context becomes, not just the place one goes to find the answer to questions, but where the important research questions themselves, as well as the answers, are located. Whereas more positivistic approaches to research tend to exercise extreme rigor in manipulation of data and relatively less in the formulation of research questions, ethnography is concerned first and foremost to discover the important questions to be answered.

In making culture my primary heuristic construct, I start with two important assumptions about people and their social interactions. First, I assume that people by and large act rationally, in that their behavior and point of view is grounded in an attempt to make sense of the world they are experiencing. Secondly, I assume that patterned behaviors are doing something for the group. In some way, although individuals may not be consciously aware of it, some need is being met through these activities. One concern of ethnography is to uncover these unconscious impetuses to behavior. Doing this not only provides explanations but, in bringing them to the attention of actors, creates new room for change.

Dependence upon participant observation in gathering data follows logically from these goals and assumptions. It is only possible to understand the worlds of participants and the meaning of phenomena in those worlds through first-hand experience, by participating in those worlds. On the other hand, since many of the social meanings of behaviors and events are not part of the conscious repertoires of group members, it is necessary to also maintain an outsider or observer perspective. Being able to consciously assume both of these roles, in some combination, is crucial to good ethnography.

To sum up, an anthropological view of literacy will build upon the results of ethnographic inquiry. This in turn seeks to explicate the meaning of literacy-related issues to participants without starting from preconceived notions about these meanings. It asks, "What is going on?" and "What does this mean in the lives of people involved?" It seeks these answers by participating in their lives while at the same time observing and interpreting from the outside. Some of the results of this approach are discussed below.

The Problem of Illiteracy

With remarkable shrillness, the press, educators, and politicians are inundating us with reminders of the tremendous illiteracy problem and of the dire consequences it portends. As discussed earlier, the essence of the popular view of the problem is that tests, and other indicators, show a large number of Americans who have never gone beyond the fifth-grade reading level and thus are considered to be functionally illiterate—meaning that, presumably, they cannot do the necessary literacy work to function adequately in our society. As a result they cannot be employed to their full potential, participate in the enrichment literacy brings, or adequately carry out their responsibilities as part of the enlightened electorate.

Thoughtful anthropology cannot deny the reality of an illiteracy problem. However, it does see the issue quite differently from this popular view in a number of respects. At the beginning of this essay I referred to the new illiterates created by the changes in our economy. At first blush calling them "new illiterates" may appear to be an inaccurate reference. After all, these workers have been unable to read or write for all their lives. Would it not be more accurate to simply describe them as "newly-discovered illiterates?" I deliberately chose the original phrasing to illustrate two important facets of illiteracy overlooked in many approaches currently popular. First, illiteracy per se is not necessarily a problem, and secondly there are a number of different kinds of illiteracy. It makes little sense to speak of illiteracy as a monolothic social issue.

The Problem with the Illiteracy Problem[2]

That the problematicality of illiteracy is contextually determined is unarguably true. That poverty is at least one element of the context making it a problem (that is to say, if one is poor the chances of his/her illiteracy being a problem increases) is also true. These truths are, however, simplistic. Illiteracy (as well as literacy) takes on valences according to a complex set of factors characteristic of a particular social context. This complex can be conveniently referred to as the group's culture of literacy. (See Smith, 1983, for a fuller discussion of this notion.)

Different cultures of literacy will have different notions as to what counts as literacy. We have found, for example, that in some school contexts writing that is not part of the official teaching-learning routines is not considered writing and children who are highly proficient in it are sometimes considered nonwriters. (Gilmore, 1983a, calls this "sub rosa literacy," and Fiering, 1981, calls it "unofficial writing.") Differing values may also be placed upon the abilities to read and write and these skills themselves may be seen as appropriate or inappropriate for varying tasks or for various classes of people. I, for instance, was raised in a context where being tagged "a reader" (as opposed to "a doer") was not complimentary for a young male and where, for most tasks, book learning was seen as a poor substitute for learning by doing. This was true despite the fact that everyone in the family could and did read.

---

[2] I am particularly indebted to the Scollons for helping think through this issue. They made a similar point about the language situation for Native Americans in Alaska (Scollon & Scollon, 1982).

A particular culture of literacy also exhibits its own notions of appropriate displays of literacy, style, and manner of acquisition and uses. Not only does this problem with the problem of literacy make futile the formulation of a monolithic attack upon it, but insisting on seeing illiteracy, defined as inadequate display of skills on a predetermined task, as inevitably a problem can have deleterious consequences for individuals.

Our own research in West Philadelphia has described individuals who were convinced that they were nonreaders and so referred to themselves, with the attendant lowered self-image despite clear "objective" evidence to the contrary. One of the research team, herself a neighborhood mother, compared carefully the out-of-school reading of boys who said they were non-readers and those who said they were readers. She found few observable differences in the quantity or quality of the reading they actually did. The non-readers' self-perceptions were at least reinforced, if not engendered, by teachers who tended to see them as poorer students (cf. Robinson, 1982). It is impossible to determine the extent to which labeling of individuals who cannot read or whose reading and writing is not "counted" affects their view of themselves and ultimately determines important aspects of their career paths.

None of this is to say that illiteracy is not a real issue that deserves a great deal of attention and effort. To address it effectively and to insure that the cure is not worse than the disease, however, we must be sensitive to when and how it is a real problem for individuals. The displaced steelworkers became functionally illiterate when their literacy skills were inadequate for the new life contexts they were thrust into. They were not functionally illiterate prior to this and it is quite unlikely that they would have responded had a basic literacy program been designed for them.

One other issue needs to be addressed at this juncture. While I am suggesting that reading below "fifth-grade level" does not constitute an illiteracy problem per se given the contemporary social realities, I am not suggesting that we should be content to leave people to be "happy in their ignorance." While illiteracy may not be the cause of most poverty, it can be an excuse for inflicting it. This in itself provides sufficient reason for working to eliminate it. This view also provides the basis for a campaign that succeeds neither at the expense of individual dignity or at the price of self-blame.

In summary, I am proposing that "the problem of illiteracy," as popularly conceived, is in itself a problem that must be addressed before any significant success can be attained in overcoming illiteracy.

Multiple Illiteracies.   In addressing this problem we must start by delineating the various illiteracies that exist. At the recent hearings on illiteracy conducted by the Philadelphia Mayor's Commission on Literacy, referred to earlier, a single morning witnessed testimony about the problem of a successful automobile mechanic who had to get help in consulting repair manuals, the plight of recent southeast Asian immigrants, public school students turned off to reading and writing, and minority recruits to banking who couldn't get out of entry-level positions. Each of these represent qualtitatively different phenomena that call for radically different understandings and solutions.

This claim is based on the assumption that illiteracy is not simply a single problem taking on various forms in different contexts, but a social issue defined and valenced by social context. This can be illustrated by some speculation on the examples listed immediately above. The auto mechanic may have no problem at all making a good living. While his inability to read may well be an inconvenience, it is conceivable that his being unlettered but knowledgeable about cars draws attention and even a certain kind of respect. His illiteracy may at the same time be a cause of suffering no less painful because it is private and personal.

The Southeast Asian suffers an entirely different kind of illiteracy. His or her problem may well not be one of not knowing how to read but of not knowing English and could well entail a serious lack of communicative competence as well. (By this latter I refer to a general ignorance of the rules governing appropriate uses of various tools of communication used by Americans. Cf. Weinstein, 1982, for a fuller discussion of this issue.) He or she may have no problem of self-concept whatever and may even be able to turn his or her inability to read and write English into an advantage.

On the other hand, the school student may be turned off by the social and psychological price demanded for the acquisition of school literacy. This can range from ridicule of his friends, to betrayal or denial of his family and his cultural identity. The minority bank employee may well not trust (often with reason given the realities of daily existence) the executive's promise of "advancement if deserved." In both of these latter two cases it would be an error to view the illiteracies as primarily problems of skill development. They are both social problems which are unlikely to be remedied by programs designed to teach the skills of reading and writing. Much of our recent urban school experience is itself poignant testimony to this and the bank executive who testified at the commission hearings referred to earlier found this to be true of his workers. His bank had initiated a literacy program for its entry-level employees but the attempt had failed because, as the executive put it, they lacked motivation.

The Causes of Illiteracy

Exclusion.   In a most provocative paper, John Ogbu (1980) argues persuasively that one of the important factors keeping minority children from learning to read and write is the caste system they must contend with. The daily realities they experience belie the school and mainstream promise that school success will lead to a better life. They soon encounter, as have their parents and most of the adults they know, the very real ceiling society imposes upon their attempts to move up or out, a ceiling that is based on color and concomitant attitudes not on ability to read and write. From the minority student's perspective, learning to read will not only be a waste of time but will entail accepting the humiliation inherent in subordinating one's self to the demands of the dominant culture's system of schooling.

In other words, for the population described by Ogbu, illiteracy is not the cause of exclusion from the promise of the American dream of a good life but the result.[3] This argument is consistent with the findings of ethnographic research into illiteracy. Heath (1980) has suggested that children come to school, not to learn to read, but they read to learn. Given the fact that learning is a primary human adaptive response, it is virtually impossible to be raised in a society as literate as ours without knowing how to "read" by the time one enters elementary school.

This position appears inconsistent with the high incidence of illiteracy reported in older children and adults. At the most fundamental level, of course, the apparent inconsistency reflects a discrepancy between ability to read, that is, to look at a written text and decode its meaning, and what counts as literacy. The latter is usually a school-defined phenomena and is measured by test performance. To become literate, in reality, means conforming to the demands of school with all this implies. The spate of recent ethnographic research has amply documented the subtle processes by which certain groups of students are excluded from access to school learning resources and the expectations of success enjoyed by other classes. (Cf., for example, Rist, 1973; McDermott, 1974.)

To summarize therefore, not only are many of those who will comprise the ranks of the illiterate excluded from the kind of life context in which becoming literate will make sense, but they are further excluded from access to the very pathways to literacy recognized by society.

Cost Benefit Ratio.   This exclusion not only makes it difficult to be able to even conceive of the possibility of becoming literate, and in addition puts serious obstacles in the way of any such effort, but it also adds to the cost often demanded for admission to literacy.[4] Indeed, assessment of cost benefit ratios frequently becomes a major consideration in determining whether one will do the necessary to be counted as literate.

In our research (Smith, 1983; Gilmore 1982), we detailed the way in which one elementary school carefully used its perceived control over access to literacy, and concomitant admission to better post-elementary schools as a basis for negotiating parent and student display of "appropriate attitudes." The stakes, of course, were far greater than simply the display of a good attitude. In many cases what the school was in reality requiring was the betrayal of cultural allegience. The children were black and the behaviors that the school counted as indicating "bad attitude" turned out upon close scrutiny—and school personnel were largely not aware of this—to also be those behav-

---

[3] Something similar seems to happen to children at the other end of the spectrum—the upper middle class. Many of them have parents who can recount versions of Horatio Alger's stories. They, by their own efforts, made huge successes of their lives, became heads of corporations, founded businesses, were able to acquire nice homes that inevitably appreciated in value, and so on. The children, perceiving themselves as caught up in the high-tech revolution, are convinced that the same opportunities do not exist in their own worlds. Consequently, the promised rewards for hard work in school are greater than the perceived reality they experience. (I am indebted to a comment by Dr. John Crosby, Superintendent of Schools in Radnor, Pennsylvania, for bringing this notion to my attention.)

[4] "Admission to Literacy" is a phrase introduced by Perry Gilmore (1982, 1983a, 1983b) and serves to highlight the fact that literacy is a state that is socially conferred and differentially defined. Attainment of the state, as defined in specific contexts, may be carefully controlled.

iors that were also seen as displays of black culture. (See Gilmore, 1982, for a fuller analysis of "attitude.")

This expected betrayal, or in some cases even abandonment, of cultural or ethnic identity may take several different forms. If the peer culture attaches a strong negative valence to being a "reader" or "writer," attempts to move kids in these directions will inadvertantly entail expecting the child to become a "lame" to his peers as a consequence of becoming literate.[5] To take another example, if child's parents are relatively unschooled, requiring them to check homework as proof of caring or of having a proper attitude—whether or not they are expected to correct it—can result in a loss of face with one's own children. These are indeed heavy costs to demand for admission to a state that is taken as an inherent right by a majority of society.

None of this is to suggest that teachers should not have as a goal the development of readers and writers, or that schools should not require parents to check homework. This analysis is offered as explanation for some of the common problems reported in teaching literacy skills. If it is a plea for anything, that would be for the exercise of sensitivity to, and respect for, the subcultural realities of children's lives in and out of school.

For adults acquiring literacy skills may involve still additional costs. First, to take advantage of the many "basic literacy" courses that have begun to spring up among us, one must publically admit to being a failure and to having a serious problem. This can be particularly traumatic in subcultures where face is important and can be exacerbated when family relationships risk being affected.

A second price that may be exacted is that of having to suffer the humiliation of "being taught." A learner, is almost always, by definition, a one-down status relative to that of teacher in our society. Being labeled "illiterate" in itself is humiliating for most and having to assume the role of student can serious multiply that sense for an adult. This becomes all the more a problem when the teacher is young and/or the learner is expected to participate in a class with others.

This latter point deserves additional comment. The potential humiliation of having to display one's ignorance in public recitation is only one part of the issue. For certain adult populations, the "trial and error" approach to learning characteristic of American schools conflicts with the learning style they consider appropriate. By "trial and error" approach I refer to the common practices of exposing learners to a corpus of material or knowledge and then devising a way—for example, by exam, written exercise, or recitation—for them to display their grasp of it. The teacher then points out errors in the display and the learner is expected to make necessary corrections in the next demonstration. For many adults the proper way to learn and to display that knowledge is to observe, then rehearse in private, and only make a public display when one is relatively sure he or she has the knowledge or skill mastered.[6]

---

[5] "Lame" was originally the black vernacular term Labov reported used in New York in the mid 1960s to negatively characterize individuals considered outside of the social group. It has found its way into sociolinguistic literature to more generally characterize these individuals (Labov, 1972).

[6] A similar problem has been reported among Native Americans who have great difficulty with modern schools (cf. Philips, 1972).

While the common justification offered for trial-and-error teaching in pre-adult schooling is its assumed efficiency, the tacit message conveyed is that children's individuality need not necessarily be respected and that they do not, by right of birth, merit respect. The message is no less clear for adults and even lacks the economic rationalization. It may, however, add greatly to the cost of admission to literacy and immeasurably increase the difficulty of the learning task.

To summarize, while it is commonplace to list the presumed costs of illiteracy, an anthropological view also concerns itself with understanding the less obvious social and psychological costs of literacy acquisition. Of crucial importance is the recognition that those costs may be not only exceedingly steep but that they are differentially assessed. For some segments of our society being literate is indeed a birthright which is only squandered with effort. For others, however, it can only be earned at the price of self-abnegation, betrayal of heritage, and of hard work against constantly shifting odds.

Some Applications

It should be clear from the above discussion that an anthropological approach to illiteracy proves an eminently useful framework for developing solutions to the various problems it poses, beginning with a specification of these problems. It, of course, suggests that no single solution is possible nor would one be desirable. Nevertheless, despite the complexity, literacy and illiteracy, when examined from an anthropological perspective, exhibit several characteristics which can contribute to understanding a variety of literacy-related issues.

Illiteracy as a Relational Problem. Fundamental to an anthropological perspective is the notion that illiteracy is not primarily a technological but a relational issue. The task of becoming literate should not be viewed as one of merely acquiring a set of skills. The presence or lack of skills is the result of a real or perceived life context that makes their acquisition either worth or not worth the effort. This fact holds several implications.

Foremost among them is a realization of the limitations of programs whose major objectives are to simply teach reading and writing skills. While such programs may boast dramatic results for individuals, from a broad social perspective they are inevitably more symptom alleviation than cure. This fairly obvious fact notwithstanding, far and away most of the effort presently underway to address "the illiteracy problem" is of this type. That we would be content to deal with symptoms is not surprising since addressing the underlying causes would call for serious and painful social changes. Among these would be a questioning of our society's very mandate to education which is nothing less than the accurate assessment and efficient development of skills.

Ethnography, at least implicitly, questions even this mandate. In this it contrasts with more traditional educational research which most frequently focuses on understanding the way this mandate is executed rather than on understanding the mandate itself and its meaning or effects. This questioning is a result of the inherent comparative character of ethnography (cf. Hymes, 1983). While many ethnographers of education have never done field work in another society and while such fieldwork is not a sine qua non of good ethnography, an ethnography of education based in cultural anthropology can not avoid comparing the mandate of American schooling with that of other possible educational arrangements.

A result of this kind of comparison, to take just one example, would be that findings that identify differences in the learning processes of nonmainstream learners would not inevitably be interpreted as calling for the design of teaching techniques that alter or remediate these processes, that is, that see the differences as problems. Rather, research conclusions would be embedded in enough rich context to offer practitioners a range of choices that would not be readily apparent without the ethnographic lens. The Michaels and Cazden study of discourse style in kindergarten sharing time (this volume) provides a good illustration. She found that minority children typically engage in what she calls "topic-association" discourse while teachers look more favorably upon "topic-centering." Furthermore, children whose discourse is topic-centered tend to do better in the acquisition of school literacy than do the others.

One reaction to this finding would be to suggest that teachers should devise ways to teach the minority children to develop skill in the topic-centered style valued by the schools. A cogent case can be made for doing just this as insurance against excluding them from jobs and roles that require topic-centered styles of talking. However, her studies contain enough description of the contexts and analyses of the situated meanings to demonstrate that the problem is not with the discourse skills per se but with their use in particular contexts. As a result teachers can use the research in guiding and in legitimating the search for ways to build upon the styles children bring instead of simply leaving them to conclude that the difference is a deficiency that must be remedied. Such solutions remove the blame and the burden for change from the child.

An ethnography of literacy (or illiteracy) that is true to its cultural roots, will examine, without preconception, both the social consequences of the particular illiteracy under investigation and its various levels of meaning to individuals. It will be sensitive to the entire web of relationships human beings find themselves enveloped in. It will not, a priori, control out any segments of this web no matter how trivial they seem. Such rich understandings will not always lead to solutions that are essentially technological, i.e. that consist of more responsive or efficient methods of teaching. Rather they will promote serious questioning of basic assumptions and examination of the invisible consequences of behaviors and relationships.

Literacy as Rational Choice.   If an important principle to be respected in seeking solutions to the problems of illiteracy is care in properly locating the problem in the web of relationships characteristic of learning contexts, rather than in the teaching technology available or in the failings of learners, it follows that sensitivity to an individual's perceived position in that network and ability to shape those relationships is also crucial. Much of the recent concern for addressing illiteracy appears to overlook the fact that what is perceived as possible and desirable, that is rational, for individuals in one set of contexts may not be for others.

For example, the much touted success of several third world literacy campaigns has led to the suggestion that we emulate them. The reason behind this reasoning appears to be that literacy is empowering and that if we could only mobilize large numbers of people and send them forth to teach significant inroads would be made in resolving the illiteracy problem. However, a crucial factor, and one that is frequently overlooked, in the success of these programs, such as those promoted by Paulo Friere and the Cuban or Chinese campaigns, was the role of the power structure. In every case the campaigns either enjoyed the proactive support of the government or held forth credible promise of changing it. In other words, those in power—who were often newly installed revolutionaries—and the illiterate population both saw the acquisition of literacy as supporting their own goals.

In our own society, few literacy programs have the avowed goal of social transformation and, in general, the government's support is more symbolic than substantive. Furthermore, not surprisingly, given what appears to be normal for mainstream participants in any society, those in a position to make policy tend to see difference as disorder, a threat to security. It would be unusual for them to appreciate that one's social identity and assessment of social reality might be so bound up in illiteracy that they would find their most reasonable choice to be maintaining loyalty as against the perceived unlikelihood of real gain from change.

Therefore, while the desire for empowerment, which can take many forms, turns out to be a significant motivation to becoming literate in our own society, the simple promise will often not suffice. I have listened, for example, to a bank officer complain that despite his company's best efforts to help functional illiterates overcome their limitation so that they could progress beyond their entry-level employment, the workers lacked motivation and the program failed. His complaint could be construed as patronizing. While there is no doubting his and his company's sincerity in their concern and effort, they may have been unaware either of the perceived limited effects of the literacy they were promoting or of the costs it might entail for individuals.

A bank promotion is by no means always seen as serious empowerment. How many who start employment with identifiable "literacy deficiencies," even if they are remediated, can hope to attain positions of real decision-making power in a bank? In addition, when the motivation to becoming literate is that it gives an individual a competitive edge and the most frequent competitors turn out to be peers, the offer of promotion upon becoming literate is not seen as simply empty. It also becomes a temptation to betray one's most important support system. It is quite possible that the failure of the bank's basic literacy program had little to do with motivation but reflected an accurate reading of the realities of corporate employment.

The above notwithstanding, there is some reason for encouragement in the evident realization of many that illiteracy in others is not good for society as a whole. It may well turn out that for their own interests, bankers, industrialists, and political leaders have a need to increase participation in the literacy culture of technology. In responding to their own need it will be rational for them to take into account the rationality of those they seek to change. To succeed they must know; what can make it rational for those others to change, given their actual, whole situations? An anthropological view can begin to provide answers.

The Pedagogy of Literacy.   Paulo Friere (1983) has argued that before one can learn to read and write the word he or she must be able to read and write the world. As I have indicated in a number of different ways in this essay, an anthropological view of literacy and illiteracy suggests that a particular individual's reading of his or her world will in large measure determine whether the price of becoming literate is worth paying. An individual's personal history and peculiar life context also determines how he or she feels about being illiterate and what it will take to change. Since illiteracy is integrally tied to the web of relationships providing life support, it is part of the delicately balanced adaptive apparatus we tamper with only at serious risk. Learning to read is not like putting on a new suit of clothes. It involves a reorientation to and a restructuring of one's world.

Starting from this premise an anthropology of the pedagogy of literacy would concern itself with at least the following:

The range of learning styles accomodated by the particular approach. For example, group drill and recitation sessions, patterned after elementary school classrooms, may prove inappropriate for adult learners and may have unexpected meanings to nonmainstream learners.

The extent to which each individual's own reading of his or her world is respected as legitimate and accurate, recognizing that no one else experiences it.

What counts as learning and what is really being learned. Although different pedagogies establish their own notions of what they will consider learning to be, anthropologists see individuals as definitionally learners (we can't not learn). We can thus say that some of us learn that being illiterate makes most sense while others learn to read and write. An ethnographer will be concerned to explain both levels of learning.

The kind of relationships facilitated. While American education appears preoccupied with finding a workable set of pedagogical techniques, the anthropology of teaching looks behind the techniques to the kinds of relationships they promote. A pedagogy that reduces literacy to a set of notions or skills that are seen as only capable of being mastered through teaching, for example, can serve, sometimes inadvertently, to reinforce the existing inequality in status between the teacher and the taught and effectively subvert the process of empowerment. Instructional groups can be used, as they have been by Friere in his literacy campaigns, to encourage people to read and write about issues that are of burning concern to them. The group arrangements are designed to provide individuals with support and encouragement. On the other hand, group instruction can be used simply to increase pedagogic efficiency and result in students finding themselves called upon to publicly display incompletely mastered skills in what they see as hostile environments.

CONCLUSION

Anthropology brings an important and eminently useful perspective to literacy and illiteracy. By starting from the assumptions that behavior normally represents individuals' attempts to make sense of the worlds they, and they alone, experience and that the persistent patterning of behavior reflects its social sanctioning, they are able to develop insights into a number of literacy-related issues.

The very problem of illiteracy is seen as extremely complex including the discovery that there are any number of different illiteracies and the realization that under some conditions illiteracy is not in itself a problem. The causes of illiteracy are also seen as multiple, frequently results or symptoms of social and economic exclusion, rather than themselves causes of the exclusion, rational choices made upon weighting costs and benefits. This perspective can also provide a useful set of principles for understanding the pedagogy of literacy. It can examine the extent to which individual learning styles and the legitimacy of a persons reading of his own world are respected, reveal unconscious and unexpected results of particular approaches, and examine the nature and effects of relationships promoted by particular pedagogies.

REFERENCES

Friere, Paulo. (1983, Winter). The importance of the act of reading. *Journal of Education* (special issue *Literacy and Ideology*), *165*, 5-11.

Fiering, Susan (1981). Commodore School: Unofficial writing. In Dell Hymes (Principal Investigator), *Ethnographic monitoring of children's acquisition of reading language arts skills in and out of the classroom*. Final report to The National Institute of Education, Washington, D.C.

Gilmore, Perry. (1982). *Gimmee room: A socio-cultural study of attitudes and admission to literacy*. Unpublished doctoral dissertation, University of Pennsylvania, Philadelphia.

Gilmore, Perry. (1983a, Spring). *Sub rosa literacy: Peers, play and ownership in literacy acquisition*. Paper presented at the American Educational Research Association Annual Meeting, Montreal.

Gilmore, Perry. (1983b, Winter). Spelling Mississippi: Recontextualizing a literacy-related speech event. *Anthropology and Education Quarterly, 14*, 235-256.

Heath, Shirley Brice. (1980, Winter). The functions and uses of literacy. *Journal of Communication, 30*, 123-133.

Hymes, Dell H. (1983). What is ethnography? In Perry Gilmore & Allan Glatthorn (Eds.), *Children In and Out of School*. Washington, DC: Center For Applied Linguistics.

Labov, William. (1972). The linguistic consequences of being a lame. In *Language in the inner city*. Philadelphia: University of Pennsylvania Press.

McDermott, Ray. (1974). Achieving school failure: An anthropological approach to literacy and social stratification. In George Spindler (Ed.), *Education and cultural process: Toward an anthropology of education*. New York: Holt, Rinehart and Winston.

The National Commission on Excellence in Education. (1983, April). An Open Letter to the American People: A Nation At Risk: The Imperative for Educational Reform.

Ogbu, John U. (1980, July). *Literacy in subordinate cultures: The case of Black Americans*. Paper delivered at The Library of Congress Conference on Literacy, Washington, DC.

Philips, Susan U. (1972). Participant structures and communicative competence: Warm Springs children in community and classroom. In Courtney B. Cazden, Vera P. John, and Dell H. Hymes (Eds.), *Functions of language in the classroom*. New York: Teacher's College Press.

Rist, Ray. (1973). *The urban school: A factory for failure*. Cambridge, MA: The MIT Press.

Robinson, Andrea. (1982). Observations on the environment and lifestyles of a declared non-reader and two declared readers. In David M. Smith (Principal Investigator), *Using literacy outside of school: An ethnographic investigation*. Final Report to The National Institute of Education, Washington, D.C.

Scollon, Ron, & Scollon, Suzanne B.K. (1982, Spring). The problem of language problems in Alaska. *Society*.

Smith, David. (1983). Reading and writing in the real world: Explorations in the culture of literacy. In Robert Parker & Frances Davis (Eds.), *Developing literacy: Young children's use of language*. Newark, DE: International Reading Association.

Weinstein, Gail. (1982). Some social consequences of literacy for Southeast Asians in West Philadelphia. In David M. Smith (Principal Investigator), *Using literacy outside of school: An ethnographic investigation*. Final Report to The National Institute of Education, Washington, D.C.

Author Index

Subject Index